VOLUME I

# THE CHURCH OF APOSTLES AND MARTYRS

HENRI DANIEL-ROPS

TRANSLATED
FROM THE FRENCH BY
AUDREY BUTLER

IMAGE BOOKS

A Division of Doubleday & Company, Inc.
Garden City, New York

Image Books edition 1962
by special arrangement with E. P. Dutton & Co., Inc.

Image Books Edition Published February 1962

H. Daniel-Rops: *L'Église des Apôtres et
des Martyrs,* first published in France by
Librairie Arthème Fayard, 1948

Henri Daniel-Rops, historian, novelist, critic, essayist, and member of the French Academy, has for the past decade been engaged upon a work of monumental proportions, his *Histoire de l'Église du Christ* (*History of the Church of Christ*). Both the secular and religious press have been unanimous in their praise of this work. *Best Sellers* said of it:

"It brings to the Catholic laymen of the world, and generally to readers of all faiths, for the first time a popular history of the Roman Catholic Church in the context of the great events which have occurred in the history of total Western civilization. It will constitute a veritable new correlation of the effect of Christianity upon the thinking and action of contemporary peoples at all periods *anno Domini* . . . this is a reference work which has had no precedent in either form or content."

*The Church of Apostles and Martyrs*, the first volume of this extraordinary series, traces the growth of the infant Church from the time of the Apostles through the fourth century; *The Church in the Dark Ages*, the second volume, covers six turbulent centuries of Catholicism, from the fall of the Roman Empire to the rise of Charlemagne; *Cathedral and Crusade*, the third volume, presents the centuries from 1050 to 1350, which saw the rise of Norman and Gothic architecture, the birth of universities, the development of Christian philosophy, and the conversion of Northern, Central, and Eastern Europe. Subsequent volumes trace the history of the Church from the Renaissance to the present day. Each of these superb volumes is a complete unit in itself and requires no previous study of earlier parts or of the full series.

*The Church of Apostles and Martyrs*, complete and unabridged in two Image Books volumes, illuminates completely, clearly, and inspiringly the most stirring and heroic period of the Church's infancy, growth, and early maturity.

"The *History of the Church of Christ* is sure to be the most popular Church history series in text and reference. An event in the world of books." *The Catholic Bulletin*

# CONTENTS

## MAPS

ACKNOWLEDGMENT

Through the courtesy of His Eminence, the Cardinal Archbishop of Westminster, and of Messrs Burns, Oates & Washbourne, Ltd., and Messrs Sheed & Ward, Inc., of New York, the scriptural quotations are in the translation of Monsignor Ronald Knox, copyright 1944, 1948, and 1950, Sheed & Ward, Inc., New York, N.Y.

# CHAPTER I

# 'SALVATION IS TO COME
# FROM THE JEWS'

## THE 'BRETHREN' OF JERUSALEM

AS THE reign of the Emperor Tiberius was drawing to its close, that is to say around A.D. 36 or 37 according to our calendar, a certain rumour gained currency among the Jewish communities scattered throughout the length and breadth of the Empire, and fanned them to a feverish pitch of excitement.

At the time all was at peace in the Mediterranean world which Rome had refashioned according to her own particular principles over the past three hundred years. Everything within the massive Empire gave an impression of ordered well-being and of permanence. It was true, of course, that the emperor, who was now more than seventy years of age, was living a life of voluntary seclusion among the rocks of Capri, where he had had a dozen or so luxurious villas built to suit his fancy. There he frittered away the autumn of his life in debaucheries and sadistic diversions, while, weary of his base dealings and his denunciations, the senatorial aristocracy looked anxiously towards the island whence little ever came save sentences of death. But the bloody whims of the elderly misanthrope had no effect whatsoever on the State's equilibrium; Rome was quiet, the subjection of the provinces was complete, and trade was prospering wonderfully on the high seas and along the great imperial roads.

It was exactly the same in Palestine, the smallest of the imperial provinces. There too nothing out of the ordinary seemed to be taking place. Law and order held sway at Jerusalem, thanks to the authority of the suspicious and sporadically brutal imperial procurator, Pontius Pilate. Part of the Jewish community accepted the Roman protectorate willingly, and force compelled the rest to acknowledge it. The Jews continued to lead the same lives that they had led for five hundred

years past, lives regulated to the minutest detail by religious
rites and observances, according to the rigid principles of the
Torah, and under the ever-watchful eye of the Sanhedrin.
Who could have believed that this abstruse piece of news,
whose validity was disputed as soon as it became known, and
which was being borne to the four corners of the earth on
'the wings of the birds,' would turn the foundations of the
Roman world upside-down, and that less than four centuries
later the entire Empire would regard it as the revelation of
ultimate truth?

This extraordinary message emanated from a small group
of Jews in Jerusalem. Anyone meeting these men in the temple
courts or along the steep alleyways of the Holy City would
have found them indistinguishable from the rest of the faithful. Their faith was certainly very much alive and most exemplary in character: they could be seen at the temple constantly, usually meeting under Solomon's Porch (Acts v. 12
and iii. 11; cf. also John x. 23), piously reciting the lengthy
*Eighteen Benedictions* each day at sunrise and at the ninth
hour, strictly observing the sabbath[1] and all the regulations
regarding ritual, even to fasting twice in the week,[2] according
to the ancestral custom of the Pharisees.

They did not belong to the ruling classes, and they had no
dealings with the priestly caste or the elders. Distinguished
men who maintained friendly relations with them, such as
Nicodemus, were few and far between. For the most part they
were very humble folk, all coming into one category. In a
word they belonged to the *Am-ha-rez*, to that element of the

[1] In Matt. xxiv. 20 we read: 'You must pray that your flight may
not be in winter, or on the sabbath day.' In Christ's day the sabbath
rest was indeed most strictly observed.

[2] During His lifetime Jesus' disciples were reproached because they
did not fast. Jesus replied to this: 'Can you expect the men of the
bridegroom's company to go fasting, while the bridegroom is still
with them? As long as they have the bridegroom with them, they
cannot be expected to fast; but the days will come when the bridegroom is taken away from them; then they will fast, when that day
comes' (Mark ii. 19–20). In the primitive Church we shall come
across this custom of the bi-weekly fast, which had been introduced
into Judaism by the Pharisees. The Temple Pharisee refers to it in
his monologue in the famous parable about the Pharisee and the
publican (Luke xviii. 12).

population which the erudite Scribes and the wealthy Sadducees regarded with suspicion and contempt. Several of them had come originally from Galilee, a fact made immediately apparent at Jerusalem by their rough country accents. But some came from other districts of Palestine too, and others from distant Jewish colonies in pagan lands, from Pontus and Egypt, and from Libya and Cappadocia; there were even Roman and Arab proselytes amongst them: they were an odd assortment of folk!

Close observers might have noted that they held frequent meetings apart from the rest of the community, where they took part in ceremonies which remained Jewish in their externals but to which they imparted a new significance. There were their communal meals, for example, where the ancient rites were given a strange and different interpretation. A wonderful harmony existed between all their members. At first they called themselves the *disciples*, because they had had a master, a founder; later they adopted another expression which seemed more in keeping with the mysterious communion which sealed their bond, and henceforth they described themselves as the *brethren*.

Several very different sects already existed within the framework of Judaism, yet these men did not form themselves into one more such sect. They did not affect the outward austerities of the Pharisees, who were perpetually seen with their 'phylacteries' around their brows, wearing mourning apparel and walking with deliberate solemnity, and they did not spend their days carping about the thousand and one precepts which dictated the sabbath rest. Nor did they flee from the world, like the bands of Essenes who had established real monastic colonies in the lonely wildernesses around the Dead Sea, who fasted rigorously, forswore women, ate no meat and dressed in undyed flax cloth. They did not even constitute themselves into an independent synagogue, a *keneseth*. Groups of not less than ten of the faithful were permitted by the Law to do this, and the practice had been adopted by several small cliques of Jews who had come to Jerusalem from far-off places and who liked to pray to God among their own fellow countrymen whenever they were not taking part in the collective ceremonies in the temple. The people with whom we are con-

cerned made no attempt whatsoever to isolate themselves, to
cut themselves off from their fellow men: quite the contrary;
their ranks were open to all, and their leaders never ceased
calling on pious souls to join their little band. Had one wanted
to link them with any of the religious streams which already
existed, the only one which would have been approximately
suitable would have been the movement known as 'the Poor
of Israel,' the *Anavim*.[3] The *Anavim*, who were scandalized
by the ostentatious luxury of the priestly caste, yet who were
too illiterate to be included among the Pharisees, used their
humble zeal to fight against all that seemed to them evil in
the Chosen People. They based their way of life on the maxim
so perfectly expressed by the Psalmist, and on it alone:
'Blessed are those who fear the Lord, and follow his paths!'
(Ps. cxxvii. 1).

What, then, was the bond which held together the faithful of this extremely ill-defined community—a bond so strong
that no outward barrier was needed to preserve their coherency
of purpose? And why did its members remain grouped together in Jerusalem, just as if, in that unchanging seat of
divine action, some event was in process of being accomplished
of which they alone possessed the secret?

### 'THE GLAD VOICE OF THE HERALDS'

The answer lies in one short sentence, which expresses in
a nutshell their entire faith: 'The Messiah is come amongst
us!' The world has let this slogan grow stale; today it has lost
its sense of mysterious revelation, its shattering novelty. To
assess the force it then possessed we must delve down to the
hardy roots of ancient Jewish tradition, and experience to the

[3] Certain writers have maintained that a kind of organized community existed which was called 'the Poor of Israel' (A. Causse, *Les
Pauvres d'Israel*, Strasbourg, 1922). But nowadays this thesis has
few supporters. The *Anavim* movement is seen, rather, as a general
attitude of Judaism, at its simplest and most traditional, a current
of thought stemming from deep in the Jewish soul, humble and
utterly faithful, which expresses itself in several Old Testament
Psalms as well as in various noncanonical texts such as the Psalms
of Solomon and the Testament of the Twelve Patriarchs.

full that surge of love and fearful awe felt by every devout
soul at the mere mention of the Messianic coming.

The Messianic idea had its origins far back in Jewish history. At first it was bound up with the national dogma of the
Jews' privileged position as God's Chosen People; their faith
in it spanned the centuries in the promise given of old to the
Patriarch Abraham by Yahweh, and subsequently repeated by
Him on several occasions: to Jacob, in the dream at Bethel,
to Moses, on the smoking summit of Mount Sinai, and to
the Hebrew kings in all the splendour of their capital at Jerusalem. Even when misfortune breathed her deadly breath over
the Chosen People, nothing could make this living water of
faith run dry. Quite the contrary: the ancestral conviction was
now more powerful and more precisely defined than ever before, and it became the Jews' one source of hope and consolation. The great prophets referred to it again and again. In
one magnificent chapter (the eleventh), Isaiah conjured up in
detail the time when the 'fresh root from Jesse's stem' would
be a 'signal, beckoning to the peoples all around.' Ezekiel visualized the dead being restored to life, and the new Jerusalem arising from the ashes of the old. The Book of Daniel
treated the idea in its entirety, and described the divinely ordained climax, the foundation of God's kingdom upon earth
through the restoration of Israel's ancient glories and the establishment of a nation of saints.

It was after the return from the Exile that this grandiose
vision really assumed individual characteristics. Obviously the
ancient Promise would be fulfilled by God, but not by Him
directly. In order to realize it, the Most High would make use
of a sacred intermediary, an *Anointed One*, a *Messiah*, a
*Christ*. Thus man's timeless, fundamental inclination to em-
body the dearest of his dreams in living beings whom he could
understand and love came to coincide with the national dogma
of the Chosen People. In this way—confused, contradictory,
yet conspicuously present in every mind—the image of a supernatural being who would deliver Israel from her enemies,
fulfil her destiny and realize the work of Yahweh began to
dominate Jewish life and thought more and more.

At the beginning of the first century of our Christian era,
there is no doubt whatsoever that the Messianic idea sus-

tained everything that was finest and purest in the Jewish soul. It was a time in which temporal hopes seemed vain and discredited; the descendants of the Maccabees had drowned in their own bloodbath; the Promised Land was now divided between petty Herodian princelings and Roman officials. Yet not a single Jew even considered giving way to despair. Far from it: we only have to open the Gospels to feel for ourselves the quivering tremor of hope which never ceased pulsating through and through the entire Jewish race. What was the question which the priests and the Levites came to ask John the Baptist, as he preached on the banks of the Jordan? They wanted to know whether he was the Messiah. What did Andrew rush to tell Simon? 'We have discovered the Messiah!' And the Samaritan woman, also, drawing water at the well, proclaimed her faith in the idea with simple sincerity: 'I know that the Messiah is to come: and when He comes, He will tell us everything.'

Naturally enough, the different sections of the Jewish community interpreted the Messianic picture in a number of different ways. Each man's idea of it was coloured by his temperament and his education. A fanatical nationalist imagined the Saviour as a kind of second Judas Maccabeus, as a man who would show His enemies no mercy. A Pharisee saw Him as a supremely virtuous teacher, the living incarnation of the sacred Law of Moses. The common people, who were always hungry for the miraculous, surrounded Him with a hazy mass of supernatural attributes. And every now and then some adventurer would spring to the fore, taking advantage of the violent fervour of the Messianic belief, and would summon his fellow Jews to enact the immediate realization of the Promise. Taken chronologically, these upstarts' names were Judas, Simon and Athronges; each in his turn stirred up rebellion for a few weeks and then collapsed under the blows of the Roman javelins, guardians of the existing political order; but the Jews never gave up hope that one day the true Messiah would indeed appear.

One particular type of literature, which was extremely widespread in the period between the second century B.C. and the first century A.D., sought continual inspiration in the Messianic theme: works of this kind are known as *apocalyptic* writings.

The starting-point of apocalyptic literature is the biblical Book of Daniel, and its climax the Apocalypse of St John. Apocalyptic works abounded everywhere at this time, expressing themselves in a strange kind of poetry, packed with semi-sublime, semi-nonsensical dissertations in which the heart-stirring dream of an anguished nation mingled with intellectual speculations which were entirely divorced from the disciplining boundaries of scientific knowledge. The most concrete and most temporal Messianic concept served as a basis for various eschatological doctrines which claimed to reveal the ultimate ends of man's existence and the final meaning of the cosmic dramas. These books, which the Church was to remove from the Old Testament canon,[4] constitute a strange, compact, harmonious collection, and the *kabbal* and the *zohar* are extensions of it. The Book of Enoch, the Book of Jubilees, the Testament of the Twelve Patriarchs, the Ascension of Moses —the Psalms of Solomon, where the pious intention is more perceptible, stand slightly apart from these—and the Book of Esdras, a later work—all these apocryphal books undoubtedly had a profound influence upon the Jewish thinking of their epoch. They show the extent to which the Messiah's coming was imagined and awaited, in the Israel of those days, as a shattering revelation, which would be accompanied by a violent overthrow of the existing order of things. Men sang: 'Happy are they who live in the days of the Messiah, for they shall behold the happiness of Israel, when all the tribes of Israel are met together again!' But in hushed tones they also whispered that the coming of the Anointed One would be accompanied by dreadful portents, that 'blood shall drip from the trees, the stones shall speak, and many parts of the earth shall be rent by the abyss.' And the joy of those who waited was mingled with fear.

It is essential that we grasp this psychological mood, where simple faith, living piety, the desire for revenge, a secret fear and the popular taste for the fantastic were all interwoven, the whole forming a strange, spiritual erethism, if we are to under-

---

[4] However, it should be noted that the Book of Enoch, which was deeply revered by the primitive Church until the fourth century, is cited in the Epistle of St Jude, and that the Abyssinian Church regards it as canonical.

stand what the awaited coming of the Messiah signified to a Jew living in the third decade of the Christian era. And only by so doing can we sense, too, the feelings of awe and amazement which would overwhelm him on being told that the moment he had been waiting for so long had now arrived.

'Blow ye the trumpet in Sion, the famous trumpet of the saints! Proclaim the glad voice of the heralds in Jerusalem, for God is merciful to Israel in his visitation! Stand up on high, Jerusalem! Behold your children, for the Lord is gathering them in from the East and from the West. Yea, from the North, they come to the joy of their God, and he gathereth them also from the distant isles. He has bowed down great mountains, to make their way easy, and caused the hills to flee away, and the cedar-groves have sheltered them as they passed by. God has made sweet-scented trees to breathe upon them, so that all Israel might pass by, prepared for the visitation of their God. O Jerusalem, clothe thyself in thy garments of glory, and make ready thy gown of holiness. For God has promised great joy to thy people from this day forward and for evermore. May the Lord fulfil his promise made to his prophets in days gone by, and may he raise up Jerusalem for all eternity for his name's sake!' (Psalms of Solomon xi.)

Such was the prayer of the devout Jew. And those who belonged to the community of the 'brethren' responded by declaring that these things were already come to pass, that 'the glad voice of the heralds' had already resounded among the Palestinian hillsides. And one of them, Simon, surnamed Peter, who acted as if he were their leader, had, while speaking one day before a large audience, given his listeners that precise information which they still found so difficult to admit: 'Men of Israel, listen to this. Jesus of Nazareth was a man duly accredited to you from God; such were the miracles and wonders and signs which God did through him in your midst, as you yourselves well know. This man you have put to death; by God's fixed design and foreknowledge, he was betrayed to you, and you, through the hands of sinful men, have cruelly murdered him. But God raised him up again, releasing him from the pangs of death; it was impossible that death should have the mastery over him. It is in his person that David says: "Always I can keep the Lord within sight; always he is at my right hand, to make me stand firm. . . ." Let it be known, then, beyond doubt, to all the house of Israel, that God has made him Master and Christ, this Jesus whom you crucified' (Acts ii).

## FAITH IN JESUS AND HIS SPIRITUAL PLEDGES

Whence came the conviction which these men asserted in such certain terms? Jesus of Nazareth, He whose human destiny and divine mission had been so perfectly summed up in those few simple sentences of Peter's, had actually declared Himself to be the Messiah. In one decisive moment, when, after being brought before the High Priest, He had been obliged to frame the reply upon which His life depended, He had not hesitated to claim the title of Saviour for Himself. 'Art thou the Christ? the Son of the blessed God? Jesus said to him, I am. And you will see the Son of Man sitting at the right hand of God's power, and coming with the clouds of heaven' (Mark xiv. 62).

This was the very sentence which had made the Jewish leaders decide to deal harshly with Him and sentence Him to death, for in their eyes it constituted blasphemy. A testimony thus sealed with blood might well be considered one of the utmost importance; but has history not seen a score of adventurers who have been ready to sacrifice everything, even their lives, in pursuit of an empty dream?

During Jesus' lifetime His followers' belief in Him was not hard to understand. All those who had met Him declared that He radiated a power which was quite unique, a power in which spiritual radiance combined with tenderness, an inexplicable power which dominated men's minds, filling their hearts brimful of love, a power which overwhelmed their souls and bore them beyond the boundaries of self. Countless indeed had been the men and women who had felt themselves linked to Jesus as soon as they met Him, just as if He had been waiting for them from the beginning of time, calling them each by name. From that moment onwards they would abandon everything relating to their old way of life and become utterly transformed.

But when Jesus was dead, how could men really go on thinking that the man crucified on Calvary was indeed the conqueror of time? The answer is that the wonderful mystery of man's faith in Jesus, a faith in which reason and Grace both play their part, already existed in those far-off, primitive times. Later this same faith was to blaze forth in all its glory in those tragic days when thousands of souls, brought face to face with the executioners of Rome, would show that it meant more to them than anything else, more even than life itself. It is a faith which travels down the centuries in the silence of our Carmelite and Carthusian houses, and in the unknown sacrifices made by Christians working in the mission-field and among the poor and the outcast.

However, those who had followed the living Jesus were but ordinary men; they had their weaknesses and their limitations, just as we have. When the Great Council decided to crush the movement led by Jesus of Galilee, its action seemed crowned with instantaneous success. Jesus' little band of followers scattered, terror-stricken. The disciples' leader himself denied his Master. Only a dogged handful of adherents, mostly women, remained at the foot of the Cross; the rest fled, hiding (so one rumour had it) in one of the Grecian-style tombs built near the foot of the ravine outside Jerusalem. Why then did a number of pious Jews, men who were honest citizens of the Holy City, remain loyal to the memory of this unsuccessful agitator whose punishment by the authorities ought to have struck them as eminently proper?

The members of the community of the 'brethren' countered questions like these with a reply based upon the supernatural realities which were to be a manifestation of the Messianic era. Yes, they believed in Jesus the Messiah in spite of everything, in spite of the terrible end to which His earthly life had come. Their belief that He was the Messiah was founded not on some commonplace bond of sentiment but on the various proofs of His heaven-sent character with which they had been provided. There had been three supernatural pledges of this kind. All the books written by the first generation of Christians, *Gospels*, *Acts* and *Epistles*, grasp their importance and show that it was upon these pledges that their writers' faith rested.

The first of them had been given by Jesus Himself the day before His death, on the evening of Holy Thursday. Joining the disciples in His last Passover Supper, He had broken bread and taken a cup of wine and given thanks, saying: 'This is my body, given for you. . . . This is my blood, shed for you.' By this action He put into sacramental terms a lesson which He had already stressed on several occasions. He had warned His followers at least four times of the tragedy in which His earthly mission would end, emphasizing the inevitable necessity of His death, and the sacrificial meaning that it was to possess. The wonderful lesson at Capernaum on the bread of life had stated this exactly long before: 'It is I who am the bread of life. . . . If anyone eats of this bread, he shall live for ever. And now, what is this bread which I am to give? It is my flesh, given for the life of the world' (John vi. 48 ff.).

No one had understood Him then. Blinded by the Messianic vision which was the one most widely held in Israel at that time—the vision of a gloriously triumphant Messiah, whose victory had been predestined by the Most High—the disciples, including Peter himself, had refused to believe in the necessity of the final oblation. But once it was an acknowledged fact (and as soon as that first quite understandable moment of human bewilderment and panic had passed) the death of the Master became an immensely important part of His followers' faith. In the first place it confirmed Jesus' prophetic gifts in a most striking fashion. Secondly, it established a bond between Master and followers which nothing would ever be able to sever, for it was a bond based on their partaking of His divine life, just as He had promised. Finally —and once again Jesus had stated this Himself—it was the sign of a New Covenant. For many devout Jews, who were well read in the Scriptures, the necessity of sacrifice had always been connected with the mystery of the Covenant, from the time of Abraham's to that of the Paschal Lamb: thus they were able to grasp the true significance of the sacrifice on Calvary. And just as Israel had, down the centuries, drawn her strength from her unshakable belief in the Ancient Covenant with God, so, in the same way, the faithful followers of Jesus were to step out into history sustained by the certainty that their Master's death was for them the pledge of the New Covenant.

All the more so, since the supernatural character of His life had been vividly proved to them in the most astonishing of all the miracles: the Resurrection. When, on Easter morning, the good women who had come to visit Jesus' tomb had found it empty, and had hurried to tell the news to the grief-stricken disciples, the astounding truth had dawned upon them. Not immediately, however. The fact had seemed so incredible that some hesitated to admit its authenticity. They distrusted women's tales of this type. Shortly afterwards Thomas actually asked to see the risen Master for himself before he would believe it. However, the Resurrection was soon confirmed by numerous eye-witnesses, acquiring a decisive position in the new faith and becoming the corner-stone of its doctrinal fabric.

Thus, as we have already seen, Peter solemnly proclaimed it as an indisputable certainty. When it was necessary to find a replacement for one of the group which directed the little community—a replacement for Judas, the traitor who had subsequently committed suicide—it was expressly stated that the substitute would be 'a witness of his resurrection' (Acts i. 22). Much later on, when writing to a group of His faithful, the greatest of all the heralds of the new faith was to tell them: 'If Christ has not risen, then our preaching is groundless, and your faith, too, is groundless' (St Paul, 1. Cor. xv. 14).

Now what exactly did this pledge of the Resurrection mean? It was not just a personal promise, '. . . the first-fruits of all those who have fallen asleep' (1. Cor. xv. 20). It was not simply a satisfaction of man's ancient yearning, a yearning expressed in one way or another by all the great prophets of Israel, Isaiah, Daniel, Ezekiel, Job: 'From this skeleton, reclothed in flesh, I shall see God!' Nor was it merely an answer to the half-mocking, half-troubled statement of the pagan Seneca: 'It would need a resurrected man to make me believe in immortality!' No: it established within the hearts of all the faithful the absolute certainty of their ultimate victory. For since Jesus had kept the most difficult of His promises, and had indeed risen again on the third day, it followed that He would most certainly keep all the rest too, and especially His promise that He would 'overcome the world' and that His followers would witness His coming again in glory.

Moreover, had the faithful not seen the first manifestation of this apotheosis with their own eyes? Forty days after that Resurrection morning—forty days during which Jesus had given countless astounding but at the same time unquestionable proofs of His survival after death—the Apostles had, on the Mount of Olives, seen Him 'lifted up, and a cloud caught him away from their sight . . . into heaven' (Acts i. 9 and 11). And was not this Ascension, also, symbolic of His divine character? For 'no man has ever gone up into heaven, except one who has come down from heaven, the Son of Man, who dwells in heaven' (John iii. 13).

Now reference to such obviously Messianic deeds as these involved Jesus' followers in numerous serious disputes with their fellow Jews. Would they have the strength to hold fast to their beliefs, to run counter to almost the whole of established opinion, which rejected the Messianic character of their Master, to resist the authority of generally accepted ideas? To sustain them they had been given a third pledge. Once again it was a fulfilment of one of the Master's own promises, for He Himself had told them that He would send them the truth-giving Spirit. 'It will be for him, the truth-giving Spirit, when he comes, to guide you into all truth' (John xvi. 13). This promise had been realized at Pentecost. It was the day on which the Jews were celebrating God's revelation to Moses; now a still more important revelation took place. The Apostles had gathered together, when 'all at once a sound came from heaven like that of a strong wind blowing, and filled the whole house where they were sitting. Then appeared to them what seemed to be tongues of fire, which parted and came to rest on each of them; and they were all filled with the Holy Spirit, and began to speak in strange languages, as the Spirit gave utterance to each' (Acts ii. 2–4).

In order to understand the full meaning of this further Mystery, it is necessary, once again, to refer back to the Judaic prophetic tradition which permeated all these men. The effusion of the Spirit was to be the final sign of the Messianic era. The Anointed One had always been envisaged as the messenger of the Spirit, and that Spirit would spread forth all around Him, transforming the world and summoning men to a new life, a life of heroism and sanctity. Thus Ezekiel had written (xxxvi. 26 ff.): 'I will give you a new heart, and breathe a new spirit into you; I will take away from your breasts those hearts that are hard as stone, and give you human hearts instead. I will make my spirit penetrate you, so that you will follow in the path of my law, remember, and carry out my decrees.'

The coming of the Holy Spirit, therefore, had really been the third supernatural pledge, and the most decisive one. From that moment onwards the followers of Jesus had no longer been just a brotherly community, but a body—a body that was both human and superhuman—of chosen souls, completely renewed in Christ, and ready to face any dangers that might confront them for the sake of their faith: later on this community was to be called the *Church*. All the early Christian texts demonstrate the importance of this fact. On the one hand St Paul was to say: 'A man cannot belong to Christ unless he has the Spirit of Christ' (Rom. viii. 9). On the other, St Peter, as he hesitated before receiving some converted pagans into the bosom of the faithful, confessed: 'Who will grudge us the water for baptizing these men, that have received the Holy Spirit just as we did?' (Acts x. 47). So, after Pentecost, the faith of Jesus' followers had not only become more steadfast, but was imbued also with the will to win new souls. These folk now felt instinctively that, within the bosom of the Jewish community whose life and rites they shared, they constituted a new kind of men, a new race, destined to spread their faith throughout the world. Henceforth they bore within them that strength which gives a determined minority its triumphant audacity.

This had been made abundantly manifest immediately after the effusion of the Holy Spirit had taken place. Talk of the phenomenon had drawn a crowd around the house where the Apostles were meeting—it so happened that the feast of Pentecost had brought many visitors into Jerusalem—and the sight of all the confusion, and the polyglot orations of these folk, had made them a laughing-stock for the mob. Some mocked them, saying: 'They have had their fill of new wine' (Acts ii. 13). But Peter drew himself up to his full height and went out to face the crowd. He was afraid no longer: never again would the cock-crow of denial sound for him. It was now that he proclaimed his faith, his steadfast faith in Jesus the Messiah, for the first time, in the phrases which we have already read. This is the moment at which Christian history begins, a beginning marked by this first vindicatory declaration, which is, at the same time, a declaration of war upon the world.

## A TRULY COMMUNAL COMMUNITY LIFE

For anyone wanting to learn about the beginnings of the spread of Christianity, about the way of life of the first community which gave shelter to the Gospel from its very birth, the New Testament offers one outstanding document, the book entitled the Acts of the Apostles. Written but a short time after the events it describes—about A.D. 60–4—by a man who, although he was not an actual eye-witness of all that he wrote, was nevertheless steeped in the most vivid Gospel tradition, it is a work of quite unique interest. True, it is somewhat incomplete. This is because it was impossible for the author, conscientious though he endeavoured to be, to know the whole story and to set down all the vital information from the facts at his disposal, because his origin and his personal ties[5] encouraged him to dwell more particularly on the action of this or that leader rather than on the community as a whole. Above all, like every other document belonging to primitive Christianity, his book was not written with any intention of satisfying the curiosity of the future historian, but simply in order to exalt the faith. And yet, within the limits which it voluntarily sets itself, what an incomparable witness it is! No one who reads it can remain unmoved by it! Of course there is no trace here of that supernatural brilliance which we find throughout the Gospels, shining out from the figure of Jesus Himself; the whole account makes the reader acutely conscious

[5] See Chapter II, section: 'Christ is Proclaimed to the Gentiles.' In the Acts Sts Peter and Paul are in the forefront of events, but the other Apostles are almost entirely ignored. On the book of Acts and its author see Chapter VI, section: 'The Apostles' Own Actions and Writings.'

of the immense void left by the Master's physical disappearance. But it is an inspired work none the less, a book written by man, and describing men's actions, and as such it reaches to our very souls. Surely no other document will ever be found that conjures up a lovelier or more thrilling picture of a Christian society which appears almost free from worldly bonds, and which, despite the flaws inherent in our fallen nature, is so truly striving to realize God's kingdom on this earth!

How many of these early Christians were there? It is almost impossible to answer this question. In Acts (i. 15), St Luke actually mentions the figure of 120, and St Paul (1 Cor. xv) talks of 500 people in all who had seen the risen Christ. But though these figures refer to the very origins of Christianity, to the weeks immediately following Christ's death, there is no proof that they include all the members of the young community. Following St Peter's first speech, the Acts tell us that 3,000 people professed the new faith at one fell swoop (ii. 41); soon after this it was a question of 5,000 followers (iv. 4). If we take the view that *c.* A.D. 35–7 Jerusalem contained some thousands of believers, but that they were still only a tiny minority in the city as a whole, we should probably be reasonably near the truth.

Then, too, we can only build up a general impression of the organization which these first Christians possessed. They certainly did possess one, there is no doubt of this: all human enterprises presuppose organization, and the very success of Christianity on the temporal plane demonstrates that its growth obeyed that profound historical law which insists that every movement desirous of expansion must have solid ranks, a principle of command and a plan of action, all this working in close relationship with its doctrine, and, moreover, forming an integral part of it. Now Jesus Himself had provided His followers with all these things, and for those of us who really know how to read the Gospels, one of the most astounding aspects of His earthly ministry is this gigantic practical effort of organization and education which He carried out, and whose consequences have lasted into our own day.[6]

---

[6] This is one of the aspects of Christ which has not been studied very much; yet it is one of the most enthralling, and may well be the one which is most investigated in the future. Jesus was not simply

Moreover, the institutional foundations laid by Him are clearly visible in the primitive community. We get the impression that the Apostles, His first witnesses, the men whom Jesus had Himself chosen and established, enjoyed, naturally enough, enormous moral authority. The fact that He had limited the number of this little group to twelve certainly has symbolic value, for scarcely had Judas's suicide become known when Peter asked the rest of the group to co-opt a replacement for him. This took place even before the sacred wind of Pentecost had breathed through the young community, and when the apostolic college put forward two candidates, the Holy Spirit acted through selection by lot to choose Matthias (Acts i. 15, 26). Peter clearly occupied a leading place among the Twelve. We shall often see him acting as he acted on the occasion of his election to this position: he is the one with whom the initiative always lies. Aside from him, there is really no one, save John, the son of Zebedee, who stands out particularly strongly. This pre-eminence of Peter, which was to have considerable importance, on account of its consequences for the entire history of Christianity, was yet another fact which rested on the express declaration of the Master. He had wanted to give His organization a hierarchic principle, and He had deliberately chosen Simon, this prudent, generous-hearted, steadfast man, as 'the rock . . . upon which I will build my church.'[7]

---

the mighty caller of souls, author and spokesman of sublime doctrine and supernatural victim that we all know: He showed, too, that He was the wisest of founders, the most accurate of teachers and the most efficacious of men of action. He gave His followers a solid basic instruction worthy of a military academy or a missionary course; He taught them the tactics they were to use. Thus in every respect it is correct to say that *the Church was born of Christ*; both the institutions and the dogmas which were to develop as the centuries passed by have their roots in His teaching, and, from its beginnings, the Church presents that dual character which it has retained until our own time (and which makes its history so hard to understand), being simultaneously a manifestation of faith, the mystical body of the living God and also a collection of human institutions, which have themselves been willed by God. (In his earlier book, *Jesus in His Time*, the author has tried to bring out this aspect of Christ's work.)

[7] This is not the place in which to take up yet again the well-worn argument on the authority of the Gospel passage (Matt. xvi. 13-20)

There were certainly a number of aides, or assistants, close to the Apostles, and these appear to have constituted a kind of secondary grade in the hierarchy. Were they related to the enlarged college of the Seventy (or Seventy-Two), which Jesus Himself had founded during the second year of His ministry, when He saw how numerous His followers were becoming? Were they the origin of the *presbyters* whom we shall soon find in all the Christian communities? What exactly was their position? It is not possible to give an exact answer on any of these points.

We also get the definite impression that another authority existed within the Jerusalem community, alongside the apostolic authority and perhaps upon quite a different plane, an authority deriving from a different set of personalities, notably from James, known as 'the brother of the Lord,' meaning that he was Jesus' first cousin. Eusebius, the first Christian historian, who lived in the fourth century and who described the far-off origins of the Church from traditions other than those of the Gospels and the Acts, was to lay great stress upon the part played by this extremely saintly personage, who 'drank no wine or intoxicating beverages of any kind . . .' and who 'spent so much time kneeling in prayer that the skin of his knees was worn as horny as a camel's.' In view of this picture, ought we to regard James as the leader of a specifically Jewish trend of thought, desirous of enclosing the new faith within the most narrowly legalistic framework, and more or less openly opposed to that party in the apostolic college which preferred the spirit to the letter? If this were so, the institutions of the new community would very rapidly mirror such a difference in the interpretation of Jesus' message; and this, as we shall see, did indeed occur.[8] But it is undoubtedly an exaggeration to view what, at the beginning, must have

in which this choice is expressed. Suffice it to say that the Catholic Church's reasons for holding its authority to be irrefutable are set out in Chapter V of the author's *Jesus in His Time*.

[8] Traces of this kind of duality can be seen in the Apocalypse (xxi. 13, iv. 4, v. 8). In the heavenly Jerusalem the visionary sees the twelve names of the apostles inscribed on the twelve foundations of the city wall, but the 'elders' are seated around the throne of the Lamb upon twenty-four thrones.

been merely a difference of emphasis in terms of a visible clash of personalities. There were far too many solid links binding the faithful together for any natural human reactions to be able to compromise at all seriously the wonderful unity which all possessed at this time.

As in the case of the details of practical organization, we cannot comment as precisely as we should like upon the rites and observances which were characteristic of the religious life of the first of the faithful; however, it is possible to pick out three fundamentals which were eventually to form the bases of Christian religious life: baptism, the laying on of hands and the communal meal.

Firstly, baptism. The Acts, like St Paul's Epistles, presuppose that it took place in all the first churches as a matter of course, and that every new adherent received it when he was admitted into the community. Why? The reason is obvious: Jesus Himself had received baptism at the hands of John the Baptist, and subsequently His own disciples had administered it. But the Christian rite certainly possessed some characteristics peculiar to it alone. The Johannine baptism had differed from other Jewish religious ablutions and from the *mikweh* rituals, because it had been a 'baptism of penitence.' Christian baptism, too, included the will to renew the soul, and to achieve spiritual purification thereby, but it comprised more than this. The Acts declare 'Be baptized, every one of you, in the name of Jesus Christ, to have your sins forgiven' (Acts ii. 38), and at Ephesus we shall see St Paul meeting some of those who had been baptized by John, showing them that the rite in which they had participated was not enough, and baptizing them again 'in the name of the Lord Jesus' (Acts xix. 5). Ought we to assume, then, that those baptized into the new faith, according to a formula which has been lost to us, had to recognize the Messiahship of Jesus, and to renounce the national sin committed against His person?[9]

The supernatural action of baptism appears to have been

[9] The actual baptismal rite is not described in the Acts, nor, moreover, in the Gospels. But the *Didache*, a Christian text dating from the end of the first century, informs us that, although normally administered by immersion, it could also be given, exceptionally, by aspersion.

completed by another ceremony: the laying on of hands. Here again we must go back to a very ancient Jewish custom, of which the Old Testament contains innumerable examples, a custom used when it was necessary to confer a supernatural efficacy upon some individual, be it the authority of the head of a family or the power of a king (e.g. Gen. xlviii. 17). It had been a custom with which Jesus was familiar (Mark v. 23; Matt. ix. 18, xix. 13, 15; Luke iv. 40, xiii. 13). Renan saw it as the sacramental act *par excellence* of the Church in Jerusalem, but this is probably an overstatement; it is certain, however, that it was a rite repeated many, many times during the history of the early Christians (Acts vi. 6, viii. 17–19, ix. 12, 17, xiii. 3, xix. 6, xxviii. 8). Exactly what was its meaning? It is difficult to determine this precisely. In all probability it was intended to correspond to a direct transmission of all the gifts which the Holy Spirit had imparted to the first disciples at Pentecost, gifts of Grace, enlightenment, courage and wisdom. Thus while baptism opened the gateway of truth to the believers, the laying on of hands, by confirming them, allowed them to follow along the road that lay beyond it.

The most moving of these ancient rites is the communion. It was also one of the most frequent. The early Christians 'occupied themselves continually with the apostles' teaching, their fellowship in the breaking of bread, and the fixed times of prayer' (Acts ii. 42). These communal love-feasts were proper meals. On this point the text is quite categorical: 'They took their share of food' (Acts ii. 46). But did they also have a far more exalted meaning, like the present-day eucharist? The communal meal is regarded in every country in the world as a rite of association; among the Jews it was the custom to break bread with solemn ceremony at the start of the sabbath repast, and to consecrate it to the Lord. In the Christian usage there was certainly more to the rite than this, and though the Acts do not establish any precise relationship between these communal ceremonies and the commemoration of Christ, it is extremely probable that such a connection existed in the minds of the faithful. Otherwise why was the sentence spoken by Jesus at the last Passover Supper, 'Do this for a commemoration of me' (Luke xxi. 19), included in the Gospels?

How clearly we can see them, these first believers, 'breaking bread and praising God,' alternating the *Marana Tha*, the traditional 'Come, O Lord,' with the hosannas which proclaimed their certainty in the Messianic fulfilment, thus uniting the past history of their race with the future of their faith, and, as they partook of the bread of life, feeling with all the fervour of their ardent faith that this was much more than a commemorative rite: this was, indeed, a participation in the divine life itself. It must have been through the communion that these early Christians became fully conscious of what they were—of what they had in truth been ever since the Holy Spirit had breathed upon them. They came to understand that they were more than a friendly assembly, a pious gathering or a school of philosophy—they were, in fact, a society of men, living in Christ and for Christ, a community of saints, a Church.[10]

This desire to live in Christ, through Him and for Him, was indeed the sole object of their existence. Although we can only grasp at the broad outlines of the constitution and observances of the first Church, there is one human reality which compels our attention with a strength born of its irresistible conviction whenever we examine its features. It is the reality of a wonderful effort, made by all the first Christians, to put the precepts of the Master into practice, an effort by each individual to realize that total regeneration which Jesus had demanded of His followers. The whole text of the Acts is dotted with exquisite little sentences which give a most vivid picture of this atmosphere of generosity and fervour. 'Gladness and simplicity of heart' (Acts ii. 47) are everywhere. 'There was one heart and one soul in all the company of believers' (Acts iv. 32). In these early days that sweet and humble charity and brotherly love which St Peter was to praise so highly in his first Epistle were really and truly practised. And proof that

[10] 'The recognition of Jesus in the breaking of bread testifies to the connection which existed from the beginning between faith in the Resurrection and the eucharistic ceremony. Faith in the Resurrection and faith in the presence of Jesus in the midst of his followers were both affirmed simultaneously in the communal meal.' These sentences draw their particular importance from the fact that they were written by Alfred de Loisy, a man who can hardly be suspected of complaisance (*Les Actes des Apôtres*, p. 217. Paris, 1920).

this picture is no fairy-tale idyll, but a true and factual record, is shown by the fact that the author of the Acts never once hesitates to point out its darker side, letting us see how, when human nature regains the upper hand, a thread of misery and sin sometimes makes its appearance.

Christ was still there, very close to His faithful followers. Many of the leaders of the little community had known Him well. They could recall personal memories; they would relate what they had seen and heard in the days when He was teaching on the shores of Lake Tiberias or among the crowd in the temple court. They collected all the known details of His life, and in this way a catechesis was drawn up and fixed in oral tradition long before it was written down to become the Gospel. The faithful sensed the Master present in their hearts; like Mary Magdalene and the disciples at Emmaus before them, each felt the reality of Him with a certainty that was completely overwhelming, and a burning, passionate fervour. 'Master!' (John xx. 16); 'Stay with us, Lord!' (Luke xxiv. 29).

Spiritual life blossomed with a brilliant intensity. Men rivalled one another in their efforts to attain a state of sanctity. Signs of God's grace seemed to spring up everywhere. Prodigies and miracles multiplied. The Lord's promise was being fulfilled all the time, unceasingly: 'If a man believes in me, as the scripture says, Fountains of living water shall flow from his bosom' (John viii. 38). And since the apocalyptic image, which was deeply ingrained in the Jewish soul, was subconsciously mingled with these tangible impressions, men asked themselves whether the return of the Master in glory were not just around the corner, and if they would not soon be seeing Him reappearing from out of the heavens, in a glorious and terrifying manifestation of His divinity. Yes, indeed! It was high time that the faithful emulated the wise virgins in the parable, and checked the oil in their lamps and prepared their souls ready for the Bridegroom's coming!

One important characteristic of this era of primitive Christianity, upon which comment has often been made, stemmed simultaneously from the ideal of brotherly love and from the conviction, held by certain Christians at least, of the imminence of Judgment Day. The Acts tell us that the faithful were accustomed to put their possessions into a common pool. 'All those who owned farms or houses used to sell them and bring the price of what they had sold to lay it at the apostles' feet, so that each could have what share of it he needed' (Acts iv. 34, 35). In this way, the precept which Jesus had laid down for the rich young man devolved into a rule for the whole community: 'Sell all that belongs to thee, and give to the poor; so the treasure thou hast shall be in heaven.' The example of one man, Joseph called Barnabas, whose generosity seems to have been infectious, is quoted in terms of admiration. By contrast, the Acts recount the horrifying tale of one married couple, named Ananias and Sapphira, who attempted to trick the Holy Spirit by pretending to hand over all their belongings to the community, a thing they were not in fact bound to do, while at the same time they kept back a part of them. It is recorded that divine justice subsequently struck down each of them in turn (Acts v. 1-11). Although no actual law insisted upon this practice of property-sharing, it appears to have been a general one. The term 'Christian brotherhood' was no empty phrase at this time.

Such is our picture of the first Christian Church. And these moving impressions were to endure down the centuries in Christian tradition—a model that men would later strive after and yearn for with regretful and nostalgic longing.

## 'It is Impossible for us to Refrain from Speaking'

The development of the Christian community very soon brought its problems. The first of these concerned the young Church's relations with the Jewish world of which it formed a part. As we have already seen, the first of Christ's flock most certainly did not set themselves outside obedience to the Torah. Had not Jesus Himself declared that He had come 'not to set them aside [i.e. the law and the prophets] but to bring them to perfection'? Had He not actually proclaimed that 'heaven and earth must disappear sooner than one jot, one flourish, disappear from the law' (Matt. v. 17-19)? It was only natural that the Christians should pay great attention to the temple prayers and ceremonies, that they should in fact be even more attentive and receptive in this respect than many of the other Israelites, for belief in the Messianic fulfilment had exalted their souls and brought them nearer to God.

However, albeit imperceptibly, a split must soon have made itself felt between the Christians and the rest of the Jews. Even though they did not desire it, but simply because they were living a life in Jesus, their practical existence was to become distinctly different from that of those Jews who did not believe in Him. For instance, the weekly religious festival, the sabbath, whose every detail was devoted to prayer, fell on a Saturday. We know that, in so far as they were Jews, the first Christians observed it. But alongside it they were obliged to recognize another festival, that of 'the Lord's Day,' on which they commemorated the Resurrection: in the Epistles of St Paul (1 Cor. xvi. 2), in the Acts (xx. 7), and even in the non-canonical text known as the *Letter of Barnabas*, dating from about 132, we find evidence that the 'first day of the week' was a Christian festival. In the result, rivalry occurred between these two equally holy days, and gradually it was Sunday that prevailed.[11] In ways such as this the first Christians were to become conscious that they were Jews who were different from the rest of the Jews, and to show these differences quite clearly.

Yet these divergences in attitude, which were of considerable importance among the most formalist of peoples, were as nothing compared with the fundamental opposition which, sooner or later, was bound to range a watchful officialdom against the heirs of the crucified Christ. The sacerdotal authorities in Jerusalem might have been able to ignore a handful of fanatics who were intent merely upon harking back to their memories among themselves; from the moment, however, that it became apparent that the Christians were

---

[11] This first change led to another. The Jews fasted on Thursdays; the Christians preferred to fast on a Friday, the day of the Passion, on which 'the Bridegroom was taken.' The most austere of all Jewish traditions, that of the Pharisees, recognized another fast-day, Monday; the Christians chose Wednesday, the day on which the Passion drama began, as their second day of expiation. The substitution of these new observances for the old was not completed until the end of the second century. In the *Letters* of St Ignatius of Antioch and in the *Didache*, i.e. prior to 150, there are still signs of conflict between Sunday and the sabbath.

carrying on a seemingly successful missionary endeavour they
were forced to put themselves on their guard. In declaring that
Jesus was the Messiah, the members of this community were
not simply branding themselves as rebels against God and the
law—for their leader had been condemned by the sacred tribunal on a particularly heinous charge, albeit according to a
procedure which no one was very anxious to discuss. They
were not simply ridiculous—since it was patently obvious that
the major proofs bearing witness to the Messianic fulfilment
had not in fact appeared, for the Roman soldiers still paced
the walls of the Antonine fortress and Israel had not recovered
her ancient glory. No, they were worse than this: they were
attacking something about which nations are always particularly sensitive; they were attacking national pride, and, among
the Jews, national pride was an integral part of the nation's
belief in its divinely ordained mission.

The whole of the Jewish Messianic tradition seemed to lie
heavily upon the conscience of the priests, that tradition
which was deeply rooted in the heart of a people who
had suffered five centuries of oppression, that desire to regain
self-respect, liberty and strength; and it was for this reason
that the priesthood decided to punish the new community
severely. So many Jewish texts gave expression to the tradition:
'Send us a king, O Lord, a son of David, and let him reign
over thy servant Israel, and gird him with power so that he
may humble the ungodly rulers . . . and destroy the sinful
Gentiles!' (the apocryphal Psalms of Solomon, xvii. 23–7).
It was true that the Holy Books contained certain references
to the Messiah which were of a very different kind, notably
that in Chapter LIII of Isaiah, according to which the servant
of Yahweh would suffer and die, wounded 'for our sins'; many
of the rabbis knew this perfectly well. But this idea seemed so
repugnant to them, so out of keeping with the mighty picture
of biblical Israel, guided by Yahweh towards glory, that they
were loath to admit its validity: some of them even wondered
whether these prophetic sentences might not refer to someone
other than the Lord's Anointed. In the second century, during an argument with St Justin, the Jew Tryphon was to utter
the following remarks, which sum up the anti-Christian state
of mind perfectly: 'We are aware that the Scriptures tell of a

suffering Messiah who will return in glory to receive the
eternal kingdom of the world. But just try to prove to us that
he had to be crucified, to die so ignominiously and so infa-
mously, to die actually accursed by the Law—for we cannot
even begin to consider such a thing!'

Consequently conflict was inevitable, and the book of Acts
gives an example of this conflict in its very first chapters (iii
and iv). The incident probably occurred very shortly after
Pentecost. Peter and John were going up to the temple for
prayer at the ninth hour. They had already crossed the Court
of the Gentiles, which anyone could enter, even the uncircumcised, and the noisy clatter of the money-changers' tables, the
traders selling animals for the sacrifices, the inquisitive sight-
seers and the ordinary passers-by. They were just climbing the
stairs to the inner court when a paralysed beggar asked them
for alms. 'Silver and gold are not mine to give,' replied St
Peter, 'I give thee what I can. In the name of Jesus Christ of
Nazareth, rise up and walk!' (Acts iii. 6).

The news of the miracle spread rapidly through the city.
Crowds rushed to Solomon's Porch and surged around the
healer. The Apostle seized the opportunity to speak to the
people. He declared that the astonishing cure had indeed been
effected in the name of Jesus, that selfsame Jesus who had
been crucified to death on the Cross. He reiterated his faith in
Jesus, the Messiah. Those who were listening to him now, those
who had killed the Master, and even their leaders, had sinned
through ignorance. But now let them repent and show themselves converted!

At this point the priests and the commander of the temple
guards arrived. They seized the Apostles and threw them into
prison. On the following day the Sanhedrin met, presided over
by Annas the high priest; Caiaphas, of ancient memory, was
there too, and probably several of those who had condemned
Jesus. They questioned Peter, who was afire with the Holy
Spirit. He talked on; he braved the wrath of the Tribunal:
'That stone, rejected by you . . . has become the chief stone
at the corner. Salvation is not to be found elsewhere [i.e. except
in Jesus]; this alone of all the names under heaven has been
appointed to me as the one by which we must needs be saved!'
(Acts iv. 11, 12). The Sanhedrin seems to have been cautious

rather than ferocious. Perhaps it was merely being astute. Surely this agitation would soon die down of its own accord! The two men were forbidden to preach and teach in the name of Jesus. And then it was that Peter and John made the reply that was to become the fundamental axiom of Christian propaganda: 'It is impossible for us to refrain from speaking of what we have seen and heard!' (Acts iv. 20). It was better to obey God than men.

In this way the opposition between the Jews of the Torah and the Jews of the Cross became more and more glaring. Very soon now the relative mildness of the Israelite leaders would come to an end, to be replaced by an ever-increasing severity. Peter and John were to have personal experience of this hardening in attitude when they began preaching the Good News again. They were arrested a second time, and on this occasion beaten with rods. On the one hand, the authorities in Jerusalem, and very soon those elsewhere too, were to fight the missionary efforts of the new message with all the means in their power; on the other, the first Christians, faithful to the Master's teaching, refused 'to hide their light under a bushel.' They could not keep silent! The more they were persecuted, the more steadfast and courageous they became, 'rejoicing that they had been found worthy to suffer indignity for the sake of Jesus' name' (Acts v. 41).[12]

## THE NEWS SPREADS BEYOND JERUSALEM

Christianity began to expand from the moment of its birth: its expansion has never ceased, and never will. This expansion is the most striking characteristic of its whole history. The

---

[12] The Apostles' second arrest is marked by a very odd incident. One eminent Scribe, the Rabbi Gamaliel, heir to a long line of Doctors of the Law and the grandson of the famous Rabbi Hillel, intervened on Peter's and John's behalf. Why? In the interests of justice? Because he had secret Christian sympathies (this was the traditional belief in the Middle Ages)? Or because he was anxious to embarrass the Sadducees? We do not know. At all events his line of argument is interesting. 'Have nothing to do with these men, let them be. If this is man's design or man's undertaking, it will be overthrown; if it is God's, you will have no power to overthrow it.' The more progress Christianity made, the more like a 'work of God' it appeared, and success thus engendered success.

Church is no fixed thing, defined and marked out once and for always; she is a living force which continues to grow, a human reality which develops within society according to what may be called an organic law. For she knows full well how to adapt herself to the circumstances around her, to make the conditions of time and place serve her own ends, to be prudent in her audacity and gently persuasive even in the breaches that she causes, never once losing sight of her sole object, namely the establishment of the Kingdom of God.

The first signs of expansion came within the narrow confines of Jerusalem itself. But the very strength of the new movement's enthusiasm quickly made it overspill the city boundaries. And this happened almost straight away, throughout the whole of Palestine and the lands immediately surrounding it. Accustomed as we are to modern methods of communication, it is difficult for us to picture the importance of the journeys which the peoples of the Ancient World were able to make, with neither cars nor railways to help them. Only those of us who have lived in the East or in Arab territory can really understand the astonishing mobility of these races who seem to ignore the fatigues of travel and to despise our European home-loving instincts. Right at the beginning of the Gospel we see Mary, even though pregnant, making the long journey from Nazareth to Ain-Karim to visit Elizabeth, then a few months later travelling ninety miles once again to go to Bethlehem, and finally fleeing to Egypt along the frightful route through the Negeb, only a little while after her Child's birth. All this with nothing but the aid of an ambling donkey. It is essential that we picture the people of Israel continually travelling about within the boundaries of the Holy Land, the roads thronged with caravans and mules, the squalid caravanserai packed with travellers and merchandise. All these journeyings and rendezvous gave opportunities for that exchange of gossip so beloved of Eastern peoples, an exchange that causes news to travel as swiftly as if it had wings.

One of the principal reasons for these comings and goings was a religious one. Devout Jews were accustomed to go up to Jerusalem for the various religious festivals. The Passover in particular drew crowds to the city of David which were comparable in size to those which now flock to the major places of Christian pilgrimage, or, in the case of Moslems, to Mecca. Flavius Josephus maintains that in certain years 255,600 lambs were sacrificed there, and since there was one sacrificial victim for every ten pilgrims, this would appear to correspond to a human wave of more than two million souls. These pious visitors came from every part of Palestine, and when the festival was over they would set off home again, intoning the verses from the Psalms: 'From the Lord deliverance comes to me, the Lord who made heaven and earth . . . the Lord protect thy journeying and thy home-coming henceforth and for ever' (Psalm cxx). And when they arrived home they would be sure to relate all they had learnt in the Holy City to their less favoured neighbours who had not had the good fortune to tread the sacred temple courts as they had done.

These movements of traders and pilgrims, which certainly must have played a decisive part in the initial spread of the Good News, were not restricted to the Promised Land alone. Palestine was but one tiny fragment of Rome's vast territories, and the whole country could easily have been turned upside-down by the news of the arrival of the Messianic era without the rest of the world being remotely aware of it had not an extremely important geographic link existed between her and the rest of the Empire: this was the link afforded by the dispersal of large numbers of Jews beyond the Palestinian frontiers, a phenomenon generally known by its Greek name, the *diaspora*.[13]

It should be remembered that, for a long time past, groups of Jews had been induced to settle in foreign lands. Even before the Exile a Jewish colony was living and trading in Damascus. In the sixth century B.C. the successive deportations of Samaritans to Assyria and defeated Judeans to Babylon had left thriving colonies along the Euphrates and the Tigris, which extended as far as the Persian plateaus, as the books of Tobias and Esther bear witness. Subsequently a number of other factors had tended to further this dispersal of population: Alexander had attracted Jews to Alexandria, his new capital; his land concessions had given rise to a real colony of them in

[13] For a more detailed study of the *diaspora* see the author's earlier work, *Jesus in His Time*, Chapter III.

Mesopotamia; the Seleucids, though they behaved as persecutors in Palestine itself, had encouraged Jewish settlements in
Anatolia; and when Rome took prisoner the Jewish contingents
serving under Antiochus Epiphanes, she established them in
Italy. Thus every historical disturbance for centuries past had
encouraged the *diaspora*.

At the beginning of the Christian era Jewish communities
probably existed in every single imperial province, and this
process of dispersal was to continue for at least another hundred years. Already the book of *Sybilline Oracles* was saying of
Israel that: 'The whole earth is filled with your people, even
the seas!' Flavius Josephus was to declare that 'it would be
hard to find a single town without Jews in it,' and this is confirmed by Strabo in almost identical terms. And St Augustine
was to quote the following sentence of Seneca's: 'The habits
and customs of this rascally race have taken root in every country under the sun!' In actual fact traces of the Jews can be
found both in Babylon and in Delos, in the holy isle of Greece,
where they built a synagogue, as well as in places as far apart
as Sardis and Roman Gaul. In Egyptian Alexandria they
were so numerous that two of the city's five residential districts
were regarded as their preserve. In North Africa they converted
some of the Berber tribes, and one French author[14] has even
maintained that, by crossing the Niger via the Saharan oases,
they may have taken there the germs of the extremely bizarre
civilization which the Peuhls or Fulbes were to bring to fruition
in the kingdom of Ghana.

Is it possible to make some estimate of the numbers involved in this *diaspora*? Obviously we ought not to take any
serious notice of Philo's exaggerated statement on this subject.
He asserts that the Jews formed half the human race, and that
in the countries in which they had settled their number almost
equalled that of the original inhabitants! But there is no doubt
whatsoever that a very large number of Jews did live abroad,
the number involved being far larger than that of the Jewish
communities in pre-1939 France or Germany. A very modest
estimate sets their number at about one and a half million,
scattered over both the Middle East (including Egypt and

14 See M. Delafosse, *Les Noirs de l'Afrique*. Paris, 1922.

Syria) and the rest of the Empire. With a total imperial population of about fifty-five million, this would mean that the Jews represented nearly three per cent of it. Consequently the phenomenon of the *diaspora* is of considerable historical importance, especially in relation to the religious history of this period.

For, although they were scattered among so many different races in this way, the Jews of the *diaspora* did not mix with the natives of the countries in which they lived. On the surface they fitted into the life of their adopted land, for they would speak its language and accept its secular customs. However, grouped together as they were in their synagogues, where they gathered to comment on the sacred Torah, and guided by a council of elders and an elected leader, they jealously preserved their spiritual independence. Unlike the Italians or the Poles in modern America, they were far from constituting an amorphous mass, with no precise organic bond holding it together. They were still a branch of the Chosen People, separated from the ancient trunk by historical circumstance, but remaining faithful to it and constantly demanding spiritual nourishment from it.

Relations between the homeland and these dispersed Jews were close and constant. For all of them Jerusalem remained the Holy City, the spiritual capital in which beat the heart of the Jewish nation. The exiles turned towards Jerusalem to say their prayers, and all dreamed of returning there one day. The Sanhedrin, too, retained its supreme authority so far as the emigrants of the *diaspora* were concerned. Appeals to it could be made from the decisions of the local synagogue tribunals. From the age of twenty every Jewish male, wherever he lived, had to make an annual payment of one didrachma to the temple, this constituting a kind of religious tax; moreover, in every town in the world where Jews were living, collecting-boxes existed to house the often considerable contributions which, when complete, were ceremonially conveyed to the Holy City; in a series of ordinances Augustus had actually guaranteed the freedom of this transfer of wealth. And on the great festivals boat-loads of Jews would come from every corner of the Empire, Jews who could truly claim: 'There are Parthians among us, and Medes and Elamites; our homes are in

Mesopotamia, or Judaea, or Cappadocia; in Pontus or Asia, Phrygia or Pamphylia, Egypt or the parts of Libya around Cyrene' (Acts ii. 9). These pilgrims would arrive in the Holy Land at Joppa or Caesarea, and, as they disembarked, all piously kissed their native soil.

In order to guess the speed at which the Gospel message spread, it is absolutely essential to take into account this constantly moving human stream, these perpetual comings and goings. Very soon now the Jewish communities of the *diaspora* would be bidding a welcome to Christians fleeing from persecution in Jerusalem, or to Christian missionaries on their travels; but already, almost immediately after Jesus' death, the story of His life had sped around the world, borne by Jewish pilgrims. And men repeated this story one to another, in places like the Jewish quarter of Messina, or the back streets of Rome. The Spirit of God had breathed upon mankind and had sown its sacred seed therein.

## HELLENISTS AND JUDAIZERS

But very soon this spontaneous expansion of Christianity was to come up against a new difficulty. No longer was it just a question of wrestling against the suspicions of evil-minded enemies of the faith: it was now necessary to decide between two tendencies existing within the bosom of the Christian community itself, each of which seemed equally respectable, with all the risk of dissension and secession that such a choice entailed. Increasing numbers of Jews from the *diaspora* had become Christians while in Jerusalem; Christian cells were being founded all over the Empire, in the very heart of the Jewish communities there; and it was this fact which was soon to raise some very serious problems, in both the theoretical and practical spheres. The future of the Church and the faith would depend very largely upon the solutions which were found for them.

Once again we must look at the matter against the background of Jewish history if we are to understand it properly. For quite a long time now two schools of thought had existed alongside one another in Israel, each of which regarded foreigners in a totally different light. The first was rigidly par-

ticularist. It insisted proudly upon the Jewish tribes' unique
position as God's Chosen People. It stressed, with some justice,
that only the Jews' savage resistance to pagan contamination
in the past had allowed them to survive and to fulfil their
mission. It passionately advocated the complete separation of
the sacred Jewish nation from 'those races accursed from their
beginnings' and regarded the least contact with them as a
defilement. The *Letter of Aristaeus*, a third-century Jewish
document, declared: 'The lawgiver enclosed us within the
iron walls of the law in order that, being pure in mind and
body, we might not mingle in any way with other nations.'
This particularist feeling varied from straightforward revulsion to active hatred of the non-Jew, and resulted in an exclusivism of which there are many authentic examples in the
Bible. On the whole it was the attitude held by the Jews of
Jerusalem and Palestine. They lived very close to the temple,
both physically and emotionally, keeping green the bitter
memories of all the sufferings which the different foreign invaders had inflicted upon the Holy Land. These Jews were
superbly uninterested in the outside world and had no desire
whatsoever to be considered citizens of it.

However, another school of thought had always existed in
the Israelite world, parallel to this one—a school which was
universalist in attitude, and which regarded foreigners with
respect. Its advocates welcomed any man of goodwill into the
Israelite fold, and were not disposed to hurl anathema at all
pagans indiscriminately. Such an attitude of mind carried the
most generous-minded Jews in the same direction as that
which Jesus was to take. These men took the promise made to
Abraham very seriously: 'All the races of the world shall find
a blessing through thy posterity!' Similarly, they laid stress
on the prophecy of Jeremiah, which foresaw a time when all
nations of the world should know God, and on the injunctions
given to Jonah when he refused to bear the tidings of God
to the Ninevites. For these universalist Jews the mission of the
Chosen People was clearly set out in the wonderful words of
the aged Tobias: 'If he [i.e. Yahweh] has dispersed you among
heathen folk who know nothing of him, it was so that you
might tell them the story of his great deeds, convince them
that he and no other, is God all-powerful' (Tobias xiii. 4).

And indeed it was among the dispersed communities that the universalist tendency was strongest. In Jerusalem itself adherents of universalism were the exception rather than the rule; men referred in tones of scandalized astonishment to the extremely learned Rabbi Gamaliel, one of the most illustrious Doctors of the Law, who had learnt Greek, who consorted with pagans and who had gone so far as to bathe in the waters of the baths dedicated to the heathen idol Aphrodite, just as if they were any ordinary pool! In the *diaspora*, on the other hand, Judaism had undergone a slow transformation during the passage of the centuries, even though it remained bound to the temple by several strong links. It became willing to assimilate new ideas. Its members spoke the new language of the day, Greek, which was the essential commercial tongue, to the very point where they forgot the Aramaic of their forefathers and only preserved their Hebrew for liturgical purposes. To these dispersed Jews pagan civilization had offered not only its temptations and its charm, but also its opportunities of spiritual enrichment: they no longer regarded it purely as the Devil's kingdom. Quite the opposite: discounting a few apostates who allowed themselves to be engulfed in it, body and soul, the majority of devout Jews in the *diaspora* dreamed of leading it to Yahweh one day.

Alexandria, in Egypt, was the principal centre of the universalist school. There, in contact with the Hellenic world at its most subtle and refined, the enormous Jewish colony had produced some extraordinary spiritual plants, whose roots still rested in the soil of the Mosaic Law, but whose shoots had pushed their way up right into the midst of the Greek sky. There, according to a tradition whose details are symbolical rather than strictly factual, Pharaoh Ptolemy II had had the Jewish sacred books translated into Greek by seventy scholars. Their efforts were said to have been completed within seventy days, and all, miraculously, coincided exactly. These scholars are known to us as 'the Seventy,' and their text, the 'Septuagint,' was to have a wide circulation. There too a school of Jewish exegetists existed who sought to find in the Pentateuch an answer to all the serious problems of Greek philosophy, and who regarded the Old Testament heroes as the incarnate symbols of reason and wisdom—of the virtues as defined by

Plato and the Stoics. And there, above all, lived the great Rabbi Philo,[15] Christ's contemporary (he was born in 20 B.C.), who was both a loyal Jew, so devoted to his nation's cause that he was willing to risk his life for it, and, at the same time, a philosopher imbued with Plato's doctrine of ideas ('the most blessed Plato' he called him), with the Pythagorean symbolism of numbers, and with the Stoic theory of ultimate causes, who consciously endeavoured to put Greek culture to the service of his faith.[16]

This universalist trend brought its natural result: proselytism. Pagan souls were attracted to the cult of the one true God, and though proselytism occurred on only a moderate scale in Palestine itself, it was rampant in the *diaspora*. If Flavius Josephus can be believed, 'large numbers of pagans zealously practised various Jewish rites—the weekly day of rest, the fasts, the kindling of lamps, and even the prohibitions concerning food.' We see some proselytes and *God-fearers* of this kind in the Gospels, the centurion at Capernaum, for example. But this extension of Judaism had its difficulties and encountered some resistance. Rigorist Jews distrusted the converts. Moreover, the rite of circumcision was obligatory upon any male who wished to become a true child of Yahweh and a full member of the Jewish community, and a large number of would-be proselytes drew back when faced with this.[17] So,

---

[15] Philo's religious ideas, and the influence they had, are studied further in Chapter VI, section: 'The Need for Philosophy.'

[16] Other Jewish texts, also originating from the *diaspora*, show the same tendencies. The *Letter of Aristaeus*, dating from between 221 and 203, interprets the message of the prophets of Israel in a universalist sense by admitting that any man can achieve salvation provided that he lives a virtuous life and believes in one single God, the Creator. The Psalms of Solomon, written some sixty years later, while attacking the ungodly most vigorously, likens *wisdom*, the Greek *sophia*, to the Spirit of God. The Fourth Book of Maccabees, which belongs to the same epoch, is a curious mixture of philosophic arguments and biblical quotations. A number of Judeo-Hellenic prayers, too, link the conviction of Israel's divine election with a generous, 'cosmopolitan' impulse, which seeks the reconciliation of the whole earth and of every nation within it in God's bosom.

[17] Consequently women proselytes were more numerous than men. The 'God-fearers' accepted the moral principles of Judaism but not circumcision.

torn between an exclusivism which was to become increasingly violent right up to the time of the catastrophe known as 'the Jewish War,' and a universalism which, though admirable, dared not go to its logical conclusion and declare that there were no longer 'circumcised nor uncircumcised,' the Jewish conscience seemed poised in a state of unbalance.

The same dilemma, transposed on to the Christian plane, soon arose in the communities born of Jesus. However, here the elements of opposition were not so clear-cut: it is the mighty call to freedom that we hear throughout the Gospels, the call to remission and salvation which is addressed to all, regardless of their origin. The one lesson which seems fundamental is that taught the Apostles by the Master in the days following His Resurrection: 'You, therefore, must go out, making disciples of all nations, and baptizing them in the name of the Father, the Son and the Holy Ghost, teaching them to observe all the commandments which I have given you' (Matt. xxviii. 19–20). Never at any time did Jesus preach anything which encouraged isolationism, particularism or religious exclusiveness.

But the most generous and all-embracing of teachings could become constricted when it passed into the Jewish mind, permeated as it was with traditional, and in a way legitimate, national pride. 'Salvation is to come from the Jews,' Jesus had told the woman of Samaria (John iv. 22). Sentences like these fell upon soil only too ready to receive them. Consequently a stream of thought remained active within the Christian community which tended to interpret the Good News in strictly Jewish terms, to impose upon future Christian converts the same rites as had been imposed in the past upon the synagogue proselytes, notably that of circumcision—a stream of thought which, in the last resort, risked imprisoning Jesus' message within the boundaries of one tiny Jewish sect. This current was so strong that St Paul himself had to deal carefully with the susceptibilities which it aroused in men's hearts. But against it were ranged the truth of Christ's teaching and the dynamics of history. The exclusivist tendency would be vanquished: in the Church of Christ the Hellenists, that is to say, the converted universalist Jews coming very largely from the *diaspora*, would eventually prevail over the Judaizers, who were overmuch shackled by fetters of mistaken loyalty. But the life of the community was to be severely shaken by the conflict on several occasions before universalism finally won the day.

## THE SEVEN DEACONS AND THE MARTYR-DOM OF ST STEPHEN

Despite its discreet reporting, one incident in the book of Acts gives a clear forewarning of the consequences of this opposition between Hellenists and Judaizers. 'At this time, as the number of disciples increased, complaints were brought against those who spoke Hebrew by those who spoke Greek; their widows, they said, were neglected in the daily administration of relief' (Acts vi. 1). This seemingly unimportant note is actually of great significance. The credibility of the whole book can be judged from such details as this. In so many ways the Acts is an account of the sublime, but its author has been careful not to exaggerate its idyllic atmosphere. The communal life of the early Christians raised a number of very mundane problems concerning administration and the distribution of the community's wealth: human nature, sanctified though it might be, occasionally displayed its baser side. The Hellenists were afraid, in this instance, of being treated as second-class Christians, particularly in connection with the allocation of relief. Here, in the practical sphere, is the manifestation of that spiritual friction which we have already noted.

These complaints soon became so pressing that a solution to the problem was a matter of some urgency. When, in the fifth century B.C., one section of the Roman populace, the *plebs*, had declared itself dissatisfied with the existing regime and had threatened secession from the Republic, a special class of magistrates had been set up, chosen from its members and entrusted with protecting its interests: these were known as the Tribunes of the Plebs. The same reasoning led the early Christian community to give the Hellenists similar pledges of good faith, by choosing various officials drawn from the *diaspora* groups, who relieved the Apostles of a number of administrative duties as well as making sure that both sections of the Church were equitably treated.

This was how the *deacons* were instituted. Their foundation was actually proposed by the Twelve themselves, with the approval of the whole community. The deacons were seven in number. Perhaps this was because the municipal councils in all Jewish towns consisted of seven members, or possibly because the second miraculous multiplication of bread performed by Jesus in the hellenized territory of the *Decapolis* (Mark viii. 1–9), a famous incident illustrative of the conversion of non-Jews, was effected with seven loaves, and when the multitude had fed seven hampers of crumbs were left. All seven deacons were Hellenist in origin. Their names are proof of this: Stephen, Philip, Prochorus, Nicanor, Timon, Parmenas and Nicolas: the last named was actually a proselyte from Antioch, in other words a Greek who had been converted to Judaism. What role were these new auxiliary leaders of the community going to play? Obviously they would assist in its administration; but they would certainly take part in the work of preaching and conversion too. There is no doubt of their sacerdotal character, for their choice was followed by a ceremony in which the Apostles placed their hands upon the deacons, invoking the blessings of the Holy Spirit upon them. Thus consecrated, they could not be regarded simply as officials performing a material function, but took their place in the ecclesiastical hierarchy, and in the Church to this day the title of deacon remains associated with the sacrament of holy orders, of which it forms an integral part.

In bringing about the foundation of the order of deacons the Hellenists had done something extremely important. And there is no doubt that the whole affair was carried through under the stimulus of the Apostles themselves, for it was they who had put forward the idea in the first place. Peter, in particular, must have played a large part in the matter, and we shall soon be seeing him acting in liaison with one or other of the deacons, notably with Philip. This is a sign whose importance should not be underestimated: whereas Jesus' relations, who, justifiably enough, exercised great influence in the first Church, seem to have held ideas which were more or less imprisoned within the narrow Jewish framework of their personal background, the Twelve Apostles, the repositories of the Word, sensed early on that it was essential for the faith to break free of this framework. Furthermore, as is always the case in undertakings of a very ambitious nature, one decision

PALESTINE IN THE EARLIEST DAYS OF THE CHURCH

led to another, and an action embarked upon for only limited objectives brought with it new possibilities of development. These deacons, upon whom the community had just conferred such an important role, were all youngish men, more receptive to new ideas, more interested in missionary efforts, and less

fettered by Hebraic conformity. They were to give the infant
Church a new and vigorous stimulus. In Acts the account of
their election is followed by this significant comment: 'By now
the word of God was gaining influence, and the number of
disciples in Jerusalem was greatly increasing' (Acts vi. 7).

The story of *Stephen* (Acts vi. 8–vii. 60) gives a very clear
picture of the dynamism which the deacons brought into the
Church. This ardent soul, radiant with courage, was the first
of that vast procession of wonderful men and women whom
Christianity was to enrol in the service of her cause, and who,
having found the bliss of life in Jesus, deemed it quite natural
to sacrifice that life for Him. Stephen was a Hellenist, and
may have even been of Alexandrian origin.[18] At all events
he was equally at home among either philosophic doctrines or
Hebrew traditions, and he was a marvellous personification of
the new spirit within the Church, which was intent upon
fresh conversions and which had decided upon certain necessary breaks with the Jewish past. He knew how to talk to
the non-Jew better than the Judaizers did; but as a result he
dealt far less gently with the sensitivities of the old adherents
of the Torah. Whenever St Peter preached to the crowds in
Jerusalem he applied himself first and foremost to the task of
showing them that Jesus had been the Messiah, the ultimate
fulfilment of all that Israel stood for. Stephen, however, remembered best the Gospel sentences which said that one could
not pour new wine into old skins, and that a tattered cloak
might not be patched with new material. Pious Jews were quick
to grasp his meaning. Here was a more dangerous enemy!
The formalists of the *diaspora*, in particular, were in no doubt
of this. 'This man is never tired of uttering insults against
the holy place, and the law' (Acts vi. 13).

The Sanhedrin met. Probably the Jewish authorities felt
more independent than usual at this particular time, for Pontius Pilate had just been recalled to Rome to account for

[18] This has been suggested on account of the knowledge which he
seems to possess of the doctrines of Philo, which were particularly
fashionable in Alexandria at this time, and also because he uses the
word *wisdom* four times in his speech, in the sense in which it was
currently understood in Jewish circles in Egypt (the biblical book
of Wisdom comes from Egypt).

various recent and over-obvious atrocities, and was now defending his actions—not very well—before Caligula. It was the opportune moment to try to smash the growing sect. Stephen was led before the judges. Not for one instant did he desire to save his own head. He was not remotely interested in defending himself, but only in proclaiming his faith so loudly that all could hear him; this was to be the attitude of all the martyrs who followed him. His speech was a magnificent one, its line of argument firm and strong. He linked Christ's message with everything in the Scriptures which had heralded its coming, and he set it out in terms of a logical conclusion: but there was more to it than this—his actual courage was superb. He rattled out accusation upon accusation against the predestined, but unfaithful, Jewish nation. And he concluded his long apologia with these damning sentences: 'Stiff-necked race, your heart and ears still uncircumcised, you are for ever resisting the Holy Spirit, just as your fathers did. There was not one of the prophets they did not persecute; it was death to foretell the coming of that just man, whom you in your times have betrayed and murdered; you, who received the law dictated by angels, and did not keep it!' (Acts vii. 51–3).

This was too much. The Jews answered his provocative speech with howls of rage. Stephen knew well enough what end awaited him. Already, so he told his accusers, he saw the heavens opening, and the Son of Man standing at the right hand of God. Blasphemy! More blasphemy! At this the exasperated audience fell upon him and dragged him away. The Roman procurator would know nothing of this illegal execution: or anyhow, there would be nothing that he could do about it. What this impious creature deserved was death by stoning, the supreme penalty for blasphemy. The stones soon began to fly, striking down the heroic deacon, who prayed aloud to Jesus, begging Him to forgive his torturers. A young Pharisee stood in one corner, watching the scene and grinning: his name was Saul, and he stepped forward and offered to look after the executioners' cloaks. 'And now behold,' Jesus had said, 'I am sending prophets and wise men and men of learning to preach to you; some of them you will put to death and crucify, some you will scourge in your synagogues, and persecute them from city to city. . . . Believe me, this generation shall be held answerable for all of it' (Matt. xxiii. 34–9). Thirty years later, when Jerusalem did indeed become the 'uninhabited house' predicted by the Master, the blood of this first martyr would be dearly paid for in a massive flood of suffering. But in giving Christianity the first of many witnesses sealed in blood, Stephen's martyrdom was to contribute a very great deal to spreading the Good News far and wide.

## The Work Done by St Peter and Philip the Deacon

The outbreak of persecution which followed Stephen's execution did not halt the missionary efforts of the Christians. 'Stephen was buried by devout men, who mourned greatly over him' (Acts viii. 2); an action which provides evidence that the Christians were not to be frightened by the assaults of orthodox Jewry. The Hellenists, who were the main targets of attack, left the Holy City, and sought temporary refuge in their countries of origin. And in this way the deed which had been intended to crush Christian expansion once and for all was in fact to do a great deal to further it. 'You are to be my witnesses in Jerusalem and throughout Judaea, in Samaria, yes, and to the ends of the earth' (Acts i. 8), Jesus had told His disciples. The resurrected Lord's prophecy was about to be fulfilled.

In the beginning Christian missionary endeavours had been directed solely at the Jewish communities, whether Palestinian or Hellenist. This had been an essential first stage which had given the movement solid foundations upon which to build later. Jesus Himself had explicitly indicated the necessity of a preliminary procedure of this kind, for when the Twelve had first begun their work of conversion He had forbidden them to go to the pagans or the Samaritans, and had ordered them to concern themselves with the lost sheep of Israel alone (Matt. x. 5). Later on, when the Christian community had been strengthened by a few years of quiet endeavour of this sort, it could become more ambitious, and go beyond the confines of the Chosen People, thus obeying the Master's final instructions, to preach the Gospel to 'all nations.' And so it is that we must visualize these first missionaries of the new faith, full of enthusiasm and unflagging courage, setting out along the roads leading from Jerusalem, travelling probably in twos according to the custom instituted by the Master (Luke x. 1–16; Mark vi. 7–13). They journeyed without money or food, wearing but a simple tunic and sandals, and carrying a staff. Should men refuse to receive them, they would shake the dust of the uninviting place from their feet and set off again, bearing the Good News still further afield. Their strength derived from one wonderful hope; had not the Son of Man promised that He would return even before their travels were completed (Matt. x. 23)? The first Christians took this text quite literally, taking it to mean the immediate future.

The deacons seem to have played a most important part in the first expansion of the Gospel beyond the narrow confines of Jerusalem. The Acts tells us a great deal about the actions and methods of one deacon in particular, *Philip*. Philip was a magnificent missionary, continually on the move, always receptive to the Holy Spirit, and quick to turn any circumstance to the advantage of his cause. He was the kind of worker every human undertaking yearns for, one of those pioneers who clear the ground and pitch the first tents, and hold the fort until others are ready to come and exploit their conquests and build permanently.

We find him going into Samaritan territory first of all, to carry the Word of God to the people there (Acts viii. 4–25). This action, which does not seem particularly astonishing to us, would have been more than surprising to the Jews of the day: they must have regarded it as a considerable scandal. Everyone in Jerusalem and the other pious Jewish communities detested the Samaritans, descendants of a pack of pagans, heretics, unclean folk whose very water, according to the rabbis, was 'more impure than swine's blood.' The Jews had never forgiven them for having built a temple at Gerizim, in days gone by, which had rivalled that of Sion, and there had been great rejoicing when John Hyrcanus had razed their capital to the ground in 128 B.C. The disciples had made their own feelings on the Samaritans plain enough to Jesus Himself, when He had spoken in friendly fashion to a Samaritan woman; what in the world would the faithful in the Holy City think of the deacon who attempted to convert these accursed people?

At this time the city of Samaria was at the height of its splendour. Pompey had rebuilt it and created it a free city; Gabinius had fortified it; Herod the Great—how like him, thought the Jews sarcastically—had given it a pagan appearance by erecting classical colonnades, temples and theatres there, and had renamed it Sebaste, in order to flatter his master, Augustus, whose name in Greek was *Sebastos*. However, the common people had retained a lively though somewhat peculiar religious faith; they were indeed awaiting the coming of the Messiah, as the woman at the well had told Jesus, but they were also easily moved to enthusiasm by a miracle-monger or a pedlar of magic. This was no easy material on which to work.

But Philip succeeded with it. 'The multitude listened with general accord to what Philip said' (Acts viii. 6). His progress was marked by miracles: 'There were many possessed by unclean spirits, and these came out, crying aloud; many, too, were healed of the palsy, and of lameness, and there was great rejoicing in that city' (Acts viii. 7–8). Jesus had told the Samaritan woman, at the foot of Mount Gerizim, that 'the time is coming when you will not go to this mountain, nor yet to Jerusalem, to worship the Father . . . true worshippers will worship the Father in spirit and truth' (John iv. 21–3). His prediction was fulfilled in Philip's baptism of the Samaritans.

The news of this success reached Jerusalem, and the community there was deeply stirred by it. But its joy was probably mingled with a certain amount of anxiety. It was decided to send two Apostles to Samaria on a tour of inspection. Peter and John were chosen to go, a choice which clearly shows that the matter was considered a very important one. Here we see the first example of a method which appears to have been used systematically on subsequent occasions: missionaries were sent out, allowed to make a start with the work of conversion and then brought under the control of other, more important personalities, who checked on the conditions in which their work was being carried on, and ensured that links were maintained between the missionaries and the parent community in the capital. Moreover, there was another reason why the Apostles' visit was quite indispensable. They alone possessed the power of invoking the blessings of the Holy Spirit on the new Christians in the rite of laying on of hands. And so Peter and John arrived in Samaria, gave their approval to Philip's work, confirmed those he had baptized, and returned, highly satisfied, to Jerusalem, preaching the Gospel in the villages through which they passed.[19]

We next hear of Philip on the road to Gaza, travelling in the direction of Saron and the country of the Philistines (Acts viii. 26–40), directed thither by an angel of the Lord. Even while travelling he never lost sight of his mission—namely the spreading of the Gospel far and wide. He happened to obtain a lift in the chariot of a friendly passer-by, and discovered that his pleasant driver—an Ethiopian eunuch, who was a courtier of Candace, Queen of Meroe, in the Sudan—was an enthusiastic reader of the sacred books of Israel. Philip offered to explain them to the eunuch. He gave him a fervent commentary on the famous passage in which Isaiah prophesies the coming of the suffering Messiah (Isa. liii. 8), and so persuasive was he that the stranger was converted to Christianity there and then, asked to be baptized and received the sacred water by the very roadside. The time was never too early nor the setting too strange to win a soul for Christ.

Philip finally arrived in Caesarea by way of Azotus. There

[19] One curious incident took place during Philip's mission to Samaria. A certain Simon was living there at the time. This Simon was a magician, a profession then very common throughout the Empire. Moreover, he was a highly successful magician, so much so that his nickname was 'great angel of God.' When Philip began preaching and converting, Simon too 'had found faith and been baptized,' though this was not necessarily a sham act on his part. But what exactly happened when Peter and John came on their round of inspection? Did they pick out those on whom they laid their hands? And did they refuse to invoke the Spirit upon this manipulator of suspect forces? At any rate, the disappointed Simon offered to pay them if they would agree to give him the power of granting the blessings of the Holy Spirit. (The expression *simony*, meaning a traffic in sacred things, derives from this proposition.) Peter, of course, refused vehemently, and threatened Simon with various dire punishments. The magician must not have been wholly bad, for he answered the Apostles humbly enough: 'Pray for me to the Lord, that none of this harm you have spoken of may fall upon me.' One obscure tradition, related by St Justin and Eusebius, claims that St Peter was to meet Simon the magician again in Rome, where he was insulted by him a second time.

he established himself, influencing all the region around with his preaching of the Good News; we shall be meeting him again later on, still in Caesarea, when St Paul passes through the town (Acts xxi. 8–9). Christian communities were subsequently founded in western as well as northern Palestine. And, once again, Peter set out to inspect them. He would meet recent converts, dwell among them for a little while, and strengthen them in their faith. Two miracles which he performed in Philistine country, the healing of a palsied man at Lydda and the raising of a woman from the dead at Joppa, contributed a great deal to increasing the influence of the new faith. It now extended beyond the circles of Hellenist Jews and began to reach the souls of the Gentiles too. And thus occurred an incident of great importance, which, in a way, pointed the direction in which the future Church would go.

The book of Acts describes this incident in detail, which is ample proof that its author considered it of capital importance (Acts x and xi). In the Italian cohort which formed part of the Caesarea garrison was a centurion whose name was Cornelius, 'a pious man who worshipped the true God,' in other words a Roman who was sympathetic towards the religious ideas of Israel. One night an angel appeared before him and bade him send men to Joppa to ask after a certain Simon surnamed Peter, who was lodging with a tanner in a house close by the sea there. Cornelius immediately dispatched two of his servants and one of his soldiers, probably all 'God-fearers' like himself. Next day, towards midday, whilst these messengers were drawing near the city, Peter, who was praying on the house top, fell into a trance. The heavens opened, and he saw a great cloth laden with all kinds of food, things both clean and unclean ritually, and he was invited to eat even of the foods which were impure. His loyal Jewish soul revolted at the tempting offer, but the voice spoke to him three times in all, making him understand that he was to ignore the Torah precepts on legal purifications and obey the command of God.

These laws concerning pure and impure foods, formulated by the Torah, may seem trivial enough to us. But they were far from trivial to a Jew of this epoch, and the least significant of believers was ready to die, like the seven brother martyrs in the Second Book of Maccabees (vii. 2), rather than transgress them. Consequently Peter was still feeling deeply puzzled about the matter when Cornelius's messengers knocked on his door. On following them to Caesarea, he found himself in the presence of the centurion, who told him of his dream. The Apostle's eyes were suddenly opened. Now he understood what God had been trying to tell him during his strange trance. It was essential to transcend the Jewish legal precepts, which related only to the letter of the law, and to yield to the spirit. In the eyes of the Torah this pagan who longed to know Christ was impure; to sit at his table would constitute defilement. And yet God desired that Peter should welcome him, baptize him and make a Christian of him. Peter still hesitated, for the decision disturbed him very much. At that moment a supernatural phenomenon occurred, a kind of little Pentecost; the Holy Spirit descended upon the whole company in visible form, and, submissive to God's will, without perhaps fully understanding the importance of what he was doing, Peter turned down the road which was to be the Church's path of triumph. He baptized Cornelius, going beyond the bounds of Jewish observances, and thus, in this one action, transcending the whole law.

This deed was of tremendous significance. The Judeo-Christian elements in Jerusalem regarded it with something akin to terror. When Peter returned to the capital they hurled all kinds of questions and reproaches at him. 'Why didst thou pay a visit to men who are uncircumcised, and eat with them?' The Apostle explained, relating all the deeds done by the six men who had gone with him on the journey, and describing the descent of the Holy Spirit. How could he be more rigid in his attitude than the Spirit of God? In the end he won his case, not simply on the question of the right which he had arrogated to himself of breaking the Torah and eating in the homes of unclean Gentiles, but even on the question of the baptism that he had given the pagan Cornelius. The conflict between the two fundamentally opposing tendencies in the Church, the particularist and the universalist, thus ended in this instance to the latter's advantage. Probably the Judeo-Christians regarded it simply as an exception, justified by Cornelius's exceptional moral character, and resistance to further attempts to increase these deviations from the law remained so great that even Peter sometimes let himself be diverted from his course.[20] No matter! The decisive choice had been made, the choice which St Paul, in his genius, was to exercise so magnificently.

## HEROD AGRIPPA, THE PERSECUTOR

In human affairs it often happens that at the very moment when a change of direction is imperative, circumstances in which the will has no part at all provoke the decision, and force the mind to break with its former habits. Thus in the lives of separate states foreign matters often exercise a decisive influence upon internal affairs. For the primitive Christian community the difficult problem of choosing between these two warring tendencies within it was to take a vital step forward towards its solution, because external events forced it to prepare for the future at the very moment when the foundations of the past were crumbling to dust.

The wave of persecution unleashed by the incident of St Stephen had never completely died away. The Christians, whether Judaizers or Hellenists, were always threatened by it, whether the period in question was one of calm or of renewed violence. And in the year 41 persecution broke out more strongly and systematically than ever before, thanks to the policy of Herod Agrippa I, who was now once more King of Israel. This unsavoury person was a son of Aristobulus and Berenice, and a grandson of the great Herod and of the Mariamne whom the bloodthirsty Idumean had loved, murdered and then mourned so deeply. His father had been one of the tyrant's final victims. Herod Agrippa was educated at the court of the Emperor Tiberius, where his life of debauchery, scandals and gambling debts had astounded a circle which was not as a rule easily shocked. In 37 he had been arrested on the orders of the aged misanthropic emperor, and had spent some months in prison. But his companion in debauchery, Caligula, had ascended the throne shortly after this, and Herod Agrippa had obtained from him the title of king and the two tetrarchies of northern Palestine, and later, after the de-

20 See the incident in Antioch, described in Chapter II, section: 'The Problems of the Past,' and Gal. ii. 11.

position of Antipas, Galilee and Peraea. Claudius had added
Judaea and Samaria to these in 41, thus reconstituting the
Herodian kingdom in Herod Agrippa's favour.

As soon as he arrived in Jerusalem, this loose-living creature,
who was certainly no fool, ostentatiously affected great religious zeal in an attempt to win popular goodwill. Flavius Josephus tells how, on his entry to the city, 'he had sacrificed
many animals as a token of thanksgiving, without forgetting
the least of the law's regulations, and had had a gold chain,
presented to him by Caligula, and weighing as much as the
iron one with which Tiberius had manacled him, deposited in
the Holy of Holies.' Perhaps this behaviour was motivated by
more than political cunning alone, for the psychology of the
Herodians always seems to have been highly complex. The Talmud records how, on one occasion, Herod Agrippa, while celebrating the festival of tents, was reading through the entire
text of Deuteronomy, according to the custom observed in sab-
batical years (40–1 was one of these), when he came to this
sentence: 'You must not let an alien, who is not of your blood,
bear rule over you.' On seeing these words, this half-Bedouin
monster was suddenly deeply ashamed that he, a man of mixed
blood, should be ruling over the holy Israelite nation, and he
dissolved in such a flood of tears that the people's sympathy
was touched, and they protested their loyalty to him in loud
acclamations.

This religious zeal explains his attitude towards the Christians. For the first time anti-Christian persecution acquired
a systematic character which it had not previously possessed.
In the past violent reactions against the Gospel message had
been of a sporadic nature. Now 'Herod exerted his authority
to persecute some of those who belonged to the church. James,
the brother of John, he beheaded' (Acts xii. 1–2). The James
concerned was one of the sons of Zebedee, whom the Gospels
mention many times; for the first time an Apostle, one of the
Twelve, was shedding his blood to bear witness to Christ.
Following Clement of Alexandria, Eusebius describes how this
martyrdom was the occasion of a stirring incident which was
often to be repeated in the heroic age of the great persecutions.
James's denouncer, who accused him before the religious tribunal, was so overwhelmed by the Apostle's courage that he

was converted there and then, and declared himself to be a Christian. He was led to execution along with his victim, and begged James to forgive him. James reflected for a moment. 'Peace be with thee,' he said, and kissed his former accuser.

Peter himself was arrested at the same time as James. His importance in the community must have been well known, for extremely important precautions were taken to guard him. Four squads of four soldiers took turns in watching him in the prison, for his trial had to await the end of the Passover celebrations.

But God had many other tasks for the prince of Apostles still to do. 'And now the day was coming when Herod was to bring him out; that night Peter was sleeping with two chains on him, between two soldiers, and there were warders at the door guarding his prison. Suddenly an angel of the Lord stood over him, and a light shone in his cell. He smote Peter on the side, to rouse him; Quick, he said, rise up; and thereupon the chains fell from his hands' (Acts xii. 6–7). Peter was dumbfounded and thought he must be dreaming. But the angel straightway led him out of the city, past the heavy iron gate, which opened to them of its own accord. The Apostle was free, and the angel, having completed his task, left him.

After some moments of thought and prayerful thanksgiving the Apostle slipped silently down the darkened streets, and reached the house of Mary, the mother of Mark, a house which, when we think back to the events of Christ's arrest, must probably have been in the most outlying suburb of Jerusalem, near Gethsemane.[21] He knocked on the door. A servant-girl, whose name was Rhoda, came to answer, but on recognizing the Apostle's voice she was so overjoyed that she

---

[21] At the time of Jesus' arrest, 'there was a young man following him, who was wearing only a linen shirt on his bare body; and he, when they laid hold of him, left the shirt in their hands, and ran away from them naked' (Mark xiv. 51). The Gospel according to St Mark is the only text which records this scene. Many critics regard it as a personal memory, a kind of discreet signature, and it has been suggested that the little plot of Gethsemane may have belonged to Mary, the mother of Mark, who had often accompanied and helped Jesus. The situation of the house would thus have been admirably placed for a fugitive like Peter, who was anxious to conceal himself.

forgot to open the door. Instead she ran back inside to give the news that Peter was here. Inside the house some of the faithful were gathered for prayers. Their reaction to Rhoda's news was unanimous. 'Thou art mad!' But the girl insisted. 'It must be his guardian angel,' the worshippers retorted. However, Peter went on knocking. At last the door was opened to him, he was recognized and joyfully acclaimed. He raised his hand and asked for silence. The Lord had miraculously freed him from prison: they must not jeopardize the chance he had been given.

In the course of its narrative this vivid and fast-moving chapter of Acts (xii. 3–19) tells us many interesting details about the primitive Christian community. Here we have this little body of believers, meeting at night in order to escape the notice of the police, putting its trust in God alone. Among those present we can make out the young Mark, the future evangelist, later to be the companion of St Paul. It should be noted that Peter, when freed, orders his followers to 'give news of this to James and the rest of the brethren.' This statement probably refers to the elders grouped around the 'brother of the Lord,' and would seem to imply that they occupied a definite position of authority in the community. The chapter ends, ironically enough, with the account of Herod's angry disappointment when he learned that his captive had vanished, and with the petty tyrant's death. He was smitten by an angel of the Lord, tortured, according to Josephus, by frightful intestinal pains, and finally died, his body eaten up by worms.

Why, for what duties, had God miraculously saved his servant's life in this way? The Acts simply say that Peter 'went elsewhere.' But subsequent events of Christian history make the meaning of this episode much more comprehensible. 'And still the word of God grew strong and spread wide' (Acts xii. 24). Far from slowing down the Church's expansion, Herod's persecution helped it. Because it was more serious than previous persecutions, it gave the Christians an even greater incentive to leave the Holy City and to seek refuge in other areas. In this way the Good News was soon to spread far further afield. One particular Christian community outside Palestine was to receive a fairly large proportion of the refugees and to acquire a position of pre-eminence thereby. This was Antioch, and tradition says that Peter himself was one of those who made their way there. Now Antioch was a Greek city, naturally universalist in attitude. When she replaced Jerusalem as the capital of the new faith, she necessarily carried Christianity in the direction in which she herself was going. This fact was of considerable historical importance, and would become obvious enough in the future, when the Holy City of David crumbled beneath the blows of the Roman conquerors.

## ANTIOCH

Antioch at that time was one of the most splendid cities in the whole Empire, ranking third or fourth in importance, and capital of the Roman province of Syria. Since its foundation by their ancestor in 300 B.C., every one of the Seleucid kings had taken pains to enlarge and embellish it. Its fortified walls stretched into the plain, enclosing about one hundred and fifty acres there; then they climbed up the sides of Mount Silpius, whose rose-coloured slopes were crowded with tier upon tier of white-terraced houses, the gardens dotted with cypress and box, and the temples of Pan, Aphrodite and Aesculapius. Antioch was situated at the opening of the gorges through which the Orontes slipped by Mount Amanus, in the very footprint, so legend had it, made by the giant, Typhon, when he was fleeing from the wrath of Zeus. It was one of the crossroads of the Empire, at the head of an estuary, and acting as a bridge across it. The desert camels which came there from Baalbek, Palmyra or Mesopotamia brought immense quantities of merchandise to its warehouses, and these goods were subsequently put aboard vessels sailing all over the Empire, leaving Syria either from the nearby port of Seleucia or from the quays of Antioch itself. Extremely wealthy, cosmopolitan, and, like most Greek cities, fairly dissolute in its morals, Antioch was one of those meeting-points of civilization—a place where ideas and cultures met and mingled, a breeding-ground of syncretism—of which there were many in the East at this period.

There was a large, old-established Jewish colony there. Flavius Josephus asserts that it numbered fifty thousand souls, which would amount to a fifth or a sixth of the whole town, a real settlement. These Israelites were engaged in trade. They spoke Greek and lived in Greek style, but they retained the faith of their fathers, holding services in their four synagogues and settling their affairs there among themselves, under the direction of an elder known as the Alabarka.

This Jewish *diaspora* community, which outwardly looked like so many others, had already received the Christian faith at some fairly recent date. 'Meanwhile those who had been dispersed owing to the persecution that was raised over Stephen had travelled as far away as Phoenicia and Cyprus and Antioch, without preaching the word to anyone except the Jews. But there were some of them, men of Cyprus and Cyrene, who, when they found their way to Antioch, spoke to the Greeks as well, preaching the Lord Jesus to them' (Acts xi. 19–21).

So it is abundantly clear that in the community at Antioch the fundamental problem of the choice between Jewish particularism and Christian universalism had been solved. If this Church did still contain two groups of converts, the one Judeo-Christian, the other Greek-Christian, relations between them were certainly good, better than at Jerusalem, for here the Jews were a minority on foreign soil; Chapter II of Paul's Epistle to the Galatians tells us that the whole community ate together, in other words here too the Torah precepts on purity had been transcended.

Did this disturb the Church at Jerusalem when the facts were reported back to it? Did Antioch rekindle the fears engendered by the incident at Caesarea? Or were those at Jerusalem merely anxious to verify the joyful news of the Gospel's success in this Syrian town? At all events it was decided to send someone to inspect the Christian community there.

The man chosen for the task was that same Joseph, now renamed Barnabas, 'the man of encouragement' whose charity had been so greatly admired by the community at Jerusalem. He was 'a good man . . . full of the Holy Spirit, full of faith' (Acts xi. 24). He was to show that he possessed wisdom too. Being Cypriot in origin, he had naturally spoken Greek since birth, but by race he belonged to the tribe of Levi, which the Eternal Yahweh had always blessed and summoned to serve Him. We should pay tribute to this Gospel messenger, who has been largely eclipsed by the brilliance of Paul, but who knew so well which was the right road to take at one of the most difficult crossroads in the Church's history. Barnabas reached Antioch, made contact with the leaders of the community there—Simon called Niger, Lucius of Cyrene, and Manahem, foster-brother of Herod the tetrarch, all of whom are mentioned a little further on in the Acts (xiii. 1)—surveyed the success of Christian expansion among the Jews, the proselytes and, above all, the pagans, and concluded that such a success could only be the work of the Divine Will. The conclusions of this inquiry therefore implied approval of the methods followed at Antioch.

So, some twelve to fifteen years after the death of Christ, this Syrian Christian community appears to have been a most flourishing one. One fact, which is recorded by St Luke, underlines the importance of this group; the term *Christians* was first used in Antioch. 'And Antioch was the first place in which the disciples were called Christians.' Probably it was little used at the start, for administrative purposes, except as a nickname. Aside from the sentence announcing its origin (xi. 26) the Acts themselves only use it on one other occasion (xxvi. 28), and in the primitive texts it is found only in the Epistle of St Peter (iv. 16). But its meaning is clear enough: these people were growing in number. How was one to describe them? As Jews? But they were not all Jews, and those who were were no ordinary ones. Well then, since they quoted *Christ* as their authority they might as well be called *Christians!*

The most venerable Catholic tradition, which is emphasized by the celebration, on 22 February, of the festival of 'St Peter's Chair at Antioch,' categorically links the development of this community with the presence there of the Prince of Apostles. Peter certainly made a number of visits to Antioch (for example, see Gal. ii. 11). Is it possible to claim that on the morrow of Herod Agrippa's persecution he established himself on the banks of the Orontes and actually transferred his 'see' from one city to the other? Jerusalem, Antioch, Rome—Christianity was to pass through these three stages, from the tiny exclusive community in the Holy City to the universalism of the *cathedra Petri.*

At all events Antioch was wonderfully situated for the
Word of God to radiate from her in all directions. And she
was to play a fundamental role just when the extension of
Christian missionary work was essential. The influence of Jerusalem had enabled the Gospel to touch Samaria and Saron.
Now it was necessary to go on and attack the Hellenic world,
and in this way Rome herself would eventually be reached.
Antioch, the new centre of the universal Church, was to maintain close relations with Jerusalem for a long time to come:
when terrible famine devastated Palestine it was the Syrian
Christians who organized relief for their stricken Hebrew
brethren. But these relations were simply feelings dictated by
friendship and respectful loyalty. Henceforth Christianity set
its face towards horizons larger than those of the Promised
Land: Jerusalem might disappear, but the paths of God were
still there, ready for the faithful to tread.

## THE END OF JERUSALEM

But whilst the new faith was preparing to shine forth into
the world with an incomparable radiance, we get the impression that in Palestine itself its development was paralysed.
From about the year 50 onwards we no longer find the enthusiastic animation of bygone days among the Christians there.
Henceforth the Palestinian communities seem to vegetate in
dark obscurity, and even that in Jerusalem itself does not glitter very brightly.

Was Jewish national pride the insurmountable obstacle
here? At this period it grew noticeably more inflexible, and
whipped itself up into a frenzied passion. Gradually the ex-
tremist schools of thought within the Jewish community
gained the upper hand. Notable among these were the
Zealots, an ultra-Pharisaical sect whom Flavius Josephus describes as having 'a fanatical love of liberty, and recognizing
no master save God.' The Zealots contained a revolutionary
group knows as the Assassins, who were devotees of the cudgel
and the dagger, who constituted a law unto themselves, and
who dispensed summary justice of a retributive and repressive
kind; they dealt expeditiously and violently with all pagans,
Samaritans or aristocratic Jews whom they considered to be

Roman collaborators. The nation which was being simultaneously embittered by foreign subjection and shaken by a thousand wild fantasies became progressively more and more violent. 'An ambiguous prophecy, found in Holy Scripture, which
stated that a man of their race would rule the world at this
time,' in other words a misconstrued Messianism; this, according to Flavius Josephus, was the fundamental cause of the
dramatic tragedy which was soon to engulf all Israel.

This hardening of Jewish feeling increased orthodox opposition to Christianity. A new tragedy struck the Church at
Jerusalem. Despite Agrippa's campaign of persecution it had
managed to survive, guided throughout by James, 'the brother
of the Lord,' who had been surnamed *Oblias*, meaning 'strong-
hold of the people,' on account of his just and upright behaviour. Some twenty years after Agrippa's persecution anti-Christian feeling in Jerusalem came to a head again, owing to some
cause of which we know absolutely nothing. This in itself
would not have had any practical consequences if the Roman
procurator, who had been re-established in Palestine[22] ever
since Herod Agrippa I's death, had been at his post in the
Antonine fortress. But Festus was dead; Albinus, his successor,
had not yet taken over his command. The fanatics took advantage of this interim situation.

In 62 the high priest Annas, son of the man who had been
high priest at the time of Jesus' crucifixion, felt himself strong
enough to crush the Christians. He had James arrested and
condemned by the Sanhedrin. We know the details of the
tragedy from Josephus and also from Hegesippus, the me-
morialist and Christian historian, who was writing about the
middle of the second century. James was made to climb to
the topmost pinnacle of the temple: then he was ordered to
abjure Jesus. When he refused, solemnly and loudly, in language similar to that used by Stephen in like circumstances,
he was hurled to the ground below. Since this fall did not
kill him men began stoning him, and finally, despite a few
well-meant protests by some of the bystanders, he was finished

---

[22] While the petty despot's son, Herod Agrippa II, after spending
his minority in Rome, obtained the semblance of kingship over the
territory of Lebanon and Bekaa. He was to reign from 50 until
about 100.

off with some heavy blows from a grindstone. This was an illegal execution, and as a result Annas was deposed from the high priesthood.

Four years later a worse punishment was to fall upon Israel. Driven to desperation by the brutality and cupidity of two successive procurators, Albinus (62–4) and Gessius Florus (64–6), and inflamed by the speeches of the Zealots, the Jews rebelled against Rome. First of all there were riots at Caesarea, followed by disturbances in Jerusalem itself. In the early days of the revolt Rome did not take these incidents very seriously. Herod Agrippa II was warned of the dangers by the conservative-minded Jewish aristocracy, and he dispatched a troop of soldiers to try to re-establish law and order. All in vain. The Antonine fortress and Herod's palace were set on fire and their defenders massacred. At the same time Roman garrisons in several parts of Palestine were attacked. Roman reprisals and fresh Jewish outrages followed one upon the other. The chief priests fell beneath the blows of Jewish fanatics, Annas being the first to die in this way. We can get some idea of what the situation must have been like by comparing it with the violence which occurred in Palestine just before the foundation of the modern state of Israel after the Second World War. During the winter of 66–7 the Roman legate in Syria, disturbed by the turn which events were taking, landed on the coast with twelve legions, and penetrated as far inland as the walls of Jerusalem. But the Jewish guerrillas exhausted his army, and he was forced to beat a retreat. The Chosen People believed that they had recaptured the glory of the Maccabees in this single blow, and at Jerusalem silver shekels were struck bearing the date of 'the first year of freedom.'

Rome could not tolerate such a situation for long. In spring 67 Nero sent Vespasian, who was an excellent general, to Palestine. He appeared in the Galilean plain with sixty thousand men. But as soon as he had to tackle the mountainous regions he in his turn suffered reverses: one of these, it was said, cost him eleven thousand soldiers. Two years slipped by, and now the Empire was fully occupied at home by the troubles which followed Nero's death. Then at Easter 70 Rome took the matter up again, really determined to finish it for good this time. Vespasian sent his son Titus, with all the necessary troops and machines of war. The fanatical Jews who were determined to fight to the death were in possession of the temple, under the leadership of John of Giscala; but in the upper part of the city the supporters of a less savage policy, who were not yet liquidated and who were commanded by Simon-bar-Giora, were resisting them. The two factions united to form a common front against the legionaries. And the siege began.

When it ended, five months later, after scenes of indescribable horror, Jerusalem was in ruins: the temple had been gutted by fire; thousands of corpses rolled beneath the hoofs of the steeds belonging to the victorious Nubian mercenaries of Rome. Of the Jewish resistance forces only a few insignificant groups remained, skulking amid the debris, and these would all succumb within three years. Judaea became a Roman province, separated from Syria, and occupied by a legion which was stationed at Jerusalem. The Sanhedrin and the high priesthood were abolished. And, as a cruel irony, Rome continued to demand the religious tax which world Jewry had formerly paid to the temple, but she collected it instead on behalf of the treasury of Jupiter.

Did these frightful happenings disturb many of the Christians scattered throughout the Empire? We do not know. The earliest converts had retained close relations with Jerusalem, regarding it as their spiritual metropolis: but these links had become gradually weaker as time went by. Quite probably many Christians saw the tragedy in the apocalyptic perspectives which were so commonplace at the time, as a judgment of God, a punishment for the crime committed against the Messiah, the fulfilment of the prophecies which Jesus Himself had made about the unfaithful Jewish people.

Meanwhile, if Eusebius is to be believed, 'the people belonging to the Church in Jerusalem received a prophetic warning to leave the city before the war began, and to go to Peraea, to the hellenized city of Pella. It was there that the faithful disciples of Christ retired.' This measure must have been ordered by Simeon, one of the sons of Cleophas (here we have another of Jesus' relations), who had succeeded James. Thus a few centres of Judeo-Christianity survived, after a fashion, in the Jordan villages. Eusebius preserves the list of thirteen bishops who, according to him, succeeded Simeon when the latter perished on the martyr's cross; all have Jewish names. But these communities can have had little or no influence on the rest of society.

The capture of Jerusalem contributed to a further worsening in relations between the Christians and the Jews. From that moment onwards the antagonism between them was all too obvious. Tacitus may well be describing an instance of it in his *Histories*[23] when he reports that during a Council of War, held on 9 August 70, at which the question of finding an opportunity to destroy the temple was discussed, Titus called to mind 'the conflict between these two sects, notwithstanding their common origin.' It was now that the Jews began formulating the traditions which were to be written down in the Talmud at a considerably later date. Here they showed their hatred of the new believers, 'apostates and traitors,' declaring that not only ought a loyal Jew to do nothing to help any of these people if one of them fell into a well, but adding that a good Jew would actually throw such a person in. About the year 80 the Rabbi Gamaleil—the second of this name— and Samuel the Little introduced a verse into the famous prayer, *Shemoneh Esreh*, which we can still read: 'Let the Nazarene and the Minim perish utterly!'—meaning the Christians.

The final act in the Jewish tragedy put the finishing touches to this mutual hatred. In the future too many Christians, forgetful of Christ's teaching, were to argue from these events that they were fully entitled to pay back tenfold the Jews' hatred of their co-religionists. At the beginning of the second century the Emperor Hadrian (117–38), who was a patron of the arts and a great builder, decided to reconstruct Jerusalem, which, at that time, was nothing but a simple garrison town, and to rename it Aelia Capitolina. The city he proposed to build was a completely pagan one: the places which had been sacred to Yahweh would be defiled by the statue of Jupiter, and, according to tradition, Venus would be enthroned on Golgotha. The remnants of the Jewish nation

---

[23] The original passage is lost, but it is quoted by Sulpicius Severus in his *Chronicle*.

could not tolerate outrages such as these. Rallying under a pseudo-Messiah named Bar-Cochba, and supported by Rabbi Akiba, they plunged into revolution. It was an absurd revolution, born of despair. The reign of terror it produced lasted for three years, and it was directed not merely against Rome but, as Justin tells us, against the Christians, 'who were executed if they refused to abjure and insult Jesus Christ.' In the end the legions re-established order; Bar-Cochba was executed, and the survivors of his insane revolt were scattered. Under pain of death the Jews were no longer allowed to go to Jerusalem, save once in four years, on the anniversary of the destruction of the temple. Then they were permitted to go and weep by the famous walls, an observance which can still be witnessed today.

Some time after these events a new Christian community appeared among the Graeco-Roman elements which had settled in Aelia Capitolina and in other parts of Palestine. Led by bishops bearing Greek names, it was to make the message of the Cross bloom again in the very place where it had first been planted. But this new Church had little in common with the primitive community of bygone days: a new spirit ruled in it, a spirit which, between times, had triumphed throughout the whole Church.

Harsh repression—the classical world's principal defence against the monotheism of Palestine—succeeded in completely destroying all Judeo-Christian missionary work. But communities of this type were to survive in the Empire for some three hundred years to come.[24] St Ignatius of Antioch warns the true Christian against those who are over-zealous in following Jewish observances: 'Anyone who is still following Jewish practices today is admitting that he has not received the Grace of our Lord. Away with the bad, old, sour leaven!' And the au-

---

[24] One curious detail: persistent traces of Jesus' relations can be found among the Judeo-Christian communities in Palestine. During Simeon's episcopate the Emperor Domitian had a search made for the descendants of David, and, according to Hegesippus, two grandsons of the Apostle Jude, 'of the Lord's race,' were brought before him; moreover, since they were harmless peasants, Domitian sent them back to their homes, and they survived in some Christian community or other until Trajan's time. In the third century Julius the African was to meet more descendants of Jesus' family.

thor of the *Letter of Barnabas* goes much further, and takes
up a position which was to be that adopted by large numbers
of Christians, from the Fathers to Claudel, maintaining that
the sole heirs of Israel's mission now were the disciples of the
new law, and that the Jews themselves 'have forfeited the testament given them by Moses.'

Isolated, shut in on themselves, cut off from the living waters of the main stream of Christianity, many of these Judeo-
Christian communities were to allow themselves to become
contaminated by false notions, and to drink from tainted
sources. Some suspicious tendencies were apparent as early as
Simeon's time, and very soon we shall be rejoining the stagnant remains of what was once such a pure stream by way of
the history of Christian heresy. We shall find among these
isolated communities the Ebionites, a savage, puritanical sect,
who denied the divinity of Christ, His Virgin Birth, and, above
all, justified Jesus solely because, they alleged, He had rigidly
followed the Torah precepts. There were the Mandeans, too,
who may have been a branch of the Essenes, detached from
the main body of the sect. Groups of these are still in existence
today on the Lower Tigris, and some authorities regard them
as the descendants of John the Baptist's followers. But their
sacred book, the *Rechter Ginza*, which was not compiled until
long after the sect's foundation, gives little information about
its original doctrines. And there were the Helchassites or
Alexites, disciples of a certain Helchassai or Alexis, who lived
during Trajan's reign, and who claimed to have received the
revelation of his weird doctrine from an angel who was forty-
five miles tall. Here Jewish observances, Christian dogmas and
magical practices jostled together in an absurd jumble. None
of these deviations was to have any influence upon authentic
Jewish tradition, or, *a fortiori*, on the Church. Later on
Gnosticism and Manichaeism would absorb the bulk of these
troubled waters.

## 'SALVATION IS TO COME FROM THE JEWS'

As the Church at Jerusalem and the Judeo-Christian communities disappear beneath the sands of history, should we

not pause for a moment to remember them, and to pay them our homage? These believers who had been born in the shadow of the temple were, it is true, dominated by it over-much; they did not always manage to see where the true light lay, and their tragic fate is ascribable to a divinely ordained logic, which rendered their eclipse essential. If Christianity had listened to them it would have remained nothing more than a little Jewish sect, and possibly by now it would have been discussed only as one more historic curiosity, like the Rekabites or the Essenes. But can we ever forget the devotion and the courage which these Judeo-Christians showed in the decisive days when the mustard seed had barely germinated, and when the frail little plant of Christianity so badly needed defending and protecting? Can we ever forget those admirable followers of the Torah, men like Stephen and James, who shed their Jewish blood to become Christian martyrs? 'Salvation is to come from the Jews!' The Master's Word was fulfilled through these early Palestinian communities, and the foundations of the faith thereby established.

Moreover, Jewish influence upon the primitive Church remained considerable. The more one studies the history of the Christianity of the catacombs, the more one notices its myriad links with Judaism.[25] Each of the four Gospels contains countless quotations from or allusions to the Old Testament, references averaging at least three hundred in number in every case. As we shall see, Christian liturgy and Christian prayer are directly related to the religious customs of the Chosen People. And what were the symbols used by these Christian communities in which former pagans far outnumbered those of Jewish origin? On the walls of the catacombs we find scores of illustrations taken from the Old Testament, the Hebrew sacred books: Adam and Eve, Noah in the ark, Abraham's sacrifice, Jonah cast up from the whale, or Daniel in the lion's den. This link is still proclaimed by the Roman Catholic Church today, when, on Holy Saturday, she turns to the words of the Fourth Prophecy and beseeches the Almighty that all the nations of the earth may become sons of Abraham, fashioned in the likeness of Israel.

But what we see today as a legitimate loyalty and well-de-

[25] See further in Chapters V and VI.

served tribute could easily have become a dangerous and limiting rigidity. In order to obey the command of Christ, and throw itself heart and soul into the great adventure of universalism, Christianity had to understand that the law's boundaries must of necessity be overstepped if it were to fulfil itself completely. At the time when Jerusalem was crumbling beneath the blows of Titus and the Judeo-Christians were witnessing their own end, the creative synthesis between the past and the future had already long been made. The Church had discovered her right path. That this was so was principally due to the work of St Paul.

# CHAPTER II

# A HERALD OF THE HOLY
# SPIRIT: ST PAUL

## THE ROAD TO DAMASCUS

HOW CLOSE he seems to us, this man whom the Divine
Light struck down on the road to Damascus—defeated, yet,
through his very defeat, overwhelmed by a profound antici-
pation of Grace—for, after all, we ourselves are still treading
that same Damascus road today! He is, after Jesus, the most
vivid and complete of all the New Testament figures, the man
whose face we can visualize most clearly. The problems on
which he burnt his fingers are the problems which perpetually
beset us too. And whenever we listen to the least important
of his sayings, we recognize that tone of unforgettable confidence attainable only by those who have risked their all.

For eight days now he had been wending his way along the
sandy road from Jerusalem to Damascus. A strange fury possessed him, that religious fanaticism and uneasy conviction of
being in the right which can make the human heart so bitter
and so violent. He had left the largely uncultivated valley of
the Upper Jordan for the plains, where the dead, dry grass
grated on the baked earth. On his left Mount Hermon reared
its perpetually snow-topped peak against an arid sky. Soon he
would be nearing the oasis, with its grey-green sycamore-trees
and the scent of jasmine and roses, and the lush jumble of the
well-irrigated orchards sheltering beneath the swaying shade
of the tall palms. It was a summer's day, and noon was fast
approaching.

Suddenly a light flashed down from the sky, enveloping him.
He fell to the ground, and he heard a voice saying to him:
'Saul, Saul, why dost thou persecute me?' Stuttering, he asked:
'Who art thou, Lord?' And the voice responded: 'I am Jesus,
whom Saul persecutes!' Dazed and trembling, the man murmured: 'Lord, what wilt thou have me do?' And the answer
came: 'Rise up, and go into the city, and there thou shalt be

told what thy work is!' Saul staggered to his feet. The brilliant
sunshine had vanished, and for Saul it was succeeded by total
darkness: though his eyes were open he could no longer see.
His travelling companions stared at him, struck dumb with
astonishment; they had heard a confused murmur of voices,
but had been unable to make out any distinct words. Saul,
however, had understood, and the understanding was to remain with him for the rest of his life (Acts ix).

He was a young man at the time, possibly an extremely
young man—a small, undistinguished-looking Jew. Certain
apocryphal Greek texts dating from the second century, and
known as the Acts of St Paul, have left us a description of him
which is scarcely a flattering one.[1] 'He was of short, stocky
build, with bandy legs; bald, his heavy eyebrows meeting between the eyes, and his nose hooked.' The description is typical of many of his race. But a strange power shone forth from
his face. It was actually said of Saul that sometimes he seemed
more like an angel than a man.

Among men and women whom nature has not endowed
with perfect physical health we often find an intense spiritual
power, all the more violent and passionate because of its association with this bodily frailty. Saul was one such person. He
lived for his soul alone. Throughout his life we shall see him
finding supreme fulfilment in tension and in conflict. Nothing
man-made could destroy him: in 'affliction, or distress, or persecution, or hunger, or nakedness, or the sword . . . we are
conquerors, through him who has granted us his love' (Rom.
viii. 35–7). The description fits the saint himself perfectly.

How did he feel, as he stood there in the sudden darkness,
this man whom God had just summoned by name? It was as
though he had been stabbed to the very soul. His had been a
thankless task, 'kicking against the goad.'[2] But now he sud-

---

[1] Possibly this 'description' derives from a kind of passport which
the missionaries of the primitive Church may have possessed, so that
they could be identified by communities to whom they were not
known.

[2] Acts xxvi. 14. Aside from the famous passage in Acts ix. 1–19,
the vision is described in the book on two other occasions, in almost
identical language, Acts xxii. 3–16 and xxvi. 9–20. There are also
several allusions to it in the Epistles. As for the phenomenon itself
and the physical illness which succeeded it, medical research has

denly realized that henceforth he must learn to live with this
open wound, this 'thorn in the flesh,' whereby the truth had
reached him. What did this sudden malady mean in human
terms? Several medical explanations have been proposed, including hysteria and epilepsy, but on close examination all
appear completely unacceptable. One of the most obvious
symptoms of hysteria, which in any case is a disease which is
little understood, is the way in which the sufferer is incited to
a kind of continuous pathological mimicry. There is absolutely
no trace of that in this highly original and genuine personality,
all of whose decisions clearly stem from a most lucid mind.
And as for epilepsy, whose two principal characteristics are
the occurrence of sudden violent breaks in the logical sequence
of human actions and the fantastic delusions which quickly
fade from the memory—what possible connection can such a
disease have either with this perfectly balanced and unified
life of efficacious service or with the objective precision with
which St Paul viewed his own visions? No, the facts are quite
plain, as unchallengeable here as in the later cases of Joan of
Arc or St Francis of Assisi: the call which was to snatch Saul
from his old self did not echo from within the limbo of a mind
that bordered on dementia; it had actually sounded, on an
Eastern high road, amid the arid sunshine of a July day.

Still completely blind, Saul set off on his journey again, and
entered Damascus. Beyond the massive tower which guarded
the city gate stretched a broad road, called Straight Street,
which led up to a temple; porticoes formed by Corinthian
colonnades ran along each side of it. A certain Jew named
Judas lived in Straight Street, a member of the very large
Jewish community which lived a highly prosperous life in this
Arab city, and which was extremely well treated by Aretas, the
local potentate. Saul established himself in Judas's house—it
would probably be more accurate to say that he collapsed on

---

proved that this fairly long period of blindness cannot be in any
way connected with the consequence of desert sunstroke. Some authorities have linked it with the blindness produced by 'electric glare.'
Here blindness is due to an excessive glare of light on the retina and
to superficial burning of the cornea, resulting in mucro-purulent dis-
charges. (For this information the author is indebted to the French
ophthalmologist, René Onfray.)

the doorstep of it—and there he stayed, bewildered and silent, his unseeing eyes staring out into the punishing darkness, refusing all food and drink, waiting and praying.

However, another man, who lived in Damascus itself, had also received a command from heaven: his name was Ananias, and he was one of the tiny circle of Christians which already existed in the town. The Lord appeared to him in a vision, saying: 'Rise up and go to the road called Straight Street; and inquire at the house of Judas for a man of Tarsus, named Saul. Even now he is at his prayers: and he has had a vision of a man called Ananias coming in and laying hands on him, to cure him of his blindness.' Ananias made so bold as to remonstrate: 'Lord, many have told me about this man, and all the hurt he has done to thy saints at Jerusalem; and he has come here with authority from the chief priests to imprison all those who call upon thy name.' But the Lord cut him short. 'Go thy errand; this is a man I have chosen to be my instrument for bringing my name before the heathen and their rulers, and before the people of Israel too!'

Ananias's information was quite correct. Saul had indeed left Jerusalem as the sworn enemy of everything Christian—backed by an express order from the priestly caste there—an order for which he had pleaded himself—an order to persecute to the death all those in Damascus who belonged to the new faith. Ever since taking up residence in the Holy City he had appeared extraordinarily pharasaical in attitude even for a Pharisee, and had set himself up as a determined adversary of the Galilean and His followers. Saul was in fact that same bitter, arrogant young student whom we have already seen standing guard over the cloaks of the executioners whilst they stoned the martyr Stephen to death.

There is, of course, more than a little excuse for these violent sentiments. The mind that can query an issue on which opinion has already been passed needs exceptional courage, independence or enlightenment. His very make-up made belief in a humiliated and vanquished Messiah more difficult for Saul than for most people. Nothing could shake this abrupt young man, with his downright religious nationalism and intrepid fanaticism, and all we know of his character makes it easy to guess how the intransigence of opinions of this kind could ally, in his case, with his own intellectual certainty and with personal pride.

However, the matter is not entirely straightforward. Is it possible that, despite its terrifying suddenness, the episode on the road to Damascus had already been prepared for deep down in the soul of the man whom God was choosing as his own? When later on we read the texts in which Paul discusses the Law and its problems it is hard to resist the conclusion that the first tremor which was to break open his closed soul may have lain here.

The Israelite Law was an extremely hard burden for any scrupulous person to bear. Could one ever be completely sure of being free of its hundreds of prohibitions? Those who wore its 'intolerable yoke' were always afraid that they might have sunk into sin, even without knowing that they had done so. And what was the good of it all? What results did it achieve? In short, did these detailed practical observances do anything to solve the real problems of mankind? Did they help to lessen that feeling of unbearable misery which is the lot of the human race? What use are formal principles when set face to face with the anguish of life? Had not the Law itself, by inflicting various principles upon man, in other words by opening his eyes to material subtleties, torn him from his original innocence and thrown him into the heart of this complexity of contradiction and despair in which he had lived ever since? This problem was to plague so many mystics and poets, from St Augustine to Rimbaud, from Origen to William Blake, and it may have been the problem which made the heart of this young Pharisee so savagely fanatical. Possibly he already suspected that the love of Christ could solve these enigmas, and the violence of his attack upon the Christians may have been due to the fact that, in attacking them, he felt he was fighting against something in himself.

On the road to Damascus, as he strode out into the miraculous darkness, he knew that he would soon receive the answer to all his soul-searchings. The fact that this answer was to be brought to him by the very folk whom he had hated most was perfectly natural, complying with the mysterious law of reversion which always unites the executioner and his victim. One of the Galilean's followers came and stood close to him: Saul heard his voice. 'Brother Saul,' said Ananias, 'I have been sent by that Lord Jesus who appeared to thee on thy way as thou camest here; thou art to recover thy sight and be filled with the Holy Spirit.' And immediately Saul's sight was restored to him.

Thus occurred the event which is usually known as 'the conversion of St Paul.' It can only be fully understood within the perspectives of the spiritual drama, in which the soul makes a choice which changes it completely. The man who had known defeat on the road to Damascus did not alter his religion or his outward appearance; he did not leave the temple, under whose shadow the young Church still lay. Saul's conversion was a conversion according to the French seventeenth-century understanding of the word, being similar to the cases of Pascal or Rancé, for example; it was the man deep within him who changed. Jesus had told His followers that they must be transformed: the change of heart must be total. He whom Saul was to obey henceforth was that Jesus who had condemned the proud, the hard-hearted and the self-satisfied. Saul himself had been all these three things. From now on he was never able to find enough time to bear witness to his love for that Lord who had loved him sufficiently to strike him to the heart.

## A YOUNG JEW FROM HELLENIZED COUNTRY

Tarsus, where Saul was born some time between A.D. 5 and 10, was one of the many brilliant yet slightly austere cities which, as the result of Alexander's conquests, the development of Greek civilization and the increasing wealth of society, deriving from the Pax Romana, had become very numerous throughout the whole of the Middle East. The town was situated at the foot of Mount Taurus, at the very mouth of the gorge which the River Cydnus had bored into this formidable mountain barrier. It guarded the gateways to Cilicia, and everyone and everything going towards Syria or the lands of Mesopotamia had to make a halt there. Today it is eight miles from the coast, owing to silting caused by alluvial deposits; but in the first century A.D. it was still a centre of maritime trade, linked to the outer harbour of Regmo, and easily accessible to the ships of the day. It was beautiful, ancient and prosperous. St Paul was to show his pride in the place of his birth, calling it 'no mean city.' Its square white houses and numerous statues were set amid luxurious gardens, for water was not scarce in Tarsus. Modern historical research links its extremely ancient origins with the Hittites and Phoenicians, but in Saul's day various names from mythology were associated with it—Semiramis, Sardanapalus and even Aphrodite herself. During a halt on his lightning march across Asia, Alexander the Great had bathed in the icy waters of its river. And, half a century before Saul's birth, in 41 B.C., its quays had witnessed a mysterious, scantily clad young queen, who had just seduced a Roman dictator, stepping ashore from a sumptuously decorated gold and purple trireme.

The Graeco-Egyptian image of Cleopatra well matches the cosmopolitan character which Tarsus shared with all the other hellenized cities, places that ranged from Antioch to Pergamum, from Corinth to Alexandria. All kinds of different elements had been superimposed upon the original Assyro-Persian ethnic base, particularly since the time when the Seleucid kings had first become interested in the city. Henceforth the Greeks dominated Tarsus, but they were Greeks of very mixed blood. Aside from the Greeks the Jews were fairly numerous in the town. They had arrived there in especially large numbers in the time of Antiochus Epiphanes; though grouped together in their own community, here as everywhere else, they were no isolated bloc, in the sense of a ghetto; they took part in all the public life of the city, even in its administration. This was the background into which Saul was born, and against which he grew to manhood.

One tradition, which has little evidence to support it, although it is reported by St Jerome in his *Illustrious Men*, claims that the parents of the future Apostle had been deported to Cilicia after Varus had, with great brutality, re-established order in Palestine in 4 B.C. following the disturbances in Galilee. Saul's later claim to be 'Hebrew' would, if this were so, be true in the most geographic sense of the term, since he might well have been taken from Israel into hellenized territory during his infancy. The name Saul, which he received at his circumcision, was a traditional name in his tribe, that of Benjamin, made famous a thousand years earlier by the first king of Israel. (In his dealings with Gentiles Saul had to use the hellenized form of his name, *Paulos*, as was the custom among the Jews of the *diaspora*.) At all events, if this family of Galilean Jews had in fact been forcibly removed to the banks of the Cydnus, they had been remarkably quick to adapt themselves to their new surroundings, for, at the time of Saul's birth, all the available evidence suggests that they belonged to the wealthy merchant class, which was a kind of provincial aristocracy. Better still, they had obtained Roman citizenship.

This is such an important fact that it needs strongly emphasizing. The *ius civitatis* was a privilege which Rome gave fairly sparingly to her provincial subjects or to various favourites whom she wanted to reward in some way. Sometimes the privilege was awarded to whole cities at a time, and it was a right which could also be bought, though the price was very high. It conferred upon its holder full civil rights, the opportunity of being elected magistrate and special guarantees in judicial matters, in particular the right of direct appeal to the emperor from any sentence awarded by a lower court. Consequently a Jew who was a Roman citizen escaped the inferior status which his race was normally accorded, and was even free from the jurisdiction of his fellow Jews. As we shall see, St Paul was to make good use of this prerogative. How had his family obtained this right? Had they bought it? Had they received it in return for some service rendered to one of the Roman dictators? After all, Pompey, Julius Caesar and Mark Antony had each in turn traversed the eastern shores of the Mediterranean, building up parties of their own supporters wherever they went. We do not know. Whatever its origin, this precious privilege not only helped the Apostle in a practical way during the course of his missions, but encouraged him to regard the Roman Empire not as the instrument of intolerable oppression, but as an actively glorious thing, as a powerful organization to which it was right and proper that men should be loyal (see the Epistle to the Romans, Chapter XIII), and which served to further the designs of God.

Was the trade which he followed throughout his missionary life, in order to 'maintain himself by the labour of his own hands,' the trade of his father before him? The term *sken-opoios*, or *tabernacularius*, can be taken to mean either a weaver of the materials used in tent-making or the man who sews the separate pieces together. In either sense it denotes a man of very humble occupation, whether his tool be the carding machine or a pair of scissors. Such a trade seems over-modest, in view of the social status of Saul's family, and some critics have suggested that Saul may have adopted it only on the morrow of his conversion, after breaking with all his relations. But we must not forget that in Israel manual work went hand in hand with intellectual study quite naturally, and that the most famous Doctors of the Law had earned their daily bread by tailoring and by all manner of other humble occupations.

Saul, then, grew up in a city, and a Greek city at that; this is obvious to anyone who reads his Epistles. The day-to-day life of Tarsus had a profound effect upon his character, and provided him with hundreds of references to urban activities, such as trade, the law and the stadium games, whereas Jesus, who was a simple Galilean peasant, always referred to things close to nature, to the sighing of the wind, the falling rain or the joyous flight of the birds. Saul's background gave him his knowledge of Greek, which he spoke fluently, and also his fairly extensive culture, which enabled him to quote not merely a sentence of Menander's but even the verses of the Stoic Aretas and the Cretan poet Epimenides. Not one of the Twelve Apostles was ever capable of anything like this.

Did Saul's native city exert a still more determinative influence upon him? Various historians of comparative religion have often asserted this, as an easy explanation for certain parallels between Paul's teaching and some pagan thinking. Tarsus was indeed an intellectual city—'surpassing Athens and Alexandria in its love of knowledge' according to Strabo. Its university was so important that ever since the reform carried out by Athenodorus, a Tarsus man by adoption and the tutor of Augustus, the professors there had controlled the city's municipal life and administration; Stoic doctrine, as elaborated by Zeno of Cyprus, Aratos of Cilicia, Chrysippus and Appolonios (Tarsus men themselves), was taught there with official backing. But we have no proof whatsoever that the

young Saul ever attended any of these pagan schools, which
were highly suspect to every Israelite, and particularly so to a
Pharisee, such as Saul was; and if pagan doctrine did have any
influence upon him, it was *a contrario*, leading him to oppose
it heart and soul. As for the religious forms which, at Tarsus
as elsewhere throughout the Eastern world, mingled together
in a syncretism which was as impassioned as it was confused,
it is even less conceivable that such practices could have made
the slightest impression upon a young man who, as all our
evidence shows, was utterly faithful to the cult of Yahweh
and the sacred Torah. Before the mystical outbursts of the
Tarsus mob, fanned to exultation point by the rhythm of the
flutes and the dulcimers, or the stake at which the ancient
Baal of Tarsus, Sandam, was burned each year, or the 'bull-
baptisms' where the disciples of Mithras, the Persian god,
wallowed in their victim's blood, it is highly improbable that
any true Israelite could have felt anything save deep disgust.

The truth is that Saul grew up in spiritual surroundings
where Judaism was at its purest, completely and utterly faithful to the precepts of the law. His family were Pharisees, and
this had a very important effect upon him. For though Jesus
denounced the guile and over-prevalent hypocrisy of these
casuistic and formalist people, justice impels us to recognize
that many spiritual virtues existed among them too—their
total submission to Divine Providence, their constant desire
to live according to the Word, even if this Word was misin-
terpreted by them.

When he was fifteen or sixteen years old Saul's parents sent
him to Jerusalem to study under Gamaliel, the greatest Pharisee of the age, who, as we have already seen, was quite outstanding in his breadth of understanding and his generosity of
mind.[3] Saul must have passed some years, at least, sitting at
the learned man's feet—a custom which is still observed today
by the Moslem students of El Azar, in Cairo—listening to
Gamaliel's detailed, interminable instruction in the law. It is
all too clear that he did not adopt his teacher's gentleness—
at least, not straight away—but he certainly learnt from him
the methods of an extremely skilful dialectic, and possibly,

[3] See Acts v. 34 and also Chapter I, p. 35, note 12.

also, certain concepts regarding human nature, life and death, nature and sin. Much later on he was to discard all the empty sophistry he had acquired, but he would continue to draw on the method of argument learned so long ago. Above all, he was to find out from personal experience that an overzealous application of the letter can lead to a certain withering of the spirit.

In this way, by virtue of his very origins, Saul appeared truly predestined for the role which he was to assume. Typically representative of the spirit of the *diaspora*, he was, on the one hand, the incarnation of Judaism at its most authoritative, at its truest and its most glorious, while at the same time sensing the need to go beyond it; on the other, he was familiar with the Gentiles, and was able to assess the dreadful void in the souls of those who, as he himself put it, had the world about them 'and no God' (Eph. ii. 12). He was at the meeting-point of two civilizations, like his native city, at the point of rupture and of attack. Men who are destined to change the course of history always present the same picture; they are tied, by their innermost roots, to the society they are attacking; it is from some personal experience that they discover the need for its destruction and replacement by something new.

## THE YEARS OF APPRENTICESHIP

Thus, 'born of his mother's womb and instructed by the Grace of God,' Saul found himself miraculously invested with the duty of announcing the new faith, the coming of the Messiah and His message of love. Almost certainly he must have made his personal testimony straight away to the little community at Damascus, which had taken him in and succoured him; but he showed no signs of any arrogant anxiety to hurry to acquire a leading role in the new Church. He was to pass many long years preparing himself for the task to which the Master had called him. He meditated, he explored the foundations of his thinking with scrupulous care, he defined various positions and experimented with different processes of thought. The vision on the road to Damascus probably took place between 32 and 36;[4] the great missions undertaken by the Apostle of the Gentiles did not begin before 45 or 46.

These years of apprenticeship must have been filled with remarkably intense study, judging from their subsequent results! They opened with a mysterious episode which St Luke does not mention at all in his book of Acts but which the saint himself was to refer to many years later, when writing to his Galatian friends. Saul went to 'Arabia' and remained there for a long time. One immediately thinks of that retreat in the wilderness with which Jesus inaugurated his ministry; one imagines the new Christian dwelling alone on some isolated plain or mountain top, compelling the old Saul within him to come to terms with this terrifying new being who had been impressed upon his soul; but we know absolutely nothing of what his feelings were during this extension of his drama, at this time when all his thoughts must have been falling into place. We know even less of this episode than we know of Christ's stay upon Jebel Karantal.

Saul returned to Damascus, and there began to preach about the Messiah and about his own faith, speaking in the synagogues, to which he had easy access. This could not fail to cause considerable astonishment. 'Why,' said everyone, 'is not this the man who brought ruin on all those who invoked this [i.e. Jesus'] name, when he was in Jerusalem? the man who came here for the very purpose of arresting such people and presenting them to the chief priests?' Ordinary folk in the mass have little understanding of sudden conversions such as Saul's, and find it hard to forgive those who change sides too quickly. Damascus Jewry hatched a plot to kill the turncoat; guards were posted at the city gates to prevent his escape; but Saul's friends helped him to make his getaway by lowering him over the city wall in a fish-hamper—not a very glorious method of departure! Long before, when telling Ananias of the man to whom he was sending him, the Lord had said: 'I have yet to tell him how much suffering he will have to undergo for my name's sake.' Here was the first example of this suffer-

---

[4] Different sources fix the date at different times between 32 and 36. If it is acknowledged that Stephen's martyrdom took place in 36, the vision on the road to Damascus must in all probability have occurred in the same year.

ing, the first lesson in the depth of human hostility to the true believer.

From Damascus Saul went up to Jerusalem, where other equally formative experiences awaited him. What was he going to do in the Holy City? All the evidence suggests that he hoped to meet there those who had seen the Resurrected Lord, and to establish close relations with them. He was greeted with suspicion. Naturally enough, the little community of Jerusalem Christians, with its vivid memories of Saul the persecutor, at first hesitated to believe in the Pharisee's vision and his subsequent conversion. Its suspicion did not cease until Barnabas, who had, as we know, considerable authority in the young Church, and who, being a Cypriot by birth, may even have been acquainted with the man from Tarsus, declared himself Saul's guarantor. Saul was then received into the community and henceforth 'he came and went in their [i.e. the Apostles'] company at Jerusalem, and spoke boldly in the name of the Lord.'

But at once fresh difficulties arose. It is hard to understand the exact meaning of these from the account given in Acts (ix. 29). This merely tells us that 'he preached, besides, to the Jews who talked Greek, and disputed with them, till they set about trying to take his life.' Does this reference concern Greek-speaking Jewish Christians, or Greek-speaking orthodox Jews? If the latter, then Saul would be colliding against the same resistance as that encountered by Stephen, and would be running the very risks that the martyr had run before him. If the former, he may have intervened in the discussion between the two conflicting tendencies that existed within the Church at Jerusalem, and have irritated certain folk by showing himself over-respectful towards the law, over-anxious not to shatter essential loyalties. 'A Guelph among the Ghibellines, a Ghibelline among the Guelphs'—really independent minds always find themselves in this position. Just when the situation was becoming really tense, Saul had yet another vision, showing him the next path to follow. Jesus appeared before him and gave him some quite explicit orders: 'Make haste, leave Jerusalem with all speed; they will not accept thy witness of me here. . . .' And, as the persecutor of days gone by confessed, with bowed head, that certain of the objections to him seemed understandable enough, Christ gave him his real task: 'Go on thy way; I mean to send thee on a distant errand, to the Gentiles!' (Acts xxii. 17 ff.).

Now it only remained for Saul to make himself ready for the missionary role to which God was calling him. This was the fourth stage in his apprenticeship. After a brief stay in his Cilician homeland, where, so several commentators aver, he met with nought save rebuffs, and even had to make a complete and permanent severance from his nearest and dearest, he was introduced to his life of apostleship in 42 or 43 by that same Barnabas who had given him such a brotherly welcome on his arrival in Jerusalem.

As we have already seen,[5] Barnabas had been sent by the Apostles to inspect the new Christian community in Syria. He soon found himself in need of assistants; he remembered the young man from Tarsus, whose virtues, ideas and general attitude to life had seemed to mark him out for great things. He went and sought him out in Cilicia, and brought him back with him to Antioch.

Consequently it was in Antioch that Saul concluded his studies in the art of apostleship, under the guidance of a truly wise and good teacher. Antioch, we must remember, was the city in which the essential development in the Christian missionary outlook was even now taking shape. It is quite clear that Saul played his part in bringing this change of plan into being, and in making the town on the Orontes the heaven-sent stage in Christian expansion which, as we have seen, it soon became. The Acts (xi. 26) records that he took part in all the Church gatherings at Antioch alongside Barnabas, instructing many people in the faith, and that, when famine became rife in Jerusalem, it was Saul and his friend, once again, who were chosen to take the mother Church the relief collected by her far-distant Syrian daughter.

Saul's tutelage under Barnabas lasted two years. It must have completed his long period of preparation for the great task ahead, since immediately after his stay in Antioch Saul set out on the first of his great missionary journeys. The years of his apprenticeship were over. Henceforth he went out, secure

[5] See Chapter I, section: 'Antioch.'

in the armour of his faith, ready to conquer the world for the Cross of Christ.

But any account of Saul's transformation into Paul would be incomplete indeed if it neglected to point out that all this physical effort and practical application were firmly bound up with the Apostle's continuous participation in the divine. The greatest mystics all admit no division at all between practical action and transcendent knowledge. Ever since the moment of Saul the Pharisee's conversion on the Damascus road, his whole being had been given to God and submerged in Him; many years later he was to say that it was no longer himself who lived, but Christ who lived in him. From this genuine incorporation, whereby the God-Man unites with those who believe in Him, and which, in stated form, was to be the lynchpin of Pauline theology, the Apostle himself was to derive all his finest qualities. It was at Antioch, some time between 42 and 44 in all probability, that he enjoyed an unforgettable ecstatic experience, which he later described in a brief account that forms one of the basic pieces of the mystical literature of all time:

'There is a man I know who was carried out of himself in Christ, fourteen years since; was his spirit in his body? I cannot tell. Was it apart from his body? I cannot tell; God knows. This man, at least, was carried up into the third heaven. I can only tell you that this man, with his spirit in his body, or with his spirit apart from his body, God knows which, not I, was carried up into Paradise, and heard mysteries which man is not allowed to utter' (2 Cor. xii. 2–4).

What was it that he learnt on this occasion? What overwhelming revelations were imparted to him? A noble modesty of soul prevented him from ever divulging the smallest details to anyone. In any case no human words, even when spoken by a saint, can adequately express divine illuminations of this kind! Yet fourteen years afterwards, when the saint was led to tell his friends in Corinth of his long-past experience, we can still feel him choking with the emotion that the memory engendered: it must have been a decisive moment indeed, the moment in which the Master finally consecrated him to the task to which He had called him.

## CHRIST IS PROCLAIMED TO THE GENTILES

Let us take a closer look at this sickly little missionary, who is henceforth to be plunged into that itinerant but wonderfully fruitful existence which was to be his for the remaining twenty-two years of his life, and which was to culminate in the martyr's crown. Surely no other human being has ever devoted himself so whole-heartedly to any cause, or given himself so selflessly to the service of a single ideal. Saul was a soldier of God, a fighting champion of the Good News, and his own life was completely merged in the doctrine which he preached. His days were packed with an almost unbelievable fund of activity. He was continually on the move, preaching, arguing and converting. New churches sprang up wherever he went; he had no sooner brought a new community into being than he was off again to sow the seed elsewhere; and yet he still found time to write, or rather dictate, countless letters of advice or remonstrance to his spiritual children, the infant communities that were scattered far and wide throughout the Empire.[6] What marvellous success was his during those

[6] Tradition has handed down to us fourteen Epistles of St Paul, and the canon of the Scriptures has grouped them all together. They are often classified into three types: (a) The Great Epistles: Galatians, First and Second Corinthians, Romans, and also the two Epistles to the Thessalonians; in these texts St Paul deals primarily with doctrinal questions, with the problem of 'justification,' Christ's return in glory, and other theological problems which troubled the early Christian communities; (b) The Epistles of Paul's Captivity: Colossians, Philemon, Ephesians and Philippians. In these the Apostle hinges his whole philosophy upon Christ and upon His role in the world and in history and upon the part He must play in the regeneration of every individual believer; (c) The Pastoral Epistles: the First and Second to Timothy, and the Epistle to Titus, all of which deal with the administrative problems of new communities, and which set them on their guard against temptations and error. (The Epistle to the Hebrews is outside this grouping.)

St Paul must have written many other letters; he himself refers to several which are now completely lost, or of which only fragmentary traces remain.

Are the Epistles contained in the New Testament all genuine? Here is how Canon E. Osty sums up this extremely controversial ques-

twenty odd years, and how few were his failures! Through him all those elements in primitive Christianity which were still little more than vague intentions, an instinctive obedience to the Master's orders, were to become formulated into method and doctrine. The man who had received the Master's call on the road to Damascus was to play a divinely ordained and indispensable role in the history of the whole Christian Church.

What resources had he at his command with which to carry out a task of such magnitude? Like nearly all those who are doing or have done great things somewhere in the world, his material resources were small. He was but a humble Jew, making a livelihood by the labour of his own hands. But he was also a man of boundless courage, whom nothing could daunt —neither the 'thirty-nine strokes of the whip,'[7] nor flogging, stoning, nor the fear of death; he was ready to endure anything—the perils of the sea or the desert, threats from Jews or Gentiles, hunger and thirst, cold and tempest. It was the immensity of his faith that gave him this massive strength—a faith of which it was said that he who possessed but a particle of it could move whole mountains. Qualities of this kind shine out from those who possess them, and they explain the supreme authority—which in several instances was overpower-

---

tion, in his excellent edition (in French) of the Epistles: '1. The vast majority of critics admit the authenticity—in their entirety, more or less—of Galatians, Romans, First and Second Corinthians, First Thessalonians, Colossians, Philippians and Philemon. 2. The majority of non-Catholic critics refuse to regard the other Epistles as St Paul's own work, though certain passages of varying importance are fairly freely attributed to him. 3. There is no doubt these latter Epistles contain certain differences of language, style and dogmatic emphasis. 4. But these differences are easily accounted for by the differences in situations and in subjects under discussion, by the altered conditions in which the Apostle wrote them, and by the amazing flexibility of his genius. The sum total of these differences is as nothing against the almost unanimous witness of scriptural tradition.' (On the Epistle to the Hebrews see note 23 at the end of this chapter, p. 130.)

[7] According to Jewish law, the penalty consisted of forty strokes, but the last stroke was never inflicted, for fear that it might kill the victim.

ing in extent—enjoyed by this man who dubbed himself a miserable weakling.

At first sight he was probably not very prepossessing. Though capable of deep, almost paternal, affection, and of unstinting generosity, he remains nevertheless a rather forbidding character. Renan considered him a hard man, in contrast to his 'gentle Galilean master.' But those who criticize his sternness have understood nothing of this ardent nature, so utterly committed to struggles in which no mercy could be expected. The man who wrote the Epistle to Philemon was to show himself possessed of exquisite tenderness. The flood of sensibility and surge of charity which carried St Paul along could sustain a thousand outbursts of anger too: the real way to love humanity is not to yield to its weaknesses and contradictions, but to strive for its well-being, even despite itself, and despite one's personal prejudices.

St Paul's work can be divided into two main periods, depending on the boundaries within which he moved. During the first period he confined himself to the Middle East, to Greece and Asia Minor, to the areas around the Aegean Sea; during the second (from 60 onwards) circumstances obliged him to operate from Rome. But in each case he was working outside the Palestinian sphere of influence, among men who did not dwell in the shadow of the temple, men who were either hellenized Jews or converted pagans—the 'nations' to whom Jesus had commanded that the Gospel should be brought, the Latin *gentes*, which tradition has turned into *Gentiles*. The problems that Paul had to face changed from one period to the other, the perspectives did not remain the same throughout. During the second phase, infant Christianity was to find itself in opposition to the centralizing authority of Caesar, running counter to imperial bureaucracy and Roman pragmatism. The first phase had thrown Saul into the heart of the classical world, permeated as it was by Greek thought and Eastern anarchy, troubled, for three centuries past, by religious doubts, moral decadence and social unrest, a world to which Rome had been able to give administrative order but not peace of mind.

Most commentators single out three important missionary journeys made by the Apostle of the Gentiles for separate attention. But this distinction really seems to be somewhat arbitrary, since the gaps between them all were singularly short, and none of these truly prodigious raids carried out in the Master's service differed from the others in either intention or resources. The Apostle probably made them all largely on foot—and who else can claim to have travelled some nine thousand miles in this way, all in the space of thirteen years! The first mission lasted from 45 to 49; Paul went first to Cyprus, and then crossed to the mainland of Asia Minor, travelling over the mountain plateaus of Pamphylia, Pisidia, Lycaonia, through the towns of Pisidian Antioch, Derbe, Iconium and Lystra and so back to Antioch. The end of 49 saw him in Jerusalem again, where a very important meeting of the Church was taking place, which was, in fact, the first 'Council.' Immediately after this he set off again for Asia Minor, visiting the Christian communities which already existed there, and subsequently pushed forward into Galatia, to preach among some Celtic peoples, closely related to the Gauls, whom the Aryan migrations of long ago had thrown up on these distant shores; then, urged ever onward by the Holy Spirit, he took ship and crossed into Europe. Here he visited Macedonian Philippi, Thessalonica, Athens and Corinth. At the end of the autumn of 52 he set sail homewards from Corinth, passing through Ephesus and so back once more to Antioch. Finally—six months later—came his third journey. This time he went back on his former tracks, continuing the work of evangelization begun at Ephesus, returning to Greece to call upon his friends at Corinth, journeying as far westward as the shores of the Adriatic, then travelling back to Jerusalem via the islands of Mitylene, Chios, Samos and Rhodes, and the ports of Syria and Palestine. Pentecost was approaching when he arrived in the Holy City, where his destiny awaited him, in 57.

In a *tour de force* of this kind it is hard to know what to admire most—Paul's courage, perseverance or wisdom, for all were essential elements of it. The impatient modern tourist who rides across Asia Minor in the comfortable coaches of an express train finds it difficult to visualize the difficulties and dangers that must have beset these slow apostolic perambulations. The Taurus passes and the desert tracks were equally unsafe, for both were infested by bandits. On the mountain plateaus—where all the towns were more than three thousand feet above sea level—the winter was extremely hard, but the summer, which was unbearably hot, was even worse. It needed a stout heart to face up to all the risks and hardships imposed by nature, but these, all the same, were less serious than the perils for which man was responsible.

For wherever it was carried out, the work of evangelization ran up against obstacles that often proved to be very difficult ones. In all the towns that the Apostle visited, events tended to follow a pattern that varied very little from place to place. At the beginning, the Jewish community, to whom he spoke first, and then the Gentiles, who always listened with interest to any new religious teaching, would afford him a sympathetic enough hearing. But all too soon opposition groups would become apparent, whether of Jewish traditionalists, convinced pagans or even, prosaically enough, the various traders who dealt in sacrificial animals or idolatrous statues, and whose living was threatened by the new doctrine. And this would lead to a crisis whose violence varied from town to town, and so to persecution. To stand fast, to persevere, to return to areas from which he had been forced to beat a temporary retreat, Christ's missionary practised a spiritual strategy of astonishing efficacy in a truly marvellous fashion. Like all really great men, he would yield to realities and draw useful lessons from every experience he went through. A rebuff such as the one he had at Athens would encourage him to take a decisive step forward. It is this mixture of flexibility and firmness which one admires most of all, coupled, of course, with his constant intellectual self-searching and elaboration of doctrine. Action did not hamper this spiritual development; on the contrary, it provided the occasion for it.

For the same man who was continually on his travels over sea and over land found time to produce those decisive texts known to us as the *Epistles*, which are veritable masterpieces of Christian philosophy and outstanding monuments to the inspiration of the Holy Spirit. When we read Paul's letters to the Thessalonians, the Galatians, the Romans or the Corinthians, we can see that these are not encyclicals or official instructions but really personal messages, which were probably

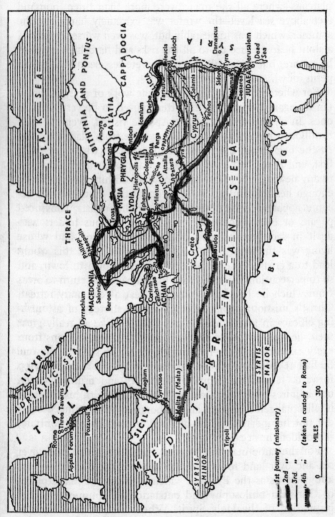

THE JOURNEYS OF ST PAUL

| 1st Journey (missionary) |
| 2nd " " |
| 3rd " " |
| 4th " (taken in custody to Rome) |

0    MILES    300

dictated rapidly under the pressure of events (their 'oral style' suggests this very strongly), and which were intended to be read aloud to the assembled faithful. Everyone who heard them would take the contents to be meant to apply to him person- ally. The astonishing fact is that Paul formulated a definite doctrine in these letters of his, a doctrine which combines sound logic with spiritual elevation, and which clearly springs from the innermost depths of his soul.

It is easy to see how such a man created affections and loyalties wherever he went. A little group of faithful souls gathered about him, just as men had gathered around Christ long before, who were determined to share his risks, and to assume the responsibilities of a common existence. Should one of them fall by the wayside, or turn from his duties—like Mark, for instance, who was troubled and disheartened by the un- known dangers of the first Anatolian mission—someone else would at once replace him. There was Titus, an 'uncircum- cised' pagan, and one of the first believers; Silas, a Roman citizen, who was Paul's companion on his second journey; Timothy, the beloved disciple; and there was Luke, the Greek physician, a highly intelligent and sensitive man, who, many years later, was to write the third Gospel and the book of Acts, from which we derive the bulk of our knowledge of Paul. There were the faithful women too: Lydia, the devout Macedonian, and Priscilla, a Corinthian Jewess, who, with her husband Aquila, sheltered and fed the Apostle and later went to Ephesus, to prepare the way for the Lord there. We get the impression that Paul had a kind of general staff grouped around him, trained to put his philosophy into practice, as well as to transcribe his thoughts into words and hand them on to others. What shines out most clearly through the ac- counts of these journeys of his is this wave of fervour and enthusiasm which makes our own hearts warm to read of it, a wave of feeling similar to that which we have already seen in the community at Jerusalem, and which has simply been transposed here on to another structure.

## The Holy Spirit Works through
## St Paul

It is impossible to try to follow the events of these thirteen years step by step. The Acts bring them to life as a vivid panorama of swift-moving action, alternately realistic and grandiose, the whole conveying a most powerful impression of authenticity. Even comic episodes are not wanting from the narrative. For instance, there was the incident at Lystra, on Paul's first journey (Acts xvi. 8–18). After the Apostle had healed a man there who had been crippled since birth, simply by uttering a few words, the crowd acclaimed him as the god Mercury, and insisted on dragging him towards a pagan altar (as for the worthy Barnabas, he was considered a suitable Jupiter!); Paul only rid himself of this embarrassing enthusiasm after some difficulty. But sublime deeds carried him along wherever he went: visions and dreams were sent him, and the Almighty performed many miracles to succour His faithful servant in times of trouble. Outstanding among these was the supernatural event for which Lystra once again provided the background. A crowd gathered around Paul again, but this time its attitude was hostile; though stoned, and left for dead, writhing on the ground, the Apostle managed to rise to his feet, and his wounds healed miraculously (Acts xvi. 19); but what of those sores on his hands, his feet, his brow and his side, which remained permanently open? These were brands that marked him as the Master's own, of that there can be no doubt, and Paul was to bear them on his body until the day he died.

Amid the rapid succession of events which comprise a life such as this, there are a number of episodes which it behoves us to study in some detail, either on account of their own special significance, or because of the implications that they carry. First of all, there is the episode involving the Apostle's change of name, which took place at Cyprus, right at the beginning of his missionary life (Acts xiii. 4–13). Cyprus was known as the island of love, Aphrodite's country. The goddess was said to have been born from the sea-spray off the island's shores, and she was remembered in the erotic rites and religious prostitution which still existed there in Paul's day. The missionary had a meeting in Cyprus with Sergius Paulus, the Roman proconsul, who was yet another of those many aristocrats who are intensely curious about religious matters. With the proconsul was his favourite, Elymas, who was also known as Bar-Jesus, who claimed to be a magician. By putting the fraud to confusion, Saul won the Roman official over to Christ's cause, and immediately afterwards, perhaps out of friendship for his convert, he permanently adopted the cognomen of Paulos which he had used jointly with his Hebrew name ever since boyhood. Henceforth *Saul* disappears from the scene altogether, giving way to *Paul*. When we consider the importance which the Jews, like all the other Eastern peoples, attached to personal names, which they regarded as being endowed with a kind of supernatural worth, this choice must be viewed as something considerably more than a mere title of convenience: it is the outward sign of a spiritual intention, showing the Apostle's total acceptance of that extremely specialized mission which the Almighty had assigned to him, namely the bearing of the Gospel to the Gentile world.

Indeed, all the greatest moments of Paul's life are linked with this intention. He was, in truth, the man destined to free the Gospel from its Jewish framework and to prepare the way of the Word of Christ to be spread to the four corners of the earth. During his first great mission he rapidly converted large numbers of former pagans to Christianity, and the problem of the relationships between the new faith and the ancient law, or, to be more accurate, the choice between Mosaic observances and adherence to Christ, became more and more pressing. Once again it was Paul who, by instigating the calling of the Council of Jerusalem in 49, led the Church to settle the matter once and for all, and, in doing so, to opt for the future. It was a splendid moment indeed when all these men, so different from one another, and yet all motivated solely by the desire to be utterly faithful to Christ, agreed on their decision, with a truly premonitory feeling for the future interests of the whole Church (Acts xv. 1–33).

A year went by. The Apostle had set off on his travels again, had spent some months in Galatia, where he was taken ill, and had twice felt that the Holy Spirit was impelling him in a direction contrary to that which his reason bade him take. Eventually he reached the plains of Troy, and, turning his gaze westwards, he thought of the Europe that lay on the far side of the narrow straits. He did not know where to turn next; his mind was tortured by uncertainties. But a force far greater than himself urged him forward towards this unknown world where the Gospel seed had still to be sown. Standing on those same shores where Achilles had given his life to defeat Asia, and where Alexander had landed on his way to conquer the old continent, Paul realized that all these lands were still closed to the Gospel message, and he felt himself divinely called to work them for Christ. Then, in the night, he had a vision, bringing him the divine command for which he was waiting. In a dream he saw a Macedonian standing before him, wearing the cloak and high helmet that were typical of his countrymen. He spoke to the Apostle: he begged him to come and bring the light of the Gospel to the children of the West. And, in that moment, Paul made another of the great decisions of his life (Acts xvi. 9–10).

Yet though there are many great episodes of this kind in the Acts, those which touch us more deeply are the ones in which the mighty Apostle seems no longer sustained by supernatural power, and infallible in his every action, but closer to ordinary mortals, more our own height. We warm to see him using a difficulty or a defeat as a means of taking a decisive step forward, worrying about his work in a wholly human way, and even yielding to very humble feelings of distress, fearing that the worst is about to happen, and then overcoming all uncertainties and marching firmly forward towards his appointed destiny.

On his arrival in Athens, in the autumn of 50, Paul was to experience the most resounding defeat of his whole career. By now Athens was no longer the splendid capital it had been in the days of Pericles and Phidias; three-quarters of the city was in ruins. The place swarmed with idle bystanders. It was one of those centres of intellectual decadence where extreme intelligence had petered out into a philosophy which was a complete negation of everything, and it attracted a dazzling coterie of young folk, drawn from all over Thrace, Italy and

Greece proper, who spent their time in reading, arguing and playing games. Certain aspects of present-day Oxford and Cambridge, or some of the more 'advanced' intellectual circles of modern Paris, give a rough idea of what the atmosphere of Athens society must have been like at the time. Was the Apostle at all disconcerted by these unaccustomed surroundings? Everything about them proclaimed the new enemy he had to fight—that pagan humanism, which tacitly cancelled out God, the beauty of the blue and gold scenery, the endless treatises on this or that empty philosophy, and, high up on the summit of the hill, at the top of a flight of giant steps, the little honey-coloured temple which, so the Greeks believed, housed the spirit of wisdom. But as yet Paul did not know how to battle with such an adversary. Tactfully he tried to link his religious instruction to references which were current in Athenian circles; he suggested that the 'unknown God' to whom the pagans dedicated their altars was really the Messiah, the God made man. But as soon as he proclaimed the news of the Resurrection his audience burst into ribald laughter. On this subject the Greeks shared the view of Aeschylus: 'Once the dust has drunk a man's blood, there can be no more hope of resurrection for him.' Someone shouted mockingly: 'We must hear more from thee about this!' (Acts xvii. 16–34).

It was a hard lesson, but it bore fruitful results. Paul took his leave of the city of learning, pondering upon this rejection, and he understood its moral. Up to now, surely, had he not set too much store on reasoning, upon demonstration through logical proof? God brought him to realize that it was necessary to bring a different kind of message to this world of sin that he had to conquer. And this message he set out in unforgettable form in the First Epistle to the Corinthians: here Paul makes it quite clear that Christianity is neither a philosophy nor the kind of worldly wisdom argued over in treatises, that it appears positively absurd when viewed in the light of human reason—'to the Jews a discouragement, to the Gentiles, mere folly.' Christianity is a fact which transcends all logic, whose reality is inscribed upon man's very soul. A Christian does not seek to prove the Cross; he lives it. Consequently the only news which the missionary must needs spread is that of the triumph in defeat, the news of the crucified Son of God.

The world has not yet fully comprehended this lesson, which Paul was to see applied in practical form immediately after his defeat in Athens. Corinth was the next stopping-place on his road—Corinth, the city of ill fame, with a reputation not unlike that of the Marseilles dockland of our own day, where the street-girls paraded openly and shamelessly under the interested eye of the 'Corinthiasts'—the pimps—and where the most popular religious cult was that of Aphrodite Pandemos, who was served by yet another set of prostitutes, sacred ones this time![8] Yet, by a miracle, the message that had failed so abysmally in the capital city of intellectualism succeeded in this place of ill-gotten wealth and debauchery. A Christian community sprang into being there, which was so rich in faith, so fervently spiritual, that it was always to remain dearest to Paul's heart. Nothing could prevent its growth, not even the hostility of the Jewish community, ever on the watch here as elsewhere, which resulted in the Apostle's arrest.[9] Here we have yet another of the Holy Spirit's lessons, revealing the

[8] Corinth had been destroyed by the Romans in 146 B.C. and in Paul's day only a few traces of its past glory still remained: the fountain of Pirene, the temple of Apollo, of which six columns survive to this day, and the tomb of Lais, the famous courtesan, which stood side by side with that of Diogenes, the great cynic. In 46 B.C. the city was rebuilt by Caesar and colonized by 'an assortment of ill-gotten slaves,' according to a contemporary description. Under Augustus it became the capital of Achaia once more, and was filled with countless monuments in the heavy Roman style, temples, basilicas, theatres and arenas, and many ruins dating from this period are still standing. According to Mommsen, Corinth was 'the least Greek of all Greek cities.' It certainly contained a large Jewish colony, for a synagogue, dating from the first century A.D., has been found there.

[9] This incident is of considerable importance in helping us to establish St Paul's chronology. The book of Acts tells us that he was brought before the proconsul of Achaia, Gallio, who, after questioning him, categorically refused to become involved in this purely Jewish quarrel. Now Gallio, a relative of the philosopher Seneca, has left behind a number of inscriptions, one of which, found at Delphi, enables us to fix the date of his proconsulship exactly: spring 52. By this time Paul had already spent eighteen months in Corinth (Acts xviii. 11). Consequently we can conclude that he arrived there in the autumn of 50 and left again in the autumn of 52.

truth that is as valid today and every day as it was to the Greeks of Paul's epoch: that a sinner is closer to God than a skilful arguer (Acts xviii. 1–17).

We all know of men who although capable of conceiving some great project are incapable of bringing it to fruition. St Paul's genius was quite complete: he possessed every kind of gift, and he was as capable of supervising an enterprise and carrying it through to a successful conclusion as he was of setting it in motion; his stay in Ephesus is proof of this (Acts xix). He reached the great Greek metropolis[10] in the spring of 53, at the beginning of his third mission, and he stayed there two years, contemptuous of all the risks he was running in so doing, unafraid of the 'ravening wolves' he had to fight. The Christian community which he had found there on his journey back from Corinth seemed to him to be full of great promise for the future, but to be exposed, also, to considerable risk. A certain Alexandrian named Apollo had already brought the Good News to Ephesus, but his instruction on the subject contained serious gaps. Paul remedied these, corrected any errors made by Apollo, removed all tendencies towards magic and, by his preaching and miracles, established the faith there on solid foundations. At the same time he did not forget the other communities that he had founded. He knew all too well that they needed his continual and firm supervision if they were to continue along the straight and narrow path. In all probability (the matter is one over which critics argue a great deal) it was from Ephesus that he sent his moving letter of

[10] At this time Ephesus was as important a place as Alexandria, and was one of the greatest of all the Eastern cities. She possessed the most thriving port in Asia Minor; even today, among the sanddunes and swamps which have separated her from the sea, the ruined town contains some striking fragments of its past splendours, both Roman and Christian. Its temple of Diana, one of the 'wonders of the world,' attracted crowds from all over the Greek dominions, who came to take part in the great ceremonies performed in honour of the chaste goddess. It was during one of these festivals that a seller of statuettes and little votive temple models unleashed a popular riot against Paul, forcing the Apostle to leave the city. However, by this time his work there was done (spring 56).

encouragement to the Galatians, who had been much troubled by Judaizing missionaries, urging them to reject the ancient servitude of the Law once and for all; from Ephesus, too, that he wrote to his beloved Corinthians, threatened at that time by internal discord, and inwardly tormented by the age-old corruptions of the flesh, sending them his wonderful message in which love and virtue are reconciled with one another. These two years in Ephesus illustrate most clearly the full-blooded realism of the great mystic, and show to what extent the Holy Spirit can be translated into practical, detailed actions.[11]

And now we come to the last stage, to the final great chapter of these thirteen years. It occurred at the end of the Apostle's third journey. Paul was making his way back to Palestine, having, so it seemed, done his work well. All the same, his heart was troubled by strange forebodings. All these years he had preached for Christ, toiled for Him and suffered for Him. Was this enough? If the Lord's will was to be fulfilled absolutely, was not something else needed besides? Was he not being called upon to seal the mystery of our Lord's Passion with his own blood? During the last months of Paul's third mission the human side of the Apostle's nature stands out very clearly indeed. He is sorely troubled and anguished in spirit. When his Ephesian friends came to visit him at Miletus, he told them that this was the last time they would ever see him; he knew this with certainty, God had told him so. He foresaw the tribulations that awaited him. Did he draw back, or hesitate, even for an instant? No. At Tyre some of the faithful, who were anxious on his behalf, tried to prevent him from continuing his journey; but he refused to linger, and whilst they knelt on the shore in prayer, imploring his blessing, he embarked on his way to that cruel fate that he accepted so sublimely. In short, just as the second stage of his life is about to commence, a stage marked by sadness and suffering, a stage in which, by bearing the Word of God right into the heart of the Roman world, Paul is to carry out in full the mission entrusted him by Jesus long ago on the road to Damascus,

11 St Paul's work at Ephesus was to be carried on by St John the Apostle, who, as we shall see, ended his days there, and exercised enormous influence on the city (see the next chapter).

the Apostle has learned the greatest lesson of all: truth, if it is to prevail, must be sealed by the martyr's blood (Acts xx. 17–36).

## An Art Form Inspired by the Holy Spirit

We should dearly like to know more about the means of conversion used so triumphantly by this man who was able to bring the Gospel light to such large numbers of very different kinds of people. We still possess some of his texts, and in quantity they almost equal those describing Jesus' own teaching. And yet, when we read them, we feel most strongly that they present but an incomplete witness of the whole, and that the true Paul lies somewhere beyond these dialectic developments and lyrical fragments, somewhere beyond all these fine-sounding sentences. Whenever we are dealing with a man of action—and St Paul is that, first and foremost—words and writing always fall short of the real thing: we must add to these the magnetism of the man's gaze, the force of his actions, the weight of his silences and the sound of his voice, either lowered in irony or raised in anger—in short, everything about a man that compels our attention and brings him to life in our imagination.

Was Paul really a born orator? Probably he was, in the Eastern sense of the word; after all, he had been educated by the rabbis, and was therefore superlatively trained to use the rhythmic phrases, repetitions and alliterations which we today consider fundamental characteristics of the Jewish method of spiritual expression. All the same, this is far removed from the Western definition of oratory. Did not the Apostle himself, in one of his Epistles (2 Cor. x. 10), say that he regarded himself as a 'poor orator'? Perhaps he was merely saying this out of a sense of humility. However, great powers of eloquence are generally associated with men of superb physical appearance. We have already noticed that Saul was utterly lacking in this respect, and it is probably more accurate to depict Paul as one of those little Jews whose voice begins to grate with emotion as soon as any strong feeling seizes him, rather than as a kind of Roman orator, speaking in powerful, ringing tones.

Was he even a born writer? Not in the classical sense of the term. He is certainly no model for the schoolboy to copy. Although his Greek was not nearly so incorrect as Renan claims, it was neither very pure nor very literary; it was the language spoken by the masses, the kind of Greek heard all over the Middle East, closely resembling that of Polybius or Epictetus, interspersed with racy popular catch-phrases and one or two Aramaicisms. It is only too easy to find fault with Paul's style: there are his ill-balanced sentences, sometimes enormously lengthy and involved, sometimes breaking off in the midst of a train of thought, and the series of clauses, clumsily linked by *and . . . and . . .* Such flaws are very apparent. Bossuet called Paul 'that ignoramus in the art of self-expression.' And yet anyone who studies this impassioned prose at all seriously cannot fail to be struck by its impetus, its spontaneous upsurge of emotion, and by that perfect fusion between feeling and style which is the hallmark of the real literary genius.

Whoever reads St Paul is bound to admire not only the saint's rare gift for striking expressions, which are dotted throughout his paragraphs, and which glitter there with fantastic brilliance—profound truths, descriptions which have become standard—phrases like 'the man of sin,' 'the thorn in the flesh' and 'the folly of the Cross.' We admire, too, those extracts which seem complete in themselves, their every word so packed with meaning that one would not wish to change a single adverb in them, and so convincing that as we read them we fancy we can hear the very ring of their author's voice.

'Here is a secret I will make known to you; we shall all rise again, but not all of us will undergo the change I speak of. It will happen in a moment, in the twinkling of an eye, when the last trumpet sounds; the trumpet will sound, and the dead will rise again, free from corruption, and we shall find ourselves changed; this corruptible nature of ours must be clothed with incorruptible life, this mortal nature with immortality. Then, when this corruptible nature wears its incorruptible garment, this mortal nature its immortality, the saying of Scripture will come true, Death is swallowed up in victory. Where, then, death, is thy victory; where, death, is thy sting?' (1 Cor. xv. 51–5).

This passage is justly famous. The sweet lyricism of the Holy Spirit breathes right through it. But there are many others which are equally splendid, such as the following, which defines the characteristics of human love as God sees them:

'Charity is patient, is kind; charity feels no envy; charity is never perverse or proud, never insolent; does not claim its rights, cannot be provoked, does not brood over an injury; takes no pleasure in wrongdoing, but rejoices at the victory of truth; sustains, believes, hopes, endures, to the last' (1 Cor. xiii. 4–7). What prodigious psychoanalysis is contained in these three short verses!

But more admirable, even, than these isolated flashes of brilliance is the force and undeniable richness of Paul's writing as a whole. It contains an incredible concentration of feeling, and anyone remaining unaware of this shows himself not merely deaf to any appeal of the Spirit but blind to literary merit too. It is true that St Paul is often obscure, and hard to understand; St Peter admits this in his second Epistle (2 Peter iii. 16) and the fact can be verified by any one of us. The meaning of his message is still being studied; two thousand years of commentaries have not nearly finished clarifying it completely, and several of his texts suggest innumerable contradictory themes. This difficulty stems not simply from the methods that he uses, i.e. the ancient Hebrew practice of setting down thesis and antithesis, one after the other, fairly and squarely, without attempting to harmonize them into a logical synthesis. Its primary cause is the violent pressure of Paul's spiritual feelings. These sometimes bring him to use the aptest of expressions, and inspire sentences of sublime poetry, but on other occasions they prove too much for the ordinary mortal in him, and he lapses into almost incoherent stuttering.

St Paul's written work demonstrates once again that very fact which is proved also by the events of his life; that he was not merely a great preacher, like so many others, and a prodigiously gifted orator and skilful dialectician besides; but that he was truly imbued with the Holy Spirit. 'Since we live

by the spirit, let the spirit be our rule of life,' he wrote in
his letter to the Galatians: he himself lived these words in
his own life, and, in addition, his every word was inspired by
the Spirit. His writing is but the expression of that overwhelming Presence which dwelt within him, springing spontaneously
from his lips. Perhaps this message, which we find so hard to
understand, was equally difficult of comprehension to the man
who was its spokesman. Long before, Amos, the prophet of
ancient Israel, had described how God had ordered him to
'Go and prophesy!' This was the same profound command
felt by the Apostle Paul when, awed by the power that he
realized was housed within him, he murmured: 'Is it really
I who am capable of all these things?' (See references in 2
Cor. ii. 16 and iii. 5.) No other art form was ever to give so
great an impression of having been dictated by the Spirit as
the writings of St Paul.

### A Spiritual Message that is Closely Bound up with the Practical

It is correct to say, then, that St Paul was indeed a herald
of the Spirit. But the question immediately arises: a herald of
what kind of Spirit? After all, many things are made to claim
kinship with 'spiritual values,' and some of them are nothing
but meaningless word-play. The Spirit, as St Paul understood
it, has no connection whatsoever with that logical abstract so
sought after by philosophers. It has nothing in common with
the will-o'-the-wisp from the cavern of Platonism. It is no nebulous dream. The Spirit whom Paul serves is He who has given
the Apostle's life its meaning, who works in man like a transforming power, and who has made His Presence felt in the
midst of society and at a given moment in historical time.
This is the Holy Spirit, the Word of God, who became man,
being born of a virgin, lived His earthly life, and died upon
the Cross.

Christianity is, fundamentally, both a transcendent explanation of the world and a living force, making a practical im-
pact upon that world. This dual message is perfectly presented by St Paul. As we have already seen, the character of

his apostolate corresponds with it exactly. Bergson aptly remarked that the greatest mystics are always people possessed of plenty of common sense, their feet on the ground, leading effective, active lives, and quite the opposite of ineffectual daydreamers: and he cites the examples of St Augustine, St Francis of Assisi, St Joan of Arc and St Teresa of Avila. St Paul was made of the same stuff as all these. His message was simultaneously bound up with the most practical of realities and linked with the loftiest of metaphysical speculations.

*Pretty Questionable.*

Consequently, when considering the content of the message which St Paul brought the world, we must beware of regarding it as we would regard a philosopher's doctrine. A philosopher seeks to realize his thinking in written form. The whole meaning of St Paul is distorted if his theology, his moral philosophy and his metaphysics are studied outside the context of the concrete conditions in which he was led to formulate them, removed from the practical circumstances which occasioned them. There is no *Paulinism* in the sense in which one talks of *Kantism* or *Bergsonism*. There is instead a man who reacts to definite events with definite ideas born of those events, but whose thinking is so inspired and so wonderfully coherent that it seems as if it has been laid down in set form long before the events in question took place.

St Paul's doctrine invariably takes shape and expression as the result of some particular fact connected with his apostolic work or with the life of one of the early communities that he served. The preoccupations of the Thessalonians with regard to man's ultimate ends led him to define his philosophy in relation to this problem and to state his views on the second coming of the Son of Man. The moral lapses that occurred in Corinth furnished a starting-point for those arguments in which Paul's doctrine of sin unfolds itself with a majesty that is quite sublime. Later on certain tendencies towards Judeo-Phrygian syncretism which he observed in one or two Christian communities encouraged him to emphasize the portrait of Christ as Christ Himself describes it.

And it is this which gives his message its practical and intensely human aspect, which makes it so perpetually alive. We tend to imagine this man as being lost in his dreams and visions. Nothing could be further from the truth. He was continually laying down axioms of practical conduct which hold good for societies of every epoch. He tackled the most mundane of problems, that of work, for example, in connection with which he uttered the following famous sentence (which was to be reiterated, later on, by Lenin!): 'The man who refuses to work must be left to starve!' (2 Thess. iii. 10). Marriage was another subject which he treated in detail, fixing its character, principles, obligations and boundaries with a precision and psychological insight that have never been surpassed since. And he dealt equally fully with many problems of social and political life, the relationships that ought to exist between parents and children, and many other topics besides. There is scarcely a single important subject of human interest that is not covered in the writings of St Paul.

Thus his message can be considered from two points of view: either in the sense that he brings brilliant, inspired answers to the eternal questions of mankind; or in the sense that he intervenes in history and ends by throwing the existing human order of things into confusion. As far as the first sense is concerned, what Christian can refrain from confessing how much he owes to this little Jewish genius from Tarsus for his understanding of certain anxieties of the human soul, and for his grasp of this or that spiritual need? Who can forget the illuminating synthesis which he made between death and sin, between our efforts towards goodness and our chances of survival? or the moving description of charity which we have just been reading in the First Epistle to the Corinthians? or that continual evocation of man's misery, which is redeemed and assuaged by the promise of salvation? All this touches us so closely: St Paul is at the very heart of our most secret inward conflicts.

The second point of view, regarding which our perspectives are limited in this section, shows how this message of Paul's effected a radical change of plan not only in the Church but throughout the world of his own age. But it must be emphasized that, so far as Paul himself was concerned, these two points of view co-existed, and were indistinguishable from one another. It was because he was so utterly dedicated to the service of the Holy Spirit that St Paul was to transform the world, and, parallel with this, we must not forget that it was in solving questions of an immediately practical nature that he was to formulate doctrines whose validity would be eternal.

## THE PROBLEMS OF THE PAST

Right from the start St Paul's active role in practical Christian affairs had brought him face to face with primitive Christianity's decisive problem: the problem which, on the tactical plane, was manifesting itself in the awkward relations existing between 'Hellenists' and 'Judaizers,' but which, taken in its widest sense, was forcing the Church to make a choice between the narrow confines of a minor Jewish sect and the limitless horizons of the universalism that Jesus had preached. The young Saul must certainly have encountered this problem from the first moment of his entry into the Church. Had not Barnabas, his Christian mentor, been sent to Antioch to look into the decision taken on the subject by the city on the Orontes? And on Saul's first visit to Jerusalem following his conversion, had he himself not taken part in some heated debates between the two opposing schools of thought? It so happened that no one was better qualified than Paul to provide a perfectly well-founded solution to this most difficult problem of conscience.

His education, like his ancestry, had been utterly Jewish in character. During his years as a scholar among the Pharisees he had made a thorough study of the Hebrew Scriptures, and he never ceased to practise them and to quote them with a kind of easy fluency. He was a fully fledged Doctor of the Law, as well grounded in exegesis and theology as in law and moral philosophy, and a true 'rabbi,' when he became a Christian. And indeed he was to remain faithful to Israel as long as he lived. Every time the occasion presented itself he declared his pride at belonging to the Chosen People, at being part of Abraham's posterity, a member of the tribe of Benjamin, as 'Hebrew-speaking as my parents before me.' He actually boasted of having been 'so fierce a champion . . . of the traditions handed down by my forefathers' (Gal. i. 14), and of having always showed himself beyond reproach 'in observing what the law commands' (Phil. iii. 6). Even when his fellow Jews treated him as their enemy, he refused to hate them:

he reiterated that 'the visible presence, and the covenant, and the giving of the law, and the temple worship, and the promises' (Rom. ix. 4) were their inheritance. He loved them, and he pitied them.

But, at the same time, Saul the Jew found himself prepared to break out from the over-rigid boundaries of Israel. Tarsus, his home town, was far too criss-crossed by Western influences for him to have remained unaware of the fresh breezes blowing in from the world at large. Gamaliel, his Pharisee teacher, had always shown himself the most open-minded of men, and the least inclined to sectarianism. Consequently everything that was finest in him led Paul to link himself to that universalist current which spanned the tradition of the ancient Israelite prophets. This was a tradition forgotten by all too many, but from which Paul, with his genius, was to create a wonderfully fruitful synthesis.

When the Council of Jerusalem assembled in 49, probably at Paul's request, what exactly was the Apostle's intention? He wanted the Church to face her problem fairly and squarely. It was so serious that a continued indirect approach to it, at the dictation of circumstances alone, was useless. It was essential to make the agreement entered into by Peter at Caesarea, in the individual case of the centurion Cornelius, an agreement subsequently repeated in the decision taken by the Christian community at Antioch, a definite principle of Christian missionary endeavour. By all means, argued Paul, let those Jews who became Christians retain the observances prescribed by the law, and let them retain, in particular, the rite of circumcision: it was right and proper for them to do so. But Gentiles who wished to be converted should not be compelled to go through the Jewish stage in the process first. Such compulsion was a mistake from the tactical point of view, since the rigours demanded by the Torah discouraged many well-disposed souls; and, in the spiritual sphere, since the law had been 'superseded' by Jesus, why cling to *petty detail* when the *basic requirement*—faith—was present?

This was the attitude adopted by the first assembly of the Church. Nothing in our evidence suggests that there was the slightest disagreement between Paul and the Apostles, the original repositories of Jesus' message, upon this vital point.

Quite the reverse. Their agreement was swiftly sealed. Years later Paul described the scene in his Epistle to the Galatians: 'Those who were reputed to be the main support of the Church, James and Cephas and John . . . joined their right hands in fellowship with Barnabas and myself' (Gal. ii. 7–9). An order was set down in writing, fixing the principle and stating exactly which of the Jewish observances should be retained. Thus the Pauline concept on this vital subject resulted in these profound trends within the Christian conscience, which until then had barely been formulated, being set up as a part of Christian doctrine.

The Apostle of the Gentiles was to retain the same attitude towards this subject all his life. Although he adapted himself to differing circumstances with uncanny flexibility, he was, at the same time, as steadfast as a rock upon matters of principle, while taking care neither to irritate nor to scandalize in practice. For instance, Timothy, his disciple, had not been circumcised in infancy, although possessing a Jewish mother. Paul had him circumcised, so that pious Jews should have no ground for dubbing him an apostate; but Titus, on the other hand, who was Gentile in origin, was never circumcised. Paul himself, on his final visit to Jerusalem, was to undergo the traditional purification ceremonies at the temple in order to assuage the anxieties of the Judaizers.[12] But at Antioch, when St Peter seemed to be taking sides with the most rigid of the Judaizers, and abandoning the true path of Christian universalism, it was Paul who, kindly but firmly, corrected him; as Tertullian wrote, this was 'but an error of attitude, not of doctrine,' but it could well have had serious consequences. Paul stopped Peter from committing such an error (Gal. ii. 11).

On the practical plane, then, it is true to say that St Paul succeeded in setting Christianity along the right road. But those who view his thinking solely in terms of a simple decision concerning tactics and propaganda sadly misunderstand the real message that this man of genius sought to give the world. Though settled in the best possible way, the dispute

[12] See section further on in this chapter: 'Paul's Arrest at Jerusalem,' p. 116.

between Hellenists and Judaizers left a wound behind it in the Christian soul.

On the one hand it was essential to go beyond the boundaries of Israel, yet on the other it was equally essential to remain faithful to the race which had been the first to receive the Promise, which had given the Messiah to the world and from which Jesus Himself had declared that salvation would come. It was a serious problem of conscience. How can we best understand the mystery of the chosen, yet rebellious, race, the dramatic contradiction between its rejection of Christ and the perfectly respectable causes of that same rejection? The argument is set out, with moving severity, in the ninth, tenth and eleventh chapters of the Epistle to the Romans, with its visionary conclusion: Israel has rejected Christ, but her sin was supernaturally necessary; through her salvation has come to the world, through the Redemption and the sacrifice of Christ's blood. When the last hour has sounded, salvation shall surely come to the Chosen People, the people which have sinned, but are now forgiven. 'How deep is the mine of God's wisdom . . . how inscrutable are his judgments, how undiscoverable his ways!'

Vast perspectives such as these are far removed indeed from pettifogging details about this or that observance, or circumcision! But how was the unity between the ancient law and the new message to be realized in the souls of the living now, before the coming of the Last Day? Here again Paul had the answer.

Sin has laid a heavy, oppressive debt upon the shoulders of mankind. The law is this debt. But now Christ has come into the world and taken the whole burden upon His own shoulders. He died for this downtrodden humanity; He rose again into freedom and light so that all those who believe in Him may share in the Redemption. The ancient law made the human soul acutely aware of its miserable state—even while completely absolving itself from any interest in it! Yet, imposed from outside as it was, it was totally incapable of redeeming humanity, of giving it peace or consolation. The love of Jesus alone performed this miracle. Consequently justification no longer lies in the law, but in faith—faith rendered efficacious by charity, in other words by good works. The Christian who gives himself wholly to Christ, who lives according to Christ's love, will be saved. This is the admirable doctrine which is set out in the Epistle to the Romans, in that to the Galatians and in a large section of the Second Epistle to the Corinthians. Not only has the problem of the past been solved, but the solution provided by St Paul bears the whole of the Christian future within it.

## OPTIONS ON THE FUTURE

The great Apostle's real concern—indeed his only one—was for the future of Christianity. He knew full well that numerous difficulties lay ahead. 'I see a great open door before me, whose access leads to efficacious action; but the adversaries there are many.' Here we see the mark of the true genius: Paul possessed the ability to see the obstacles even while they were still concealed in the limbo of the future, and to provide the means of overcoming them long in advance.

It was in Greece that Paul encountered the first of the many problems which Christianity would have to resolve when, having once gone beyond the bounds of Jewry, it began to attempt to penetrate intellectual paganism, the paganism of the schools and the philosophers. The adversary here was no longer the formalistic legalism that imprisoned the soul in a strait jacket in which the Spirit wilted and faded away; this enemy was pagan humanism, 'worldly wisdom,' which claimed to grasp the divine solely by intellectual exercises, or which enclosed it within a naturalism where its transcendency melted away to nothing.

We have already seen how, in the unforgettable words of his First Epistle to the Corinthians, St Paul had broken once and for all with the basic assumptions on which all humanistic paganism rested; and how, in proclaiming the 'folly of the Cross,' he had given Christianity a new method of thought. Here again the spiritual revolution was complete. Paul had solved the problem of the relationships between pagan and Christian humanism. Had the new faith tried to find a foothold among the ordinary religious and philosophical concepts of the day, it would have remained but a vaguely reformist doctrine, differing only a little from the pagan mysteries and the theories of the pagan humanist scholars: it was this total inversion of positions, word for word, which enabled it to make the decisive break with classical tradition. The Gospel of Jesus Christ conquered the classical world precisely because Paul proclaimed it to be a 'folly' and an absurdity from the viewpoint of traditional logic.

Yet it is impossible to ignore the fact that in preaching thus Paul at the same time attacked and condemned for ever two of the gravest of human temptations—the first being the sin of intellectual pride, the second that of yielding to the sluggardliness innate in man's nature. The 'folly of the Cross' humbles man's spirit and shows him his true limitations; by insisting on the suffering of the flesh it makes him fully aware of his wretchedness and frailty. So just as he told the Jews to 'believe and love!' St Paul bade the Gentiles: 'Humble yourselves! Submit to man's condition!' These few words contain many of the fundamentals of the Christian religion, and in so far as it can be said that Christianity has changed humanity, it has done so by introducing these principles into it, principles so admirably stated by St Paul.

Thus St Paul's writing proves in most striking fashion that a spiritual doctrine can be fully efficacious in human society only when it rigidly obeys its own principles. Furthermore, it was the most essential theological concept of Paulinism which, in a historic sense, was to enable the new-born Church, called to take the place of the Roman Empire, to realize the two mental operations without which no revolution is conceivable: namely, the promotion of a new type of man and the projection into the future of a new sort of society. To use the classical German expression: the *Weltanschauung* of young Christianity was born of the metaphysic, the theology and the mysticism of St Paul.

'With Christ I hang upon the cross, and yet I am alive; or rather, not I; it is Christ that lives in me!' (Gal. ii. 19). The Apostle's triumphant cry is the perfect expression of the ideal striven after by all the great mystics: self-identification with the divine. But at the same time it is the definition of a Christian. What is meant by the term 'Christian'? Surely, a man who lives in Christ. As a result he is no longer 'Greek or Jew'; he is a Christian—the one word is all-sufficient. Thus, thanks to St Paul, this new breed of men—this *tertium gens*, as it was subsequently to be called, which was to replace the pagans and the adherents of the Old Law—would fully find its own feet: the new type of man had been born. And the new society was defined too, simultaneously, that society which was to take the place of the Jewish community, the classical city-state and the universalist Empire of Rome, the society composed of all those who lived 'according to the Spirit,' through Christ and in Christ: this new society was, in fact, the Church, 'the body of Christ,' redeemed and sanctified humanity. It is quite true that the immense edifice of Pauline writing contains several other ideas besides these, all of which marked a step forward for the whole of Christianity in the understanding of the truths revealed by Jesus—notably Paul's ideas concerning dogmas such as that of the Trinity, and his views on the sacraments, e.g. on the eucharist. But these are of secondary importance: the essential of Paulinism lies in its desire to outpace the past, in the creative synthesis of old and new which we have just observed. The first Christians had understood all this deep in their hearts; they had wanted to live with Jesus; they had known instinctively that they were the good seed from which mighty future harvests would spring forth; but these feelings had never been built into a formal body of doctrine. That was the task which St Paul was called to perform.

And if we want to assess the really explosive force of this doctrine, we should turn to one of those aspects of it in which St Paul shows himself at his most far-sighted: to his famous theory of Christian liberty, which is scattered throughout all his writing, and implied in its every word, especially in his Epistle to the Romans and his First Epistle to the Corinthians. How does St Paul conceive this liberty? Not as a kind of puffed-up independence and licence, as a sort of anarchy. Far from it. We have seen already that he was a man who appreciated law and order, and who respected, in their own fields, the hierarchies of society and the State. True revolutionaries scorn futile revolts. The Christian, according to Paul, is free because, thanks to Jesus, he has conquered the world, his own passions and even death itself. What does it matter whether he be the subject of one of the most oppressive of states, whether he be slave or captive? The Christian is the free man *par excellence*, and nothing can take this freedom from him. When St Paul made such declarations as these the logical consequences of his spiritual principles, he had not yet collided with the might of Rome, and he never stated that the Empire of the She-Wolf would one day be overcome by the Cross. But his principle embodied this inevitable conclusion. The Christian soldiers who, in the name of this Christian liberty, would claim the right to love their brethren, even their enemies—the martyrs who, in the name of this Christian liberty, were to die rather than sacrifice to 'Rome and Augustus'—were to deal imperial domination its death-blow. On this point, too, St Paul's doctrine seems to have had conclusive results.

## JESUS OR PAUL?

One question remains outstanding, since it is the one which, so far as contemporary religious criticism is concerned, has led to the adoption of various positions which are completely unacceptable to the Catholic. Paul's message was indeed of supreme importance to the future development of Christianity. Was it sufficient on its own to ensure this development? The mighty Apostle's philosophy is admittedly highly original and extremely powerful. Is it actually independent of the vast collection of ideas which had made up Christianity from its very beginnings—and, in particular, independent even of Christ Himself? This is the thesis which has been maintained by certain critics. Some hold that the Hellenist Jew from Tarsus was the real 'inventor' of Christianity.[13] They assert that he seized on the figure of Christ (who, they say, neither believed that he was God nor taught any such thing) and distorted the true picture into the theological portrait of the

---

[13] Needless to say, such critics claim to see in Paul various Hellenistic influences, traces of Greek philosophy or Greek religious thought. When studying Paul's youth we have already noted the improbability of any such influences from a psychological point of view. Regarded objectively, they are completely absent from his writing.

Saviour that we know today.[14] The other class of critics, which
consists mainly of liberal Protestants, believes it is possible to
oppose the Christianity of Jesus, which they declare to be
purely moral—'evangelical'—to the Catholicism of Paul, the
master-dogmatist and theologian. Both schools of critics are,
in their own peculiar way, denying the supernatural qualities
of Christ by attributing a process of divinization to men, to
'the first generation of Christians' and to the author of the
great Epistles.

The true facts accord ill with these theories. In the first
place St Paul never ceased referring back to Jesus, declaring
again and again that he proceeded from Him, and that he was
but acting in obedience to the divine voice which spoke to him
in his visions. This could, of course, be but a dialectic artifice;
but when looked at quite objectively these declarations of
Paul possess ample practical confirmation. After all, Christianity existed long before Saul was converted. Peter was in charge
of the Church at Jerusalem, and Barnabas was teaching at
Antioch. Now Paul was wholly accepted by these other
Christians: we can find no single trace of dogmatic conflict
between him and them. If the Christianity preached by the
Apostle of the Gentiles had not followed the traditional pattern to the letter, who knows what violent opposition he might
have encountered? It is quite true that there is a difference of
emphasis beween the Gospels (especially the Synoptic Gospels) and the Pauline Epistles, and that the transition from
Gospels to Epistles is marked by a distinct progress in the
definition of Christian doctrine. But this stems from the difference in personalities, and from the variations of background and intention: a Galilean carpenter, whose audiences
were humble fishermen from Lake Tiberias, would not express
Himself in the same terms as a Roman citizen who possessed
a smattering of Greek culture, and, similarly, one would
hardly use the same language as that used in preaching to the
Palestinian poor, the *Am-ha-rez*, when arguing with students
schooled in Greek philosophy. St Paul did indeed define, elaborate and enrich—but his every word was in the direct tradition
of Christ. Jesus told His disciples: 'He who is to befriend you,

[14] This is the position systematically maintained by the French
author Charles Guignebert, especially in his *Le Christ*.

the Holy Spirit, whom the Father will send on my account, will in his turn make everything plain' (John xiv. 26). Father Allo quotes this sentence in his admirable conclusion to the argument on this subject: 'The Holy Spirit has made everything plain through the mouth of St Paul, more than through any other man.'

One reality alone resides at the heart of this message of Paul's, and in the centre of this doctrine which surpasses all philosophy. Indeed, it is through it alone that the world is to be transformed. It is the reality of the crucified Jesus.

## PAUL'S ARREST AT JERUSALEM

The crucified Jesus! He it was whom St Paul was, henceforth, to succeed in rejoining, in the course of this, the final stage of his wandering life. Shortly before Pentecost, in the year 58, he ended his third great missionary journey and landed in Palestine, at Caesarea (Acts xxi. 7–14), where, as we know, a solid nucleus of Christians existed. As was his custom, he stayed at the house of a friend there. In this case the friend was Philip, the admirable missionary who, as we have already seen, had settled permanently in Caesarea, along with his four daughters, 'unwedded maids who possessed the gift of prophecy.' A disturbing incident in Caesarea matched the tragic forebodings which had been weighing heavily upon the Apostle's soul for many months past. A certain 'prophet,' called Agabus, sought out Paul, seized the Apostle's girdle and bound his own hands and feet with it, saying: 'Thus speaks the Holy Spirit, The man to whom this girdle belongs will be bound, like this, by the Jews at Jerusalem, and given over into the hands of the Gentiles!' It was a symbolic action, after the manner of the Old Testament prophets; thus, long ago, had Jeremiah walked the streets, yoked like a mule, in order to predict the Chaldean conquest of Israel; likewise Isaiah had stripped himself naked to make it clear in what state the Israelites would be left in the days of divine wrath. None of those who witnessed the scene failed to understand the meaning of this prophecy, and all begged the Apostle not to go up to Jerusalem, but to remain in Caesarea with them. But how could the man who was guided by the Holy Spirit escape his divinely ordained destiny and refuse to see it through to the bitter end, even though such a refusal might have enabled him to save his own life? 'What do you mean by lamenting and crushing my spirits?' answered St Paul. 'I am ready to meet prison and death as well in Jerusalem for the name of the Lord Jesus.' Then the Christians of Caesarea understood the meaning of this sacrifice, and, with aching hearts, they murmured: 'The Lord's will be done!'

Agabus's prophecy was soon to be fulfilled. Paul may have had two worries preying upon his mind, as he toiled up to the Holy City: firstly, that he might be regarded with what amounted to distrust by the leaders of the Church at Jerusalem, who, as we have seen, remained Judaizers; and secondly, that his presence in the town would provoke a violent reaction among the fanatical supporters of the ancient Law of Moses.

The first of these anxieties proved completely unfounded (Acts xxi. 17–25). On his arrival in Jerusalem Paul went to see James, 'the brother of the Lord,' to give him an account of his work in the lands beyond the Palestinian borders. When they had heard him, all the 'presbyters' of the Jerusalem Church praised God and congratulated Paul on his efforts. However, they warned him that he had a number of opponents in the Christian community in the Holy City. To appease these they advised the Apostle to give public proof of his loyalty to the Mosaic Law: Paul showed great wisdom in bowing to their advice by making a traditional retreat as a *nazir*.[15]

Unhappily, however, the other danger was all too apparent. The very sight of the man who had battled so vigorously against the Torah aroused the fury of the Jewish formalists (Acts xxi. 27–40 and xxii). They hated the Apostle. Prominent among these fanatics were Jews from Asia Minor, with whom Paul had often come into conflict in the course of his

---

[15] In Israel the *nazirs* were men who consecrated themselves to the Lord by making three vows: to refrain from cutting their hair, to drink no wine and to abstain from sexual relations with women. In Christ's day these vows seem to have been of a temporary nature only, and were not binding for life. Some critics have suggested that Jesus may have been a *nazir*, but this is hardly likely. However, it seems very probable that John the Baptist was one.

missionary journeys. These people were well versed in con-
ducting intrigues. They accused Paul of some vague sacri-
legious act, such as bringing an uncircumcised and therefore
impure Gentile into the inner court of the temple, to which
only Jews of pure Hebrew blood were allowed access. 'Here is
the man who goes about everywhere, teaching everybody to
despise our people, our law, and this place!' (Acts xxi. 27–30
and ff.).

A violent commotion broke out. Voices were raised and
blows struck. It was typical of those Eastern scuffles where the
outside observer finds it hard, amid the bitter shouts and
frenzied gesticulations, to understand what the two sides are
arguing about. And Lysias, the Roman tribune, who was
watching over the city from the heights of the Antonine tower,
and who saw the uproar and rushed down into the street
below to restore order, understood the situation less than anyone. First of all he took Paul for an Egyptian bandit who had
escaped from prison, and then, when the Apostle had explained
who he was, he allowed him to put his point of view to the
crowd. But after Paul had, in a long speech in Aramaic, convinced his audience of his Jewish ancestry and Jewish connections, and had apparently lulled its suspicions, he went on to
declare that he had been called by God to carry the Word to
the Gentiles. At once the shouting broke out again, and the
disturbance recommenced; the soldiers had to drag Paul away
from the scene in order to save him from the fury of the mob.
The Roman officer's patience was now exhausted. He had the
agitator taken into the fortress, probably to the very room
where Jesus had been questioned by Pilate—'Let's get the
matter settled, and find out what it's all about!' Clearly Lysias
was thinking along these lines. A few well-aimed strokes of the
flagellum would make this fanatic see reason and persuade him
to explain his case properly.

But at this point Paul made a formal protest. He spoke to
the centurion who was about to have him beaten. Was it lawful, he said, to scourge a Roman citizen, who had not even
been sentenced? The man was nonplussed, and scented danger.
Long ago, one of the worst accusations brought by Cicero
against Verres had been precisely this: that Verres had
treated a Roman citizen in an ignominious fashion—and the

fact had weighed heavily against the propraetor of Sicily. The
soldier prudently referred the matter to his commander, who
came to see Paul himself. 'What is this? Thou art a Roman
citizen?' 'Yes,' said Paul. 'Why,' answered the captain, 'it cost
me a heavy sum to win this privilege.' 'Ah,' said Paul, 'but I
am a citizen by birth.' And at this Lysias, much impressed,
had the Apostle released from his bonds (Acts xxii).

But this was far from being the end of the affair. The
Roman official was anxious to get it settled, and, above all,
to shift the responsibility for it on to someone else. Suppose
Paul and the Jewish leaders were confronted with one another?
Would this be the best way out? This time dissension broke
out within the heart of the Sanhedrin itself: for Paul cun-
ningly raised the question of the resurrection of the dead, a
point on which Pharisees and Sadducees were divided. At this,
priests, scribes and doctors all fell to squabbling, shrieking
and shouting among themselves (Acts xxiii). This was no
solution! And it was becoming increasingly risky to keep
Paul in Jerusalem: had not various young Jewish fanatics
hatched a plot against his life? So Lysias decided to rid himself of this prisoner who was such an embarrassment to him.
He sent him, under heavy escort, to Caesarea, which was the
residence of the imperial procurator himself (Acts xxiii. 23 ff.).

The procurator was a certain Felix, brother of Pallas, the
famous freedman friend of the Emperor Claudius, a man
whom Tacitus calls 'cruel and depraved, exercising royal power
with the soul of a slave.' Felix dared not ill treat Paul, who
was protected by the *ius civitatis*. But he kept him in prison
for a long time, possibly with the secret intention of extorting
a ransom from the Apostle.[16] Then Felix was replaced by
Festus, an honest but weak individual, who dared not free
his prisoner, and thought of ridding himself of him by sending him back to Jerusalem, which would probably have meant
Paul's death.[17] At last, making use of his privilege as a citizen,

[16] Paul's stay in Caesarea is not given much mention in the Acts.
It was probably during these two years that Luke, Paul's faithful
companion, questioned numerous eye-witnesses of the Gospel incidents, and collected the material which he was to draw on three
years later in Rome, when writing his Gospel.

[17] One incident illustrates the prestige which St Paul possessed at
this period. As he was about to leave Caesarea, Agrippa II, the Hero-

and weary of the interminable delays in this trial which was really no trial at all, Paul appealed to Caesar, and demanded to be sent to Rome (Acts xxiv. 2, xxv. 3, xxvi).

Next, therefore, it is his picturesque and romantic voyage to Rome which the Acts describes to us, a voyage that was both fruitful and thrilling, and which lasted from autumn into spring. The account reads like a catalogue of adventure stories, and contains so much information about classical navigation that Nelson once declared that he had learned his profession from it. Paul left Caesarea under the sympathetic supervision of a centurion named Julius, together with a large escort of legionaries. Luke sailed with him as well, and so did Aristarchus, another loyal Christian friend of the Apostle's. They sailed via Syria, Lycia, Crete and Malta. Wherever they stopped the little missionary group founded new Christian communities, such as the one in Crete, which is remembered in the splendid basilica at Gortyna. What adventures the travellers had, and what hazards they underwent! Off Crete, near the island of Cauda, they ran into a storm. This harried them for fifteen days: it fell to Paul to reassure the crew and force them not to abandon ship, and even to direct operations. The Apostle's stay in Malta is remembered in the famous anecdote about the viper, which was to be a favourite subject for artists in the Middle Ages, on

---

dian prince, landed there with Berenice, his sister. Agrippa at once wanted to see this man whom everyone was talking about, displaying that morbid curiosity so often shown by members of societies which are dying towards those who are supplanting them. Moreover, a very curious conversation took place between the Apostle and the petty ruler. Paul described his conversion and his call from God. Festus, the Roman procurator, who was present, shrugged his shoulders: 'Paul, thou art mad; they are driving thee to madness, these long studies of thine!' The Apostle then turned to Agrippa, reminding him that he too was a Jew. 'The message which I utter is sober truth. The king knows all this well enough; that is why I speak with such confidence in his presence. None of this, I am sure, is news to him; it was not in some secret corner that all this happened. Dost thou believe the prophets, King Agrippa? I am well assured thou dost believe them!' Agrippa was embarrassed: he did not want to be explicitly disloyal to his race, but he had no intention of appearing foolish in front of the Roman. He extricated himself from his dilemma with a joke: 'Thou wouldst have me turn Christian with very little ado!'

account of its symbolic value: the reptile, which was hiding beneath some firewood, darted out and fastened itself on the saint's hand; but he shrugged it off into the fire, and it was clear to everyone that it had not harmed him: neither sin nor evil had any power over such a man as this. The obvious authority which radiates from the Apostle is very striking throughout the whole of this voyage: by a certain combination of inner unity and spiritual strength this one man compelled obedience from everyone around him, even from his enemies.

It was in spring 60 that, having left Malta in a vessel whose 'sign was Castor and Pollux,' Paul first saw the Bay of Naples looming up on the horizon. There before him rose the smoking peak of Vesuvius and the slopes of Posilipo, clad with pines, like so many black parasols: the long-awaited shores of Italy, where, as he knew, the supreme witness would eventually be demanded of him.

## St Peter and the Church at Rome

There is no doubt whatsoever that this Roman community of Christians to whom the Apostle of the Gentiles was about to offer his presence and his message was already held in high esteem by him. It was no mere chance that had made him desire to be sent to the Eternal City, and Festus the procurator had, in so doing, unwittingly served to further the designs of God. Some time before, when he was at Corinth, Paul had written the Romans his famous letter in which he told them that he would one day come and visit them, in which he praised their 'faith . . . renowned throughout the world,' and in which he expounded to them the essentials of his doctrine concerning sin, the Redemption, divine justice and the power of faith. All this is set out here in such a complete and wonderful fashion that, when Christian tradition subsequently fixed the canon of the New Testament, this text was placed first of all the Epistles, despite its chronology, as a kind of model and starting-point for the reader. All this would seem to indicate that the great missionary understood perfectly that if Christianity was to succeed in conquering the world the Cross must be planted in the very spot where the world's heart beat most strongly.

In the great cosmopolitan city which Rome had by now become, all the peoples of the Empire jostled one against the other, intermingling. Out of a possible total of a million inhabitants, how many were pure Latins? Very few! But a goodly sample of long-haired Gauls and African Negroes forgathered there, as well as Spaniards, Greeks, Syrians and Dalmatians: it did indeed offer a fine field of action for the Apostle of the Gentiles!

Among all these heterogeneous groups, the Jewish community was remarkable for its cohesion and its strength. Though it could not claim to equal its counterpart at Alexandria, it must have comprised at least forty or fifty thousand souls: in 4 B.C. the Jewish delegation which had gone to see Augustus had numbered 8,000 men, and Tiberius had raised a levy of 4,000 soldiers from the Jews for his expedition to Sardinia. Since the time of Caesar—who had proclaimed them his 'friends,' and whose death had been loudly lamented by them—the Jews had been protected by all the rulers of Rome in turn. These Jews were mainly traders and small craftsmen. Their homes were scattered throughout the city, and, contrary to a belief long held by historians, they did not live all together in one single area, in a ghetto. They lived not only in Transtiberine Rome, but in the Suburra, the Martian Field and along the approaches to the Capena Gate. They possessed about a dozen synagogues and several cemeteries, from which archaeologists have recovered a number of their characteristic *graffiti*, seven-branched candelabra, and the chests in which they kept the sacred Torah.

It was in this society of Jewish shopkeepers that the first Christian community in Rome was born. How and when? We know very little about its origins. Had the good seed of Christianity been borne from Palestine by a few pious Roman Jews who had gone on pilgrimage to Jerusalem, and been converted to the Christian faith while spending the Passover there? Did an expedition of Christian missionaries go to Rome from Antioch as well, around the time when Paul was residing on the banks of the Orontes? Some authorities think so. Ought we to take into account, too, the normal cross-current of ideas which was natural in a great empire like Rome's, with its excellent communications? All these causes must have been working simultaneously in Rome, as everywhere else, each in its own way helping to spread the faith there. At all events, by the time Paul was about to join it, in A.D. 60, this Christian community gives the impression of being already extremely important, and, like the Jewish colonies elsewhere, had attracted around it numbers of 'God-fearers' and proselytes who had been won over from paganism to monotheism.

We know of only one anecdote relating to the earliest days of this community, and that is a detail told us by Suetonius:[18] he states that, during Claudius's reign (probably c. 49), there were various violent disturbances within the Jewish colony in Rome, 'prompted by Christus.' This is a very vague statement, written by a man who knew nothing about the topic he was discussing, but it enables us to imagine the incident quite clearly—the arguments and jealousies that must have arisen between the Jews of the Temple and the Jews of the Cross, their brawls, and finally, to put a stop to it all, an imperial decree, exiling the trouble-makers. The fact reported by Suetonius is confirmed in the Acts of the Apostles, for there the reader encounters, in Aquila and Priscilla, St Paul's friends and protectors in Corinth, Jews who had been turned out of Rome (Acts xviii. 2); it proves the vitality of this first group of Christians in the Eternal City, and the turmoil aroused by the work of evangelization.[19]

However, to explain a success which history was gloriously to confirm, can this Roman community not claim an origin other than that of some unknown pilgrim returning from Jerusalem? The Church believes that it can, and this view is not simply that of Catholic tradition alone, but is shared by liberal theologians such as Harnack, and by Protestants such as Lietzmann. The man who contributed most to this eminent foundation, long before St Paul disembarked at Pozzuoli, was

[18] This is a very important fact, since it is one of the earliest non-Christian texts to mention Jesus.

[19] Were there two tendencies, which we have seen elsewhere, consisting of Judaizing Christians on the one hand, and those with universalist conceptions on the other, within the very heart of the Christian community at Rome? It would appear so, since, in his Epistle to the Romans, St Paul goes to the trouble of explaining the providential role of Israel to his correspondents, probably to avoid the implication that his philosophy had been influenced by fanatics.

none other than the very person to whom Jesus had entrusted the task of directing His Church—the Prince of Apostles, St Peter, the ancient 'rock' of Christianity.[20]

Unhappily our information about the actions taken by the Prince of Apostles after his stay in Antioch[21] is extremely scanty. Origen, whose sayings have been reported by Eusebius, asserts that Peter visited Pontus, Bithynia, Cappadocia and Macedonia, and some indication of this can be seen in the fact that the First Epistle of St Peter is addressed to the Christians of these same provinces, which, in the eyes of the primitive Church, proved that a bond existed between the Apostle and these lands. Likewise proof of his visit to Corinth can be found in an allusion in the First Epistle to the Corinthians (i. 12), in which St Paul speaks of those who cry

[20] St Peter's stay in Rome constitutes one of the most delicate subjects of discussion relating to this period of Christian history, a discussion that is the more lively because a precise relationship between the Church at Rome and St Peter is obviously of prime importance so far as the origins of papal authority are concerned. If we refer to the work of the Protestant historian, H. Lietzmann (*Petrus und Paulus in Rom*, Berlin, 1927), we must conclude quite definitely that by the end of the second century the tradition of the stay of the Prince of Apostles in the Eternal City, and his subsequent martyrdom there, had become firmly established. All the literary documents of the period agree on this point: a text by the clerk Gaius, who was writing *c.* 200 and who has been quoted by Eusebius; the famous *Liberian Catalogue*, begun about 235, giving the list of the bishops of Rome, which was continued until the fourth century and the pontificate of Liberius (352–66); the letters of St Irenaeus, Bishop of Lyons *c.* 180, and of Bishop Denys of Corinth, belonging to the same epoch. The two oldest known texts are the famous *Commentary on the Sentences of the Lord*, in which Papias, the aged Asian bishop of Hierapolis, who had known the Apostles' immediate disciples, declares that Mark summarized Peter's preaching in Rome in his Gospel; and a letter from St Clement, pope and martyr, who, writing to the Corinthians *c.* 95, speaks explicitly of Peter's and Paul's martyrdom at Rome. Moreover, archaeological remains prove that the Christians in the catacombs venerated the memory of the two Apostles. Thus so far as the actual fact of the stay is concerned the matter seems settled. As for the length of this stay, and the dates which can be assigned to it, all serious historians, whether they are Christians or no, confess that here they are in the realm of pure hypothesis. Eusebius places Peter's arrival in Rome in 42, and his martyrdom in 67.

[21] See Chapter I, section: 'Antioch.'

'I am for Cephas,' and who are virtually in conflict with the Christians who look to him; in the middle of the second century, Bishop Denys of Corinth stated explicitly that his Church had been founded by Peter and Paul.

It is absolutely certain that the Prince of Apostles came to Rome, and even that he arrived there at quite an early date in Christian history; it is certain, too, that he stayed there for a very long period, about twenty-five years, a stay broken only by various brief absences, notably by his journeys to Jerusalem; likewise there is no doubt whatsoever of his martyrdom in the city which he was to consecrate with his own blood. But beyond these facts we know nothing definite.

By the year 60 Peter was an old man; if it is allowed that he was born roughly at the same time as Jesus, he must now have been around sixty-six or seventy years of age; he was certainly ten or fifteen years older than St Paul. Though his actions do not seem to have had the violence or verve of those of the man from Tarsus, we can, from the little we know of them, visualize that, though different, they must have been no less efficacious! We have a picture of a saintly man, laden with years and fame, still bearing on his face the radiance of that light which he had received on the day of the Transfiguration, an old soldier of the Gospel, whose presence alone constituted a lesson in the faith, making his way from city to city, blessing, healing, exalting souls and bringing the peace of Christ into men's hearts. This wisdom of Peter's was sorely needed: beside the vivacious strength of Paul, the swift-burning flame of Christianity, was the solid stability of Peter, the Church's foundation-stone.

But there was certainly no conflict between the two men, even if, as has been stated all too often, two different schools of thought were apparent in all the early Christian communities, consisting of the partisans of Peter on the one hand and of Paul on the other; around great leaders factions accentuate or, if required, invent differences and partialities. On every occasion when we are able to watch them working together we see these two witnesses of the Spirit agreeing absolutely on the essentials: namely the glory of Christ and the spreading of the Word. All else stems merely from human pettinesses, from certain differences in education, social background and temperament, and is of little real significance. At Rome, whilst Peter was preaching primarily to the Jewish community, St Paul probably worked mainly in Gentile circles, among the soldiery, the minor officials, and even the prostitutes; their action would thus have been parallel and complementary. The medallion engraver whose work has been discovered in the catacomb of Domitilla was right indeed when, by showing the Prince of Apostles and the Apostle of the Gentiles face to face, he joined in bronze these two men whom the same faith and the same destiny had united so completely in the Spirit.

## FREEDOM OF THE SPIRIT

St Paul landed at Pozzuoli in the spring of the year 60 (Acts xxviii. 11 ff.). Oh, joy! There was a Christian community there, and Julius, the kindly centurion, allowed his prisoner to remain a week in the port in order to preach to his brethren. Then the little procession set off again, following the Appian Way, but already news of its landing had spread far and wide. Numerous groups of Christians hastened to meet it, some travelling as far south as Forum Appii, some forty-three miles from Rome, and others to the Three Taverns, which was still a good thirty miles from the city! Surely this is proof—if proof were needed—of the fame which surrounded the Apostle at this time. People were avid to have the experience of listening to him.

Paul was handed over to the praetorian soldiers entrusted with the duty of guarding accused persons who were making an appeal to Caesar, and was placed under 'military surveillance'—*custodia militaris*—but it seems that the fairly stringent rules governing this surveillance were relaxed in his case. Probably he had to endure being chained to his jailer by an iron chain fettered to his wrist. Probably, too, he was not allowed outside his dwelling: visits to friends and to the Christian communities in the city would be forbidden him. But instead of being held in the official *castra praetoriana* he was allowed to live in a house he had rented, where anyone was free to come and see him. Here he was to stay for two years.

Perhaps there is no other period in the whole of his consecrated life which gives such an impression of completeness, fulfilment and greatness as that given by these two years spent in captivity. The finest of men feels himself completely free even when he is in physical bondage, for the freedom he possesses is none other than the freedom of the Spirit; and for this wonderful lesson, which, down the centuries, has enabled tens of thousands of men and women suffering the hardships of slavery or languishing in prisons or concentration camps to find a means of freedom through the very cruelty of their physical experience, the world is deeply indebted to St Paul.

As soon as he arrived in Rome Paul established his authority in an extremely important speech (it is reproduced in the last chapter of Acts, which breaks off immediately afterwards) in which he reaffirmed several essential points in his teaching, stressing in particular that he remained a loyal Jew, faithful to his people, that he was in no sense a renegade, but stressing too that the Word of God was to be given to humanity as a whole, and that the Gentiles were to receive it. For two years (probably his actions ran parallel with those which St Peter would have been undertaking at the same time) St Paul filled the role of a real leader in this community to which he imparted his own burning and inspired enthusiasm. Quite a little company of faithful Christians grouped themselves around him. There was Luke, of course, Paul's 'beloved physician,' who, as it happened, wrote his Gospel and the book of Acts during the course of these years in Rome; and Timothy, whom the Apostle called 'my own son in the faith,' and who was his constant helpmate; and Mark, towards whom Paul's former grievances were now forgotten[22] and who was also in process of writing a Gospel; and Aristarchus of Salonica, and Epaphras, who had come from far-off Colossae, on the Armenian borders, at the foot of Mount Ararat, and Tychichus of Ephesus, who was to be one of Paul's missionaries, and many others! All the Churches which the great Apostle had founded during the course of his missionary

[22] Because Mark had deserted him when he was about to cross Asia Minor during his first mission, St Paul had refused to take him with him on his second journey.

journeys seem to have sent witnesses of their continued loyalty to be near him in Rome at this critical time.

There is no doubt whatsoever that this imprisonment, as St Paul himself declared, 'only had the effect of spreading the Gospel further.' Conversions occurred even among the soldiers who guarded him. The curious, and those who thirsted for the truth, came to look at him, and some of them went away Christians. Among these must have been men like Eubulus, Pudens and Linus who actually seem to have belonged to the old Roman aristocracy—and it was Linus who was one day to become St Linus, pope and martyr, first successor to St Peter. Conversions even took place among those 'who belong to the Emperor's household,' and these St Paul reports with justifiable pride (Phil. iv. 22). The influence of this imprisoned man radiated far beyond his jail; for the power of the Spirit is utterly invincible.

His influence extended to the outside world in yet another way, through the letters which he continued to write his spiritual children, letters addressed both to the communities he had founded and even to humble individuals, and which dealt with points of doctrine or moral attitudes. These are known as the *Epistles of Captivity*; they possess an extraordinary simplicity and beauty, and exude a far more tangible human warmth than the great *Dogmatic Epistles*. It is as if this vehement Apostle and impassioned messenger of the Spirit has, on entering middle age, succeeded in realizing full maturity, and acquiring a new gentleness towards his fellow men. The enchanting Epistle to Philemon dates from this epoch. Here the Apostle is interceding with a Christian slave-owner, begging the latter to deal mercifully with one of his runaway slaves, whom Paul has converted to the faith and is sending back to him. 'Make him as welcome as thou wouldst myself,' he asks. The whole lesson of the universal love that Christ taught is contained in these few simple, trusting lines, transposed on to the practical plane. For in the eyes of God there are no longer masters and slaves, but only brothers in Christ Jesus.

## THE WITNESS OF BLOOD

At the end of his letter to Philemon St Paul had written as follows: 'Be prepared, meanwhile, to entertain me; I hope, through your prayers, to be restored to you.' This forecast was an accurate one. After these two years of house arrest he was, in all probability, acquitted by the imperial tribunal. At all events he was set free. What was the date of this liberation? It probably occurred before 64, since that was the year in which the violent wave of persecution against the Christians was unleashed by Nero, following the burning of Rome. St Paul's stay in Rome had, in fact, coincided with the years that marked the turning-point in the Beast's reign, years in which, having watched Burrhus die (many said that the emperor had him assassinated), exiled Seneca, his old teacher, and then divorced and put to death his innocent wife, Octavia, the crowned monster embarked on the path of madness which was eventually to destroy him. About 62 while Burrhus was still alive, the acquittal or discharge of a Christian leader would be quite conceivable: it would no longer be so two years later, with the notorious Tigellinus in charge of the emperor's affairs.

As soon as he was freed the great missionary set off on his travels again. He knew full well that he had but been granted a temporary respite, that death at the hands of the executioner would eventually be his fate, and so he was anxious to make haste to visit those lands where the Gospel message had still to be spread, and, above all, to see once more the communities which had been born of his previous labours. The book of Acts fails us from this point onwards, and we therefore know very little about Paul's last journeys. Did he go to Spain, as he had wanted to do? Thirty-five years later, St Clement of Rome seems to imply that he did. By studying the Epistles to Timothy and Titus we can follow his footsteps through Greece and Asia, and we thus know that he visited Crete, Corinth, Ephesus and Nicopolis. The three Epistles dating from this period, which are known as the *Pastoral Epistles*, are quite obviously the final instructions of a man who knows that his end is near, and who wants once more—and with what fervour!—to advise the disciples who are to continue his work, in order that 'the Spirit of God, who dwells in you' shall be well and truly safeguarded.

It seems likely that Paul was arrested for the second time at Troy, and transferred from there to Rome. Whatever the circumstances of his rearrest, it is certain that his Second Epistle to Timothy, a most moving document, was written from the Eternal City.[23] This time his imprisonment was a harsh one. Severity towards the Christians had become the rule, and there was no longer any question of compromise. The captive Apostle was thrust into the depths of a frightful jail known as the 'Tullianum,' a place where the Romans did not hesitate to put their prisoners, and there he suffered dreadfully from the cold, and even more bitterly from the enforced solitude. As in all persecutions, fear had caused numerous ravages in the Christian community: apostasies oc-

[23] We are passing over—with but this brief mention—the Epistle to the Hebrews, which, in Catholic bibles, is placed after St Paul's other Epistles. The Catholic Church attributes this document to St Paul, but other Churches do not admit his authorship of it as definite. There is no doubt at all of its Pauline inspiration, but when compared with the other Epistles it shows marked differences in style and vocabulary. Some critics have suggested that it was actually written down by one of the great Apostle's disciples, working from notes of Paul's sermons. In this connection Father Prat has put forward the name of Barnabas. The most tempting hypothesis is that of Father Marcel Jousse, the well-known originator of 'rhythmo-pedagogic' studies. Basing his argument on the linguistic characteristics and rhythmic construction of the Epistle, he confirms that it is genuinely one of St Paul's own works, but states that its drafting must have differed radically from that of the other Pauline texts. As a Jew dictating his letters in Greek, St Paul usually let the cadences which were a part of the normal oral technique of the rabbi, and which he had learned from Gamaliel, creep through into his style, but when his secretaries transcribed his thoughts—'transcribing from oral dictation, on the spot'—they would summarize the typically Jewish turns of phrase in a more direct fashion. However, when writing to his racial brethren, the 'Hebrews,' St Paul would have dictated the last Epistle in Aramaic; and it would be from this document that one of his disciples, translating at leisure from the already written text, would have produced the final result which we now possess as the Epistle to the Hebrews. The result, therefore, would be a work 'of Greek style, which reveals a master in the Hellenic language,' in other words something rather different from the rest of Pauline literature. (See Marcel Jousse, 'Judâhen, Judeen, Judaïste dans le milieu ethnique palestinien,' in the review L'Ethnographie, No. 38, 1946.)

curred, as well as actual betrayals or defections in which worldly prudence overcame the demands of the Spirit. Naturally there were many wonderful examples of loyalty too—that of St Luke first and foremost—but as he reported these melancholy facts the Apostle could not conceal his deep sorrow.

And yet a marvellous hope remained to him, hope of that martyr's death which he knew was to be his and which would mark the complete fulfilment of his Christian witness: the longed-for moment when his blood would flow 'in sacrifice' for Jesus! 'The time has nearly come when I can go free. I have fought the good fight; I have finished the race; I have redeemed my pledge; I look forward to the prize that is waiting for me, the prize I have earned. The Lord, the judge whose award never goes amiss, will grant it to me when that day comes' (2 Tim. iv. 6–8).

Our texts tell us nothing of Paul's trial, sentence and subsequent death. Did he have a proper trial at all? Was he charged with being 'an instigator of dangerous innovations,' according to the customary formula? Was he given the legal safeguards due to a Roman citizen? All this remains a mystery, and hurried and illegal measures against prisoners were commonplace during these years of police terror. The most ancient tradition of the Church records that he was beheaded on the Ostian Way, by the sword, in accordance with the privilege that the *ius civitatis* gave him. It also links the death of the Prince of Apostles with that of the Apostle of the Gentiles in both time and significance: for St Peter must have been executed at the same time (or within a day of Paul); but his was the servile death accorded to a humble Jewish vagabond. He died on a cross, having in his humility asked to be hung there not upright, as his Divine Master had been hung, but upside-down, his head dangling towards the earth. Symbolic traditions say that Paul was put to death 'near a cedar' and Peter 'near a terebinth-tree': thus the two loftiest trees of the Church were struck down at one fell swoop. But nothing could stop the Spirit from living on. At St Paul of the Three Fountains, folk still talk of the three springs of living water that gushed from the severed head of the Apostle, as it bounced three times upon the ground. . . .

The liturgy of the Church, which links St Peter and St

Paul in two festivals, celebrated on 29th and 30th June, goes back, so it seems, to a very ancient tradition, since these dates were chosen in Constantine's time to commemorate the removal of the two precious bodies from the Appian Way to the catacombs,[24] a deed carried out in 258. Later on, while St Peter's body was taken to the Vatican, to the place of his execution,[25] that of St Paul was replaced in the spot where he

[24] Numerous archaeological finds have been discovered near the Appian Way, in the Catacombs of St Sebastian, close to the basilica of the same name. An inscription of Pope St Damasus, dating from the end of the fourth century, says that 'St Peter and St Paul' rested there.

[25] In 1949, in the course of an address to a gathering of students, Pope Pius XII stated: 'The site of St Peter's tomb was and *still is* beneath the central point of the gigantic cupola of the basilica.' These words came as confirmation of those contained in a lecture given on Vatican Radio in 1942, which had already revealed that a place of Christian worship had been found under the basilica built by Constantine. Signs of the devotion of the faithful were proved by the numerous *graffiti* and tombs there. The words also confirmed the statement made by the Holy Father on the occasion of his episcopal jubilee, in which he had revealed that traces had been found of the 'trophy' built over the Apostle's burial-place. The existence of this trophy was noted in a text by the priest Gaius, written in the second century, and subsequently repeated by Eusebius, the historian. Thus it seems fairly certain that the official announcement of the discovery of St Peter's tomb only awaits a favourable occasion.

Ancient tradition has it that St Peter was martyred in Nero's Circus, not far from the Via Cornelia. The circus was situated approximately in the area where the Basilica of St Peter and the Vatican stand today. Obviously the discovery there of Christian *graffiti* and tombs is a solid argument in support of ancient tradition: moreover, an inscription found on one mausoleum proves that once there had indeed been a circus on the site. Finally, why should Constantine have decided to build his basilica here, despite the poor geographic conditions, despite the clay soil that made drainage so difficult? Tradition must have been the governing factor. Was it only the place of martyrdom? Or the site of the tomb as well?

Here again tradition confirms that, after being buried in a cemetery close to the place of martyrdom—the cemetery where his immediate successors would also have been interred—St Peter's body was moved to the catacombs of St Sebastian at the time of Valerian's persecution in the third century. These catacombs were on the Appian Way, and here too the body of St Paul, who had been beheaded on the Ostian Way, would have been brought. However, there is no agreement among scholars as to the date at which the bodies of the

had borne his last witness. The splendid Basilica of St Paul outside the walls preserves the memory of the 'testimony' of the Apostle of the Gentiles, whilst the Trappists of the Three Fountains watch over the spot where his blood flowed, amid the eucalyptuses and luxuriant foliage of their monastery garden.

St Paul's martyrdom completed his life and gave it the

---

two Apostles were carried to the places where the basilicas dedicated to them stand today. Some assert that St Peter's body was already back in the place where it had first been buried, straight after the Apostle's death, at the time when Constantine had the primitive basilica built, in whose construction, so tradition avers, the emperor worked personally, with his own bare hands. Others, who include Monsignor Belvederi, the eminent archaeologist, say they have reason to believe that the body of the Prince of Apostles did not return to what are now named the 'Vatican grottoes' until the sixth century. It has been suggested that the emperor had the saint's tomb recovered with a heavy bronze sarcophagus. But this has not yet been proved conclusively.

In the sixth century St Gregory of Tours relates: 'The burial-place is under the altar, and it is extremely well concealed. But anyone wishing to pray there has but to open the little iron gate which encloses the holy places and to walk over the tomb. Passing his head through a small opening, he can utter his wishes, which, if reasonable ones, will be granted.' This suggests that at this epoch the tomb was quite visible, and that pilgrims were accustomed to climb down far enough to enable them to touch it with objects tied to the end of pieces of cord. In this way they could claim to possess a relic which had been in contact with the burial-place of the Prince of Apostles. The last eye-witness accounts of the tomb date from the ninth century.

In 846 the basilica was pillaged by the Saracens; in 993 it was seriously damaged in a dreadful fire, and in 1527 it was again sacked by the mercenaries of the Constable de Bourbon.

A tradition which has always been firmly held in Rome insists that the tomb has never been profaned. Truth to tell no one can yet confirm this, save the Pope himself. . . . For who else can be certain that the works undertaken during the building of the existing basilica did not interfere with the venerable tomb? Only archaeological evidence can provide confirmation or denial of this. But prior to 1941 no systematic excavations had been undertaken in the central part of the Vatican basilica. Only sporadic, haphazard diggings had been attempted, whenever it had been necessary to reinforce certain sections of the structure. This happened in 1594, under Clement VIII, during the construction of a new papal altar, then under Paul V, for the rebuilding of the covered 'Confession' in the basilica, and again in 1626, under Urban VIII, for the erection of Bernini's four

final meaning that it needed. It was scarcely conceivable that the witness of the man who has been called 'the most important after the Son' could have failed to bear a supernatural resemblance, that it could have been fulfilled in any way save through blood and suffering. During the centuries that followed, thousands of other martyrs were to be reunited with Christ through violent death, and their blood was to be the

colonnades. One of these enterprises gave rise to a curious incident, which is reported by Tonizio, one of the chroniclers of the basilica. A fall of masonry occurred, and through the crack in the ground could be seen the famous gold cross which, it was said, Constantine had had inlaid in the heavy stonework built over St Peter's burial-place. Pope Clement VIII, accompanied by an architect and three cardinals, of whom St Robert Bellarmine was one, went down into the cavern below the basilica (if Tonizio can be believed) and, after inspecting the tomb, ordered that the crack should be sealed in his presence, and the whole incident kept secret. To understand this decision we must take into account the reverential awe in which St Peter's tomb was held. Men believed that frightful punishment would fall on all those who dared to disturb the burial-place.

During the succeeding centuries no one tried to penetrate the secret of the Prince of Apostles' tomb. Then, about sixty years ago, Father Grisar, a well-known archaeologist, received permission from Pope Leo XIII to make certain researches, which resulted in some extremely interesting, though inconclusive, findings concerning St Peter's tomb. Another attempt was about to be made, under Benedict XV, when, at the last moment, the Pope withdrew the permission to dig under the altar of the Confession, a permission he had previously given.

Operations were recommenced quite by chance, and this time they were followed up with new vigour. The occasion was the installation of the monument to Pius XI in the 'Vatican grottoes.' It was so large that it could only be erected by removing some eighteen inches of the floor of the grottoes themselves. This operation revealed a burial-ground of extraordinary richness, whose existence had scarcely been suspected by anyone. Its exploration began forthwith. Pius XII, who at once deeply interested himself in these discoveries, appointed a commission to direct excavations, whose principal members were Fathers Ferrua and Kirschbaum, Professor Josi, Apollonii Ghetti the architect, and Monsignor Kaas. These excavations have been extremely difficult, since they are being made directly under the enormous mass of the basilica itself, and are often carried out by hand. It is well known that, in order to prevent any indiscreet disclosures and premature gossip, the Pope insists on a promise of absolute silence from all working on the project.

Thus not a great deal is known of the results obtained so far. The

'seed which brings forth Christians.' But St Paul holds a special place among them; did he not, with proud humility, call himself 'an apostle of Jesus Christ, by the will of God, in furtherance of that promise of life which is given us in Christ Jesus'? The Church has confirmed this privileged position. Of all the saints who never knew Jesus in the flesh, he alone is called Apostle, and is given the same title and the same position as that accorded the twelve faithful who had es-

---

area of excavation stretches from the covered Confession, where the statue of Pius VI stands, as far as the boundary of Constantine's basilica, whose remains have been discovered a little beyond Bernini's inner colonnades. As for the results themselves, all that is known is that traces have been found of the 'trophy' venerated by the faithful during the first three centuries of our era as the burial-place of the Apostle, as is made clear by the *graffiti* which have been discovered all around it. In 1942 a large number of coins, going back to the first century A.D. and belonging to many areas of Europe, were found. This confirmed the existence of the burial-place, for these coins represent the traditional offerings left by pilgrims.

One important statement has been issued by Apollonii Ghetti: 'In the present state of excavations it can be confirmed that, despite earth-tremors and fires, despite wars, the barbarian invasions, and the pillaging that went with them, despite demolitions and reconstructions, despite all the architectural vicissitudes of the basilica, the tomb has been preserved, thanks to man's determination and the manifest intervention of Divine Providence.'

Recent publications have dealt with the discoveries made in the pagan part of the burial-ground. Some very fine urns, inscriptions and tombs have been found: those of the Caetanni, Marci and Valerii are among the most beautiful. There is even one Egyptian mausoleum, with a splendid alabaster amphora. And these discoveries confirm the tradition mentioned earlier, according to which the body of the martyr must have been laid to rest in a cemetery near the circus.

But one question has still not been answered, and its answer is probably being reserved for the most august voice of all: it is 'Are the remains of St Peter still in the tomb?' Cianfarra, Rome correspondent of the *New York Times*, has published a sensational article in which he states that not only has the tomb been discovered, but the bones of the Apostle also. He alleges that they have been found in an urn, in the midst of coins dating from the epoch of the death of the Prince of Apostles. He adds that the Pope now keeps these bones in his private chapel.

The story has been neither confirmed nor denied by the Vatican. *Quotidiano*, the official organ of Italian Catholic Action, has remarked, however, that in such a delicate and important matter as this it is quite essential to rely only on explicit official information.

corted the living Messiah on the slopes around Galilee. And, as a remarkable sign of gratitude, Catholicism has inscribed his name in the collect for Sexagesima Sunday, at a place where no names, save those of God and Christ, otherwise figure.

'Apostle of the Nations.' Despite the passage of the centuries, and the shift of events, St Paul retains his title. His message has never been out-dated. Anyone who reads his brilliant pages can find countless lessons therein, whose force is as strong today as it ever was. To the modern miasma of negation and absurdity, which is the gravest temptation of the mind, St Paul would have opposed the indestructible certainty of a supernatural explanation, of a revelation according to which the enigmas of the world and of man are both perfectly resolved. Had he been confronted with the permanent disloyalty of mankind, and its universal forgetfulness of God, he would have confirmed the living reality of a Presence whom nothing can destroy and whose infinite mercy survives the darkest betrayal. He would have countered the feeling of despair which man derives from the very heart of his human condition by the promise of a conclusive victory over sin and death, by the pledge of glory and resurrection. And, in a world of violence and hatred, whose characteristics are recognizable enough in every historical epoch, he would have upheld the message of love, the certainty of the omnipotence of charity, which he had learned direct from Jesus, but which he expressed with a human fervour that no other man has ever equalled. In the little Jew from Tarsus history sees the most effective fighter that the Revolution of the Cross possessed in the early days of its struggle; yet, after two thousand years, not a word of his teaching has become obsolete, not one of his actions has lost its meaning—because this revolution is, in fact, a revolution that is never-ending.

# CHAPTER III

# ROME AND THE REVOLUTION
# OF THE CROSS

## THE SOWING OF THE CHRISTIAN SEED

NO PERIOD in the whole history of the Church is more important than that during which the Christian seed was first sown far and wide: and, equally truly, there is no period of which so little is known. In every great religious or political movement it is almost always the early years which hold the key to the whole future. Whilst men are still groping in the darkness, trying to find the right way forward, positions are being adopted, and methods developed, on which the success or failure of the whole enterprise depends. In the case of Christianity, the result is there for all to see. The Good News was spread to countless lands with breath-taking speed, and there it germinated, producing communities of immense vitality. By the middle of the second century we can point to proof upon proof of the existence of churches which were situated many hundreds of miles from the Palestine in which the Gospel message had originated. But though the general picture of this missionary endeavour is fairly clear, we can name but a few of the individuals who must have pioneered this conquest. We see them through a dark haze of obscurity.

If we read the New Testament, the spread of Christianity seems to be entirely summed up in the person of St Paul. His figure stands so much in the limelight that it appears to throw into the shade all other actions, directed by this or that other Apostle or disciple. The sheer genius of the saint from Tarsus is not the sole explanation for this distortion of perspective; it should be remembered that our best source of information for this period, the book of Acts, was written by St Luke, St Paul's friend and companion. Naturally enough Luke's text is centred on Paul. But it would be quite wrong to think of that glorious adventure, which the first dispersal of the Gospel news comprised, simply in terms of the work of the

Apostle of the Gentiles alone. St Paul never did or wrote anything that might lead us to think that he had the slightest desire to monopolize all this effort and fame for himself. As he himself wrote in his Epistle to the Romans (xii), every single Christian of the day was called to take his part in the immense work which awaited all the members of 'the body of Christ,' each contributing his own particular gifts, 'according to the special grace which has been assigned to each.'

There is no doubt whatsoever that all Jesus' immediate disciples obeyed their Master's command, and set out 'to make disciples of all nations.' An allusion in the First Epistle to the Corinthians (ix. 5) implies that the other Apostles were engaged in missionary work at the same time as Paul. But textual references to them are so few and far between that we cannot follow their progress on those great enterprises whose results are later to become strikingly apparent. Aside from a few short passages in the Acts, the Pauline Epistles, the other Epistles which bear apostolic signatures, and the Apocalypse, our most definite information on this subject derives from writers who lived significantly later than the events they describe: authors like Clement of Alexandria, St Irenaeus or Eusebius. All the details, such as they are, are to be found only in piously venerated traditions.

Of all these early spokesmen of Jesus, these men who are the living links between ourselves and the Master, one figure alone pierces the general obscurity to an appreciable extent: St John. Yet any account of his life and work is bound to contain huge gaps. He disappears from the scene after the Council of Jerusalem in 49; he reappears next at Ephesus, certainly after St Paul's death, and probably around 67. Here he would seem to have been extremely well acquainted with everything that was happening in Asia Minor, and deeply respected by the Christian communities whose mentor he was. Domitian's persecution was to find him in Rome, where, according to Tertullian, he was cast into a cauldron of boiling oil, but miraculously escaped the slightest injury. However, he was deported to the Greek archipelago immediately after this incident, to the forced-labour camp at Patmos, where he wrote the Apocalypse. Finally Nerva set him free and he returned to Ephesus. There, in the words of Clement of Alexandria,

he passed a long, serene old age, travelling through the neighbouring districts, 'consecrating bishops, founding churches,
choosing this or that man to be a priest,' and, at the same
time, guided and inspired by the Holy Spirit, writing his wonderful Gospel, and his Epistles, and repeating tirelessly, as if
it were the *leit-motif* of his magnificent Christian existence:
'My little children, love one another: such is the commandment of Christ!'

So, apart from John, from glimpses of Peter in Antioch
and Rome, and from the two Jameses, the heroic martyrs of
Jerusalem, we know nothing very definite about the other immediate disciples of Jesus, or about their work. The numerous
apocryphal Acts of the Apostles, which flourished at the end
of the second century, claimed to fill this historical void. But
the Church was to treat these with extreme caution, and to
refuse to rely on their evidence—which does not necessarily
mean, however, that everything included in these accounts is
completely false. One very ancient tradition asserts that,
twelve years after our Lord's resurrection, all the Apostles left
the Holy City, and went their different ways. This is quite
likely, since the date mentioned coincides with the persecution
of Herod Agrippa, in which James, the son of Zebedee, was
martyred and Peter thrown into prison.[1] It was at a time such
as this that the Apostles might well have set out in all directions to bear the Word of God to many different races. Eusebius, who states that he is repeating information supplied by
Origen, and Rufinus, who translated and embellished Eusebius' work, claimed to know which theatre of action was al-
lotted to each Apostle: according to them, whilst John went
to Asia Andrew made his way to the country of the Scythians
(southern Russia), Matthew attempted the conversion of the
Ethiopians, Bartholomew north-west India, and Thomas the
kingdom of the Parthians. Other traditions make certain additions to this schema. The most curious of these declares
that Thomas, by following the caravan route through Persia,
eventually reached the valley of the Ganges, where he converted Prince Mathura, satrap of the Sacians, just as the latter
was in process of founding a powerful empire in India and

[1] See Chapter I, section: 'Herod Agrippa, the Persecutor.'

Asia Minor.[2] These are certainly splendid themes, which lend themselves easily to daydreams. But a great reality shines through all these different legends: the prodigious zeal and energy of the Christians in spreading their faith, this scattering of the Good News to the four corners of the earth.

Though this Christian endeavour possessed outstanding leaders, in the persons of Apostles and disciples, we should not forget that the immense labour of thousands of anonymous believers must have been of at least equal importance in ensuring its success. These unknown folk, by their chance journeyings and meetings, must have done a very great deal indeed to prepare the way for the Lord and to begin the work of winning souls for Christ. The word mission, which is so often used to describe this first effort of Christian conversion, nowadays tends to imply a movement with a systematic plan, an organization and an administrative centre: while such factors existed in an apostolate like St Paul's, they must have been completely absent from this other type of evangelization, which was spontaneous, and largely unconscious in character. Yet its influence must have been just as decisive. In order to understand it fully, and to appreciate its effectiveness, it is really necessary to have practical experience of the kind of conditions governing the average person's life in the first few centuries of our era, to picture the constant traffic from place to place, and the never-ending individual journeys, which were unimaginably frequent and widespread, and to visualize the inns and the caravanserais, where folk from different areas met one another, and gossiped among themselves. We should also take into account the important position occupied by the Jewish communities of the *diaspora* in all the cities around the Mediterranean, and even as far afield as Mesopotamia, for these communities often sheltered the first Christian mis-

[2] At the beginning of the thirteenth century the first western explorers were to encounter 'the Christians of St Thomas' in India. There are still about 300,000 of these 'Thomasists,' especially in Malabar. Historians differ as to their origins, some considering that they may indeed be descendants of apostolic communities, and others regarding them as successors of the Nestorian churches founded in the Persian Empire at the end of the fifth century. Their university of Trichur is of some importance. (Cf. Herbert, *Spiritualité hindoue*. Paris, 1947.)

sionaries. Above all, we must seek to feel for ourselves the fierce joy and the will to conquer which was the privilege of a very young doctrine, in which the Spirit of God was still bursting forth in a galaxy of miracles.

So silent and secret was this missionary endeavour that no contemporary has recorded it. No names of any of these early heralds of the Gospel have come down to us. One day the news would simply begin to spread through some exclusive city quarter, or in one or other of the poorer districts near the walls. Who first brought it there? Was it some Jewish pedlar, some merchant from Antioch, or even this escaped slave here, who was said to have come from Cyprus or one of the Cilician cities? Might it even have been a woman? For women played a leading part in this 'whispering campaign.' People talked about the new doctrine in the shops, in the open-air markets, as well as in the stinking tanneries and the offal-yards. Some ridiculed it, others were deeply moved by it. The God who became man, the Resurrected Lord, the Consoler of all human sufferings—who was it who first mentioned His name? Then one day, perhaps, a stranger arrived in the city. He had obviously come from afar, and he spoke Greek with a foreign accent. Perhaps he commented in the synagogues upon the scriptural texts, in order to justify his extraordinary statements. More probably he attracted crowds around him in the public squares of the town, and to these he addressed not only scholarly lectures and finished sermons but improvised, heart-to-heart, popular speeches, something like those that one can still hear today at Hyde Park Corner in London. This man's talks were more picturesque and fervent, of course, since they were directed at the more emotional peoples of eastern lands. Thus the Church was born, or rather the embryo of a Church, probably comprising only twelve or fifteen believers in the first place. In the majority of cases nothing could henceforth destroy it.

Is it true that Christian missionary endeavour obeyed certain carefully considered principles, which led it to incline in one particular direction rather than in another? Where outstanding leaders were concerned, yes. It is quite obvious that St Paul did not leave the planning of his itineraries to chance; his five great halts have considerable significance in relation to his intentions and his ultimate aims. Antioch was the starting-point of the Mesopotamian caravans; Ephesus the spring-board to Asia Minor; Salonica the threshold of Macedonia; Corinth the leading port in Greece serving both the Aegean and the Adriatic; and Rome was the heart of the Empire itself. These were, indeed, 'the gateways to the world.' But what of the other, unknown missionaries? Did they follow a systematic plan as they spread the news of Jesus far and wide? No, it is clear that they did not. And yet this endeavour shows a very practical and profound understanding of the geographic, economic and political realities of the world of the day. It was extremely flexible, adapting itself readily to local customs, following the great routes of sea or river trade, occasionally taking bold risks, but never deviating in the slightest respect from its extremely firm basic purpose. This missionary enterprise does indeed give an impression of exceptional strength and continuity.

Where was the spread of Christianity most marked in the beginning? In the first place in Asia Minor, above all, and the surrounding regions. These were the areas where Paul and John preached, and they were not so very far from Palestine: many churches were to flourish there. Christian communities actually spread beyond these districts, clearing the frontiers of the Empire itself, and reaching out towards the kingdom of Edessa, or Osrhoenia, which seems to have been rapidly converted to Christianity, and towards Persia too, where some communities of the faithful existed from about the end of the first century.[3] Since Christianity had succeeded so well in these regions, was it to become an Asiatic religion, devoting itself to Asia? Far from it. Osrhoenia and Persia were to remain exceptions to the general pattern of conversions. Following in the footsteps of St Paul, who, there as everywhere, had opened up the road, the Gospel crossed the Aegean Sea and

[3] It should be remembered that, on the first Whit Sunday, the crowd in Jerusalem had included Parthians, Medes, Elamites and folk from Mesopotamia (Acts of the Apostles, ii. 9). This fact would seem to lend considerable support to the tradition which asserts the existence of a Christian Church in Persia in very early times, and to be at least as admissible as confirmatory evidence as the apocryphal accounts of St Thomas. (See the classic work of Canon Labourt, *Le Christianisme en Perse*. Paris, 1912.)

turned towards Europe. The seed sown in Greece was soon to germinate, and with the conversion of Greece came the conversion of her Illyrian and Dalmatian appendages also. Soon —probably very soon after Christ's death—the first baptisms took place in Italy, and Christian communities quickly multiplied there. Egypt, a Roman province, must have been touched by the Gospel very early on, even if she was not actually evangelized by St Mark the Evangelist, as tradition would have us believe. By contrast, Christianity penetrated the West much more slowly. Despite the illustrious sponsors which their Churches were to claim as theirs in the distant future, Gaul, Spain and Africa were not really opened up to the faith until the second century. Then, however, the manner of their conversion was superb. The pious Hermas, the author of *Pastor*, was right when, around 120, he already compared Christianity with a tree, whose branches covered the whole of the civilized world.

Thus, in the space of about a century, the Gospel had breached all the vital spiritual nerve-centres of the Empire. However, thus outlined, the curve of this Christian propagation calls for one extremely important comment. Primitive Christianity was, with but two exceptions, developed within the framework of Rome: in other words, to use Monsignor Duchesne's famous phrase, 'the Empire was its *motherland.*' Like the Roman Empire, it did not go beyond a certain boundary in the east. Like the Empire, it faced westwards. In its very progress it followed in the footsteps of Roman civilization, born in a Graeco-Oriental melting-pot, but gradually conquering the less sophisticated but healthier lands of the West. Here we have a concordance of frontiers which was to be of fundamental importance to the whole future of the Christian religion. The Church owed much of what she finally became to the Roman system: but at the same time she was soon to come into direct conflict with the might of Rome.

## IMPERIUM ROMANUM

During the first two centuries of the Christian era, that is to say at the very time when the seed of Christianity was seizing its opportunity to take root, one political reality alone existed throughout that part of the world which centred on the Mediterranean, forcing itself on every individual mind within that world: the Roman Empire. We have learned so well, from personal experience, that worldly empires all fade away in the end that it is almost impossible for us, living as we do in an unsettled age, to understand the full import of this phrase—*imperium Romanum*—and to assess all that it signified in terms of stability and greatness at that time. Neither the Holy Roman Empire, nor the dominions of Napoleon, nor even the British Empire in the days of Queen Victoria, ever gave such an impression of absolute impregnability. Only the China of the Han dynasty, which existed at the same time as the Roman Empire, was to have an equally profound feeling of utter well-being. Unique in its class, enormous and invincible, the Empire born of the She-Wolf seemed destined to endure for ever.

The patient efforts of the Latin peasant-farmers had, by this time, completely achieved their goal. The Mediterranean was henceforth a Roman sea: *mare nostrum;* no other power could now dispute its control with them. Two centuries before, Carthage, their only really serious enemy, had been defeated and devastated by Scipio. With an ease that had something almost disturbing about it, the Romans watched the overripe fruits of the Eastern kingdoms fall into their hands, one after another, whilst, at the same time, albeit with more difficulty, they succeeded in overthrowing Viriathus and Vercingetorix, and imposing their iron rule upon Spain and Gaul. Flanked by arid deserts in the east, and protected in the west by the as yet undented shield of the legions, the Empire had the opportunity to make the peoples she had defeated forget the brutality and even the iniquity of her conquests, and to pose as the guarantor of the only valid kind of civilization.

In the year 30, when Jesus died, the Empire comprised roughly one and three-quarter million square miles, and certainly contained at least fifty-five or sixty million people. It was bounded in the west by the Atlantic Ocean, stretching from the shores of Morocco to the Rhine estuary. Then, following the mighty river back to its source and dropping down the course of the Danube, the frontier which separated civilization from Germanic barbarism crossed Europe from west to east. The whole of Asia Minor served as an imperial fortress against the Parthians on the eastern border, with two Roman advance posts set in the heart of the savages' world. These were the protectorate of Armenia, ruled by one of Rome's creatures, and the small Greek vassal kingdom of the 'Bosphorus,' the modern Crimea. Finally, when Egypt and, through her, the North African provinces which she had ruled had been linked to this bloc, Syria and Palestine closed the massive circle from the centre of which a triumphant Rome could survey her vast possessions.

The first two centuries A.D. were really Rome's Golden Age. Every great state follows a progressive pattern which corresponds exactly with that of individual human lives. All the efforts, toil and sacrifices of past generations eventually bring society to a point of unsurpassable perfection, in which the race's every potentiality is fulfilled. This is the time of the nation's greatest achievements, of its geniuses and its masterpieces, the time when human groupings face the world, one after another, like witnesses of the glorious present and guides to the future. These heroic ages never last long: between one and two hundred years on average. They pass, and nothing is left for the future save the inevitable slide towards the abyss into which history hurls empires and individuals with sublime indiscrimination. For Rome, this fleeting moment of wellbeing, might and pride was the period of the Early Empire.

The Empire was built by a man of genius: *Octavian*. With prodigious intuition he had, from early manhood onwards, realized that the crisis which Rome had been suffering for nearly a century, and which had shaken her with frightful convulsions, was not merely a crisis of government, as the rivalries of men and factions might lead one to believe: it marked a decisive turning-point in her history, a point at which the very definition of all that Rome stood for needed to be thought out on completely new lines. Now that Rome had become too vast for Rome herself to control under the present system, it was necessary to modify her principles of government, to leave the narrow confines of the traditional city-state and to found an empire consisting of a vast collection of lands, in which the Eternal City would, of course, still have the leading functions of initiative and control, but without claiming any longer to enclose an entire world within her municipal framework. In order to bring the grandiose plan into being, Octavian had to destroy the Republic's ancient legal forms: the very greatest imperial schemes of history nearly always infringe on individual liberty. Octavian appropriated this liberty for the State, but he had learned much on this subject from the example of his uncle, Julius Caesar, and he knew how to retain the appearances of liberty, which were what men valued most. Did this appropriation occur on 2nd September, 31 B.C., the day of the victory of Actium, or on 1st August, 30 B.C., when Octavian's rival, Mark Antony, died at Alexandria, or in mid August, when Octavian made his triumphal return to Rome, or on 16th January, 27 B.C., when the Senate bestowed on the successful dictator the divine name of Augustus? The very uncertainty of dating shows the subtlety of the manœuvre. At all events the first emperor, the 'Master of the World,' subsequently knew, too, how to show himself 'master of himself.' Overcoming those defects in character which had previously made people regard him with bitterness and distrust, he built up an impression of spirituality in men's minds, acquiring serene greatness, and even generosity, and well deserving the hardly exaggerated tribute which one historian was later to pay him: 'Everything that men can ask of God has already been obtained for the Roman people and for the world by Augustus.'[4]

The regime thus founded endured from A.D. 14, when Augustus died, until 192. Of course changes did occur; and the characteristics which were later to be the factors determining its decline were accentuated, as time went by, even in their externals. But this evolution was a slow one: it took place by degrees; the vital centres of the Imperium were not yet threatened.

Three dynasties held imperial power one after the other, deriving from three different elements in the Empire. The first was the Julio-Claudian dynasty, comprising the relations of Augustus, and representing the old Roman aristocracy. It does not seem to have included any very outstanding men, apart from its founder: probably only one, Tiberius, showed

4 Velleius Paterculus.

real greatness, despite his extremely unpleasant moral character and all the bloodshed of his last years. Two, Caligula and Nero, were insane; and one, Claudius, was a weakling. But so sound was the mechanism set up by Augustus that it continued to function perfectly despite the deficiencies of its operators. Even if the emperor were a personal failure he possessed plenty of servants who took their tasks fully in their stride, whether they were war-leaders, like Germanicus and Drusus; Claudius's freedmen, ambitious, crafty rascals, but men who knew how to govern and were first and foremost creatures in the service of the administration; or the first counsellors of the young Nero, Seneca and Burrhus.

Then, in 69, when the lesser Italian bourgeoisie obtained power in the person of Vespasian, it brought to the throne, together with a certain narrow-mindedness, its own qualities of order, tenacity and frugality. The policy of the Flavians consisted in maintaining financial stability, organizing great public works, and making an intelligent effort to reform the moral and social climate of the Empire. The title of 'darling of the human race,' which was bestowed posthumously upon Titus after his all-too-brief reign, certainly expressed a sincere popular sentiment, and when, in 96, his brother Domitian was overthrown by an aristocratic *coup d'état*, there is little doubt that the common people in both the country and the towns mourned the death of this brutal and dictatorial ruler.

Finally, from 96 until 192, the Antonine dynasty held sway. This dynasty, which was of provincial Italian stock, presented history with a sequence of such remarkable characters that it has scarcely a single equal among all the ruling families of the world. Trajan, Hadrian, Antoninus, Marcus Aurelius: they all differed vastly from one another in both character and behaviour, but all shared the same feeling of responsibility towards the state they governed. These second-century emperors enjoyed such tranquil and unquestioned authority that many national leaders today may well regard them with envy. It was an age of financial stability and strict administration, an epoch in which government also sought to become more moral and more socially responsible. The reigns of the Antonines mark the point at which the organizing empiricism of

Rome, by dint of its wisdom and its strength, was on the verge of becoming humane.

Thus throughout these first two centuries the Empire gives an astonishing impression of solidity. Not that it did not have its jolts and jars. In the first place there were its wars, in Germany, Britain, on the Danube and in Dacia, and, in the East, against the Parthians or the rebellious Jews; no reign was without some fighting abroad. But these wars remained peripheral in character; they involved only limited forces, and they did not concern the great mass of those who lived in the shadow of the Roman eagles. Moreover, these were not wars of extension or conquest; they were directed at acquiring stronger positions, or were simply wars of a necessary and punitive type. The common people of the Imperium could largely ignore them. These were wars without 'the injuries of war.'

Political crises occurred too. There was the drama of 41, when the insane Caligula was hounded into the cryptoportico of his palace, to die there, pierced by thirty sword wounds. In 68–79 civil wars occurred, some legions fighting with one emperor against others who were supporting a rival emperor. There was the drama of 96, when Domitian put up a ferocious struggle against the assassin who had attacked him in his bedchamber, and finally fell, his fingers severed, streaming with blood. There was the drama of 192 when Commodus was eventually strangled in his bath, after he had escaped the poison offered him by his own concubine. And to these great tragedies in which the fate of the whole world was at stake must be added all those which, on so many occasions, played havoc with the Roman aristocracy, who risked the consequences of an unsuccessful plot and who were at the mercy of all the crazy whims of a prince. But it should be remembered that these bloody upheavals so stressed by the historians were no more than palace revolutions in the majority of cases, and only concerned the ruling classes, the senior officials and the courtiers who lived directly under the master's eye. The rest of the people, in other words the vast majority, only heard of them second hand, by word of mouth; they might be pleased or angry at the news, but they really only judged their political rulers by results, and, if these results were good, they remained calm and indifferent to events.

Moreover, this profound tranquillity was another thing which stemmed from the very conditions of imperial organization. As established by Augustus, and respected by the majority of his successors, it left a large measure of autonomy to the local administrations, to the various towns. Once order reigned, and everything was functioning smoothly, the imperial government did not intervene in matters of detail. This relative independence was the surest base on which to found the loyalty of the governed. And although during the first two centuries A.D. the Empire progressed farther and farther along the road towards centralization and state control, the Roman world did not yet know the defects inherent in these methods of government, defects of which it was subsequently to have most painful experience: incoherency of purpose and inertia, waste and ineffectualness. In governing from above, the Rome of this period shielded its empire from the inevitable upheavals of personal regimes.

This then was what the Imperium was like during these first fifteen decades when Christianity was springing up all over its domains. It presented an appearance of might, equilibrium and stability: these characteristics are overwhelmingly obvious to anyone who studies the masterpiece which was the Golden Age of Rome. And when we think of the frail little structure of the young Church beside this majestic Colossus it seems ridiculous to imagine that a conflict between the two could possibly result in anything other than the complete annihilation of Christianity. Yet in the struggle between David and Goliath, also, everything had at first seemed to be on the giant's side. . . .

### 'THE FEET OF THE LEGIONS HAD MARCHED FOR HIM'

Contrary to a very widely held opinion, disturbed epochs are not those which are most favourable to the expansion of a new doctrine. Times of crisis, misery and disorder can offer a revolutionary aspiration the chance to be crystallized into practical events. But in order that these events be not reduced to a more or less fruitless agitation, and to ensure that they end in a creative result, a doctrine impelling them towards their goal has to exist in men's minds well beforehand. This doctrine needs a certain period of stability in which to permeate society thoroughly. Here is one of the paradoxes of human government: by establishing order and peace within its boundaries a society makes it easier for forces within its bosom which are attempting its destruction to act, despite all the precautions it may take to prevent this. This paradox worked in favour of Christianity in the days of the Early Empire.

The splendid opportunities for missionary endeavour which the Gospel was to find within the Empire are summed up in one famous phrase: the Roman peace, Pax Romana. The early years of the Christian sowing corresponded to the most peaceful and secure period of history which the West has ever known, before or since. For we Europeans of the modern world, who have for centuries been prey to increasingly frightful and apparently inevitable wars, peace no longer has any absolute significance: to us it is merely a respite between two cataclysms. Things were very different for an imperial citizen living in the time of Titus or Trajan. Peace then was a durable reality, whose benefits could be exploited without reservations. In Spain, for example, the final agonies of the conquest were over by 19 B.C.; in Gaul by about 50; and henceforth, until the arrival of the first waves of barbarian invaders, that is to say for some three hundred years to come, no threatening soldiers were ever to set foot again in the lands which were now protected by Rome. We can understand the situation in more modern terms if we picture the West as having had no conflicts from the end of the Wars of Religion until 1900! And this external peace, during which, as we have seen, the defence of the frontiers was not neglected, went hand in hand with an internal tranquillity which was almost as total. The military crises which occurred were very short-lived, and never seriously disturbed it. At all events the prolonged struggles between rival and destructive armies, such as men had known in the days of Sulla, Pompey and Mark Antony, were over and done with! Gone too were the massacres of Roman citizens, like those actually indulged in by Mithridates in the last century of the Republic! Gone the constant pillaging and piracy that had infested land and sea routes in bygone days! Pax Romana: the literary tributes paid to this great historical reality do not want for emphasis. 'The immense majesty' of this peace, which was praised by the Elder Pliny, was very real, and Tacitus shows himself a trustworthy eye-witness of the present, as well as a prophet of the future, when he writes: 'If the Romans were ever driven out (may the gods prevent such a calamity!) what else would there be, save universal war? Eight hundred years of dogged purpose and good fortune have gone into the raising of this mighty edifice. Whoever destroyed it would be wiped out by his own act of destruction.'

The first benefit which nascent Christianity was to derive from the Pax Romana was the protection of the law. We need only read the chapters in Acts which relate to St Paul to see the part played in his missionary life by Roman law and Roman discipline. He took full advantage of his status as a Roman citizen, which allowed him to make complete use of the benefits of the imperial system. It was thanks to the laws of Rome that he escaped being massacred by various groups of fanatics on several of his journeys; it was Caesar's officials who allowed him to give God His due. For example, at Corinth it was Gallio, the proconsul of Achaia, who restored order among the Jews who had rioted against the Apostle. At Jerusalem it was the tribune, the military governor, who, by deciding to send Paul to Caesarea, ensured his escape from the plot hatched against him by the Torah zealots—his escape, that is to say, from certain death. At Ephesus it was the Roman magistrate who calmed the faithful followers of Diana when they were on the verge of tearing the Apostle and his disciples to pieces. On this occasion an extremely significant speech was made to the mob by the secretary of the city: 'If Demetrius and his fellow craftsmen have any charge to bring against them, why, we have court days, we have two proconsuls: let the two parties go to law. If, on the other hand, you have any further question to raise, it can be settled by the lawful assembly' (Acts xix. 38–9). Provided therefore that they did not come into open conflict with the basic principles of the State too quickly (and we shall see that the rupture was very far from being immediate) the Gospel missionaries could make use of the framework of legality and security which the Romans guaranteed throughout their empire in carrying out their apostolic work.

On the material plane, Rome was to put her incomparable system of communications at the disposal of the Christians. The Roman roads! The network of roads, whose main outlines had been mapped out in the days of the Republic, was the emperor's constant preoccupation. As soon as he attained power Augustus busied himself with repairing the Italian highways, and his friend Agrippa, to whom he confided the task, erected a map on the Martian Field, where even the least of citizens could admire the immensity of the Empire of the She-Wolf and the multiplicity of the roads which served it.[5] Claudius established a Minister of Communications, who took charge of the highways system throughout the entire Empire. Gaul's roads were built during Augustus's reign, and the communications network there was to be one of the most complete and intricate of all; Spain's roads were finished by Tiberius and Vespasian; Claudius built the roads in Dalmatia, and Nero those in Thrace. During the first two centuries A.D. every single emperor made some addition or other to this grandiose system. Some areas, which today possess only indifferent cart-tracks, such as parts of Asia Minor, or which can only boast one or two isolated and recently built motorways, like Tripolitania, were at that time equipped with splendid roads. From Rome to the Pillars of Hercules, or to Byzantium, or the Danube, or the farthermost tip of Armorica, these wonderful, marvellously paved highways ran their course. Proud and straight they ran, over the mountains and across the plains, like the very symbol of that indestructible net which Rome had cast across the whole world.

The sea offered an equally good means of travel. Now that the Roman warships had swept away most of the pirates it had become a safe thoroughfare. Numerous boats plied in all directions; the Mediterranean was certainly as thickly crossed with shipping lanes in those days as it is in our own. There were the heavy, slow merchant ships and the rather faster

---

[5] *Peutinger's Table*, which was famous in the Middle Ages, was simply the reproduction of one of the numerous parchment copies of this plan of Augustus's, which Peutinger, a fifteenth-century Augsburg banker, acquired for his private art collection. Another such tablet, written in Greek, can be seen in the monastery of Vatopedi, on Mount Athos.

passenger boats, some of which could carry as many as six hundred people. Shipbuilders ran into hundreds. The shipping companies had their offices not only in the ports (Ostia had twenty-five of them!) but in Rome and all the other large cities as well. There were even travel agencies, urging the idle rich to go and spend a warm winter in the hot Egyptian sun.[6] The great ports were at the height of their prosperity: in the East, Alexandria, Smyrna, Ephesus and Seleucia Pieria; in Italy, Pozzuoli and Ostia, both of which served Rome, and, after them in importance, Syracuse and Brindisi; in Africa, Cyrene, Carthage and Leptis Magna; in Greece, Corinth, Salonica and Dyrrachium (Durazzo), the last-named serving the Adriatic; finally, on the western shores of the Mediterranean, Marseilles, Arles, Narbonne, Tarragona, Carthagena and far-away Gades, the modern Cadiz, which faced the Atlantic. This list of names is revealing in itself, for it is also that of the first outposts of the Gospel. Likewise the list of Roman roads and waterways marks the route of Christianity's penetration into the various imperial territories. The economic map of the Empire and the map of Christian conquest are roughly one and the same.

Indeed it is overwhelmingly obvious that nascent Christianity was to derive considerable help from these material conditions around it. This was not simply because they enabled its missionaries to travel easily and safely wheresoever their task called them—as indeed they did—but the very play of human exchanges, which was a necessary accompaniment of all imperial business dealings, and which was immensely facilitated by these admirable communications, helped it too. Rome's object in building this marvellous network had un-

<hr/>

[6] Roman maritime trade actually ventured far beyond the boundaries, not simply of the Empire itself, but of Europe and the whole Western world also. For instance, the following relations were established with India. Augustus received ambassadors from the Punjab, and Claudius envoys from Ceylon. Every July a fleet of 120 vessels left Berenice, on the Red Sea, and sailed for India, making use of the monsoon conditions, discovered by Hippalos, a Greek sailor, and returning in November, laden with pepper, diamonds, pearls and cotton goods. Are not the traditions relating to the penetration of Christianity into India likely to be based on truth, in view of the established fact of these trading connections?

doubtedly been essentially political and economic; it existed so that the emperor's edicts could be sent out far and wide, and, conversely, so that reports from the provincial administrators could be received in Rome as quickly as possible; it also existed in order to attract to Rome—to that great emporium of warehouses and shops that encircled the Aventine—corn from Sicily and Egypt, minerals from Spain, scented woods from Asia Minor and Phoenicia, skins and woollen cloth from Gaul, perfumes and spices from the Arab countries: all those thousand and one articles that a mighty capital increasingly demands. But imperial decrees and loads of merchandise were not the only things that circulated back and forth on these land and sea routes. Naturally enough the sailors and the travellers played the same role here as they have always played elsewhere, in every age; as they journeyed from one place to another they carried ideas along with them, so that the most distant corners of the West soon learned what men were thinking many miles away in the East. Besides, among the merchandise that travelled the imperial highways there was one category that was possessed of souls and minds: the slaves, who formed an important element of everyday trade. These uprooted, transplanted folk, who were very numerous in the Empire's luxurious heyday, carried their own customs and beliefs into the bosoms of the Roman families who bought them. Quite often, if they were Greeks or orientals, and more cultured and refined than their masters, they exercised an unconscious but exceedingly strong influence upon those they served. Syrian ladies' maids had been successful missionaries of the various mystic cults from Asia which came to flourish in Rome; Christianity too was to possess many zealous adherents among the slave class.

The missionaries derived other advantages from the Roman system, and from the economic interdependence of the different regions of the Empire. As in all vast commercial systems, the means of exchange had of necessity to be co-ordinated. Gold had been established as the monetary unit when the Empire was inaugurated. By the third century its use was to become standard, a symbol of Roman sovereignty. Business men had to understand one another; it was in order to make commercial transactions easier that the Phoenicians had circulated their extremely practical alphabet, the ancestor of our own; as today English has, by force of circumstances, become the business language of the world. Likewise a man could make himself understood throughout the whole of the Early Roman Empire so long as he knew Greek. Latin (which gradually increased in importance and ended by being the dominant Western tongue from the third century onwards) was still primarily the military and administrative language. But Greek was understood by anyone who had a smattering of education: there was the popular Greek of the waterfronts, as well as the aristocratic Greek of the upper classes. This does not mean that local tongues had disappeared. Men still spoke Libyan (in other words, Berber) in North Africa, and Iberian (from which modern Basque derives) in Spain. But if one spoke Greek one could be sure of being understood either in Iconium or among the Galatians (as St Paul's example proves), as well as in Bordeaux or Trèves. When the Christians first began to write down the Gospels, they were to write them in Greek.

It is therefore easy to point to a large number of opportunities which the majestic organization of the Imperium, in the ordinary course of events, afforded for the spread of Christianity. Likewise it is true to say that the new faith had the ground prepared for it in the moral and intellectual fields. Though Rome indeed pursued a policy tending towards unification, this was not motivated by selfishness alone. 'Romanization' did occur wherever the legions went, as is still obvious to anyone today who studies the surviving ruins of identical buildings erected by the Empire in the four corners of the world. But Romanization aimed at something nobler than mere economic exploitation of the subject territories. The ancient hardy and rugged race of Latin peasant-farmers who had created the nucleus of an empire by annexing the provinces around Rome, rather in the spirit that landowners acquire new estates, had had the extreme good sense to realize that brute force had its limitations, and to put this force to the service of a particular ideal. That had happened when Greek philosophy had impregnated the Latin mind, when that Graeco-Roman synthesis had been achieved from which emerged the classical civilization which we admire so much. Consequently

the idea that the folk of the She-Wolf had been divinely ordained to pacify and rule the world had genuine nobility; in
the early days of the Empire it swelled into a universalist aspiration, into a humanism with which the 'Latin genus' liked
to identify itself. The superior happiness deriving from a common culture, the interchange of fruitful ideas, men's realization of a lucid, reasonable concept of life: Cicero was thinking
of all these when he loftily defined the world as a 'society of
the human race.' And while Roman universalism still appears
far inferior to Christian universalism, it must nevertheless
have been a kind of useful introduction to the latter, a favourable soil in which the new doctrine could take root and
grow.

The historical masterpiece that was Imperial Rome certainly contained a large number of fundamentals which
seemed extremely favourable to Christian expansion, and
those practical connections which we have already observed
between the young Church and the Empire are easily explained by Christianity's geographic placing within the imperial framework. The fact that Christianity was subject to Romanization from its very beginnings was to have far-reaching
consequences so far as its future development was concerned.
It became first and foremost a religion of the cities, since the
Empire was essentially an organization of city-states.[7] As soon
as it needed to provide itself with an administration it borrowed its ideas on the subject from the Imperium. This connection can almost be regarded as predestined, for it was to
attain complete fulfilment on the day when the capital of the
Roman world became that of the Church also, and the seat of
the Caesars that too of the successors of the Apostle Peter.

Was this a historical chance, or the culmination of a divinely ordained intention? Ever since the earliest times many
of the faithful have regarded this Roman phenomenon as
proof of a divine plan. The opinion reiterated by so many

[7] The fact that Christianity was, in the first place, a religion of
townsfolk, and that the peasantry was converted far more slowly,
is proved by the fourth-century use of the word *paganus*, which
previously signified 'peasant,' and which at this time acquired its
current meaning of 'pagan.' (See Chapter XI, section: 'St Martin
and the Conversion of the Countryside.')

modern Christians, who can judge the event in the light of subsequent history, was already intuitively understood by the primitive Church itself. Many of us are familiar with the passage in Péguy's *Eve*—a work of our own time—where the author calls to mind the magnificence of Rome, when the world 'became one enormous rotunda, governed by two thousand cohorts,' and asserts that all these material efforts had no other end save the coming of the Master, and that 'the feet of the legions had marched for Him.' But as far back as 220 Origen was already writing: 'Because God was anxious that all the nations of the world should be ready to receive the doctrines of Christ, His Providence subjected them all to the Emperor of Rome.' And this wonderful theory was set out in full in the fourth century by Prudentius: 'What is the secret of Rome's historic destiny? The answer is that God desires the unity of the human race, since the Christian religion demands a basis of peace and international friendship. Until now the whole world has been rent asunder, from east to west, by continual strife. To curb this madness God has taught all nations to obey the same laws. They have all become Roman. Now we can see men living like citizens of a single city, like members of the same family. They come from across the seas, from far-off lands, to a forum which belongs to them all; nations are united by trade, by the same civilization, and in the marriage bond; from the mingling of peoples a single race is born. Herein lies the reason for the Empire's victories and triumphs: *the Roman peace has prepared the way for the coming of Christ.*'

## THE TWO GODS: ROME AND AUGUSTUS

However, true though declarations such as these undoubtedly are, it would be quite wrong to think that the triumph of Christianity can be wholly explained in this way. A determinist conception of this story, which has but temporary and partial validity, runs, when pushed too far, into conflicting evidence just as obvious as that of the opportunities offered by Rome to the Cross: into the increasingly conscious and sensational resistance with which the Empire opposed the new doctrine. Now this opposition was inevitable: it sprang from the spiritual fundamentals which were at the heart of the whole concept of Imperial Rome, from what might be called the Empire's entire historical personality. Everything came to pass just as though God, by confiding the Empire with the task of preparing the ground for the Gospel, had, at the same time, wanted to give the Christians the opportunity to perform those acts of heroism and self-sacrifice without which no great earthly enterprise is ever successfully accomplished.

Inscriptions dating from the first emperor's reign have been found at several places in Asia Minor. On them we can read sentences like this one: 'Providence sent us Augustus, as a Saviour, to put an end to war and to regulate all our affairs; the day of his birth marked the beginning of Good News for the whole world.' And Denys of Halicarnassus writes: 'Eternal nature has set the crowning seal upon her blessings to men by offering them that supreme gift, Caesar Augustus, father of his own motherland, the divine goddess Rome: Augustus, who is Zeus the father, Saviour of the human race.' Such sentences ring strange to Christian ears: they are characteristic of the Graeco-Roman mentality, as it had been moulded by the religious beliefs of countless generations; they give a forewarning of the content of the antagonism which was soon to flare up between pagans and Christians. For a man living in the first few centuries A.D. divinity meant, over and above everything else, the supreme power which, in an often incomprehensible manner, ruled the destinies of all human beings, and upon which their fortune or their misfortune depended. This supreme power was symbolized as Fatum, or Destiny. Consequently it was natural enough that the Roman Empire, the concrete expression of Fatum—and what a happy, mighty, miraculous destiny it had turned out to be!—should be regarded as a supernatural phenomenon, and it was entirely in keeping with pagan psychology that men should thereupon invest it with a divinity of its own.

Thus at the very moment when the Empire was entering upon its Golden Age, the imperial religion was established— the cult of *Rome and Augustus*. The expression 'the divine goddess Rome' had already been commonly used for a long time past. But even though this idea was personified in sculpture by a powerful and beautiful female figure, the abstract genius and sound common sense of the original Latins implied something rather theoretical by it. In ancient Rome men had not favoured investing either human beings or worldly objects with godlike attributes: the shades of their ancestors and the qualities of genius possessed by living men were not regarded as divine. The tendency which bore to the altars the divinely ordained might of Rome, made incarnate in the man who ruled her, came from the East, following its conquest by the legions. After all, had not the Egyptian Pharaohs accustomed their people to worshipping them as the incarnation of Amen-Rah for thousands of years past? Did the Persians not regard their king as chosen from the gods, sharing their glory and haloed in their light? As for the Attali monarchs of Pergamum, had they not each possessed their own colleges of priests, even in their own lifetimes? Had not Antiochus the Great had the words 'Son of God' engraved on his tomb in the Taurus Mountains? The mighty Alexander himself would not have been able to disregard this tendency to make princes into gods, even if he had wanted to do so; as the declared descendant of Hercules, the conqueror and heir of the Achemenides, he had claimed divine honours for himself, just like the Persian Kings of Kings. As a boy, Alexander had been taught by Aristotle, and perhaps when he proclaimed his own divinity he had been thinking of the divinity of the individual soul, as laid down by Plato, of that *spirit* which Democritus held to be present in every human being. But the mob had regarded him first and foremost as the heaven-sent man, the divine hero, the symbol of power, the man who, even in scholarly Athens, was hailed with words like these: 'The other gods are far away and scarcely hear us: thee we can see, face to face!'

When we think of the very real benefits which Augustus brought his people, of the sense of deliverance felt by everyone when his triumph ended a century of bitter strife, it is easy enough to understand how the Eastern world, which was quite accustomed to making its rulers into gods, granted him the honour entirely of its own free will. In his character the Greek hero and the Saviour-God of the Asian mysteries seemed perfectly combined. But even in the West Virgil, in his Fourth Eclogue, remembering the end of the age of swords, and the world's entry into the Golden Age of Empire, seems to point to the providential being in whom the hope of humanity is made incarnate, and Ovid certainly saw the emperor as the very manifestation of divine power.[8]

In this way the imperial cult was soon to be established throughout the length and breadth of the Empire. Even while Julius Caesar was alive he had been awarded quasi-divine honours, under the name of Jupiter Julius, and his name is remembered in our modern month of *July;* on his death he was elevated to the rank of the heavenly gods. The same process occurred in Augustus's case; although the astute politician curbed his followers' enthusiasm in the capital, he allowed temples and altars to be dedicated to him in the Roman provinces, even in Italy itself; after his death the Senate had recognized him as a god and had established a college of priests for him.[9] To this day our month of *August* commemorates the god Augustus. The imperial cult continued to develop throughout the first two centuries A.D. Each successive master of the Empire was to encourage it: some, like Tiberius, Claudius and Vespasian, with a restraint that amounted to virtual embarrassment, for all three refused all tokens of adoration during their lifetime; others enjoyed it openly. Emperors such as Caligula, Nero and Domitian, for example, liked nothing better than to see the sacrificial animals burning in their honour. But all of them made much of the cult, even the wise Antonines, for it had, in short, become a brand of loyalism, the most obvious expression of the subjects' devotion to their leader.

The word loyalism is used here in its widest sense. Far more than political and administrative loyalty is implied by it, for in the Ancient World it had a real religious significance too. The man in the Greek city-state was a citizen of that city in

[8] J. Carcopino's standard work on the subject, *Virgile et le mystère de la IVe Églogue* (Paris, 1930), points out that the poem was conceived on two planes simultaneously: on the one hand it is obviously a poem composed for a specific occasion, namely, to celebrate the birth of a child of noble birth; on the other it develops in a quasi-prophetic way, using symbolism of a rather Orphean and Pythagorean kind, and imparts 'an immortal message of human hope.'

[9] Thus the temple at Vienne, in France, was erected in honour of Augustus and Livia, who were both deified after death.

the very measure in which he participated in the civic cult. As the concept of the city-state expanded, the national religion had to expand with it. Alexander showed he had already grasped this when he tried to unite his own Macedonians and the Persians he had vanquished in one religion and one race, and so had his Ptolemaic successors in Egypt, in creating one god, Serapis, from the synthesis of Osiris of the Nile and the Greek Apollo. The imperial idea of the one universal city-capital needed a religious basis: the cult of Rome and Augustus supplied it with one.

It follows from this that nothing would be more erroneous than to view this official religion as simply a rather clumsy political manœuvre, carried out to cloak the exploitation of an empire by its capital, and the subjection of sixty million people to one single individual. This cult had its deepest roots in the masses' sincere gratitude. No one was in the least angry or scandalized when the city of Rome drained the wealth of the world to enhance its own adornment, when, one after another, the emperors spent vast fortunes in rebuilding it, making it each time more luxurious than before, precisely because the *Urbs* was the visible symbol of the very idea which the world venerated most highly, and in it mankind read the meaning of its own destiny. Likewise, to house the divine master, the Palatine was covered with palaces richer, even, than temples, whose still beautiful ruins now lie shrouded in wistaria and jasmine; flattering writers spread themselves in lavish imperial panegyrics; and rumours of orgies and scandals concerning the emperor were whispered from mouth to mouth; yet all these things were accepted with equanimity by the descendants of Cato, Cicero and Brutus, because the heaven-sent ruler embodied the loftiest ideal of all that Rome stood for in a truly mystical way. In the *Apotheosis*, the deifying ceremony in which, so it was said, the spirit of the dead emperor was born heavenwards by an eagle, there to sit among the gods, the pagan soul of the pacified Roman world found a real spiritual satisfaction and exaltation. Even in the final days of the Empire, on the eve of the catastrophe known to history as the Barbarian invasions, Rutilius Numatianus, the Gallic poet, was still to invoke the image of the divine Rome, like a last citadel of salvation. The imperial cult only finally disappeared when the actual Empire it supported collapsed.[10]

Thus the fundamental cause of the conflict between Christianity and the Empire is plain for all to see. This conflict was to begin as soon as both adversaries realized that they were indeed each other's enemy. The cult of Rome and Augustus was the reverse side of all those many advantages which the expansion of the Gospel derived from the majesty of the Roman peace. To a world which enjoyed the most assured of material benefits, was it not logical that the Saviour should seem to be none other than that mighty, invincible man from whom all these benefits flowed? But, quite naturally, the Christian opposed such a concept with an unqualified *non possumus*. This religion which was so completely identified with the established order of things and with material happiness was certainly not the religion of Christ. The city which was glorified as the motherland was not the city of God. To the Christians the cult of Rome and Augustus was nothing but state idolatry, built upon man-made law, the supreme act of religious subversion, since it insisted on the giving to Caesar of the things that belonged to God. It was against this fusion of the temporal and the spiritual that the Christians were to rally. Herein lies the basic cause of the tragic struggle confronting the Empire and the Cross during the first centuries of our era. Consequently, though the Gospel did indeed find physical conditions in the Roman world extremely favourable to its initial growth, it was only through a violent break with that world that it was to fulfil its destiny therein. And when the Revolution of the Cross eventually triumphed the imperial cult disappeared from all the imperial cities; and the Empire, in fact if not in theory, disavowed the very foundations on which it rested.

## CRACKS IN THE EMPIRE'S MORAL FABRIC

However, having established the inevitability of the conflict between Rome and the Cross, the observer who considers

[10] It should also be noted that, in practice, the imperial cult was generally upheld most ardently by the very people who derived the greatest benefits from the imperial system. In the provinces the municipal priests of 'Rome and Augustus' were all Roman citizens, aristocrats or business men, or retired soldiers.

the rather surprising result of that conflict—namely, the triumph of Christianity—is led to wonder whether some cracks must not already have existed in the very structure of that majestic imperial society which was to suffer this astounding defeat. Through these the new doctrine might be able to infiltrate to the heart of the system, there to cause, or at any rate to assist, a process of decomposition. Such cracks did indeed exist. They were barely visible to the majority of people who lived at the time, but they are perfectly obvious to the modern historian. There was no question yet of society being utterly decadent, and the student who applies this adjective to the Early Empire is distorting the picture completely; but all the same it is quite clear that the fundamental causes which, later on, from the beginning of the third century onwards, were to push Rome more and more rapidly towards the abyss were already present in the Empire's Golden Age. Until 192 there was no real decline, but the 'crisis in man himself' existed long before that date.

We shall watch the symptoms of this crisis becoming increasingly defined, and its effects continually growing, right up to the tragic collapse at the end of the fourth century. It stemmed from the very conditions which had made the Early Empire the masterpiece it was. Rome had conquered the world, but what was Rome herself? She had begun as a straggling Italiot village, a market-place, where the worthy peasant families of the district met to buy and sell, a modest administrative centre to which rugged, straightforward folk came to discuss their common interests: men skilled in handling both the ploughshare and the sword, but little prepared to assume the role of leaders of civilization. Very soon the numeric disparity between this little nucleus of rulers and the vast mass of the governed became enormous, and resulted in a highly dangerous state of disequilibrium. This was all the more serious since many of the vanquished races possessed a richer conception of the world, and a more advanced civilization, than their conquerors. Consequently the East came to exercise a considerable fascination over the Romans, and they took to adopting its customs and ideas. This is what is really implied in Horace's famous sentence: 'Vanquished Greece led captive her savage vanquisher.' Greek art, Greek philosophy, oriental religions, Asiatic morals: the East was to let loose on Italy an unending flood of new ideas, and this flood brought with it things that were evil as well as things that were good.

Thus her conquests led Rome into a kind of spiritual no man's land. Her intake of spiritual ideas—all those things which form the very basis of a civilization, its interpretation of life, the conception which it has of itself—came less and less from her own ancient loyalties. As they became more cultured and civilized the Romans deviated more and more from the ideal picture of their race that they had held in bygone days, regarding it now as uncouth and old-fashioned. Their philosophy came from Greece. The splendid humanistic ideal of Roman universalism was inherited by Rome from various Greek philosophers and from the grandiose schemes of Alexander the Great. The language of the Roman ruling classes was that of Homer and Aristotle. We can get some idea of this spiritual confusion by imagining what France would be like if Arabian was adopted as the language of the educated classes, and the country's attitude to life determined by the principles of the Koran. In the Empire's early days national vitality was still strong enough to prevent this foreign contribution from sterilizing what the Latins themselves had to offer. Quite the contrary: the grafting of this Greek slip on to the Roman trunk produced some marvellous fruit. But the farther the Empire travelled along the universalist road, the more these interchanges of ideas multiplied between one province and another, and the more the Roman mind was submerged beneath Eastern influences. Politically the Empire was eventually to become the property of Asian dynasties, before ending its existence as the plaything of the Barbarians; spiritually it was all ready to welcome a new conception of the world, for its own was utterly exhausted.

This spiritual phenomenon produced its consequences in every field of human activity, but notably in the sphere of morals. In conquering the world Rome had watched those vital forces within her which had enabled her to make this conquest shrink and wither away. Could she have prevented this? No. Here is a striking example of one of those insoluble dilemmas in which fate places man, possibly to make him more conscious of his limitations. The Latin soul could only have re-

mained pristine and inviolate if the Roman citizen had remained the honest, stolid boor he had been in the far distant
past; but in that case he would not have been capable of ruling his vast empire, and from the moment that he decided to
abandon his policy of brute force his vital energies slackened.
As the centuries slipped by, from the first century B.C. until
the fourth A.D., when everything was to fall asunder, Roman
society was to give an ever-increasing impression of exhaus-
tion and bankruptcy. Its morals, like its art and its philosophy,
slowly disintegrated.[11] This is not the only example which
history offers us of a close connection between the improve-
ment of a society's ideals and the collapse of its original virtues. The reconciliation of force and morality, and the heroic
and the humane, needed nothing less than a total overthrow
of the existing order: and this was precisely what the Gospel was to provide.

Such is the real meaning of this 'moral crisis,' which historians have long been accustomed to paint in the blackest
colours. It is essential to study it rather more rationally than
this. The Gospel was not sown in the worm-eaten world of
the Late Empire, but in a society whose foundations were still
extremely sound, and which, despite some cracks in its struc-

---

[11] The decline of creative ability is, in fact, a most striking symp-
tom of the progressive sterilization of Roman society. Neither art
nor literature could remain healthy in a sick civilization. The coming
decline can be foreseen as early as the Augustan Age. The Roman
masterpieces, born of the sowing of Latin soil with Greek seed, were
produced within the space of a very short time. Then followed a
copyist epoch, an age of increasing pedantry. Though it was, in many
instances, grandiose in proportions, imperial art lived, first of all, on
the artistic capital of the final period of the Republic, then lapsed
into the pompous and the grandiloquent, and soon fell into blatantly
bad taste. The most widely read kinds of literature in the first century A.D. were not the works of Virgil and Tacitus, but the compositions of writers of anecdotes and anthologies, like Hyginus and
Valerius Maximus. Seneca's *Naturales Quaestiones* and the Elder
Pliny's *Historia Naturalis* were also popular. In the second century
popular taste turned to the neo-Sophists, the grammarians and the
lexicographers, to the scientific treatises of Ptolemy and Nichomachus:
all works which, in themselves, did not lack merit, but which had
no positively creative impulse. In this field, too, the historical role
of Christianity was to be immensely important; it was through the
Gospel that the arts and literature were to be rejuvenated.

ture, did not feel in the least danger of collapse. It would be
as foolish to judge Roman morals by the acid criticism of Juvenal, Lucian or Suetonius, or by the descriptions of Petronius
and Apuleius, as to see the whole of twentieth-century France
in terms of the satirical comedies of Bourdet or Pagnol, or the
worldly wise novels of Marcel Proust. At this early period, demoralization of the kind depicted in the *Golden Ass* or the
*Satyricon* had affected only a few sections of well-to-do society,
particularly in the large cities. A luxury-loving and corrupt
clique could offer picturesque material for the talented author
without being at all representative of its age. As soon as we
leave these literary texts, which refer only to the highest in
the land, and turn to more humble evidence—epitaphs, *graffiti*, papyrus inscriptions—it is clear that the private life of the
majority of Romans in the Early Empire offers countless examples of numerous fundamental virtues. Conjugal love, tenderness towards the weak, filial piety, brotherly affection—all
these are movingly praised. 'She spun the cloth and kept to
the house.' 'She was good and beautiful, modest, sober and
chaste. She helped everyone.' These are the kind of burial inscriptions written by grateful husbands, and one couple chose
to lie side by side beneath this touching epitaph: 'We had
but one heart.' Admirable pictures such as these inscriptions
conjure up can be seen even among the ranks of the higher
aristocracy, and around the imperial throne itself, and they
are still to be found in the future, in the age of complete
decadence: steadfast, tender wives, sons who respected their
fathers, faithful souls for whom the precepts of morality were
certainly very far from being a dead letter.

However, a society can very well contain within it both elements that are perfectly healthy and the active ingredients of
disintegration, and they can exist side by side: we see examples
of this before us today, in our own age. The Rome of the
first two centuries A.D., though it did possess virtues still practised by many good folk, bore, too, the symptoms of serious
dangers, which nothing could curb, for they stemmed from
the fundamental conditions of the Empire itself, from the
conditions that had made it so wealthy and so strong.

As a result of her conquests, much gold and many slaves
had accrued to Rome. The booty carried back from the East

by the Roman generals reached astronomical proportions; men said that Pompey's spoils ran into hundreds of millions of gold coins. Many others followed his example, and in this way regular gold-mines showered down on Rome; the tributes levied on the Eastern provinces amounted each year to some ninety million gold sovereigns. The common people received some of this manna, in the form of gifts made to the soldiers and distributions to the Roman *plebs*; the ruling classes received the largest share. And in an era when capital possessed few outlets for investment, owing to the lack of large-scale industry, gold merely enabled the common people to stop working, and the idle rich to spend riotously on dwelling-houses, food and drink and material pleasures of all kinds. The little yellow coin, which is so dangerous whenever it is not the reward for honest toil, was to cause the disintegration of Roman society in exactly the same way as, fifteen centuries later, it brought about the collapse of Spain, after the American expeditions of the Conquistadores.

In the Roman Empire another influx added to the disastrous effects caused by the superabundancy of gold: that of slaves. During the last two hundred years of the Republic, wars resulted in hundreds of thousand of slaves falling into the conquerors' hands. It was not unusual for one military campaign alone to bring in one hundred and fifty thousand at a time. This process continued during the imperial wars. In order to have some idea of the enormous size of the slave population, of the incredible proportion of society which it comprised, we should also take into account the effects of piracy, the fruitful traffic in human bodies and the normal reproduction rate of slaves who were already fixed in the servile class. During Augustus's reign slaves accounted for more than one-third of the population of Rome; in Alexandria, possibly two-thirds. The quantity of slaves available resulted in bargain prices being paid for them; an ordinary unskilled slave was worth about five hundred gold coins, a slave specializing in a particular trade, fifteen hundred to two thousand. Consequently anyone who needed a manual worker, whether he was a landowner, a business man or a craftsman, preferred to use slaves rather than free men. This proved a further cause of society's disintegration.

As a result of it a large body of people sprang up in the great cities, particularly in Rome, who were largely unemployed all the time. They consisted of uprooted peasants, free workmen who could no longer find work, freed slaves, and foreigners from every corner of the Empire. This was an excellent breeding-ground for all political cankers, and for all the forces of demoralization. The hard-working Roman of olden days became the 'client,' the parasite, paid for his doubtful loyalty by the *sportula*. The emperors were forced to reckon with this lamentable *plebs* and to deal circumspectly with it. But a people cannot make a habit of beggary and idleness without tainting its soul. Cowardliness and cruelty speedily went hand in hand with the vice which, as the popular saying so rightly remarks, engenders all the rest. Men no more wanted to defend their frontiers than to till their soil; and, as a diversion, this idle crowd was to find in the circus a theatre for pleasure in which all vestige of human sensibility was finally degraded and destroyed.

But there was something even worse than this landslide of society towards moral inertia; or, to put it more accurately, a second phenomenon existed alongside it, deriving from the same causes, and especially from the excessive enrichment of all sections of the population. Roman society was attacked in its most vital spot, at the source which sustains all societies; the structure of the family was shaken to the roots, and the birth-rate began to fall. The mother of the Gracchi had borne twelve children; at the beginning of the second century A.D. parents who had as many as three were to be praised as quite exceptional. Men shirked marriage and its obligations: had not the *orbitas*, the bachelor, all the advantages, the principal one being to assure the rich man of a permanently faithful following of expectant heirs? And, after all, he was depriving himself of nothing, since slavery provided him with bed companions who were more docile than any legal wife, and who, moreover, could be exchanged whenever he wanted! Abortion and the 'exposing' of new-born babies (in other words, their wanton abandonment) acquired terrifying proportions: in Trajan's reign one inscription gives the precise information that, of 181 new-born infants, 179 were legitimate, and that the latter figure included only 35 girls. This proves how lightly people disposed of their daughters and their bastards! As for divorce, it became so commonplace that no one attempted to provide reasonable justification for it any more: the simple desire for a change sufficed.

Was there any attempt to halt this moral disintegration? States have always shown themselves completely incapable of restoring their moral foundations once they have allowed them to weaken. The Roman rulers were far from being unaware of the peril, but their good intentions were absurdly useless, in view of the strength of the forces which were driving their society on to ruin. Augustus's example is cogent evidence of this. He promulgated countless laws with the loftiest of moral intentions, in an effort to fight the twin scourges of adultery and divorce. Did anyone take these laws seriously? Not his own family, that was more than obvious! And in addition, was it not Augustus himself who, by creating the Annonan Prefecture, which was entrusted with the task of providing the people with free food, gave idleness official sanction?[12] From time to time all the emperors would re-enact the excellent measures promulgated by the first of their line, which is proof of their complete uselessness. The dissolute morals of many of their masters, the more or less amused resignation with which Claudius or Marcus Aurelius bore their own marital misfortunes, made the common people perfectly aware of the real object of these legislative measures. At the beginning of the third century, when Dion Cassius took over the consulship, he was to find three thousand cases of adultery entered on the list of pleas, relating to Rome alone. When a crime becomes universal can it really go on being regarded as a crime?

The substitution of the State edict for the individual conscience is always a sure sign of decadence, in every country and in every age. A nation is indeed sick at heart if in order to live decently and to produce children it needs a series of subsidies and rules to enable it to do so. Livy was already

[12] The State's custom of supplying food was to grow apace; by the second century, of a population of some 1,200,000 souls in Rome it has been estimated that there were only about 100,000 heads of households who did not knock at the gates of the Annona.

writing: 'We have reached the point when we can no longer either tolerate our own vices, or the remedies which would cure us of them.' Four hundred years later St Jerome was to declare: 'The Barbarians' power is founded upon our own sins!' It was no longer for the emperor and his jurists to attempt to restore the healthy foundations of Roman society. Nothing less than a radical change in the very bases of morality itself, and in its effects upon the individual's mind, would now suffice.

## SORES IN THE SOCIAL STRUCTURE OF ROMAN SOCIETY

Exactly the same fundamental causes of decay which affected the moral life of the Roman world affected its social structure too. However powerful an impression of equilibrium and stability it might convey, there was something stultified about it. In some respects it seemed to be suffering from a number of severe internal wounds. As the last centuries of the Classical Age drew to their close, humanity suffered more and more obviously from that evil which invariably destroys civilizations: the disappearance of social values. In so far as Christianity was to put itself forward as a social doctrine (and it would be necessary for it to fix its limits in this respect with some firmness), this crisis in pagan society was to be of considerable importance to it, and would help to ensure its eventual success.

Here, as everywhere, money was the real root of the evil. The over-rapid enrichment of society, due to the conquests, had led to the rise of a thorough-going type of capitalism, very different from our own, being much more sterile and damaging than that of the modern world, since it was based, not upon industrial enterprise, which produces goods from which the whole social structure benefits, but on the monopoly of gold and land. This capitalism of the *latifundia* acquired unbelievably vast proportions, despite periodic protests on the part of this or that far-sighted individual critic: half of Roman Africa, for instance, belonged to six men alone! The men who profited most from the enormous spoils of military victory, and

THE ROMAN EMPIRE IN THE FIRST CENTURY

those gaining most from the exploitation of land,[13] were generally one and the same. In this way a very small class of extremely wealthy individuals grew up, closely connected with the government and the administration, and separated from the inferior strata of society by an enormous financial gulf.

Thus a serious lack of balance existed between a small, pleasure-loving aristocracy and the enormous mass of the people, which only received the crumbs of all these benefits of Roman civilization. The historians rarely bother to mention these deprived folk, all the unimportant artisans, unemployed workmen and cosmopolitan *peregrini*. The joys and sufferings of the *humiliores* are not so interesting as the deeds and actions of the Caesars. But if we really want to understand the mechanism of Christian expansion we must not lose sight of these insignificant folk, the carders, fullers, ropemakers and shopkeepers of all descriptions, who lived crowded together in immense four- or five-storeyed tenements, whose dark rooms only opened out on to connecting corridors. Governments scarcely ever gave them a thought, save to ensure that they remained quiet; under the Empire they were not even electors any more.[14]

Roman society was not merely unbalanced: it was rigidly fixed, and it became increasingly so as time went by. We are now very far away indeed from those republican days when

[13] Here we can see the fundamental cause of the Empire's eventual economic ruin. To a large extent the Roman system rested on the exploitation of the conquered territories. But the more Rome spent the larger she had to become. While a victorious Rome was annexing and pillaging her economy seemed prosperous. But as soon as her expansion ceased the Empire was incapable of finding sound bases for her economy again. She was virtually bankrupt, and underwent all the evils of crumbling regimes: financial embarrassment, excessive taxation and inflation.

[14] However, it should be noted that the condition of the *humiliores* was, in a sense, less hard than that of the proletariat of a century ago, during the period when modern industry was coming into being. Work, for those who practised it, had nothing in common with our mechanized work. It did not take up the whole day. As is customary in the East today, there were several rest periods. It was not brutalizing, as factory work used to be a hundred years ago, and still is today in many respects. A poor *plebs*, which still retained spiritual happiness and the joy of living, was better off than a proletariat stupefied by the machine.

every free man had his chance to carve a great career for himself in the *cursus honorum*. The masters of Rome tried to react against the dangers of social disintegration which they saw, all too clearly, before their eyes. But how? It is an old mistake in rulers of every age to imagine that a society can be saved by freezing its hierarchies. When the demagogic crisis in which the Republic had collapsed amid the conflicts of rival ambitions had ended in the destruction of the democratic system, Augustus had replaced it by a carefully departmentalized organization which rested on that most detestable of principles, a descending monetary scale. At the top were the senators, who had to possess one million sesterces (two hundred and sixty-five thousand gold sovereigns). Reserved for them were a large number of important and lucrative posts. They were to be created into a hereditary *nobilitas* by a decree of Augustus which extended the prerogatives of the 'laticlaves' to the third generation. After the senators came the knights, who had to be worth four hundred thousand sesterces. They too were a privileged class, linked with the Empire's development by their occupation of several major official positions and by their innumerable business enterprises within it. Moreover, from the reign of Claudius onwards they became the second grade of the nobility. And below them? Below them there was nothing: only the plebs, the common people, without wealth, privileges or hope.

This rigid system, which may be compared with that evolved by Peter the Great of Russia at a later date, claimed to allot each section of society its exact place in that society. In actual fact it starved it of the very thing which prevents human society from dying of what can be called structural sclerosis, of those egalitarian currents which allow men's energies and legitimate ambitions to come to the surface. The *new men*, many of whom had done much to create the Empire's glory, hardly ever penetrated its higher circles any more, save by force, when they were able to apply it. Exceptional elevations into the ruling classes are indeed quoted—cases of men of low birth, even of freed slaves, reaching the very top of the social scale—but the circumstances of these promotions are usually so extraordinary or so suspicious that they serve to shock rather than to point a lesson.

In the great cities of the Empire there was one condition
worse than that of the common people: the lot of the slaves.
This was the running sore in the flesh of the classical world.
Today it fills modern man with astonishment; but he forgets,
of course, that certain aspects of the present-day existence of
the working classes may scandalize the historian writing a thousand years to come just as much! Slavery was an absolute necessity in an economic system where energy was scarce, owing to
the lack of machines. It both supported and undermined the
regime at one and the same time. We have already noticed
how it tended to ruin the free workman, owing to the cheap
manual labour that it provided. By putting one class of human
beings in a position of complete dependence upon another, it
encouraged hardness of heart, injustice and, when one thinks
of the circumstances in which many female slaves were placed,
many types of immorality. The Early Empire tried in vain to
reconcile these two contradictory facts: firstly, its vital need of
slavery, and secondly, its increasingly strong feeling that the
institution was vicious in principle.

When considering an institution as vast as classical slavery,
there is no doubt whatsoever that the observer ought to judge
it differently in different cases, and not regard it all as uni-
formly bad. The servile state varied from case to case. Several
inscriptions show us that relationships of genuine affection
and mutual trust existed between masters and slaves. When
Seneca advised men to treat their slaves as 'humble friends,'
and the Younger Pliny confessed himself overwhelmed with
grief at the serious illness of one of his servants, their sentiments must have found echoes in the hearts of many other
slaveowners. Although the condition of slaves on the land was
often appalling, largely because they had to work in gangs
under foremen who were frequently very brutal, while the lot
of those in the mines was even worse, slaves who belonged to
the State, 'to Caesar's house,' had far less to complain of, and
domestic slaves were generally well treated. In certain cases
it was better to be the slave of a wealthy, kindly master than
to be a very poor free artisan. Moreover, a slave always possessed the hope of possible freedom in the future. This could
be obtained either by a payment or by an act of mercy on the
master's part. Once freed, the former slave could quickly

acquire equality with the free-born, or at least his children could.

But even allowing for these considerable variations in the condition of different slaves, it still remains true to say that the slave's life was a most unhappy one. It was unhappy even for those who had been slaves from birth; it was much worse for prisoners of war and victims of piracy, who continued to be offered for sale in the markets. The virtual absence of all civil and religious rights made the slave, in law, less than a man: a tool without a mind or feeling, a chattel, *res*, according to the ancient Latin juridical expression. And though it is undoubtedly true that during the first centuries of the Empire a trend of thought did exist—inspired first of all by the philosophers, and then, later on, by Christianity—which urged men to regard the slave more humanely, there was another trend, too, which was never to disappear. Some owners, impelled by mistrust or pride in their own superior position, treated their slaves with extreme severity.[15]

In fact the thing which slavery revealed most strikingly, though it was apparent in all other spheres of Roman life too, was the fundamental contradiction inherent in the very system on which the Empire was based. The universalism which the Empire had made its principle and its pride was far from being all-embracing. It merely covered a group of privileged people. The capital of the world excluded millions from its bosom. Barriers had been raised between the free man and the slave, the rich and the poor, the civilized man, that is to say the Graeco-Roman, and the 'barbarian.' The idea that loss of liberty meant that the loser no longer had any right to be regarded as a man, and the view that when a man's fortune declined he ought to be officially downgraded in the scale of values, hallowed an injustice which was infinitely deeper and

[15] The two trends are well brought out in an incident which took place in Nero's reign. An important magistrate had been murdered by one of his slaves, and, after long discussion, the Senate decided to apply the ancient law which laid down that all the slaves belonging to such men should be crucified, since they had not known how to protect them properly. However, there were so many protests at this terrible sentence that the four hundred condemned people could be executed only with an army standing guard over them to prevent interference by the sympathetic onlookers.

more fundamental than anything suffered in our own age. The imperial system rested upon a certain definition of human hierarchies; but this definition was false, even in its basic principle.

However, it would be quite wrong to think that the Early Roman Empire was a breeding-ground for revolutionary aspirations, in the sense in which we use the expression today. Lasalle's 'brazen law of wages' did not operate in terms of modern dialectic. The unprivileged masses did not react to their miserable state by revolting against it. In general their attitude was rather one of scepticism and political cynicism, which mattered little. Now and then they would give their support to some ambitious adventurer, who would appeal to the urban or military proletariat in his effort to break down the social barriers in his favour. The vague desire of the unprivileged for change showed itself, and would continue to show itself increasingly, in the form of dictatorial adventures. Such is the meaning of Tacitus's astute comment on the serious crisis of 68–9, 'The secrets of the Empire were surrendered'; for this is indeed the first occasion on which the historian can see that henceforth power is at stake between the injustice of an established order and the equal injustice of violence.

The slave class itself scarcely felt any of this new, though dim, awareness of strength. Its will to rebel was sporadic and limited in character; e.g. in 71 B.C. Spartacus the Thracian had stirred up his formidable bands of armed slaves and held the legions at bay for two years; and in A.D. 24, according to Tacitus, 'Rome trembled before an uprising of rural slaves.' But slavery was still too vital a part of the system to be seriously questioned by anyone. A thousand years were to pass before it finally crumbled away. At that time spiritual aspirations and technical progress would join hands, simultaneously enabling and compelling its suppression. In the first four centuries of our era, however, all that the millions of human beings who were refused the very name of men were waiting for was for someone to teach them to raise their heads.

## The Revolution of the Cross

Such is the general moral and social picture presented by
the Roman Empire during the first two centuries of the Christian era. One has but to consider it again at the end of the
fourth and it is immediately apparent that everything has
changed completely. Whilst the foundations of the classical
system were to be destroyed, society would, by this time, have
discovered new bases on which to live, and these bases would
be Christian ones. A new set of personalities would have
picked up the reins of government that the old, worn-out
cliques had abandoned; and these new people would be Christians. The concept of the world that had been traditional to the
pagan Graeco-Romans would have been largely discarded, and
what remained of it transformed and transfigured by the Gospel message. A change in the foundations of a system; the
replacement of one ruling class by another; a new *Weltanschauung*: these are the three very characteristics which define
a revolution.

Herein, so far as the historian is concerned, lies the supreme
phenomenon of the first four centuries A.D., the phenomenon
that has rightly been called the *Revolution of the Cross*. It is
obvious that such a name could lend itself to all sorts of mis-
interpretations, were its limits not rigidly laid down. Christianity is not, in itself, a 'revolutionary force' in the social-
political sense in which the phrase is used nowadays. It is
neither a social nor a political doctrine. Nor is it a moral
system, as understood by classical philosophy; that is to say
its moral philosophy is not an end in itself, but a result, during
our mortal lifetimes, of principles which totally transcend this
life.[16] It is no more and no less than the revelation of eternal
and complete truth, given us through the teaching, example,
death and resurrection of Jesus, who is God made man. However, at the same time, for the simple reason that it is 'the Way,
the Truth, the Life,' Christianity's contact ensures the destruction of all the things that are false, sham and outworn in the

[16] 'Be perfect as your Heavenly Father is perfect.' These were
Jesus' words, and the whole of Christian morality stems from this
simple precept.

contemporary world. Such is the real meaning of the Revolution of the Cross.

It is an eternal law of history that, in order to pass effectively into deeds, all revolution has need of three fundamental and simultaneously present attributes: a revolutionary *situation*, a revolutionary *doctrine* and a revolutionary *personnel*. In the Empire's Golden Age outward appearances hardly seemed to favour revolution. But a 'revolutionary situation is not necessarily a situation in which revolution is on the verge of starting or of being successfully concluded. It merely implies a more or less open questioning of all those moral and social standards by which people have become accustomed to live, a crumbling of old values, a change in the balance of forces which go to make up the particular appearance of a society at a certain moment in history. A revolutionary situation can exist even though open revolution is far away.'[17] This, precisely, was the sort of situation that existed in the Empire in the glorious period of the Caesars, the Flavians and the Antonines; but the more time went by the more obviously was a necessary connection established between the revolutionary situation and the underlying desire for revolution.

Christianity was to put forward the revolutionary doctrine for which the ancient world was waiting, simply because, on all the essential points which were being questioned by the human conscience of the period, on all those matters in which society was soon to be acutely conscious of its own shortcomings, the Gospel offered valid answers and solutions. The 'new birth' obtainable through baptism would assure the Christian of the renewal of vital forces which a profound, inevitable transformation of his very being had made impossible for the civilized Roman. Where all the legislative efforts of the emperors to rebuild the bases of sexual and family morality had failed, the Gospel appeal to purity was to prove successful; the crisis affecting the institution of marriage and the birthrate would be resolved at last. The Christian attitude to work placed the subject in an entirely new light by insisting that labour sanctified the individual who performed it. This com-

---

[17] The author has taken these excellent sentences from one of the finest political commentators of our age, Albert Ollivier, who formerly wrote for the French newspaper *Combat*.

pletely broke with the idleness and sloth of which the classical world was dying,[18] while Christ's terrifying condemnations of the injustices of wealth and the abuses of mammon sufficed to keep the new Christian society free of that passion for gold which was the pagan world's most serious disease. To the false universalism of Rome, with its extremely limited number of beneficiaries, Christianity was to oppose the true universalism of the Gospel, according to which there are no longer 'Greeks or Jews,' slaves and freemen, rich and poor, but only brothers in Jesus Christ. A society rigidly moulded into its hierarchies and caste privileges was to see rising up beside it another, absolutely egalitarian society, in which the humblest of believers could, by his virtues alone, attain the highest place in the episcopal system. And when, at last, the ageing Empire followed the inevitable custom of every society in decline and ground the individual increasingly harshly beneath the weight of an oppressive centralized administration, it was Christianity which, being founded completely upon the rights and duties of the individual conscience, was to step forward as the champion of the rights and liberties of the common man.

Consequently Christian doctrine was a revolutionary doctrine in the most obvious sense of the term; and, it should be added, it was also a doctrine inclining entirely towards positive action. For the ancient world had known many other doctrines which had judged life and mankind just as lucidly as that of the Christians. Stoicism is one example of these. It was a doctrine that had many adherents among the finest minds in the Early Empire. But the Stoic's lesson ended in a rejection of life, in a kind of tacit resignation from it. What Seneca desired was 'to be left in peace, living with myself alone.' Epictetus advised men to 'have need of no one, and to shun all company,' and, from the lofty heights of the imperial throne itself, where the demands of action held him prisoner, Marcus Aurelius thought nostalgically of 'that most peaceful and carefree of retreats, which man makes for himself in the depths of his

---

[18] Here it is opportune to remember St Paul's famous sentence: 'The man who refuses to work must be left to starve!' (2 Thess. iii. 10). What a complete condemnation of the Roman idlers, of the *sportula* hunters! And the fact that this sentence was adopted, word for word, by Lenin is a clear indication of its revolutionary character.

own soul.' How different, this, from the lesson which Jesus never stopped preaching, that man saves his soul only by devoting himself to others, that charity is the human action *par excellence*, that it is necessary to help one's fellow men in order to find personal fulfilment! Thus Christianity not only showed itself to be a revolutionary doctrine; it contained within it an incomparable reserve of strength to sustain the men and women who were to put its principles into practice.

Here we have the third fundamental attribute: Christianity was to possess a revolutionary personnel, that is to say men who were determined to ensure the triumph of their cause, and who made this their sole aim in life. The Church was an autonomous and complete society of its own, almost a state within the state. It possessed its own system of government, its hierarchy and organization, and its own discipline. The Church entered classical society fortified by an extraordinarily effective dialectic, which enabled it to use the conditions offered it by the Empire for its own ends, and to establish itself within the very framework of Roman society, without ever allowing itself to deviate from its path, or to contaminate its soul. Here it was, *in* this decaying world, but without being in any way *a part of* this world. To act effectively in a society man is bound to accept a certain detachment and separation from that society, as Christ had taught his followers.

He had taught them something else besides: the morality of heroism, which asked man to sacrifice himself for the cause in advance, counting his own life as nothing. The 'revolutionary personnel' of the early Christians was to consist of all those countless hosts of martyrs in whom the spirit of sacrifice would be pushed to heights normally unattainable by mere humanity, martyrs who awaited and even desired death from the circus lions or the executioner's sword in order to declare their faith. Carlyle pointed to the supreme and really revolutionary meaning of this sacrifice, when he wrote that in every age, place and situation it was the hero's characteristic to return to realities, and to rely on things and not on the appearances of things. In the first few centuries of our era reality no longer meant the Ancient World, ostentatiously strong in its outward appearances, but rotten at its roots;

reality meant that new world which was waiting to be born, and whose heralds were the Christians.

These are the elements defining the Revolution of the Cross on the historical and sociological plane. But here it is essential to hold to firm limits in comparing it—as compare it one must —with other historical revolutions. One vital difference must be emphasized, in order to make it quite clear at what point this causal examination is incapable of giving a total explanation of the Church's triumph (which is, in fact, unquestionably ascribable to a divine mystery). To win success all the revolutions of history, save this one, have made use of violence and trickery, and although their adherents may have given personal witness of rare qualities of brotherhood and self-denial, the forces which they have brought into action have given rise to the darkest characteristics of human nature, to envy and to resentment. 'Nothing is achieved without the great lever of hate,' said Proudhon. The Revolution of the Cross was the only revolution which, in intention as in methods, always appealed to all that was most contrary to man's fallen nature, and which never used the secret allies of instinct and self-interest for its own ends. It counselled its followers to love their enemies, and to forgive them their sins; it told them to be humble, to practise complete renunciation of self. What other example exists of the world transforming itself in the name of principles like these? And what other instance is there of a political victory being gained by the use of truth and justice alone? This mystery is just as deep—and, moreover, is it not the same one?—as that of the Messiah 'conquering the world' in submitting to death upon the Cross.

Thus it is very clear that it was not by ordinary methods of political and social revolution that Christianity was to enter the world. The changes in the established order, the replacement of rulers, the over-turning of current doctrines, were but consequences of that entry. Christianity is a religious revelation, and it was in fact as a religious revolution alone that it made its stand, and as a religious revolution that it was to triumph.

### RELIGIOUS CONFORMITY AND
### SPIRITUAL DOUBTS

As protagonists of a new faith, the bearers of new dogmas, what kind of religious situation were the Christians to encounter in the Roman world? To put it briefly, civilizations always die of a drying up of their religious sap, of an antagonism which grows up between the fundamental aspirations of the human soul and the frameworks in which societies seek to confine those aspirations. Had the Roman religion been established on sound foundations, had it been at one with the living conscience of the Empire, a new faith would scarcely have had the opportunity to establish itself there. But here too the cracks were manifold, and they were increasing all the time.

Roman religious life during the first two centuries A.D. presents some blatantly contradictory characteristics. If the externals alone are considered, it would seem that the citizen's whole existence was permeated by religion. Even the most sceptical of Romans did not want to dispense with all the elaborate ceremonies marking various stages in the year and in individuals' lives, with the prayers which divided up the different periods of the day, or with the whole collection of customary religious rites, precepts and prohibitions. The modern concept of *secularism* had no place whatsoever in the classical soul, where, as must never be forgotten, the traditional religion was but a sacral expression of citizenship, a token of devotion and adherence to the city-state, which was the basis of society; its priests were the civic magistrates, and, naturally enough, the great men who travelled the *cursus honorum* sought and bore titles of a sacerdotal character, those of *flamen* and *augur*, for example, even though they no longer had the slightest belief in the religious reality attached to these offices.

What did this framework of beliefs represent in terms of a living religious force? It is extremely difficult to give a judgment on this, and undoubtedly a distinction must be drawn between the most highly educated elements of society and the common people, whose reactions to it were vastly different. For both the ancient national religion had ceased to exist in a pure form. For more than four hundred years it had been adopting features suggested to it by Greece, and a series of classical identifications between Greek and Roman legendary heroes enabled the Roman Pantheon to be endowed with a mythology that the less imaginative Latins could never themselves have invented. These fables found absolutely no credence among the rulers of Rome and the educated classes. Claudius Pulcher, who drowned the sacred chickens to prevent them from giving an omen of ill luck, and Marcellus, who smilingly drew the curtains of his litter so as to avoid seeing the portents, belong to the same class as that great lady who is described by the Younger Pliny as asserting 'that she did not care a fig for Jupiter.' Greek rationalism had accustomed educated folk to reject the incredible and often immoral stories contained in Greek fable, and Juvenal was certainly summing up a generally held opinion when he wrote: 'Even the children no longer believe in spirits of the departed and an underground kingdom of the dead, or that there are black frogs in the Styx, and a boatman armed with a boathook who can ferry millions of folk across the river in one small boat!'

To what extent had this scepticism percolated the popular strata of society? It appears that the old religious rites which dated right back to the earliest days of Latin tribal government were still very much alive, and would remain so for a long time to come; there was the cult of the Lares and Penates, for example, which endured so long that Theodosius was forced to issue a decree, proscribing it specifically, as late as the fourth century, when the Empire was already officially Christian. The *Didascalia*, a third-century Christian document, attacks the Christians for their religious negligence, compared with the zeal shown by the pagans for their gods. There are countless proofs that scattered among the common people there resided a genuine faith in deities closely linked to the soil and to the natural elements, such as the ancient goddess Anna Perenna of the Tiber, whose festival was regarded by educated sceptics as but one more excuse for a drinking bout (rather as our present-day midnight revellers consider Christmas), but who was looked upon by the ordinary Italiot labourer with that mixture of faith and superstition so easily adopted by even the modern European peasant.

This mixture of belief and scepticism is admirably set out in *Octavius*, a Christian text dating from the end of the second century. Its author, Minucius Felix, attempts to put the philosophy of a typical Roman into words: 'Since we know nothing of the divine, nor of Providence, save that fortune is fickle, is it not best, in our ignorance of the truth, to remain loyal to traditional ways, to honour the gods of our fathers, those gods towards whom, since our childhood, we have been used to feeling sentiments of fear and adoration, rather than an over-familiar intimacy?' The recognition of the existence of a divine principle, of a *deus* who to some was the pantheist power of the Stoics, to others, something even more intangible, but whom it was convenient to honour by rites and forms which derived from the very heart of ancient tradition: this was the religious attitude most generally accepted throughout imperial society.

Moreover, it was on this kind of attitude that Augustus based his attempt at religious restoration, whereby he hoped to complete his great work of political reconstruction. Temples were rebuilt, altars set up again, the office of priest of Jupiter, which had been in abeyance for sixty-five years, was re-established with extraordinary ceremony, and a great celebration known as the 'jubilee games' was held, which purported to commemorate the foundation of Rome by the gods. Augustus's sole object throughout was to make use of ancient traditions in order to shore up his own power. His successors were to work along similar lines, trying either to restore or patch up the ancient religious structure which had made Rome great, or attempting to rejuvenate it by incorporating new elements into it; but always as part of the exercise of their absolute power, and for their own personal glorification.

It need hardly be added that these official practices and popular rites could scarcely satisfy those who were genuinely looking for God and for the real meaning of life. And these sorts of people were increasingly numerous. It would be utterly wrong to imagine that, at the moment when Christianity was about to enter it, the religious soul of the Early Empire was atrophied by scepticism, frozen by official formal-

ism, or degraded by superstition. These elements of decadence undoubtedly existed (and were actually fast increasing), but they were compensated for by a frequently intense
spiritual activity and a deep mystical longing, which could be
seen among several sections of society.

Once again this new religious contribution came from the
East, yet another result of the Roman conquests. It was the
Greek philosophers and the Eastern cults that taught metaphysical speculation to the old pragmatic Roman, who, in his
relations with his own gods, was so obsessed by exact calculations of sacrifices and services. Asia, cradle of religions,
opened the eyes of the Roman world to a loftier spiritual
life. Disgruntled conservatives like Juvenal might well write
angrily: 'The Orontes is pouring into the Tiber!'; for henceforth the transformation of the Roman soul was an accomplished fact. The same men who, in their role of imperial
magistrates, could be seen presiding solemnly over cults in
which they no longer believed gave their real faith to the
deities of Syria and Egypt, and ecstatically celebrated the
mysteries of Orpheus or Dionysus, or else sought to understand the world and humanity through the postulates of
Greek philosophy. Here was another sign of the fundamental
flaw which was rotting the Empire's soul; Rome started having a true religious life, in our sense of the phrase, only at
the moment when the official religion ceased to have any hold
over her people.

The intellectuals sought their answers to the great problems
of humanity in Greek philosophy. When a cultured man of
the Early Empire pondered upon God, his thought ran something like this: Is He, as Plato teaches, the perfect planner,
the abstract idea of good, intelligence in its purest form? Or is
He the prime driving force, the necessary agent, the immutable and perfect activity of which Aristotle speaks? Might He
not be merely the impersonal harmony in which Epicurus's
disciples believe, the very face of order and beauty? Or, as Stoic
doctrines maintain, the anonymous wisdom and pantheist
principle which the presence of this earth seems to pre-sup-
pose? All these ideas were to exist throughout the first few
centuries A.D. under the forms of Neo-Platonism, Neo-Aris-
totelianism and Neo-Stoicism; in other words, as the names

indicate, all tended to lose their original fecundity and purity. Moreover, they affected only a few restricted circles.

It was quite another story so far as the Eastern cults were concerned. These had penetrated the Roman mind long before the start of the Christian era, and possessed adherents among all sections of the population. As early as 204 B.C., in the middle of the Punic War, Rome had sought out the 'Great Mother,' the goddess Cybele of Phrygia, in order to make certain of a supernatural ally in the struggle against Hannibal, and she had been installed on the Palatine in the form of the black stone of Pessinonte. When Scipio had vanquished the Carthaginians at Zama two years later, the feat was regarded as miraculous, and the goddess was considered to have acquired Roman citizenship thereby. From that time onwards processions of her worshippers (*Galli*) were a regular feature of Roman life. Clad in multicoloured gowns and wearing scarlet 'Phrygian bonnets' they escorted the young fir-tree, symbolizing the transformed Atys, through the streets, bewailing his death with rhythmic shouts, and throwing violets on to his bier. Then, during the first century B.C., it had been Egypt's turn to offer Rome her gods and her festivals; the followers of Isis, goddess of goodness, the consoler, certainly soon ran into thousands. These regularly celebrated the feasts of 'the sailing of the lady' on 5th March, or, in the autumn, the liturgical drama in which the divine wife sought and found the body of her husband Osiris, which had been cut into pieces by Seth, and brought him back to life. Countless other gods and goddesses followed these, for the East teemed with deities! There were the Phoenician Astarte, the Syrian Aphrodite, the 'Beast-Goddess' of Anatolia, the dead and resurrected Adonis of Byblos, the handsome Tammuz, whom one invoked with arms upstretched. . . . This flood of Eastern gods continued to pour into Rome throughout the first few centuries A.D.: Baal of Commagene, Malagbel of Palmyra, Dusaris, an Arabian god —every single one of the deities whom Rome encountered on her triumphant progress was adopted by her in some form or other. Shortly before the beginning of the Christian era, Mithras, a deity originating in the Persian plateaus, who was discovered by the Roman armies in the East, began his astonishing career by taking root in Mesopotamia and Cappadocia, and very soon afterwards established himself in the western provinces of the Empire. Nero was initiated into his cult by the King of Armenia. The mighty Mithraic wave which was soon to overwhelm the Empire began to flow towards Rome about the end of the second century, when tens of thousands of Romans found their sole spiritual hope in the *taurobolium*.

On gaining the West all these Eastern religions assumed one almost universal characteristic, which they derived from certain cults among their number: they evolved into *mysteries*, that is to say, instead of putting themselves forward as open to all, their membership all on one level, and so following the laws and customs of the classical city-state, they kept themselves strictly to themselves, forming exclusive communities which required their adherents to undergo a specific ceremony of initiation. Did not the mysteries of Eleusis already exist in Greece, side by side with the official religion, and with adherents as far afield as Rome? And those of Dionysus-Bacchus, too, which had a special kind of attraction, on account of certain immoral characteristics? The ancient Orphic tradition, which was rich in myths and which delved deep into the mysteries of human understanding, permeated many of these esoteric cults, and occasionally gave them some sublime echoes.

What was the net result of all these complex and continually changing elements? So many aspects of this religious aspiration are naturally shocking to us: what did it really represent? A balanced judgment is difficult: the wave which seethed in the Empire's conscience was a tainted one, bringing with it not merely the noblest of hopes and fears but the most abject of depravities. But it is certainly a complete distortion of the general picture to interpret this mystical trend solely in terms of the scandals of the Bacchanalia, the rites of castration connected with the *Galli*, the religious prostitution of the female worshippers of Astarte, or even the frenzied dances and hymns characteristic of various cults. The best of these doctrines, which had all, moreover, passed through the double screen of Greek intelligence and Latin common sense, contained some very praiseworthy elements. A yearning for a more intimate religion, an ascetic effort towards moral purity, a desperate quest for a personal union with the divine: these are eminently fine ideals, and they were pursued by many sincere people. Cicero, a follower of the mysteries of Eleusis, had already declared that they 'made life happy, and enabled one to die with the consolation of a splendid hope'; this was approximately what most people demanded of this or that type of Eastern religion. All that was finest in the classical soul was yearning for *salus*, *salus* no longer regarded in the commonplace sense in which the ancient Romans had understood the word, namely as a healthily balanced earthly existence, but as the promise of a spiritual liberation and of eternal bliss. And this longing coincided with the moment when the Gospel was about to offer it the true doctrine of salvation.

## THE GOSPEL'S OPPORTUNITIES
### AND OBSTACLES

Thus in many respects the religious atmosphere prevailing at the opening of the Christian era offered a fertile soil for the sowing of the new faith. If, materially, the Roman Empire had traced the paths and marked out the boundaries within which the Gospel was to spread, it is probably also true to say that, on the spiritual plane, the whole of classical civilization should be considered a gigantic preparation for it. All those heart-searchings for truth made by past generations, from Akhenaton to Zoroaster, from Zoroaster to Plato—the spiritual current which had raised the human soul very near to God, in an ever-ascending progression from the original primitive cults associated with totemism and magic, the efforts made by so many fine minds and brilliant intellects to purify religion and to raise its standards, the increasingly strong yearning that the human soul might share in divine eternity—all these give a moving impression of a wealth of stubborn questing in the darkness, and of a forward movement towards the heart of the mystery. The fashionable passion for Asian religions and mysteries does more than simply add yet another element to an enormous total of temporary answers. It offers also a glimmer of hope for the future. The world turned eastwards, seeming to sense, in some confused way, that the light would come from there. And come indeed it did: 'There was one who enlightens every soul born into the world; He was the true light' (John i. 9). The call made by so many for a thousand years past had been heard.

Christianity contained the conclusive satisfaction of everything for which humanity had been longing in a more or less coherent fashion for centuries past. Precisely because, from its very beginnings, it appeared as a synthesis of apparently conflicting elements—the very synthesis of life itself—it fulfilled, in one fell swoop, a number of extraordinarily varied kinds of expectations. What complexity of contradictory desires had the religious thought of humanity reached at this point? It longed to know one universal God, who would go beyond the semblances of polytheism, and prove to be the essential cause and meaning of the world, on whom everything depended, and through whom everything existed. It wanted to look at the divine, not across the maze of philosophical abstractions and systems, but in the face of a being whom each individual could love, in whom each man could actually recognize something of himself. It sought to discover clear, positive answers to the fundamental questions concerning man, life, death, fate and time. The Gospel answered all these appeals of the human soul, and the Christian theology of the Incarnation, the Redemption and the Trinity, which were being gradually developed on the unshakable basis of Revelation, was to fill a need which had always existed in pagan philosophy. For the disciples of the mysteries, Christianity offered far more than they possessed, yet, at the same time, its universalist character enabled it to avoid the dangers of sectarian exclusivism. For the advocates of reason it presented itself with the absolute logic that only historical evidence could have, whilst it taught those inclined to pagan mysticism the real way of reaching out towards the ineffable, the path to spiritual reunion with the divine. It assumed and embodied all that religion had contained down the centuries, but in a decanted form, purified, freed of all taint. How limited the old religions seemed, and how ridiculous their practices, beside the teaching of Jesus the Messiah! For it was, in short, the personality of the Living God, in its wonderful purity and unique simplicity, which made one spiritual whole of all these contradictory attributes, revealing them to men in the example of His own life, through His teaching, His death and His resurrection.[19]

We must, then, take into account this ready soil and expectant need in order to understand the victory, on the spiritual plane as on every other, of the Revolution of the Cross. But here as elsewhere it is essential not to carry this idea so far as to suggest a determinist explanation of Christianity's success. In the first place this is because the undoubted religious preparation which can be observed in the classical world is not in itself sufficient 'explanation' for Christianity's triumph. During the first few centuries of the Christian era men were to witness one gigantic and strictly humanist attempt to answer all the questions posed by the soul by taking various elements from the different religions of the day and binding them together into one whole. This attempt was known as *Syncretism*. It was a phenomenon which acquired considerable importance during the third century. But Syncretism was an artificial conception, and because of this it was to be a failure. Its dogmas never went outside the bounds of scholastic exercises; they never grew into a life and a faith. 'Christianity is not a syncretism, but a synthesis, a synthesis which would never have been made without the action of an *absolutely new* element, of a new knowledge which was *not the end product* of previous religious systems. It was presented to the human mind from outside, from On High; this event was a fact whose existence was quite independent of human philosophy, and a thousand times superior to the projection and concentration that man-made philosophy could have created of its confused dreams on a purely human basis, necessitated by historic determinism. Humanity did not bear God in its womb; humanity did not engender the divine Jesus of Nazareth.'[20]

If then the religious ferment of the first few centuries A.D. does not explain the triumph of the Gospel in the theological

[19] It should be noted here that Judaism, which on several fundamental points gave the religious heart-searchings of the world answers which were perfectly correct ones, could not assume the decisive role which Christianity was to have, because its abstract monotheism alienated too many mystically inclined souls, and because its narrow legalism completely failed to possess the influential force of the doctrine of love.

[20] R. P. Allo, *L'Évangile en face du Syncrétisme païen*. Paris, 1910.

sense, it is just as true to say that, on a pragmatic plane, it was also not particularly favourable to its spread. By reinvigorating paganism, the Eastern religions had given the Ancient World a weapon against Christianity—a weapon that the pagans knew how to use. Mithraism, and later Syncretism, both attempted to fight the Gospel by entering its own territory. In the fourth century, at a time when the pendulum had already swung in the Cross's favour, Julian the Apostate tried desperately to unite all the energies and cults of paganism in order to oppose the single, unique adversary with one solid front. All the religious efforts of humanity alone had culminated only in partial truths; in one sense these half-truths helped the complete truth, while, at the same time, they offered the most insidious of resistances to it.

This was all the more so since, by its very nature, Christianity could not do what all the other Eastern faiths had done, and come to terms with the other forms of belief fashionable at the time, thus infiltrating among them by playing their own game. When the Imperium had seen its conscience being invaded by Eastern religions, its reaction had been very far from a categoric rejection. Very often it was the official authorities themselves who introduced new gods to Rome. It was true, of course, that there had been some opposition: that of the 'old Romans,' who were strongly attached to their ancestral traditions, that of the moralizers, who suspected the depraved rites of certain of these cults, and, now and then, that of a few politicians, who dreaded the moral chaos to which the Eastern invasion could lead. For example, Augustus, the conqueror of Cleopatra, had banned the worship of the Egyptian goddess Isis from within Rome's walls. But the sum total of such measures was small, and, moreover, very ineffective. Tacitus's comments on the Chaldean soothsayers and other charlatans, 'They are chased out with one hand, while the other is busy taking them up again,' was even truer of the Eastern religions. Several emperors were their adherents, and even their priests. They regarded those exotic deities, who had become acclimatized to Rome, as nothing more nor less than allies, with whom they could come to terms in order to strengthen, politically, the spiritual bases of their own authority.

But it was impossible to treat Christianity in this fashion, even though some of the emperors would have liked to do so. Christianity refused to be considered along with all the other cults that had derived from Asia. Even in those elements where some resemblance might have been found between it and them, it worked assiduously to differentiate itself from them. Its God destroyed the pagan gods; He did not mix with them. This alone was enough to make the Roman mind resist the newcomer. When the imperial magistrates subsequently accused the Christians of impiety and blasphemy, they were from their point of view, entirely right in so doing; between rigid monotheism and pantheism there was no conceivable area of agreement. And the more polytheism grew, as was the case during the first few centuries A.D., the more it was, in fact if not in theory, hostile to the religion of the one God. Thus the religious ferment was as much of an obstacle as an aid to Christian expansion: here we come back to the dialectic law which was to demand from the Christians a heavy sum of sacrifice and struggle as the price of victory.

And on this point we see, once more, the fundamental opposition which we have already observed on the political plane: the cult of 'Rome and Augustus' appealed to a large part of the mystical stream which watered the soul of the age, attracting it by its appearances of simple loyalism. Imperial idolatry rested on a pantheistic conception of the universe: once the former was destroyed the latter would collapse too. The faithful worshippers of Isis or Mithras could be monarchists in the exact sense in which the Masters of the World understood monarchy, and this, in the last resort, was why the Empire propitiated them. But between the divinely ordained authority in the sense in which the Empire was to define and strengthen itself from dynasty to dynasty, and the men who refused to acknowledge its very foundations, there was no possible area of agreement whatsoever. The only logical conclusion was opposition.

## THE BEGINNINGS OF OPPOSITION

The Revolution of the Cross had in fact begun the very day when Jesus uttered His famous words 'My kingdom is not of this world!' and when a few men had, in following His example, opted for 'the kingdom which is not of this world' in preference to earthly possessions and powers. Let Caesar reign in Rome! What did it matter? The real Master was elsewhere, sitting beside the Father, in divine eternity. The opposition between Empire and Cross was as fundamental and substantial as it could possibly have been: however, it was not immediately apparent. History proves this: societies, like individuals, never notice the germs growing within them, which are eventually to prove fatal.

At first, as we have seen, the Empire ignored the Christians: Julian the Apostate was shrewd enough to observe this; the life, teaching and tragedy of Jesus passed completely unnoticed by imperial contemporaries. The apostolic utterances would have aroused no more interest in Rome than the obscure propaganda of religious agitators indigenous to Madagascar or Ceylon does in Western Europe today. We have to wait until the year 112 before we find an official document —the letter of the Younger Pliny to Trajan—referring to the Christians, and until the year 116 for Tacitus to devote a few paragraphs of his *Annales* to them. In the early days, people who were concerned with the Christians usually confused them with the members of the Jewish communities among whom they had taken root[21] and in whose bosom they provoked a

21 Moreover, this confusion with the Jews was not particularly favourable to the Christians, for a very hostile attitude existed towards the Jews in the Roman world, running exactly contrary to the goodwill shown the Chosen Race by one or two notable political figures. Marcus Aurelius was to refer to 'this noisy, stinking race.' All kinds of ridiculous gossip was rife concerning Jewish habits. Cicero, Plutarch, Diodorus of Sicily and Tacitus are almost as stupid on this subject as avowed anti-Semites like Apollonius of Rhodes or Appion. The mob's love of malicious absurdities is well known, and it is easy to imagine what the Roman mob had to say on this subject. Why did the Jews refuse to eat pork? Because they worshipped a pig-God of course! Unless this idol was a donkey, as many averred. (This tale recurs in the calumnies made against the Christians.) The Egyptian historian Manethon reported that the Jews were descended from a tribe of lepers, and were probably not properly cured of the disease themselves! As for circumcision, it provided a wonderful topic for salacious jokes about 'the skinned ones.' And another revolting tale was also whispered from mouth to mouth: each year, or at least once every seven years, it was said, the Jews kidnapped some Greek or

number of disturbances; and though, at Rome, from 63 onwards, Nero's police seem to have discriminated against them
specifically, this was certainly not the case everywhere. Furthermore, even when Christians were recognized as such, they
were at first regarded merely as yet one more Eastern sect, on
the same level as the worshippers of Astarte or the magicians
of Chaldea. The Empire, in its role as the established authority, could not see the fundamental difference which separated
them from the other Asian devotees, or the radical threat
which they were to offer its principles.

For their part the Christians were no better aware of the
real situation facing them. They considered themselves perfectly loyal subjects of the emperor, and bore themselves as
such. 'Give back to Caesar what is Caesar's, and to God what
is God's!' This precept of Christ's gave doctrinal foundation
to a Christian loyalism of which we possess numerous proofs.
We have already seen how, in the Epistle to the Romans, St
Paul expressly commanded: 'Every soul must be submissive to
its lawful superior; authority comes from God only, and all
authorities that hold sway are of his ordinance' (Rom. xiii).

In his first letter to Timothy he actually asked that 'petition,
prayer, entreaty and thanksgiving should be offered for all mankind, especially for kings and others in high station, so that
we can live a calm and tranquil life, as dutifully and decently
as we may' (1 Tim. ii. 1–2). St Peter, writing soon after Nero's
persecution in 64, urged submission to authority nevertheless,
thus silencing the rasher spirits who were calling for rebellion,
and ordering that respect be shown to the sovereign. 'Give all
men their due; to the brethren, your love; to God, your reverence; to the king, due honour' (1 Pet. ii. 17). Some years later
St Clement of Rome was to compose a noble prayer for
princes and all those who ruled the earth; and these same
protestations of loyalty and obedience can be found again and
again throughout Christian apologetic literature, in the writing

---

Roman, sacrificed him according to their rite and then ate his heart.
As a result of commercial jealousy, which was increased by these
ridiculous stories, anti-Jewish feeling sometimes erupted into real
pogroms, such as the one which went on for a month in Alexandria
in 38, causing dreadful bloodshed. To a large extent, anti-Christian
feeling was to be moulded on anti-Semitism.

of Aristides and St Justin, for example, and even in that of the
fiery Tertullian, who was to declare: 'The Christian ranks have
never contained a single rebel, conspirator or assassin.' This
was a perfectly logical attitude, for in fact it was not in the
field of direct action that the opposition between Christianity
and the Empire existed.

Yet the fact that Christianity was above politics made it
no less certain that this conflict would inevitably appear. The
mob became conscious of its existence before the Government
did. It was human spite which first enlightened it, or, in some
areas, the sordid self-interest of some specific business concern.
The natural instinct which whips up the masses' hatred for the
nonconformists in their midst, and especially for those who
fail to conform in matters of the spirit, played the role of
policeman here, as in so many like cases. Undoubtedly the
fact that their own trade in sacrificial animals or pagan statuettes was suffering was enough to make certain folk hostile to
the Christians. In addition, as we shall see, a thousand and
one ugly rumours were popularly circulated concerning the
new sect's alleged indulgence in human sacrifice and secret
immorality. But at the back of its mind the pagan mob sensed
that the new doctrine was about to demand of it a dramatic
transformation, a complete change of heart. It hated all those
changes which the 'new race' wanted to make.

In this way, urged on by the *vox populi*, the public authorities were forced to take action. In very many instances, at
least in the early days, they did so only with extreme diffidence
and real moderation. Thus Trajan's instructions on the subject to Pliny, his representative in Bithynia, were highly circumspect. For a long time to come a number of imperial
officials were to retain an attitude of sceptical indulgence and
scorn towards the Christians; and by confusing certain expressions, such as 'Son of God' and 'Supreme King,' made out
that they were not, in fact, committing treason. But as the
Empire went further and further along the road of authoritarianism and absolutist centralization—as, in effect, it became more totalitarian—it grew increasingly aware of the gulf
which separated the Christians from official conformity, and
recognized them as its enemies. This evolution became very
marked from the end of the second century onwards, and by

this period it can be seen that it is the best rulers, those who
see the demands of their imperial office and the fundamental
needs of the regime most clearly, who are the Christians' fiercest persecutors.

Likewise, as the young Church became more conscious of its
own identity, its awareness of a fundamental cleavage between
it and the Empire was to increase. Just as Christianity had
had to make clear its differences from Judaism during the first
thirty years of its existence, in order to be able to live its own
independent life, so, during the first century A.D., it was forced
to establish itself, quite deliberately, outside the very framework of the empire in which it was developing. It did this
quite simply, merely by applying the Gospel teaching of 'the
kingdom which is not of this world.' Thus, around the year
110, the author of the *Letter to Diognetus* arrived at the following admirable formula, which put his opposition between
worldliness and godliness into words: 'Christians sojourn in a
country, but only as if they are passing through it. To them
there is no foreign country which is not their motherland, and
no motherland in which they are foreigners.' And a little later
on Tertullian declared, more brusquely: 'For us Christians,
nothing is so foreign as the Republic! We recognize but
one republic—the republic to which all men belong—God's
universe!'

Thus defined, this spiritual opposition was to lead the Christians to alter their whole attitude towards the Empire. Loyalism became mingled with an aspiration arising from the very
depths of the new Christian conscience, a hope of witnessing
the disappearance of the illusory earthly power and the establishment of God's kingdom, *hic et nunc*. Following this train
of thought, St John, in his Apocalypse, describes that same
Rome which St Paul had respected so highly as 'the woman
riding on a scarlet beast,' and the 'mother-city of all harlots,
and all that is abominable on earth' (Apocalypse xvii). One
day—and very soon, the author hoped—the world would see
this iniquitous city vanish from the earth, when the seven angels sounded their trumpets. Likewise, in the apocalyptic
book of Esdras, which is a noncanonical text, but one which
was studied a great deal by the early Christians, the writer
prophesies 'the death of the eagle, whose horrible wings, ac-

cursed pinions, evil heads and hateful talons' would disappear, so that tyranny on earth should cease and man rediscover justice and mercy.

It was now that the antagonism between Rome and the Cross became dramatically and tragically obvious. The Empire began to try to smash the new faith that was rising up in its midst: sporadically at first, then, increasingly, as part of a systematic political campaign. The persecutions started, and the long processions of martyrs were led to the circus arenas to meet their deaths. But the heroism of the first Christians was so great that violence was powerless to halt the progress of their beliefs. The martyrs who died that a new world might be born were stronger by far than the persecutors who resorted to violence in order to try to save a dying world. *Semen est sanguis christianorum*, as Tertullian was to remark. From the very moment that Rome's opposition to the Cross turned to bloodshed, that same opposition worked more efficaciously than ever to further the spread of Christianity.

# CHAPTER IV

# SACRIFICE OF BLOOD:
# THE CHURCH'S
# FIRST MARTYRS

## THE GARDENS OF NERO

ON THE NIGHT of 18th–19th July 64, the night-watchmen's trumpets resounded through Rome, giving the fire alarm. Fire was an extremely commonplace occurrence in this over-populated city. It contained far too many houses built of wood, packed far too closely together, and these offered the flames an ever-ready victim. But on this particular occasion the fire was an unusually vast one. The strong wind blew the smoke heavenwards, and the dark sky was turned to crimson. Very soon the hissing and crackling of the flames became deafeningly loud, and the fire seemed to be everywhere at once. It had first broken out among the crowded streets around the Great Circus, among the spice-booths and drapers' stalls there; it was fed by the stocks of oil kept on these premises and by a thousand and one other highly inflammable articles, and almost at once it engulfed the entire area around the Palatine and Coelian Hills. By the grey light of dawn the terrible catastrophe was already all too obvious. Gliding down the narrow alleyways, fastening itself on the poorest quarters of the city, now and then shooting up in prodigiously high cones of flame, the fire seemed to be completely irresistible. People were forced from their homes, to run hither and thither in howling groups, colliding one with another, like swarms of insects, searching, but all in vain, for a safe place of refuge. And no one stopped to think about the dead any more.

The tragedy lasted nearly one hundred and fifty hours. For six days and six nights the flames wandered at will throughout the length and breadth of Rome. When the fire was eventually brought under control at the foot of the Esquiline, after a fair number of buildings there had been completely destroyed in order to prevent the flames from getting the fuel they needed to spread further, the scene that men saw before their eyes resembled the end of the world. Of the city's fifteen districts, four had been burnt to the ground; in seven more, only fragments of wall and blackened, uninhabitable houses were still standing; the remaining four alone could be said to be unscathed. The hot, sickly stench of destruction was everywhere. And what the 'old Romans' mourned most—more than all their burnt-out mansions and their valuable personal possessions, now lost (all the Greek works of art and Eastern war loot that lay buried under the smouldering rubble)—was a whole collection of famous memories which had been a heritage from the venerable past of the city of the She-Wolf: the temple of the moon, built, so it was alleged, by Servius Tullius; the great altar and sanctuary of Hercules, consecrated in the dim and distant past by the Arcadian Evander; the temple of Jupiter Stator, which had been erected by Romulus himself; the temple of Vesta, where the city's Penates had been held in safe keeping. The catastrophe was irreparable: it seemed as though a blind destiny had wanted, not merely to wipe out the city as it was at present, but to obliterate its past as well.

What could have started the fire? It seems more than likely that it was completely accidental. The eight simultaneous areas of flame which some folk claimed to have noticed could well have been no more than the result of one fire in one solitary house being carried far afield by the wind, so fast did the flames take their hold. However, it would be wrong to exclude the possible accuracy of those contemporary hypotheses which put the whole affair down to a somewhat crude and brutal town-planning operation, an attempt to clear the capital of all its slums and enable a reconstruction to be made after the Alexandrine style, on a truly majestic scale. At all events the common people, who invariably dislike pinning the blame upon some abstract fate, refused to believe that one chance flame alone could have caused a disaster of such dimensions. A scapegoat was quickly found.

At that time the atmosphere in Rome was extremely tense. Nero's reign had passed the decisive turning-point when, after abandoning the relatively sensible path which Seneca and Burrhus, his first advisers, had done their utmost to preserve, the crowned monster was to hurl himself towards the abyss of self-destruction, surrounded by a thousand follies and drenched in waves of blood. Agrippina had been murdered on the orders of that same son for whom she had—by means of a dastardly crime—gained the throne. Tigellinus was beginning to be all-powerful; a few influential aristocrats and some of the emperor's freedmen had already succumbed to his prosecutions. The sweet-faced but savage-hearted Poppaea, whom the emperor had abducted from her husband, had just become his mistress. In order to marry her Nero had renounced Octavia, his lawful wife, after slandering her in the vilest fashion, and had eventually had her beheaded. This final crime had deeply inflamed public opinion; and the execution of the young empress, who was Claudius's daughter and a descendant of Augustus, had been marked by demonstrations which were extremely hostile to both the emperor and Poppaea. The sight of that young, severed head being borne before the royal concubine had made men's blood run cold. Rumours began to circulate concerning a mysterious punishment called down on Rome by Nero's crimes; superstitious tongues spread round the news of several prodigious happenings which were clearly of ill omen: there were tales of thunderbolts falling in all fifteen districts of the city at the same time, of uncanny deaths, of a woman giving birth to a serpent, and of a comet which was exactly the colour of blood. The emperor was at least morally responsible for the divine wrath that this fire betokened; might he not also be deeply implicated in it in a more material fashion?

People swore that this was so. The rumour that his menservants had been seen running through the slum areas of the city with burning brands in their hands gained strength. After all, he was considered quite perverted and evil enough for such a deed! His own imprudent sayings lent substance to the idea. How often had he not declared: 'A prince may do anything he likes!' It was said that on one occasion, after hearing the Greek line of Euripides, 'When I am dead, may the earth be consumed by fire!' he had retorted, in the same language: 'When I am alive!' One tale, which Suetonius preserves for us, put the crowning touch to the people's fury; it was said that while the fire was burning the emperor had been seated on the top of the Maecenan tower, dressed in actor's costume, where, his lyre in his hand, he had set to music the words of a poem he had written, about the capture of Troy and the fire kindled there by Agamemnon's warriors.[1]

The accusations gathered momentum. In vain Nero adopted a thoroughly generous and helpful attitude, throwing open the Martian Field, the buildings erected by Agrippa, and even his own gardens to house the wretches who had lost their homes, lowering the price of corn to next to nothing, and distributing it freely. Equally vainly, so far as his own popularity was concerned, he immediately began to rebuild the city, to a plan which was extremely enlightened at that time, granting large subsidies to property-owners, and mobilizing the army and the navy to clear away the debris. In the eyes of the public he was simply admitting, more and more blatantly, that he was indeed the man who had started the fire; and at this he took fright. Now it should be remembered that Nero, for all his natural cruelty and semi-madness, had always been extremely prone to fear. It was because he had been so terrified of Britannicus that he had had the latter liquidated; and he had rid himself of his own mother because her presence made him feel uncomfortable. After the fire of Rome the people's anger made his stomach writhe with fear: he had to provide a diversion, and quickly too.

The Christians supplied the answer. Why did Nero pick on them? It is very hard to say. Had measures already been taken against the new sect in the past? This is doubtful. It is true that Tacitus refers to a certain noblewoman named Pomponia Graecina who had been accused of 'foreign superstition' in 57, on account of her austere way of life and various other mannerisms, and who had been arraigned before the tribunal by her own husband, Aulus Plautius, in the name of the ancient law of Rome, but acquitted there of all the charges laid against her. Was she a Christian? It is possible that she was, but by no means certain. As for the exact motives be-

[1] This is in fact physically impossible. Nero was not in Rome at the time of the fire, but at Antium, by the sea, some seven miles from the capital. This does not mean that the play-acting braggart did not seize the opportunity to regale his court with a performance in which his poem fitted contemporary circumstances so exactly. This at any rate is Tacitus's version of the incident.

hind the persecution of 64, no one can define them clearly. Tacitus alludes to them in extremely vague terms: those accused of the crime were, he says, 'men who were abhorred for their villainous practices, and convicted of nourishing a hatred towards the whole human race.' This really says nothing save that one ought to hold these particular people responsible for the tragedy.

However, it must be taken into consideration that the language of Christianity, which was something of a mystery to the non-initiated, may well have acted as a disturbing and almost provocative influence, with its great pictures of divine wrath, of sinful cities being devoured by the flames, of universal conflagrations: with all that apocalyptic symbolism with which St John was soon to score his themes.

A number of other less obvious forces may also have been working to whip up anti-Christian feeling. When it is seen how nicely the Christians were distinguished from the Jews in the police round-up; when we remember the violent antagonisms within the synagogues themselves resulting from the movement which favoured regarding Jesus as the Messiah; and when we note the Judaizing sympathies of Poppaea and the role played by certain members of the Chosen Race in her *entourage*,[2] our suspicions are considerably aroused. However, it is also not beyond the bounds of possibility that disagreements within the heart of the Christian community—disagreements, for example, between Judeo-Christians and 'Paulinians'—had attracted police attention. Consequently it was tempting for the official authority to choose as its scapegoat the despised little Christian flock which had already been calumniated by popular gossip, and from which, moreover, it had nothing to fear.

So a surprise raid was carried out on the Christian communities. Those who were arrested first were tortured into giving away information about the rest. Their connections, their way of life, their conversation, and even their silences, could serve as pointers: the young Church had not yet prepared its members for events like these. The prisons were packed, to the point at which Tacitus could speak of a 'great

[2] This is stated by Flavius Josephus in his *Vita* (iii) and in his *Jewish Antiquities* (xviii, xx). Tacitus also mentions it (*Hist.* i. 22).

multitude' of arrested Christians, a comment which gives us some precious information as to the progress which the new faith had already made in Rome, less than thirty-five years after Christ's death. Was the confession that they were indeed the fire-raisers actually wrung from the weaker of the faithful? Does the accusation of 'hatred towards the whole human race' cover this, out of all imaginable crimes? Anyway, the juridical pretext was of little significance: Nero was far less interested in punishing a possible offence than in appeasing the infuriated mob by himself choosing the guilty and handing them over to it. Within the frighteningly fertile brain of this evil man political expediency and a personal taste for sadism united in one atrocious idea. And so began the scenes in the Vatican Gardens.

All the vilest horrors that could possibly be invented by a sadist free to indulge in completely unrestrained brutality were now realized in one fantastic nightmare of atrociousness. It was not enough merely to torture, behead or crucify the victims in Nero's Circus, which was situated where St Peter's stands today.[3] Men went hunting in the imperial parks, but it was hunting with a difference. The quarry on this occasion consisted of Christians, who were sewn into animal skins and then torn to pieces by the emperor's mastiffs. Tableaux were produced, depicting the lewdest or most barbarous scenes from classical mythology, with Christians in the character roles, forced to submit in reality to all the outrages described in the legends. And one evening, along the avenues that were thinly dotted with a sorry crowd of bystanders, and where Nero himself was promenading, clad in a coachman's livery, driving his own chariot, torches coated with pitch and resin were raised aloft and set afire to lighten the darkness: but these torches were living human beings. St Clement of Rome, who may well have witnessed this scene with his own eyes, was to retain a memory of unforgettable horror regarding that night of 15th August 64, and Tacitus himself confessed that such a

---

[3] The circus, whose foundations have been discovered, was situated where the left half of the basilica of St Peter's stands today. Its obelisk, which was removed by Fontana during the pontificate of Sixtus V, now stands in the centre of the famous piazza.

surfeit of bestiality would only make honest folk feel some pity for the Christians.

The persecution was not confined to these abominable spectacles, which were provided to entertain the riff-raff of the town. It continued in time; it extended its range. Writing, probably on the very morrow of the tragedy, to the communities in Asia, Pontus, Galatia, Cappadocia and Bithynia, in the name of 'the church here in Babylon, united with you by God's election'—in other words of Rome, which had become, like Babylon of old, the place of exile by the banks of the rivers, and the capital of grief—Peter, the Prince of Apostles, alludes to the various tribulations which, for a 'brief interval,' these far-off brethren are suffering, 'so that you may give proof of your faith, a much more precious thing than the gold we test by fire' (1 Pet. i. 6–7). He tells them specifically that, though innocent of all guilt, they may be 'punished for being a Christian,' and that this shall be their true title to glory. Consequently it is clear that Rome had no monopoly of executions. It was shortly after writing this letter that, in fulfilment of the Master's prophetic sentence, uttered so many years earlier (John xxi. 18–19), the aged Apostle went serenely to his death upon the cross. At about the same time—or possibly a few months later, no one knows—the other great pillar of the young Church, Paul, the evangelist of the pagans, perished also beneath the executioner's sword.[4]

This was what the first episode in the long, tragic drama of Christian martyrdom was like; right from the start it reached a pitch of horror which would never be surpassed, but which would often be equalled, in the future. It was all very well for Nero to disappear from the scene four years later, hunted to his death by a disgusted and angry people: the precedent

[4] It has never been possible to fix the date of these two executions with complete certainty. According to Eusebius they took place in 67 or 68, but it is quite likely that the historian only put forward these dates in order to confirm information he had previously given about the twenty-five years of Peter's Roman pontificate. It is certain that the Prince of Apostles was not among the victims slaughtered in the Vatican Gardens; he must have been martyred shortly afterwards, in the same locality, not far from Nero's Circus. (See the discussion on this subject at the end of Chapter II, and its corresponding footnote.)

created by him was to show itself all too effective. As reign succeeded reign, and dynasty followed dynasty, the example set by the half-crazed exhibitionist was to be emulated by several men who were by no means all monsters, as Nero had been. The term 'Christian' was virtually synonymous with 'execution victim' from the beginning. Between 64 and 314 every single day held for the faithful believer the ever-present threat of a frightful death: the period is divided fairly evenly into the years of active bloodshed and those of relative quiet. And every so often, during those two hundred and fifty years of history, we shall hear that cry of distress and agony rising heavenwards again, just as it had risen from the gardens of the Vatican glade in Nero's day. But from the moment of the first tortures the faith had known how to transform that cry into a cry of hope.

## 'GESTA MARTYRUM'

The account of the early persecutions forms one of the most splendid pages in the whole history of Christianity. In the mystical sense it is the one which links the Christian soul to Jesus, its model, by the closest of bonds, that of a shared experience. St Paul had aptly referred to the faithful completing the passion of Jesus in their own flesh. These early heroes gave their faith the crowning seal of a voluntary oblation, without which no truth can triumph on this earth, and they provided examples for future generations which neither the dulling effects of subsequent over-pious renderings of their tales, nor the additions made by well-intentioned commentators, have been able to nullify. Even today at least half the names contained in our Calendar of Saints belong to this period. And it is by virtue of examples such as these that Christian witness has been renewed in the form of accepted sacrifice right up to our own age, up to the names of Father Damian or Father de Foucauld.

On the whole we are well supplied with information about this long and tragic period. Because they regarded the tragedies in which so many of their number were perishing not simply as personal calamities but as striking demonstrations of faith, the Christian communities were careful, even at the height of the storm, to pass the account of them on to the rest of the brethren. They would rapidly send round to one another the descriptions, which were often highly detailed, of the various 'battles' which their members had waged, and the 'triumphs' which had carried off those whom the Divine Master had chosen for His harvest. We know of several of these accounts which were written down immediately after the events they describe: those describing the Passion of St Polycarp, for instance, or the story of the martyrs of Lyons. In addition we possess various letters dispatched by Church leaders after they themselves had been arrested and condemned to death, in order to send instructions to their priests and deacons, or to exhort their flocks to maintain their patience and their courage. It is impossible to imagine anything more moving than the words of these almost administratively precise documents, signed in the martyrs' blood.

However, tradition has not always preserved this original restraint. A well-known characteristic of popular devotion is its ardent desire to possess even the slightest details concerning the lives of the beings it most admires, particularly if those details incline to the picturesque, and not to be over-scrupulous regarding the literal accuracy of a picture, so long as the essential impression shines through it. In order that their names might continue to be profoundly revered by posterity, the heroes and saints who were the great martyrs had no need whatsoever to be torn from that sublime simplicity in which they had wished to die. But had they not already been crowned with a halo of glory while they still lived? It seemed only natural that some of the rays from their heavenly crowns should be more fully described.

Thus, quite often, our most authentic evidence does not relate to the most famous of the martyrs. All that we know of this or that great figure, of whose actual existence and sacrifice there can be no doubt, is not closely enough linked with the time in which that saint lived to be taken entirely at its face value. St Agnes is an example of this. An inscription of the learned Pope Damasus, in the catacombs, simply tells us that she lived and suffered a martyr's death; but posterity apparently knew far more about her! It has bequeathed us the radiantly pure picture of the young virgin who was dedicated to Christ from early childhood, who, at the age of ten, refused the hand of a very important suitor, who miraculously escaped the flames of the stake, and who, at the tender age of thirteen, when condemned to perish by the sword, encouraged the executioner to strike the fatal blow. By contrast pious tradition has rarely tampered with the lives of the less well known: those Christians who lived in provinces far from Rome, the ordinary anonymous martyrs who existed in their thousands during the first three centuries A.D. When some humble merchant, junior officer or gardener was tortured, it was such a commonplace event that reality alone sufficed, and so it has happened that, fortunately for us, the official proceedings relating to such cases have been preserved in their original form.

In the main, all the separate accounts contained in this hagiography appear to stress the true facts about the martyrs according to one common, four-point pattern. They all paint the pagan authorities, the emperors and the magistrates, in the blackest possible colours, and, since they have little understanding of the fundamental reasons for their hostile attitude, attribute the basest of designs to them. They multiply the variety of types of capital punishment inflicted, with a tendency to the extravagant which may well be explained by the imaginations of the executioners—or by that of their victims. They insist on the physical phenomena which accompanied the executions, and, before leading the martyrs to the conclusion of their ordeals, set out to demonstrate their invulnerability. Finally, in almost every case, the tragedy closes with a 'moral' denouement of a type which popular taste enjoys to this day; sometimes describing the dire punishment inflicted by heaven upon the torturer, and sometimes his complete change of heart before the heroism of his victim, and his own sudden conversion.

One cannot refer to this *Golden Legend* of saints and martyrs without the deepest respect and emotion. Generations of Christians have been uplifted by the pictures which these stories evoke; the stained-glass windows and sculptures of our cathedrals have preserved them in their entirety for us to see. Many of the accounts form the basis of some particular local devotion, tradition or pilgrimage, and the sum total of these venerations, repeated over a period of several centuries, has engraved in human memory many details which history has hesitated to retain. For a long time now the Church, with resolute circumspection, has reacted strongly against any excess in this torrent of miraculous occurrences. More than three hundred years ago, at Anvers in 1643, the Bollandists began the mammoth publication of their *Acta Sanctorum*, which is not yet completed. From the start they demonstrated a highly scientific attitude towards their subject, which earned them much bitter criticism, but despite this they have continually increased the severity of their tests. It is to their sentences, stripped of all exaggeration, and possessing a bald factuality that is often overpowering at first sight, that we should turn if we wish to discover the morality of Christian heroism, and the Christian view of death.[5]

## PERSECUTION: ITS JURIDICAL BASES AND ITS ATMOSPHERE OF HORROR

As carried out by Nero, the anti-Christian persecution would appear to be simply the manifestation of a sanguinary form of insanity, the frightful diversion engineered by a ruler who was in moral fear of his subjects' wrath. Had the tragedy of 64 remained an isolated case such an explanation would have been perfectly valid. But the persecution was very soon to begin again, under other emperors, and it continued until the beginning of the fourth century. Consequently it was not solely due to the regrettable chance which had placed Nero upon the

[5] The 'martyrologies' are composed of collections of the oldest 'calendars of the festivals of the martyrs.' Some of these (such as the *Liberian Calendar*, begun in 235 and continued until the pontificate of Liberius, 352–66) are very old indeed. The most ancient of these martyrologies, known as the *Hieronymian Martyrology*, was compiled in Italy during the fifth century and re-edited at Auxerre a century later. All the known manuscripts derive from the Auxerre version. The present-day Roman martyrology is founded on a compilation made at Saint-Germain-des-Prés in the ninth century, and revised by Baronius in the sixteenth century. The majority of the accounts of the martyrs which are contained in the breviary have been taken from Baronius's compilation. The scholarly Pope Benedict XIV (1740–58) declared quite categorically that the Holy See did not guarantee their complete historical accuracy.

throne and caused the great fire in the slums of Rome. This immediately raises an extremely difficult problem, and one which has not been fully solved to this day, namely, the question of the juridical bases which a people as obsessed with law as the Romans were could give to measures of this nature.

The Christians of the period themselves attacked the problem. We find it referred to in a passage of Tertullian's *Apology*, written at the end of the second century. This outlines the history of the persecution from its beginnings until Tertullian's own time. Addressing himself to the Romans, the author exclaims: 'Consult your own archives, and you will find that Nero was the first to lift the imperial sword against our sect. . . . Later on another attempt at persecution was made by Domitian, who, so far as cruelty was concerned, was a second Nero. What were our persecutors like? Why, they were wicked, blasphemous, infamous men, and you yourselves often condemn them! By contrast, of those rulers who ascended the throne and showed respect for human and divine laws, can you name a single one who waged war upon the Christians? . . . What can you think, then, of laws which have only been executed against us by impious, unjust, infamous, cruel, extravagant and insane princes, which were partially ignored by Trajan, and which Vespasian, the slaughterer of the Jews, and Hadrian, Antonine Pius and Verus never applied at all?' (*Apology*, v). This text contains not merely a skilful manœuvre, designed to throw the entire responsibility for the persecutions upon emperors whose names were universally abhorred, but a fairly powerful juridical argument besides: certainly many anti-Christian laws exist, says Tertullian, but proof that they are monstrous and iniquitous is shown by the fact that they have only been enforced by rulers who were themselves monsters of iniquity.

Unfortunately this is simply not true. Several excellent emperors, men who, in many ways, had a high regard for humanity, while they did not actually promulgate new legislation against the Christians, did not hesitate to apply the old persecution laws. Those reigns which the apologist cites as periods of well-being were, in fact, bespattered with Christian blood.

Consequently there must have been something else besides, some valid juridical instrument which bound the public authorities to deal severely with the new sect. We do not possess these texts and decrees which must have dealt with the anti-Christian persecution. When Trajan replied to the Younger Pliny in the famous letter which is studied later on in this chapter, he referred to what was either some previously enacted legislation or, at all events, an anti-Christian jurisprudence. Tertullian declares quite categorically that Nero promulgated a law against the Christians, and the fact would therefore appear perfectly admissible. But it is still necessary to try to understand on what juridical argument his decree could have been founded.

The Romans distinguished the Christians from the Jews, regarding them as dissidents from Judaism. But the fact that the Christians therefore no longer benefited from the special privileges which Israel had obtained for her members, notably the right to pray for the emperor before their own God without making an act of obedience towards the official cults, is not of itself an adequate explanation of their persecution. Crimes at common law, such as arson and so on, which the spiteful, stupid mob alleged that the Christians had committed, could well have been used as pretexts for launching the persecutions: but no thinking person or jurist took these seriously. On what grounds, then, did the Institutum Neronianum refuse Christianity the rights which so many Eastern religions had obtained from Rome, and declare the new faith *superstitio illicita*?

We can view the unfolding of events against the background of many centuries of history, and to us it is quite obvious that, from the moment of its first appearance, the Gospel message was basically opposed to all that constituted the very foundations of the Empire. But, as has been seen, neither the Empire nor the Christians were at first aware of this irreconcilable conflict between them. It is true that, according to Roman law, the Christians became liable to charges of treason and sacrilege as soon as, in their hearts, they rejected the gods of the Empire, and, in particular, on their evasion of the cult of 'Rome and Augustus.' But sacrilege necessitates a positive act: during the first two centuries A.D. there is no evidence of any Christians rushing to attack the pagan idols. And not until the third century do we find any juridical texts basing the anti-Christian persecutions on the sect's refusal to sacrifice to 'Rome and Augustus,' in other words, on the double charge of sacrilege and high treason. Therefore, at the start, the persecution cannot have rested on these foundations.

It may actually have depended finally upon the ordinary police power possessed by all Roman magistrates, upon that right of *coercitio* which allowed them to inflict summary punishment, including the death penalty, upon the instigators of public disorders. It was substantially this right which Pontius Pilate had claimed when Jesus was brought before him. But the Christians, when left to themselves, did not cause disorders; there was no class of more obedient, law-abiding subjects; if their profession of faith led to public disturbances, this was solely due to the mob's reaction to it, to demonstrations organized against the Christians, not by them. In such situations the Roman magistrates were hard put to it to apply their right of *coercitio*, a difficulty proved by the fact that on many occasions provincial administrators were to seek instructions from the emperor on this very point.

So while it can be said that the formula *christianos esse non licet*—no one is allowed to be a Christian—was admitted as a juridical principle from the morrow of the Neronian persecution onwards, no explicit bases can be provided for it. Everything reads as though the Empire was motivated by some kind of defensive instinct, which made it want to fight the new faith, even though it was still very far from suspecting it to be a revolutionary force. Conversely, Christianity, while not yet fully aware of its own potential, now assumed the role to which its Master had called it, the role of being an eternal 'sign of contradiction' among men.

The history of the persecution, therefore, must be considered in the light of the double evolution already noted above. On the one hand there is the political conscience of the Empire, which during the first three centuries A.D. was to veer towards a strengthening of the central authority, towards a crushing domination of minds and individuals, and which, as a result, was increasingly opposed to the nonconformists it harboured in its bosom. On the other there is the Christian conscience, which, by virtue of its members' communal life, the work of its thinkers and the example of its martyrs, was

to be more and more conscious of its irreconcilable antagonism
to the whole imperial structure. Only in this way can the great
spiritual division into two parties be fully understood. From
64 until 192 the persecution was to be largely spontaneous,
relaxed or accelerated at will by the imperial authorities, or
at any rate always sporadic in character, and never in the least
systematic. From the beginning of the third century onwards,
a new regime came into being. Persecution was applied by
special edicts, emanating from the Government itself and ap-
plicable to the whole Empire. The results of the second
method were unquestionably far more bloody than the first.

There is absolutely no need to regard as an historic fact
the traditional figure of the *ten persecutions*, which several
pious works still retain. The number ten, which, moreover,
varied even in primitive times, seems to have been chosen on
account of its symbolic associations. Did it not correspond
with the number of the plagues of Egypt? And did not one
read, in Chapter XIII of the Apocalypse, that the beast which
would be 'allowed to levy war on the saints, and to triumph
over them,' had 'ten horns and seven heads, and on each of
its ten horns a royal diadem; and the names it bore on its
heads were names of blasphemy'? In actual fact there were
certainly not so many as ten great systematic persecutions, but
only four or five; however, if one counted every bloody reaction made to the Christian message by the imperial authorities throughout all the Roman provinces, the number would
be ten or twelve times greater than this.

One question still remains. It is a problem which troubles
the modern mind a good deal. The fact that the Roman
Empire had its reasons—partially conscious, partially instinctive—for waging war on Christianity does not in itself explain
the appalling forms which this anti-Christian persecution took
right from the beginning, and which it was to retain even when
it was no longer controlled by a madman. Here we are touching one of the most obvious symptoms heralding the moral
disintegration of Roman society, and its future decadence.
This civilization which, in many respects, had set its humanist
ideal so high, and which had known how to express the principles behind it in phrases which are often very admirable
ones, was prepared to debase mankind, and itself, in spectacles

of unbelievable bestiality. Before the account of the tortures with which Rome regaled herself in imperial times the reader experiences the same shocked amazement that the modern world feels on hearing the details of certain horrors, which, alas! it has known how to multiply many times over all too well: one hesitates to recognize human beings, similar to oneself, in those responsible for such atrocities.

A certain taste for blood had always existed in Rome, or at any rate people were fairly accustomed to taking the sight of it for granted. After all, a religion whose ceremonies had the appearance of veritable butcheries would not have predisposed the Romans to any refinements of sensibility on the subject.[6] The custom of carrying out capital punishments in public, which was general everywhere in the Ancient World, encouraged the mob to enjoy spectacles of degrading erethism. It was quite commonplace for a slave to be beaten to death, and when a certain master fed his pet fish on human flesh not everyone thought it scandalous by any means. From the end of the Republic onwards the public's taste for blood was systematically used by the Government for the 'distraction' of the mob, or, to put it more accurately, for its debasement. In the famous phrase, *panem et circenses*—bread and circuses—the second noun is as essential as the first; the circus spectacles, that is to say collective degradation, were henceforth a government affair.

In order to stress this point fully, too many deeds of a far too ghastly nature would have to be remembered. One would need to draw attention to those mimes in which a condemned felon was substituted for the real actor in the final scene, there to offer the public the enjoyment of watching an agony that was far from being a fictitious one; playing the part of a wretched Prometheus, here nailed to a cross instead of a rock. On Augustus falls the responsibility of devising the punishment for the bandit Selouros in which lions, leopards

[6] Now and then sacrificial beasts which had not been properly butchered would escape and run amok in the crowd, gushing blood. One such incident, which was considered a very ill omen, occurred as late as the time of Septimius Severus: two black heifers chased the emperor back to the palace, with the sacrificial swords embedded in their necks.

and panthers were let loose on the naked, defenceless prisoner. This form of penalty was soon to enjoy a tremendous vogue in the anti-Christian persecutions. A law in the *Digest* lays down that all those sentenced to death in the provinces can be sent to Rome to be thrown to the circus beasts there. Then too we should have to recall all those other bloody orgies which took place in the arenas, not only in Rome, but in all the provinces as well: hunts with the appearance of slaughterhouses, where wild beasts were sent to their deaths in huge batches; gladiatorial fights in which the contenders were by no means all volunteers, and in which men killed one another in their thousands and tens of thousands, beneath the gaze of a frenzied audience. To understand this taste for bestiality, which the Roman leaders were to put to good use in the anti-Christian persecutions, the student should not forget those 'midday sessions' where the condemned were forced to execute one another until only one was left, or the *venatio matutina*, which was really nothing more nor less than a wild beasts' banquet, human flesh constituting the food. Such spectacles as these, in which the Christians were soon to be the unfortunate players, though so utterly revolting to us, were common enough in Rome. Eye-witnesses who demonstrated their disapproval of them were rare indeed.[7]

It is, in short, this complex mixture of political intention and of deliberate titillation of the mob's worst instincts on the part of the imperial authorities which explains both the circumstances of the anti-Christian persecution and its atrocious characteristics.

[7] The limits of severity which modern law binds on itself were unknown in Rome, in theory as well as in practice. Neither the victim's youth nor his age afforded any protection against capital punishment. Octavia was under twenty when Nero had her beheaded. When Tiberius had rid himself of Sejanus and had given orders that the whole family of the fallen favourite should be wiped out, Sejanus's little daughter, who was only nine years old, was violated by the executioner before being beheaded, because the law stipulated that virgins must not be put to death! In a moral climate of this sort it was small wonder that many of the Christian martyrs slaughtered on the sands of the amphitheatre were only children.

## DOMITIAN'S SUSPICIONS AND HATREDS

The second wave of persecution which was to beat against the young Church was essentially the work of one imperial will alone, that of Domitian. Despite many eminent qualities —qualities which, moreover, were hereditary among the Flavians: intelligence, an aptitude for hard work, a sense of reality and effectualness—Domitian was a thoroughly unpleasant character and the exercise of power was to increase his failings, not diminish them. He was arrogant, egotistical and dictatorial, and as soon as he encountered the slightest resistance his suspicions turned to dementia. His vanity, which was almost as great as Nero's, resulted in cruelty that certainly equalled his predecessor's. Domitian became emperor in 81, when he was still under thirty years of age, after the premature death of his brother, Titus. He immediately began to distrust large sections of his own subjects, and, ill served throughout by his continual suspicions, he ended by himself knotting together the strands of the violent opposition which, in 96, was to break upon his own head and kill him.

Domitian distrusted the Roman aristocracy, in whose eyes he was little more than a titleless newcomer, the grandson of a provincial speculator, and the colourless brother of a brilliant general, and he feared that its little campaign of scurrilous epigrams against him concealed more specific and subversive intentions. He distrusted the intellectuals, the philosophers, the followers of Epictetus and Dion Chrysostomus, who supported the right to think independently, and who spread their doctrines among all classes of society. He distrusted the Jews, who, despite—or even because of—the destruction of their capital by Titus in 70, continued to spread all over the Empire. Some of their number, such as the Herodian princess Berenice and Flavius Josephus, the historian, had actually been at the courts of Domitian's own predecessors. Finally he distrusted the Christians, whose propaganda had now emerged from the slums to penetrate the aristocracy and to affect even members of the emperor's own family.

For here is the one great fact that is revealed by Domitian's persecution: in the twenty-seven years that had elapsed since

Nero's death the new faith had greatly extended its range. It had climbed several rungs of the social scale. Certain members of the aristocracy, such as Marcus Acilius Glabrio, consul for the year 91, belonged to the Church. Christ had even sown His Gospel seed among the 'gens Flavia' itself: it is possible that Titus Flavius Sabinus, Vespasian's brother and prefect of Rome under Nero, had already been influenced by Christianity several years earlier; his son, Flavius Clemens, who was Domitian's cousin, was undoubtedly a member of the sect, together with his wife, Flavia Domitilla, and their two sons, who were the emperor's heirs presumptive.

Domitian's fury was unleashed at the beginning of 88, when the aristocracy attempted a military uprising against him, which was stirred up on the Rhine by Saturninus, with the actual support of some of the Germanic tribes there, and which was a failure. Henceforth the emperor's wrath was directed against anyone who might be suspected of wanting to oppose authoritarianism, or of being 'out of step' with the regime. Members of the nobility from near and far who had been involved in the affair were tried by a servile and terrorized Senate and either condemned to death or, if they were lucky, deported to some obscure imperial island. Then came the turn of the philosophers. Some were executed and others, like Epictetus and Dion Chrysostomus, banished. The soothsayers and astrologers, who also possessed considerable influence in Rome, suffered a similar fate.

Finally Domitian turned on the Jews and the Christians. There he adopted a manœuvre whose purpose is not very clear. Ever since the destruction of Jerusalem the Roman state had collected the ritual tax of one didrachma, which all the faithful of the Torah had formerly paid to the temple 'for Jupiter'—in other words for its own use.[8] But in reality the administrations of Vespasian and Titus had not been over-exacting in this matter. Domitian commanded that this iniquitous levy be rigorously enforced. And this time the contributors were to include not only all the circumcised Jews but also those who were regarded as 'living like Jews,' in other words all who believed in one God, including the Christians.

[8] See Chapter I, section: 'The End of Jerusalem.'

Why was this step taken? By this time any unconscious confusion between Jews and Christians on the part of the imperial authorities is no longer conceivable. Did the emperor hope that his action would arouse protests from the Christians, and that in this way he would be able to find out exactly who they were? Or quite possibly the purpose behind the extension of the levy was initially a purely fiscal one: may not the State have been aiming merely at increasing the yield, by including the Christians among those subject to the tax, and in this case may it not have been the frequent refusals to pay it which showed the police the considerable inroads already made by Christianity, and thus unleashed the persecution?

Whatever the answer, there is no doubt whatsoever that Domitian's anti-Christian action was inspired by political motives. Did the suspicious emperor smell a plot in all the Christian talk of Christ's future kingdom? The first to be attacked were members of the aristocracy: Acilius Glabrio, the consul, whose family cemetery, on the Salarian Way, was to be the most ancient of all the Christian burial grounds; Flavius Clemens, who had been suspect for a long time on account of his 'lack of enthusiasm' towards the official cult, and who, says Suetonius, was put to death 'on the flimsiest of pretexts'; Domitilla, his wife, who was deported to the island of Pandataria, and whose name still marks one of the finest parts of the Roman catacombs today. Imperial suspicion reached out as far as Palestine, hauling in the descendants of him who had been called 'the king of the Jews,' the humble sons of the Apostle Jude. They were brought to Rome for interrogation, but this eventually led nowhere.[9]

Sporadic at first, the persecution soon gathered momentum and attacked all classes of the population. Did the accusation of *atheism*, that is to say opposition to the official gods, which was lodged against Glabrio and Clemens serve as the basis for the other judicial proceedings? Was the 'Neronian law' applied here? Our information on both the mechanism and the detail of this persecution is scanty. It occupied the last years of Domitian's reign, from 92 until 96. It must have

[9] See footnote in section 'The End of Jerusalem' in Chapter I, p. 68.

been very violent, for Pope Clement, writing to the church at Corinth in 96, apologized for his delay in replying, on account of the 'misfortunes and catastrophes' which had overwhelmed the Roman community. The barbarity of the executions probably rivalled those which had taken place under Nero, when one remembers the tradition which mentions immersion in boiling oil as being one of the ordeals to which St John was subjected. The persecution affected the provinces as well as Rome itself. This is proved both by an allusion in the Younger Pliny's letter to Trajan as well as by the text of the Apocalypse, the book which St John wrote at the very height of the agony, while a deportee in Patmos, and under stress of the emotion which the sight of so many martyrs had raised in him.

As the first century A.D. draws to its close, what the Apocalypse reveals, across the grandiose orchestration of its symbolism, is the tragic atmosphere in which Christianity is henceforth to grow, continually under threat, and treading in its own blood. It shows the connection which is beginning to grow up between the Christian faith and a religious nonconformity which the secular authorities fear, for it declares that 'if anyone refused to worship the image of the best, it [i.e. the Roman Empire] had him put to death' (Apoc. xiii. 15); and finally it discloses the opposition which certain Christian elements[10] are starting to realize exists between them and that Rome which is 'drunk with the blood of saints, the blood of those who bore witness to Jesus' (Apoc. xvii. 6). 'The blood of prophet and saint lay at her doors; the blood of all that were ever slain on the earth' (Apoc. xviii. 24). Thus, in the space of thirty years, the relationship between Rome and Christianity had become clearly defined.

## Vox Populi

One non-political element was to render the Christians' position even more dangerous: popular hostility. This was not related to any logical intention, but its sure instinct knew only too well how to lie in wait for and trap its quarry at all times

[10] Not all, however: Pope Clement, who lived at this time, declared himself a loyalist. (See Chapter III, section: 'The Beginnings of Opposition.')

THE CHURCH'S FIRST MARTYRS

and in all places. Did this hostility exist as early as Nero's day? It would appear so, judging from Tacitus's allusion to the people who were 'abhorred for their villainous practices.'[11] Later on, at all events, as fast as Christianity developed, so popular hatred towards it grew. It fed upon a whole collection of false accusations, vile calumnies and legends whose silliness and unpleasantness would be laughable did we not know that all too often they resulted in the most tragic consequences.

What were the fundamental reasons behind this anti-Christian current of opinion? Probably several elements encouraged it: the austerity shown by the faithful in their daily lives; their more or less implicit condemnation of the immoral distractions of their pagan contemporaries; the secrecy surrounding their meetings, which were mostly held at night underground; popular distrust of anything poor and humble which had no influential backing; then, as the persecutions grew more widespread, the ferocious excitement of taking part in denunciation and murder, in other words the attraction of mob sadism. When the *vox populi* speaks, it is not, contrary to the proverb, always the word of God or even that of reason and common sense.

It is quite probable that the Christian rites, which were not properly understood, and scurrilously interpreted, lent themselves to some most unfortunate ambiguities. The eucharistic sacrifice, which contained such phrases as 'This is my body, this is my blood,' suggested to the ignorant heaven knows what kind of cannibal celebration. The close familiarity existing between those who called themselves *brothers* and *sisters*, and the kiss of peace which was bestowed during Christian meetings, made people think that all kinds of immorality were practised at them. The letter in which the church at Lyons tells the tragic story of its martyrdom is highly instructive in this respect. 'They said we had held feasts worthy of Thyestes; that we were as guilty of incest as Oedipus. And they accused us of other horrors that we cannot repeat, nor even think about, nor yet believe that any human beings have ever committed them.'

These odious tales were to have a long life. They were to be

[11] But Tacitus did not write these words until *c.* 116, in other words, by the time that proofs of this hostility were very numerous.

extremely prolific throughout the second century. About 150 Fronto, the rhetorician, who enjoyed enormous contemporary fame, although he was certainly no genius, and who counted Lucius Verus and Marcus Aurelius among his pupils, solemnly declared that he knew for a fact that the Christians were in the habit of rolling an infant in flour, and of forcing one of their neophytes to stab the victim in the heart and then drink its blood. After this, he alleged, the whole assembly frenziedly divided the body among themselves. To this gruesome picture he added another, depicting the collective orgies and lecheries in which, he was certain, the members of this hated sect indulged after the lights had been extinguished!

Other scurrilous tales of a rather less dangerous nature were also told. They too show what a muddled idea of Christianity the Roman masses possessed at this time. People readily declared that members of the new religion worshipped a god with an ass's head, and in 1857 a precious *graffito*, now housed in the Kircher Museum in Rome, was discovered on the Palatine, traced with a stylet on part of the plastering of a house. It depicts a crucified ass, together with this inscription: 'Alexamenos worships his god.' What was the origin of this sort of ridicule, which had earlier been directed at the Jews, and which was now taken up again and used against the Christians, with the mere addition of the cross in the latter's case? Possibly the mimes and *atellanes* in which the actors dressed up in fantastic masks made to resemble donkeys' heads, had something to do with it. Or some association with the Egyptian god Seth, a deity who was half man and half ass, may have influenced the matter; it is fact that some Gnostics were subsequently to assimilate Seth with Christ, both called 'the sons of man.' Then there is the donkey in the stable at Bethlehem, and the ass that carried the Master on Palm Sunday. Some critics have even suggested that the idea may have had some connection with a certain indecent passage in Apuleius' *Golden Ass*, in which the animal plays the role of a begetter. . . . The inventive power of the mob is invariably enormous, and wanders freely into the realm of absurdity.

It is also true that every time some catastrophe occurs, public opinion likes to be able to pin the guilt upon specific individuals or groups of individuals. This was something that

Nero had grasped perfectly. Among the pagan populace of Rome, still very close to the primitive, where superstition flourished, fear of and a taste for magic encouraged people to interpret every misfortune as the consequence of some evil spell. Were not the ceremonies held by these Christians, these night-birds, full of all kinds of suspicious incantations? Everyone knew that magic worked at night. Since the Christians were capable of anything it followed that they must be guilty of everything. Tertullian was to write: 'If the Tiber floods, or if the Nile fails to flood, if the skies darken, if the earth trembles, if famine, war or plague occurs, then immediately one shout goes up: "The Christians to the lions! Death to the Christians!"'

Finally we must take into account, too, the various specific material interests which were threatened by the Christian message, those of the traders selling pagan ornaments or sacrificial beasts, who clearly intended to defend themselves by attacking the Christians. Above all, we should remember all those private quarrels and secret jealousies which, in the guise of loyalty to the old gods, and under the protection of the imperial law, were to inflict several underhand acts of personal revenge. Frequently it was this whole hotchpotch of unworthy sentiments that set the anti-Christian operation in motion. More often than not the origin of persecution should be sought not in some action of the imperial authority, but in the howling fury of the mob, whipped up by the charlatans, the temple beadles, the pagan priests and the bazaar-sellers; it begins with the angry crowd stampeding into the places of Christian worship, into Christian cemeteries, and stealing the stores of oil and wine which the Christians kept for their poorest members; it is some probably anonymous or collective accusation which sends those suspected of 'atheism' before the magistrates, and forces the latter to act severely. At this point the juridical question comes to the fore again. In fact, very often popular prejudice overwhelmed legal precedent, and tossed it about like a wave; but to the credit of Rome's officials, it should be mentioned here that many of them, whose whole characters had been moulded by their reverence for the law, reacted strongly against such outbreaks of fanaticism. In the midst of the persecution, these men were to attempt to preserve at least a minimum of legality. This was so under Trajan, in the case of the Younger Pliny.

## TRAJAN'S RESCRIPT AND THE ANTONINE POLICY TOWARDS THE CHRISTIANS

We find the juridical position of Christianity in the Empire defined for the first time in 112, in a correspondence exchange between the Younger Pliny, the imperial legate, and his emperor, Trajan. The official's letter and his master's reply constitute the most important documents of the period on the vexed question of the purpose and range of the persecutions. They are important both because of the information which they provide on the spread of Christianity eighty years after Christ's death, and also because they explain the attitude which the entire Antonine dynasty adopted towards the Christians: this unhappy paradox of four extremely human rulers, who abhorred bloodshed, yet who, during their reigns, allowed so much innocent blood to flow.

Both actors in this scene belong to that superior type of classical manhood whose aspirations and principles have been admirably summed up by Terence in his famous line: 'I am a man, and therefore nothing human is irrelevant in my eyes.' Trajan was one of the finest emperors that Rome ever had; the unity of his character, the nobility of his attitude, his sensitive intelligence, his love of hard work, the simplicity of his personal life and his friendliness all combined to make up a personality which would be admired in any age. He gave proof of his humane feelings several times over; in the social policy which established public relief to help the poor, and instituted aid for abandoned children, and also in his decisions in respect of the penal code, where he had limits set to the period of preventive detention, erased all anonymous denunciations from the police dossiers, and gave fresh trials to all those sentenced in their absence who surrendered to the authorities. It was Trajan who uttered the well-known saying, which too many modern legal minds fail to appreciate: 'It is better to let a guilty man go unpunished than to sentence someone who is innocent.' The surname Optimus, which was bestowed on him by the Senate, was well deserved; in the

Late Empire, the accession of every emperor was to be hailed with the following ritual formula: 'May he be happier than Augustus, and better than Trajan'; and in the Middle Ages, when legend had adorned his image even more extravagantly, it was to be said that Pope St Gregory had obtained for Trajan a unique favour, God's agreement to receive the soul of the dead pagan emperor into heaven.

As for the Younger Pliny, child of the fairest region in all Italy, he first saw the light of day at Como, by the shores of the exquisite lake there; he drew from the beauty and gentleness of his native soil that optimism and generous view of the world which always encourage their possessors towards kindliness and love for their fellow men. Throughout the whole of an extremely brilliant career—and we know that good fortune encourages goodness of character—he gave ample proof of his high moral qualities. It was the same in his private life; his letters show how interested he was in the lot of his slaves, freeing them willingly, worrying when they were ill, and mourning the death of this one or that whom the fates had cut off in the flower of manhood. Between the man who, on the 'Trajan Column,' still bears the title of 'Father of his people,' and the writer who was to compose his panegyric, complete unity of feeling and intention thus existed; neither of them was a bloodthirsty brute!

Now in 112 Pliny wrote a letter to Trajan. As imperial legate he had spent the past year in the Asian provinces of Pontus and Bithynia, a vast territory around the Black Sea. He was trying to put things to rights there, after several years of over-lax senatorial administration. The character of this mission, the difficult circumstances surrounding it, and also Pliny's own character—he was somewhat cautious and very scrupulous —made it necessary for him to refer to his master on several occasions, whenever the affair in question was a delicate one. This was so in the case of the Christians.

On his travels in the eastern regions of his provinces the legate had received various complaints about them. The Christian communities in Asia Minor were the fruits of the first Gospel missions—perhaps those of St Paul himself—and they had already expanded in a splendid fashion. Christianity had modified the social life of the area to the point where it was causing the supporters of the old order considerable anxiety. People were deserting the temples, the official cult was being neglected and the trade in sacrificial animals had been affected. Some members of the sect had been arraigned before the legate, and he had judged and sentenced them. However, since he was a good jurist Pliny had found the whole business highly disturbing. Had any of the proceedings against the Christians which had been held in Rome or the provinces revealed anything reprehensible? He did not know of any that had. It did not seem to him that the people brought before him had committed any crime. But he was obviously well acquainted with the jurisprudence of his forefathers, with the Neronian Law and so on, and so he had decided to act strictly in accordance with the principle: 'No one is allowed to be a Christian!' After having been assured, no less than three times, by the accused themselves, that they were indeed Christians, he had punished this criminal obstinacy and had had the guilty executed, with the exception of those who were Roman citizens. The latter he was sending to Rome. His account covers all this: he considered he had acted rightly and properly.

But his anxiety had subsequently increased, for the affair had rapidly assumed enormous proportions. Roused by these first death sentences, public opinion made itself felt in an ominous rumbling. Information which was often given anonymously poured in to the legate, in which masses of alleged Christians were denounced. From now on a great host of people—men, women, and even children, of all classes and all ages —were dragged before Pliny's court. Pliny was far too humane to send everyone to the scaffold without first examining them closely. He had therefore undertaken a more thorough investigation than before, and he gives the results of this in his letter. Among the Christians there were, in the first place, those who claimed the name with pride; for them the issue was quite clear: they had placed themselves at the mercy of the law, which was laid down by traditional Roman jurisprudence, and which he, Pliny, had applied in earlier instances. But there was the problem of the rest as well. . . .

Here was an accused person whose denouncers claimed that he was a Christian. He denied it. Or rather he agreed that he had once been a member of the sect, but said that he had left it long ago. Put to the test, he had worshipped the emperor's portrait and the temple gods, and abjured Christ. Thinking of the accusations which were commonly circulated concerning the Christians' ceremonies and morals, the legate had tried to discover whether any of these apostates had committed any crimes or moral misdemeanours during the period in which they had belonged to the sect. All denied this, some even under torture, e.g. two female slaves, who had been deaconesses in one community. All had declared that their sole crime, in so far as they were Christians, had consisted of meeting together before daybreak, to sing psalms to the glory of Christ, to swear never to steal, murder or commit adultery, and to eat a common meal together; at least, in so far as the authorities did not prevent their assemblies from taking place at all.

Now the question which Pliny set the emperor is summed up thus: 'Is the mere name "Christian" punishable?' In this case, must the death penalty apply not only to those who acknowledge the Christian doctrine but even to those who now deny it? And he plainly suggests that a policy of clemency, by encouraging apostasy, would have the best results so far as the social peace and religious well-being of his province are concerned.

Trajan's reply to this painstaking report is in striking contrast, in its *imperatoria brevitas*, to the detailed missive sent him by his official: in three lines, and three points, he lays down the line of conduct which the legate must follow in the future. 'It is not necessary to seek the Christians out, but whenever they are denounced, and declare themselves convinced of their errors, they must be punished. However, if anyone denies that he is a Christian and proves it by doing homage to our gods, he thus obtains his pardon.' The Romans always possessed an extraordinary gift of expressing an enormous mass of juridical principles in remarkably concise formulae. The two central phrases of Trajan's reply, completed by the recommendation that anonymous denunciations should be rejected, and that the legal form of the accusations must be strictly maintained, define an entire juridical attitude. It is an attitude which is undoubtedly hostile to Christianity, but which, from

Rome's point of view, cannot be termed either unjust or in-human. The fundamental points can be summed up as follows: (1) The crime of Christianity is a special kind of crime, exceptional in character, since one has but to regret it to be pardoned, which has never been the case in relation to theft or murder! (2) The Christians' innocence of all the abominations of which they had been accused is implicitly recognized. (3) The initiative for starting prosecutions is not to be taken by the authorities; Christians must not be 'sought out.' (4) Proper legal denunications must be made against the Christians in accordance with the usual principle of classical law in this matter. (5) Apostasy—not merely past apostasy, but apostasy which takes place at the time of interrogation—is sufficient to stop the case and render the charge null and void.

From a political point of view this collection of measures was masterly: a head of state, reasoning as such, and failing to understand the astonishing power of the faith upon men's souls, might well think that they would check the spread of the new doctrine. From the humane standpoint, provided that one disregards the frightful conditions in which the 'punishment' of convinced Christians was carried out—death in the arena or forced labour in the mines—and which derive from the general customs prevalent at that time, the rescript has nothing ferocious about it. Historically it proves that at the beginning of the second century the Empire was certainly not attempting to destroy Christianity in any systematic fashion, for it had not yet recognized it as its enemy. But all the same its attitude remained somewhat ambiguous and equivocal, as Tertullian aptly noted in one ironic sentence: 'The Christian is punishable not because he is guilty, but because he has been discovered, even though he must not be sought out.' This ambiguity of attitude is always adopted by societies that have been in existence too long, and are too sure of their security, when faced with doctrines which are fighting them to the death.

Trajan's rescript was to form the basis of his successors' entire Christian policy. Hadrian confirmed its trend, in a rather less clear-cut manner. Granianus, proconsul of Asia, who was disturbed by the mob's bloodthirsty attitude towards the

Christians, had gone so far as to doubt whether it was 'just to sentence people who have committed no crime, save that of belonging to this particular sect.' The emperor wrote a reply to Granianus' successor, Minucius Fundanus, a reply which is a mixture of that scepticism and moderation which formed the basis of his character. Oh yes, the law must be enforced. But in enforcing it the authorities ought not to yield too easily to mere gossip and popular calumnies. There must be calm and prudence at all costs! Between the lines of this new rescript, which is quoted by Eusebius, one can read the formula used by many governments who fear the immediate difficulties more than future risks: 'Don't show too much enthusiasm!'

And even the 'pious' Antoninus, who reverenced the old gods so highly, was no more systematically anti-Christian than previous rulers had been. It is clear that he enforced the anti-Christian legislation of his predecessors; during his reign the interrogation of the martyr Ptolemy took place at Rome, an incident whose tragic brevity is recorded by St Justin: 'Are you a Christian? I am. Then to your death you must go!' But none of the measures taken by this devout pagan showed the slightest desire to go further in the matter of Christian repression than Trajan had done. In short, throughout the whole period of the Antonine dynasty's rule,[12] anti-Christian persecution scarcely ever went beyond the twofold desire to maintain order and not to irritate public opinion by over-tolerance.

This policy explains the character which the persecution retained throughout the second century. It was local and sporadic in character; it was never universal, nor deliberately planned. It was the mob which caused its outbreaks: in areas where the *vox populi* did not ring out against the Christians,

[12] It is curious to note that it was under the last of the Antonines, Commodus, who was a real monster of a man, that Christianity's lot was least burdensome. Though some persecutions did take place during his reign, none was on a very large scale. And it is known that he performed one act of mercy regarding the Christians who had been sentenced to penal servitude in the Sardinian mines; he had the Bishop of Rome give him a list of these wretched folk and he then sent a Roman priest to set them free. This merciful deed of his should be remembered, for in other respects his memory is singularly blackened by crime!

it did not occur; but in places where the rabble rose up in arms against the sect, the authorities followed suit. To a large extent its character was to depend on the local official who represented the imperial authority: we find some magistrates 'holding out a helping hand' to the accused, quickly and willingly setting them free provided they burnt the tiniest grain of incense before the altar of the idols; by contrast there are other, appallingly fanatical officials who pushed the processes of interrogation, investigation and torture to the furthest possible limits. The balance between the severity of imperial legal principle and the moderating desires of certain of the emperors was, in the last resort, dependent upon chance and circumstances.

## IN ASIA: TWO PRINCES OF THE CHURCH

Out of all that immense band of heroic figures who rise up, their faces marked with blood, throughout the whole of the second century, one hesitates to remember one more than another, for all those whom we see deserve our equal veneration. One would like to enumerate them all, not only those whose names are famous, and who stand out, like shining landmarks, along the martyr's road, but also all those unknown, anonymous folk, who paved the way for Christ with their own mangled, sacrificed bodies. However, all possess such similar characteristics, in their common desire for self-sacrifice and their steadfastness of soul, that to evoke but a few of them is to know them all: the same wonderful qualities are shown by the most important of bishops and the lowliest of slaves, linked by a common heroism, faith and simple goodness.

There are two men who compel our attention first of all. They stand out particularly clearly not simply because of the manner of their deaths (this might almost be considered commonplace, in the light of all the martyrdoms of the first two centuries), but because of the importance attached to their names by virtue of the eminent intellectual masterpieces which they wrote, and also on account of their high place in the ecclesiastical hierarchy: Ignatius of Antioch and Polycarp of Smyrna. Both were bishops, leaders of the Christian communities of whole cities; in those days, being a prince of the Church was a far from restful occupation, and the only advantage the bearer derived from such a title was that of finding himself specially marked out for the executioner's blows. In these lands of Asia Minor, and the neighbouring islands, where religious fanaticism had been rife for a long time past, where the imperial cult had actually come into being (at Pergamum), and where, on the other hand, as we know, Christian missionary endeavour had been very intense, and crowned with great success, it is not at all surprising that anti-Christian feelings should have been particularly violent: two princes of the Church, Ignatius and Polycarp, were to be its victims.

*St Ignatius* is a highly remarkable and engaging character, an admirable example of those revolutionaries of the Cross who never minced their words, looking events and men full in the face, clearly aware of all the risk they were taking in so doing. It is not for nothing that the etymology of his name makes us think of fire—*ignis*—a point that was noted by his contemporaries. His letters bring him to life as an energetic, picturesque figure, quick to join battle in the cause of the faith and of justice, an experienced jurist and administrator, by virtue of his considerable study of the Church's constitution, and, in his meditations on Christ and the spiritual life, an eminent theologian and mystic: he was the author of that admirable formula which so many saintly figures were subsequently to adopt: 'Let all our actions be taken with the sole thought that God dwells in us.' Then too Ignatius was a Christian witness who was very close to the apostolic generation, and he knew some of its direct representatives. So he is one of the living links that bind Christian tradition to Jesus Himself, possibly through St Paul or St Peter.[13] The blessed violence that we find in the first sowers of the Gospel seed was in Ignatius also, in its entirety.

He was arrested under Trajan, in the course of the scattered persecutions which marked the beginning of the new emperor's reign, persecutions in which Pope St Clement, St Peter's third

---

[13] In his *Panegyric on St Ignatius* St John Chrysostom says that he was made Bishop of Antioch by St Peter himself: the *Apostolic Constitutions*, a fourth-century compilation, considers that he was chosen by St Paul.

successor, was probably martyred in Rome, and in which St Simeon certainly suffered crucifixion in Jerusalem.[14] Virtually nothing is known about the events leading to Ignatius' prosecution, and we do not know whether the initiative came from the mob or from some local magistrate. As for the circumstances of his martyrdom, so many contradictions arise from the different versions of it drafted in Antioch and in Rome that it is impossible to try to correlate them: the most that can be said is that he must have perished in 107, possibly in the Colosseum, which was in process of completion at that time, during the gigantic spectacles provided by Trajan to celebrate his victory over the Dacians, in which ten thousand gladiators and eleven thousand wild beasts were put to death. But though the concrete facts regarding Ignatius' life escape us all too completely, we are excellently informed regarding the saint's psychology, and his gloriously radiant soul. His letters have been preserved for us, and they are so numerous and so wonderful that the primitive Church considered them almost canonical, placing them only slightly below those of St Paul in importance. They form one of the monuments of the Christian spirit in these early days of the faith.

The bishop was sentenced to death at Antioch, along with his two companions, Refus and Zosimus, and was sent to Rome to be thrown to the lions there. Though well aware of the fate which awaited him, he showed a fervour and an enthusiasm which can only be given a supernatural explanation. He wrote to the Christians of Smyrna: 'Even under the sword-blow, or in the lions' jaws, I shall always be close to God.' Each stopping-place on his journey to Rome provided an opportunity to spread the Word. At Smyrna he met Bishop Polycarp, who was eventually to follow him along the same bloodstained road of martyrdom. And before reaching Rome he sent the Christian community in the city a letter which Renan has called 'one of the treasures of primitive Christian

[14] See Chapter I, section: 'The End of Jerusalem.' St Simeon, St James's successor as head of the Church in Jerusalem, had succeeded in saving his little flock when the city was captured by Titus. He was 107 years old when he was denounced as a Christian and as a descendant of David (he was related to Jesus). He was tortured and crucified.

literature,' begging the faithful to do nothing to secure his freedom. They were not to attempt to obtain a pardon for him, or to enable him to escape execution. As this man faced one of the most ghastly deaths imaginable, his only fear was that he might never experience it, that he might be spared its horrors. And he cried out: 'While the altar is ready, let me make my sacrifice! Let me be the lions' prey! It is through them that I shall reach God. I am the rough wheat of God: but I must be ground in the Lions' jaws to become the pure, white bread of Christ.' The Golden Legend of the Middle Ages was to show a wonderful feeling of true symbolism when, in its interpretation of the surname of Theophorus, which Ignatius had borne during his lifetime, it declared that, when his heart was exposed, the name of Christ was found written upon it in letters of gold.

Half a century later, under Antonine, *Polycarp*, who had received the great Ignatius on the latter's way to Rome and who, after his death, had collected his letters and meditated upon his example, suffered a similar fate. We possess a great deal of information about his trial and death, from a letter which the Christian community at Smyrna wrote to their brethren in Phrygia, who had asked them to give them an account of these events immediately after they occurred. Polycarp was a very old man by now, almost ninety years old; but he was not too old to bear witness for the Spirit, and God grants those who are most physically frail the strength for the fight.

In 155 twelve Christians from Smyrna had been arrested, sentenced and executed. All save one had shown wonderful courage: in the amphitheatre one actually provoked a beast that was too lazy to devour him by slapping it! The exasperated mob called for more Christians to be punished, and Polycarp's name was shouted out by many. He was hunted for two days, and was finally given away by one of his own servants, who betrayed him under torture, and arrested. His serenity and dignity impressed even the soldiers who came to take him away. Several irregularities occurred during his trial, which was slapdash, but spectacular, in form. Some games were taking place in the amphitheatre at the time, and Quadratus, the proconsul, was watching them. The bishop was led there, mounted on an ass, and was pushed into the arena; his entry caused the tumult to break out afresh. And then the interrogation began. Its tragic simplicity is excellently conveyed in the hagiographal text. On the one hand there was the Roman magistrate, who was clearly aware that strict legality was not being observed, on the other the crowd, ready to cause a new uproar or start a riot: facing both, the saint who never flinched.

'Swear by the fortune of Caesar! Repent! Declare: Death to the atheists!'

Turning towards the mob, which was indeed truly atheist, and looking it straight in the eye, the aged bishop stretched wide his arms and cried: 'Death to the atheists!' But obviously this was not the interpretation that the Roman had in mind.

The proconsul insisted: 'Apostatize! Swear, and I will set you free at once! You have but to insult Christ.'

'I have served him for eighty-six years and He has never done me any wrong. Why then should I blaspheme against my King and my Saviour?'

'Swear by Caesar's fortune!'

'You flatter yourself if you hope to persuade me. In all truth I solemnly declare to you: I am a Christian.'

'I have the lions here, to use as I think fit.'

'Give your orders. As for us Christians, when we change it is not from good to bad: it is splendid to pass through evil into God's justice.'

'If you do not repent I shall have you burned at the stake, since you are so contemptuous of the lions.'

'You threaten me with a fire that burns for an hour and then dies down. But do you know the eternal fire of the justice that is to come? Do you know the punishment that is to devour the ungodly? Come, don't delay! Do what you want with me!'

When the magistrate had had the condemnation proclaimed by his herald, the mob could contain itself no longer. It poured down the amphitheatre steps on to the track. The sticks and faggots were soon piled high, and the Jews of the town were far from backward in helping to build the pyre. And the flames soared heavenwards, high and dazzling, like some great arc, or a sail swollen by the wind, so that the saint's body seemed like

a loaf which became gilded in the baking, or like gold and
silver tried in the crucible. . . .[15]

## IN GAUL: THE MARTYRS OF LYONS

The next scene in the great tragic drama of the persecutions unfolds in Gaul; it has a particular importance for French
Christians, since it is the first incident which brings the beginnings of Christianity in their country into the limelight.
Does this mean that the Gospel message had waited until the
third quarter of the second century before invading Gaul?
Certainly not. The soil of France had been an integral part of
the Empire for two hundred years past, linked to Rome by
important trading connections, its great ports opening on to
the Mediterranean, its interior crossed by several admirable
roads. Therefore it could not possibly have remained untouched by the Gospel sowing. Without placing too much
credence on those traditions which claim a glorious and miraculous origin for this or that church,[16] various recent archaeo-

[15] The end of the document records a prodigious event of the kind
that men dearly loved to link with these accounts of the martyrs.
When the fire proved powerless to destroy Polycarp's body, an executioner was sent for to cut it to pieces with sword-blows, but so
much blood flowed from it that the fire was immediately extinguished.
The fire had to be lit again, and only a few bones were left of what
had once been the body of the saint.

[16] It is impossible here to deal in detail with these traditions
whose charm lies in their local character and their folklore associations. The most famous is that which ascribes the foundation of the
church in Marseilles to the family from Bethany, Lazarus, Martha
and Mary, who, it is said, landed miraculously on the shores of
Provence. Not far from there the 'Saintes-Maries' preserve the names
of Mary mother of Mark and Mary Salome. Generally speaking, the
common factor in these traditions is that they form a link with Christ
Himself through the medium of people who knew Him. St Aphro-
disius of Béziers is the man who sheltered the Holy Family in Egypt;
St Amator of Cahors is said to be the pseudonym of Zacchaeus, the
good publican; St Restitutus that of St Paul of Trois-Châteaus, the
man blind from birth, whose sight was restored by Jesus; St Rufus
of Avignon, the son of Simon of Cyrene; St Martial of Limoges, the
child whom Jesus blessed. Local traditions also link other missionaries and founders with the apostolic period: St Trophimus of Arles
and St Crescens of Vienne are regarded as disciples of St Paul; St
Denis of Paris as one of those converted by the great Apostle; Rennes

logical discoveries[17] lead one to assume that Christianity must have affected Gaul quite early in the Christian era. St Irenaeus' statement that he was obliged to speak Celtic to make himself understood by a part of his flock implies that Christianity had by then already penetrated the rural areas, where Latin was not generally spoken. The Good News must have found a very early hearing among the colonies of Eastern merchants in Gaul, who conducted the main commercial business of the province. Numerous groups of the faithful certainly existed there c. 150; and a Church grew up in the form of the extremely vigorous bishopric of Lyons.

It was attacked in 177. At that time the emperor was Marcus Aurelius: his nobility of mind, his upright character and his constant concern for humanity and morality make him one of the finest figures the world has ever known, and this was acknowledged even by his own contemporaries. Can it really be true that this great Stoic, this friend of Epictetus, was the Christians' persecutor and executioner? Unfortunately, yes; and his attitude is comprehensible only if one bears in mind the jurisprudence laid down by Trajan, which Marcus Aurelius, as an emperor who was profoundly conscious of his duty as an emperor, enforced rigidly. He distrusted Christianity, viewing what he regarded as a ridiculous fanaticism through a sceptic's eyes, and he insisted that his magistrates respect the law, keeping within its limits, but also conscientiously applying the severe penalties it enjoined. He did not hesitate to call sharply to order an official who showed excessive zeal, and who violated the principle of 'not seeking out the Christians'; but

---

actually claims St Luke, and there is not a single one of those seventy-two 'secondary' Apostles who is not quoted somewhere or other in France. This is a topic which has caused many arguments, and Monsignor Duchesne has written a critical thesis on it in *Fastes épiscopaux de l'Ancienne Gaule*, Paris, 1894, 1915. See the works of L. Delisle in *L'Histoire littéraire de la France*, vol. xxix, Paris, 1884, of Monsignor Bellet on *Les Origines des églises de France*, 1898, of E. Bernard on the *Origines de l'Église de Paris*. See also Canon Griffe's recent work, *La Gaule chrétienne à l'époque romaine* (vol. i), Paris, 1947. (See also Chapter VII, section: 'Christian Expansion.')

[17] Notably an inscription preserved at Marseilles, which seems to establish the fact of two martyrdoms there, at least contemporary with those at Lyons.

when a denunciation was properly made and an indictment well and truly laid, he stipulated that justice must take its course; and his Stoic humanism did not go so far as to tempt him to prohibit the abominable spectacles in the arena which the epoch seemed to demand.

Thus 'justice took its course' in 163, in the second year of the reign, in the case of *Justin*, the great doctor of the Church. He had been formally accused by his personal enemy, the philosopher Crescens, condemned to death with a number of his disciples, and executed for having refused to sacrifice to the gods.[18] This could be regarded as a properly conducted trial. The affair at Lyons, in 177, exhibited some altogether different characteristics. It started in the neighbourhood of that great festival which, once a year, united delegates from the three Gauls round the altar of Rome and Augustus, and which coincided with a large, bustling fair. The mob, excited by waiting for the games to start, and by the kind of loose talk common at great gatherings of this kind, seized a few Christians, manhandled them and denounced them. The civil and military authorities, who were either inexperienced or pusillanimous, allowed their hand to be forced by popular clamour, and instituted proceedings against the Christians. Then, seized by conscientious scruples, the legate sought the emperor's advice in the matter. The latter set him back on the right path—namely, the path of Trajanian jurisprudence—and subsequently a proper trial took place, the accused being charged with the crime of Christian belief. However, during the course of these three phases, the persecution, though growing more legal in character, did not become any less cruel thereby. As recorded on the spot, immediately after the events, it forms one of the most appalling as well as one of the most sublime pages in the history of nascent Christianity.

It appears that various important Christians were arrested, largely chosen at random.[19] First of all they were accused of all the imaginary vices which the *vox populi* alleged they had

[18] The personality and work of St Justin will be considered further on, in Chapter VI, section: 'The Apologists of the Second Century: St Justin.'

[19] Thus St Irenaeus, the successor of St Pothinus at Lyons, does not seem to have been persecuted.

committed. Under torture one or two of the servants gave some kind of backing to these calumnies. One very young baptized slave-girl, named Blandina, was urged to subscribe to these infamies too. And because she seemed weak in body and spirit her masters were extremely apprehensive of the result. But Blandina had the strength of God to help her, and she replied: 'I am a Christian, and not one of us has done anything wrong.' Relays of torturers were employed, one after the other, to extort a confession from her: all in vain. And the Christians, filled with admiration at this child's fortitude of spirit, at the moral grandeur displayed by this humble slave-girl, realized that she was, in fact, the Master's own spokeswoman: that Master 'who holds in high esteem those whom men despise, and who considers the power of love more important than empty semblances of material strength.' And Renan was to write: 'Blandina the slave-girl showed that a revolution had taken place. The true emancipation of the slave, the emancipation through heroism, was, to a large extent, her work.'

When the trial began the first victim was Pothinus, Bishop of Lyons, who was ninety years old. He had already been very advanced in years when he had come from his native Asia to govern the Lyons community. 'His health was very poor, and his body had been so ill-used that he could scarcely breathe. But the fire of the Holy Spirit gave him strength, for he much desired martyrdom. Dragged before the tribunal, his body broken, but his spirit unbowed, he gave a splendid witness of faith there. The governor asked him who this God of the Christians was. "You shall know Him when you are worthy enough," was the bishop's reply. Whereupon he was most brutally set upon and grossly maltreated. Men kicked him, and pummelled him with their fists, showing no respect for his age; those who were standing farthest away threw anything that was near at hand at him. In this way they thought they were avenging their own gods. . . . When the martyr was eventually thrown into the prison he was scarcely breathing at all; he died there two days later.'

Models like this were an example to the rest. Heroism was catching among the arrested Christians. Some, whom fear had led as far as apostasy, were filled with self-revulsion and contempt for their accusers, and returned to the faith, openly professing themselves Christians. Men and women walked to martyrdom 'full of joy, their faces radiant with heavenly glory and beauty. Even their chains seemed like splendid jewellery, or like the golden fringes on a bride's wedding-gown. And all around them hung the sweet odour of Christ, so much so that many onlookers wondered if they were actually wearing perfume of some kind.' The kinds of execution inflicted on them were, according to the test, 'of every sort, all beautiful by virtue of the beauty of those who suffered. These martyrs were like flowers of every kind, whom their torturers wove into a crown, and who were thus offered to the Father.' Before the bloodthirsty eyes of the crowd in the amphitheatre all sorts of dreadful spectacles took place: there were not merely the usual beatings to death, crucifixions and beheadings; not only were wild beasts used, but more subtle tortures were devised, such as the iron chair, which was heated until it was red hot, and which scorched the flesh so dreadfully that the smoke and stench of human fat hung in a pall over the arena. The names of several of these heroic victims have come down to us: Vetius, who belonged to a patrician family; Sanctus, a deacon from Vienne; the humble neophyte, Maturus; Attalus, a Roman citizen hailing from Pergamum; and Ponticus, a boy of only fifteen. Blandina had been hung from a stake in the middle of the arena, 'and when they saw her, hanging there like someone crucified, and praying in a loud voice for all to hear, Christ's warriors felt their own courage increase.'

When the list of victims—about fifty in all, it is thought— was exhausted, Blandina still remained; the lions, who had probably eaten their fill, would not touch her. She and her companion, the boy Ponticus, had been taken to the amphitheatre on several occasions, and forced to watch the sufferings of their brethren, in the hope that they would apostatize. They had held firm. At the end their turn came. Like a brave mother who instils her child with her own courage, Blandina inspired Ponticus to keep faith whilst they were both being tortured. She was spared neither the rod nor the red-hot irons. When she was found to be still alive 'she was cast into a net and thrown to the bull. After she had been tossed in the air by the animal several times, and was almost lifeless,' a little breath still remained in her body. So, finally, her throat was cut. 'And the pagans themselves realized that they had never seen a woman suffer so dreadfully, nor so bravely.'

When everything was over, when the bodies of the martyrs had been exhibited and abused for six days, they were burned to ashes. These in turn were thrown into the Rhône, so that no trace of them should remain. And, being sufficiently acquainted with Christian dogmas to know about the Christian belief in life after death, but too ignorant to understand its spiritual meaning, the pagans who scattered the ashes remarked: 'Let us see if their God will resurrect them now!'

## AT ROME: CECILIA, A YOUNG PATRICIAN

Scarcely had the flames of the Gallic stakes died down when persecution flared up once more in Rome itself, during the final years of Marcus Aurelius' reign. Probably its underlying causes lay in the war weariness and nervous frustration which were felt by both the public and the Government at this time; thorny wars in Britain, on the Rhine, the Danube and against the Parthians in Armenia; dreadful epidemics; cracks in the army's loyalty. . . . Action against the Christians could play its usual role of creating a useful diversion.

It is thought probable that one of the most famous of all Christian martyrdoms can be placed somewhere within the space of these three years 178–180: that of St Cecilia. It should be noted, however, that the date has long been the subject of considerable argument, being set, according to the whim of the saint's various biographers, anywhere between the period of Marcus Aurelius and that of Julian the Apostate, a time span equal to that separating our own age from that of Louis XIV. But the martyrology of Ado of Vienne states categorically that Cecilia died 'in the reigns of the emperors Marcus Aurelius and Commodus'; and this rather late text, which dates from the fifth century, is supported on this point by an express allusion which is made there to a recent juridical decision promulgated jointly by 'the emperors,' an allusion which appears to refer to the rescript concerning the martyrs of Lyons, which could have been signed by both Marcus Aurelius and his son Commodus, since the latter had by that time been associated with his father in the government of the Empire for ten years past.

Moreover, the date is far from being the most uncertain feature in the account of this martyrdom. The *Passio Sanctae Ceciliae*, which provides the basis of it, was written three and a half centuries after the event, and its author, though full of good intentions and theological knowledge, and with considerable literary talent besides, embroiders on a deed of tragic simplicity with a well-meant sympathy which far oversteps the boundaries of discretion. Scholastic criticism has discerned many influences at work in this text, those of Tertullian and St Augustine as well as those of numerous noncanonical and apocryphal 'acts.' As we read it here the story of St Cecilia can be quoted as one of the most perfect of those 'Passions' which the medieval Christians loved so dearly. Its poetic charm cannot be denied, even though its authenticity is rather suspect. And it is as the character depicted by the artist Raphael that we today remember this stately young Roman damsel, whom writers from Pope to Dryden, from Addison to Ghéon, have made their heroine, overlooking, all too often, the supernatural radiance which shines about her face.

Cecilia belonged to one of the oldest and noblest families in Rome, to that '*gens* Caecilia' which had been linked with every famous event in the Republic's long history. Among her ancestors were men who had vanquished the Veii and the Carthaginians, and matrons who were already being held up as examples in the days of the Tarquins, as well as that Caecilia Metella, the wife of the triumvir Crassus, whose mausoleum on the Appian Way is still strikingly majestic today. Moving in this extremely aristocratic society as she did, how did it come about that Cecilia had been touched with Christian Grace 'since infancy'? Perhaps she owed her baptism to some nursemaid, to some household slave who was a convinced believer. Certainly, ever since the story of Domitilla the Gospel had continued to make progress among the upper classes. Is not the martyrdom of two patrician women, Sts Praxedes and Pudentiana, whose memory is preserved in two ancient Roman basilicas, said to date from the reign of Antoninus? Thus Cecilia grew to womanhood strong in the faith, in her parents' home, in one of those wealthy town houses that had been built after Nero's fire. The old text declares that 'under her fine, gold-embroidered gowns she wore a hair-shirt, and she carried the Gospel always in her heart.'

As soon as she was of marriageable age, her family decided to marry her to a likable young man by the name of Valerian. He too was a scion of a very famous *gens*: of the Valerii, which abounded in heroic traditions. The Valerii owned a very imposing mansion on the far bank of the Tiber, rather oddly situated in a somewhat shabby quarter of the city; here it was that Cecilia's parents planned that she should lead the life of a dutiful wife and mother; in fact it was here that she was to be martyred.

At this point miracles begin to happen. In the secret depths of her heart Cecilia had vowed herself to God alone. Why did she not tell her betrothed before she married him of the secret vow which she had made? Was she afraid of being betrayed? Or was she even then obeying a divinely ordained plan? The writer of the ancient tale is not over-concerned with psychological considerations of this kind. On the wedding eve, when all the ceremonies surrounding a worldly marriage were over, Cecilia asked God 'to keep her body and soul free from blemish' and then made a little speech to her husband, which began as follows: 'O most gentle and dearly beloved young man, I have something to confide to you, on condition that you give me your solemn oath to keep my secret faithfully. . . .' What could Valerian do save give the promise she desired, when he saw the fair face he loved so well become suddenly so anxious? And he heard the woman he adored telling him why she could never be his.

It would be pleasant to follow in all its details the delectable Latin version of the *passio*; to see the flowers from this bouquet of miracles bursting into bloom one by one. The ancient text treats all this with a simplicity and artlessness which brings to mind the style of the stories concerning the Holy Grail, as told in the French of Chrestien de Troyes. There is no doubt whatsoever that the author believed every word that he wrote, and that the strength of his convictions gives his work poetic grandeur and touching sincerity. Valerian listened to Cecilia. He heard his young wife talking of Jesus, of the Christian faith, of the angel who protected her chastity and of the supernatural love which was waiting for him too. Immediately—was it out of tenderness for Cecilia, or was it a miracle?—Valerian set off down the Appian Way, running as hard as he could to the place where he had been told that he would find a wise old man, ready to receive him into the Church. He fell 'like a corpse' at the feet of Urban, Bishop of Rome (?), who welcomed him rapturously. Whilst the saintly figure was intoning the ritual prayers over him, Valerian fell into an ecstatic trance, seeming to see before him an old man, haloed with gold, who presented him with a book, on the first page of which he read these words: 'One God, one Faith, one Baptism.' Cecilia's prayer had been answered!

This was but the first blow which the Christian virgin was to strike on the cymbals of heaven. Valerian's brother, Tiburtius, came to visit the young couple, and he was as astonished by the marvellous perfume which hung around the house as by Cecilia's and Valerian's very serious and solemn conversation. He was told that the supernatural perfume of roses and lilies was the only one existing there, and that the words they used had a very simple explanation. At once he demanded to know what this explanation was, and thereupon received a short course in Christian theology from his sister-in-law, which is more remarkable for its wonderful result than for its eloquent assurance: for Tiburtius was converted by it. 'The Angel of God has spoken through you!' he declared to Cecilia, and he too hurried away to be received by Urban.

It was now that the threads of the tragedy began to knit together. The two young men paraded their faith a little too ostentatiously. They erected burial grounds in their family gardens, where the bodies of many martyrs were laid to rest. They held Christian services in their houses. In short they were soon denounced, arrested and dragged before the city prefect, who was clearly anxious to try to save these well-born youths from the penalty the law enjoined. But the two brothers wanted to die: they were not merely awaiting the executioner's sword, but longing for it; to get it they were ready to defy every magistrate on earth, and all the Roman gods! And their attitude was so heroic, their faith so radiant, that the rough soldier who was entrusted with the duty of leading them to execution—Maximus, the *cornicularis*—was converted by their example. All three died together, the two patricians by the sword, and Maximus by being flogged to death with a leaden-ended whip.

Cecilia remained alone, widow and virgin, even stronger in her faith than before. She sought and obtained the bodies of the three martyrs, and had them buried in a Christian necropolis. Not for a moment did she waver. When her turn came to be condemned, she proclaimed her faith with pride, and claimed her penalties. The text puts the words, which are worthy of Polyeuctus, into her mouth: 'We will never deny the most blessed name we know. *Non possumus*. That is impossible. Rather than live in misery, by rejecting our God, we prefer to die and achieve supreme liberty. This truth which we proclaim is torturing you—you who are toiling so hard to make us lie. . . .'

The indomitable young woman dominated her judge. She jeered at the pagan, in phrases which call to mind the language of Corneille: 'Are these gods that you worship? Or are they blocks of wood and pieces of stone?' That was enough. Let her die! First of all her executioners tried to kill her by the method reserved for guilty noblewomen: by suffocation in her own over-heated bathroom; but when they opened the *caldarium* after transforming it into a stifling oven for the space of twenty-four hours, they found the saint as fresh and radiant as ever, praying and praising God. Would the sword suffice to kill her? The executioner, who must have been either distraught or clumsy, struck the three blows which the law authorized, and there Cecilia lay, covered with blood, her neck only half severed, but—miraculous to relate!—still having the strength to comfort her dear ones. . . .

It is from this enchanting but rather exaggerated story that the modern critic derives the fact of Cecilia's existence and martyrdom. In 1599 the body of a decapitated woman was found beneath a plaque bearing the saint's name upon it. In 1905 a *caldarium* and some ancient marble fragments were discovered beneath the church of St Cecilia in the Transteverine. One of these marbles bore an epitaph of the saint on it. These discoveries seem to confirm the basic facts of the wonderful tale, at least so far as its ending is concerned. In Christian history the real significance of this edifying account lies in its declaration of the spiritual value of virginity, of the pre-eminent importance of the woman who refuses the happiness of motherhood in order to obtain the supernatural privilege of bringing souls to her God. It is this message—which was revolutionary in relation to the classical Roman idea of woman as the social instrument of national fecundity—that one must understand when, each autumn, in the catacomb which bears her name, on that soil which she had inherited from her for-bears,[20] Cecilia is feted by the Church, and when the hymn 'Jesus corona virginum,' the hymn of the virgins and martyrs, echoes from the vaults and the mosaics there.[21]

## IN AFRICA: THE HUMBLE MARTYRS OF SCILLIUM

All the same, are we not right in selecting, in preference to the literary amplifications of the *Passio Sanctae Ceciliae*, one document which does not date, as it does, from a much later epoch; which, on the contrary, was written just after the event it describes; whose almost shorthand character makes one think of an official account, and whose stark style has some-thing overwhelming about it? This document concerns the *Trial of the Scillitan Martyrs*, which took place at Carthage right at the beginning of Commodus's reign, most probably in 180. Some critics have even suggested that this document is none other than the barely altered report made by the proconsul on the affair. At all events, it is one of the most

[20] The crypt of St Cecilia is near the Appian Way, in the area of the catacombs of Callixtus.

[21] Another episode is linked with the same period, that of the *Thundering Legion*. This is related by both Tertullian and Eusebius. The Twelfth Roman legion, which was violated in the midst of a desert and in danger of dying of thirst, was saved by an unexpected thunderstorm. We know this to be a historical fact. Christian tradi-tion asserts that this miracle was due to the prayer of the Christian soldiers, who were very numerous in this legion, since it was recruited principally in Syria; that the name *Fulminata* derived from it; and that Marcus Aurelius was so impressed by the incident that he pro-mulgated a rescript, enjoining clemency towards the Christians. But the pagans attributed the miracle to Jupiter, and there is no evidence of any such change of heart by the emperor at the end of his reign.

unchallengeable of all martyrologies: it has the authentic ring of truth.

When was Africa first touched by the Gospel? As in the case of Gaul no exact date can be given. Some catacombs found at Susa, the ancient Hadrumetum, which contain more than five thousand tombs, prove that Christianity was already flourishing in the area of present-day Tunisia in the time of the Antonines. Carthage, an extremely important commercial centre, would certainly have received the messengers of the Good News at a very early date. About 130 the Gospel must have penetrated the whole of North Africa, since the tragedy we are about to describe took place at Scillium, a tiny township in Numidia. There twelve Christians, five of them women, were arrested and sent for trial at Carthage. They were obviously all humble, ordinary folk; we know nothing at all about the personal backgrounds of any of them. In order to understand what heroism and holiness the faith could engender in men's souls in those days, it is only necessary to quote here the simple text of this account, without any commentary whatsoever.

'At Carthage, under the second consulate of Presens, and the first of Claudianus, on the sixteenth calends of August, Speratus, Narzales, Cynthinus, Donata, Secunda and Vestia appeared in the audience-chamber.

'Saturninus, the proconsul, began to interrogate them:

*Saturninus*: You can obtain the pardon of the emperor, our master, if you will but return to better ways of thinking.

*Speratus*: We have done nothing wrong. We have committed no crimes. We have wished no ill to anyone. When folk maltreated us we actually responded by blessing them. We are the emperor's most loyal subjects.

*Saturninus*: Very well. But we Romans have a religion and you must observe the same. We swear by the divine emperor and we pray for the emperor's well-being. As you see, it is a very simple business.

*Speratus*: Listen to me, I beg you, and I will tell you of a mystery that is all simplicity.

*Saturninus*: You mean you will describe a religion which insults our own. I have no wish to hear you. Rather I desire you to swear on the emperor's divinity.

*Speratus:* I do not know the deified emperor of this world. I prefer to serve God, whom no one has ever seen, and who cannot be seen with human eyes. And since I am not a thief, and since I pay my taxes, I am entitled to know my Lord, the King of Kings and Emperor of all Nations.

*Saturninus, to the rest:* Abandon these beliefs!

*Speratus:* Beliefs are evil only when they encourage murder and perjury.

*Saturninus, to the rest:* Do not be a party to this madness.

*Cynthinus:* We fear no one, save the Lord our God, who is in heaven.

*Donata:* We respect Caesar as is his due. But we fear only God.

*Vestia:* I am a Christian.

*Secunda:* I am a Christian too, and I desire to remain so.

*Saturninus, to Speratus:* Do you persist in calling yourself a Christian?

*Speratus:* I am a Christian.

'And all made the same declaration.

*Saturninus:* Do you wish for time to reflect on your declaration?

*Speratus:* One does not reflect on a decision as wise as ours.

*Saturninus:* What is in this casket here?

*Speratus:* Our holy books, and the letters of Paul, a good and upright man.

*Saturninus:* Take thirty days' grace, to reflect further!

*Speratus repeats:* I am a Christian.

'And all the rest affirmed the same.

'Then Saturninus the proconsul read the sentence on the tablet aloud: Speratus, Narzales, Cynthinus, Donata, Vestia, Secunda and all the rest have confessed that they are practising Christians. They have been given the chance to return to the Roman religion. They have obstinately refused to do so. Therefore we sentence them to be beheaded.

*Speratus:* Thanks be to God.

*Narzales:* Today, fellow martyrs, we shall be in paradise. Thanks be to God.

'Saturninus, the proconsul, then had the herald proclaim the following: I command that Speratus, Narzales, Cynthinus, Veturius, Felix, Acyllinus, Laetantia, Januaria, Generosa,

Vestia, Donata and Secunda to be taken to their execution.
*All the prisoners:* Thanks be to God.

'Thus all received the crown of martyrdom. And they dwell
now in the Kingdom of Heaven, with the Father, the Son and
the Holy Spirit, for ever and ever, Amen.'[22]

## MARTYRDOM AS A HUMAN TESTIMONY

Throughout all these accounts in the *Acta Martyrorum* the
reader is struck by evidence of a courage so sublime that,
viewed on the human plane alone, it places these tens of thousands of willing victims among the most outstanding heroes
the world has ever known. As they faced death, all, from the
most famous to the most humble, gave proof of a steadfastness
of spirit and a tranquillity which frequently aroused the admiration even of those who did not share their faith. We have
here a unique collection of witness, given by man to man,
demonstrating all that is best and purest in him.

These victims possessed no greater strength than ours with
which to face the horrible deaths which they knew awaited
them; there was no hypnotic ecstasy blinding them to the
reality of their fate. On the contrary, one of the most touching features of their suffering is the simple candour with which
the Christians themselves spoke of it. We know that they
talked about the subject among themselves in the prisons
where they lay awaiting the final moment; they wondered if
the executioner's sword hurt a great deal, if one needed to
suffer much to die; they discussed the tortures which they
realized would be inflicted upon them. But they overcame the
horror of these terrible pictures, which their imaginations so
easily conjured up. Very, very few of them wavered at the last
moment. Encouraging one another, exchanging the kiss of
peace, even more united in the moment of sacrifice than in
their everyday lives, where it was only human that discords and
dissensions should have existed, they went steadfastly to execution, bearing in their hearts that peace which Christ had
promised them.

But it is just as important to remember the meaning which
the early Christians gave to these deeds of heroism as it is

[22] Adapted from the French version of Father Pierre Hanozin, S.J.

to remember the heroism itself. There are many ways of being brave, and many reasons for facing death; there are some people whose sacrifice has no meaning behind it, being an obedience to a Nietzschean philosophy which is only seeking, by this means, a mortal achievement, a 'supreme fulfilment' of the man. In sacrificing themselves as they did, the Christians of the persecutions were pursuing a very definite object. They were giving their lives for a reality which gave those lives their whole meaning. They were, literally, *testimonies* in themselves. And for this reason, since according to ancient legal custom the testimony of the humblest folk—the outcasts and the slaves—was always obtained under torture, the word martyr has come to mean both he who testifies and he who suffers death in so doing.

Nevertheless the Christians did not in fact go out of their way to give this testimony, or to put it more accurately, they did not seek to provoke the opportunity for testifying. Marcus Aurelius was mistaken when he saw their attitude as one of vain bravado. On the contrary, several documents of the primitive Church insist on the uselessness and even the danger of ostentatious gestures. The Passion of St Polycarp records that just one of the Christians arrested with the saints was released in the lions' presence, and it was that selfsame man who had presented himself to the judges, and had enticed others to imitate his example. 'This is why we reprimand those who surrender themselves to the tribunals,' says the text. 'This is not the spirit of the Gospel.'

Not to pursue vainglory, even by means of the most complete sacrifice, but, whenever it was the will of Providence that testimony should be given not to flinch from the obligation, and to go forward steadfastly, testifying to the end: such, in its wisdom and its greatness, is the moral philosophy of the martyrs' heroism. They must accept their fate, never seeking to be revenged upon their persecutors: their act of self-denial must be based on love, just as Jesus, on the Cross, forgave his executioners; 'to live as He lived, to die as He died,' as one of the greatest mystics was to say many years later: martyrdom is the climax to a life entirely orientated towards Christian testimony, the crowning point of that life.

The martyrs testified for Christ in two ways: by their words, and with their blood. Large numbers of arrested Christians took advantage of their trials to proclaim their faith publicly, to spread the truth. This had been done long before by St Stephen, the first of the martyrs; he had countless imitators. Sometimes the testimony was in the form of quite a simple declaration of faith, like the one we have seen springing from the lips of the African martyrs: 'I am a Christian!' Or even, at the identity parade, in answer to the 'What is your name?': 'A Christian! That is all you need to know!' Sometimes it took the form of a more explicit act of faith, such as that given in Rome by St Justin in 163: 'We worship the God of the Christians. We believe that He is the one and only God, the creator of the world, and the ruler of all creatures, both visible and invisible. And we believe in the Lord Jesus Christ, the Son of God, whose coming was foretold by the prophets, who was sent to save mankind. He is the Messiah, the Redeemer, the Master of all that is good.' Sometimes, under pretext of being a legal plea of defence, it actually resembled a proper course in apologetics and theology; thus it is said that Apollonius, a wise old Christian thinker who was tried in Rome c. 180, used his trial as a platform for a genuine philosophical discussion, in the midst of a gathering of intellectuals and senators. For three whole days he spread enlightenment and arguments amongst his audience.

What were the results of this spoken testimony, and of the even more striking testimony of blood? They were enormous. There is something catching about heroism, to which the human soul, though it may not contain a great deal of nobility, is very susceptible. On several occasions Christians who were merely watching a trial in which some of their brethren were appearing were in some way or other caught up in the fervour of the latters' faith, going so far as to betray themselves by their own shouts of exaltation. This was how Vetius had given himself away at Lyons. The desire to emulate the example of others carried certain martyrs beyond the bounds of self; for what other emotion could men feel who saw their friends dying, and attaining celestial glory thereby, or sons who, like the young Origen, watched the execution of their own fathers? Sometimes they would rush, one after another, to take their place on the scaffold. Nothing links the supporters of a cause together so firmly as the bond of blood: it was the seal that ratified nascent Christianity.

Martyrdom had a no less profound effect on the pagan spectators. Probably the majority of those in the amphitheatre who watched the extraordinary spectacle of these sacrifices derived nothing from them save the gratification of their basest passions. But other feelings are also apparent. During the Passion of St Polycarp, Germanicus, one of his companions, faced the lions so bravely that a sportsmanlike admiration seized the crowd, and it all but cheered him on. Sometimes the spectators' revulsion at the suffering inflicted on the Christians was so great that their nerve broke: they ended by pitying the victims. This had happened in the time of Nero, and it was to occur again at Smyrna. Certain upright folk were indignant at seeing human beings who had committed no felony treated like criminals, and now and then this reflection alone led to a conversion. Even some of the magistrates were moved, and showed themselves not merely humane in their efforts to save the accused, but troubled, even curious about this faith which raised men to such heroic heights. And the accounts in the *Passions* and *Acts of the Martyrs* which refer to executioners being converted by the example of their own victims are too numerous and too precise for us to regard them all as literary exaggerations or mere tricks of style: it is necessary to take them more seriously, to see in them the historic proof of the Christian dogma of the reversion of righteousness and the redemptive power of blood.

'When I was one of Plato's disciples,' writes St Justin in his *Apology* (ii. 12), 'I listened to the accusations being brought against the Christians. They faced death so intrepidly, they were so fearless regarding the things that all mortals dread, that I told myself that it was impossible to believe that they really lived evil lives, spent in immoral pleasures.' This is really the most practical sense in which Tertullian's famous words should be understood: 'Christians spring from the blood of the martyrs.' The lesson of history matches that of the Gospel: 'It is the man who loses his life for my sake who will secure it!' (Matt. x. 39).

## Martyrdom as a Sacramental Act

'It is the man who loses his life for my sake who will secure it.' In this short sentence of Christ's lies the whole explanation of the heroism shown by the martyrs; their experience, their sacrifice, has real meaning only when interpreted in terms of a supernatural intention. Of course every human cause can find its fanatics, who are willing to die to ensure its triumph; but properly speaking the martyrs were not thinking of the triumph of their cause in the sense in which one speaks of 'cause' in relation to a modern political party or a philosophical doctrine; they were striving after something which transcended the struggles of the earth. They were Christ's witnesses and the soldiers of the Kingdom of God.

Thus martyrdom was not only a political fact, the logical consequence of a conflict between a revolutionary doctrine and an established order. It was a fundamental attribute of the primitive Church, a sacramental act, which was granted like a gift, like 'the Grace of Graces,' to certain privileged souls, and whose supernatural effects were transferred in turn upon the whole community of the children of God. Absolute faith in Jesus, complete trust in His Promise, charity so great that it becomes self-oblation: the three theological virtues are fulfilled in the act of martyrdom with a completeness that is unrivalled elsewhere; the entire Christian experience—moral, ascetic and mystical—finds its most perfect expression in the sacrifice of blood.

'What is the martyr, if he is not an imitator of Christ?' St Victrix of Rouen was to write in his book, *In Praise of Saints*. Later on generations of the faithful would strive to attain the veritable 'imitation.' But the victims of the Roman arenas achieved it in a single act. The martyr followed the path trodden by Jesus, just as He had foretold it to Peter: 'I am going where thou canst not follow me now, but shalt follow me afterwards' (John xiii. 36). Writing to the faithful in Magnesia, St Ignatius told them: 'If we are not all ready, with Jesus' help, to rush to our own deaths in imitation of His Passion, He does not live in us.' And, later on, the account of the death of St Polycarp contains this sentence: 'We worship Christ as the Son of God, but it is meet that we venerate the martyrs as disciples and imitators of the Lord.' This conviction was to be handed down in the Church from century to century to the present day; one can well imagine what an inspiration it must have been at a time when the possibility of the supreme sacrifice was a universal one; each person took as his model Christ, that Christ who had given His own life for all mankind. 'Thus,' St Gregory the Great was to write, 'Christ will truly become a host for us when we have made ourselves a host for Him.' And we think once more of St Ignatius' desire to be the coarse grain, ground in the mill of persecution, in order to become the pure white bread of God.

The imitation of the One Model carried with it its own recompense. As the mystical medium *par excellence*, martyrdom was the most perfect way of achieving union with Jesus. While still on earth, in the midst of their worst sufferings, the martyrs were sustained by Him, fortified by His strength. It was He who inspired the confessors of the faith to make their brilliant answers to their tormentors, and from Him derived the wonderful shouts of exultation which sprang from their lips. Quite often, at the very last, He would give them the gift of prophecy, and of supernatural visions. But, more important still, it was through death that union with Christ was achieved. As they faced execution these privileged souls bore within them the marvellous certainty that they were being freed from the bondage of their earthly bodies to be welcomed into Divine Bliss, that they were going straight to heaven. St Cyprian was to write of martyrdom that it was 'the baptism by which, on our departure from this world, we are united with God.' Moreover, this baptism of blood could make up for the lack of baptism by water. An unbaptized catechumen who died a martyr's death was *ipso facto* included among the celestial members of the Church. Commenting on the martyrs' experiences, Bossuet declared that they were 'the only adults who, it is certain, have entered straight into God's glory, the only ones for whom no prayers are needed, and who are, on the contrary, ranged among the intercessors.'

In this way martyrdom, which was the noblest way of imitating Christ, which assured the sufferer of union with Him, was, in these times of vibrant faith, the surest means of attaining perfection, the ideal of every Christian. Jesus had said: 'This is the greatest love a man can show, that he should lay down his life for his friends' (John xv. 13); this was why St Polycarp called the martyrs 'imitators of the true charity.' The blood that was shed in the amphitheatres absolved and redeemed. It assembled all the merits which man could acquire and consecrated them in the Crucified God. 'Whosoever dies for the faith,' said St Clement of Alexandria at a later date, 'realizes the perfection of charity.' After the close of the era of persecutions, and when martyrdom for the faith had lost its collective character and had become, in general, no more than an individual act—as it has, in the main, remained until the present day—St John Chrysostom was to declare: 'I have heard from our fathers that there were indeed real Christians once upon a time, during the persecutions!'

Consequently it is hardly astonishing that the martyrs occupied an important place in the primitive Church. The 'confessors,' meaning those who had given their testimony for Christ, and risked their lives in so doing, bore, while they yet lived, the reflection of the eternal light of heaven. 'The saint is synonymous with the martyr.' A special Grace surrounded them. From the depths of the prisons where they lay awaiting death they sent messages of hope to their brethren who were still at liberty. The least of their instructions was received almost as ecstatically as if it were a direct communication from Jesus Himself. Should they escape death the marks left by their floggings and the wounds on their bodies were evidence of the Grace which they had received, and a special place was reserved for them in the hierarchy, and in the administration of the various communities.[23] In particular they were regarded as mediators, chosen to reconcile to God the wretched souls who had weakened under torture and apostatized—the *lapsi*; if a *confessor* pleaded for them, then, by vir-

[23] Occasionally excesses occurred. A few 'confessors' challenged the authority of the bishops. Sometimes it was the 'martyrs' who had suffered the most before succeeding in escaping the executioners who showed themselves the least permeated by their own merits. Man remains man, even when he is bathed in an odour of sanctity.

tue of the reversion of righteousness, such folk were absolved their sin and reintegrated into Christian society.

Did the martyrs' role of guides and intercessors cease after their deaths? No, of course not. How could such a thing be, since they dwelt now in eternity with Christ, ever present? In consequence, men invoked their aid with a confident tenderness. Their bodies, in which the Lord had resided—those bodies which were a part of the Crucified Body of Jesus—rapidly became objects of a special cult, the first form of the cult of the saints. The account of St Polycarp's Passion has this to say of the saint's charred body: 'We gathered up his bones, which were more valuable than precious stones, more dear to us than gold, and we laid them to rest in a place worthy of them. There we shall meet, so far as we are able, to celebrate joyfully, with the Lord's help, the anniversary of that day on which Polycarp, through martyrdom, was born in God.' This was how the custom of celebrating the eucharist over the martyrs' bodies was to be founded. The habit of placing relics under altars is, therefore, the precise result of this very ancient observance, and the Roman liturgy preserves intact a fundamental connection of the Christian faith when, on the Thursday of the third week in Lent, on the festival of Sts Cosmas and Damian, it declares: 'In memory of the precious death of thy righteous ones, we offer Thee, O Lord, this sacrifice, which has been the principle of all martyrdom.' There is no better way of marking the affiliation which, through martyrdom, binds the mass and the eucharist to the sacrifice of the living God.

Consequently the epic of the martyrs is not merely an episode in time, now over and done with, one definite period of history. It is a fact of unique importance lying at the very heart of the Christian faith, which is bound up with the most essential parts of the Christian dogmas. Neither the Christian's rejoicing in the face of death, nor his certainty of redemption through blood, could be fully understood had we not the example of these first Christians to guide us, men and women like ourselves, who sang as they went to their deaths, preferring the faith to life itself. Even when the Church emerged triumphant, and this great chapter was finally closed, her whole history would be ennobled and, as it were, hallowed by the wonderful figures of Ignatius, Polycarp, Cecilia and Blandina, and by those of their brothers and sisters in Christ who were to follow in their footsteps for the space of another century to come. Against that false picture of a persecuting Church (which her enemies conjure up in order to denounce) there is no nobler picture that can be cited by the believer than that of the persecuted Church of the martyrs.

One place still exists where this lesson of martyrdom hangs like a living presence: the Colosseum, the amphitheatre of the Flavians, built by Vespasian. Its immense oval sweep, the three tiers of its arcades, its mighty mass of stonework yellowed by time, stand right in the heart of modern Rome, like an immutable link with the past. In the midst of the arena, on the very spot where generations of Christians gave their lives that the Word of Christ might not be an empty fantasy, there stands a very simple cross, the silent protest against barbarity, and the symbol of an eternal triumph. Here the pilgrims to Rome find, at its most directly moving, the example of their long-dead brethren. Here St Benedict Labre spent several weeks in prayer, and here too a young French girl knelt to kiss the soil with childlike fervour, before going to bury her youth in the silence of the Carmelite house at Lisieux. The air there is heavy with consoling presences. In the silence, the pilgrim seems to hear the echo of the last, halting prayer of all those unknown martyrs: 'O Christ, deliver me! I suffer in thy name!' And, in remembering the historic role assumed by these defeated folk, these seekers after the Kingdom of God who, by their death, vanquished the kingdoms of this earth, we remember that sentence of St Paul's, which so aptly expresses the guiding principle of the whole primitive Church: 'When I am weakest, then I am strongest of all!' (2 Cor. xiii. 10).

# CHAPTER V

# CHRISTIAN LIFE IN THE AGE
# OF THE CATACOMBS

## THE CHRISTIANS IN THE PAGAN STATE

WHEN WE consider the Church of these first few centuries, this budding Christianity which was threatened and attacked on every side and yet which, despite all the obstacles, swept forward with a vitality that was quite prodigious, we immediately call to mind the Gospel comparison with the mustard seed: that smallest of seeds, which grows into a large tree, in which all the birds of the air delight to build their nests. What a small, insignificant thing this Church had been, on the day her Founder died the death of a common agitator on a bare hilltop outside the gates of Jerusalem, crucified between two thieves! Less than two hundred years after this date she existed everywhere. True, she was not yet ready to conquer the whole world and blossom forth in her full strength. But already she had sunk her roots so firmly and deeply that nothing would ever be able to dislodge them.

During the second half of the second century A.D., considerable evidence exists which shows that Christianity extended and penetrated into all the areas and all the social classes of the Empire. It is not only found in Italy. Pompeii and Pozzuoli contained Christians long before the catastrophe of 79, in which many of them perished; there are Christian cemeteries at Naples dating from 150; the first bishops of Milan probably date from the same epoch; while St Apollinaris, who established the faith at Ravenna, is believed to have been a direct disciple of St Peter. From the history of the martyrs we know that, at the same time as this, Gaul and Africa, as well as Asia and its islands, contained vigorous Christian communities; some were as flourishing as that at Alexandria, in Egypt, which was to become famous for its theological studies, or as the church at Athens, in Greece, the motherland of Denys the Areopagite, or as the community at Gortyna, in Crete, where so many splendid Christian ruins can still be seen.

The spread of Christianity must not be viewed in terms of square mileage alone: for the seed went deep into the ground, putting out strong roots. At first the Word had mainly affected very humble folk, the small wage-earners, all those fullers, cobblers and wool-carders who had often been Christ's first witnesses and martyrs. It had proved the comforter of men of low degree, of people like Fortunatus, Achaicus, Urbanus, Hermas, Phlegon and Stephanus, all of whose names, clumsily carved upon their tombs in the catacombs, reveal their humble birth. But many wealthy Romans, the aristocrats of imperial society, had soon followed their example. The heroic testimony given by Glabrio and Flavia Domitilla under Domitian, and by Vetius at Lyons under Marcus Aurelius, is ample proof that the aristocracy had been genuinely touched by the new faith. During the second century the Christian ranks included senators like Apollonius, senior magistrates like Liberalis, the consul, and intellectuals like Justin, who were all capable of speaking in the Forum. Tertullian was undoubtedly telling the truth when he asserted that the pagans were furious to see that Christ's followers included 'people of all classes.'

Is it possible to obtain an accurate estimate of the proportion of Christians in relation to the total population of the Roman Empire? Not really. A frequently quoted passage from Tertullian's *Apology*—written at the end of the second century —gives them enormous numerical importance: 'We appeared only yesterday, and now we fill your cities, your homes, your squares, your municipii, the councils, the tribunes, the decuries, the palace, the Senate and the Forum: we have left you nothing save your temples. Should we secede from you, you would be terrified by your own loneliness!' But here it is obviously necessary to make allowances for some literary licence, since some sixty years later Origen was to say that the Christians were still 'very few in number' in relation to the millions of people who lived in the Empire.[1] The Christians of

[1] It is equally difficult to take the number of martyrs as a basis for calculation. Those enumerated in the texts fall into a number of units, totalling a few score; some fifty at Lyons, a dozen at Scillium. But we

the second century, therefore, constituted only a minority group, albeit a singularly active one. It was a minority which was never to cease growing until it became, in the fourth century, a decisive majority.

This proliferation of Christians raised very numerous problems regarding the relations between the faithful and the pagans. One picture, which is too frequently considered a complete explanation of the question, and which is suggested by the single word, *catacombs*, tends to represent these early believers as a race of troglodytes, spending the whole of their lives underground, hiding from their enemies, and leaving their subterranean hideouts only to go and die amid the sunlight of the amphitheatres. Although it is true that the catacombs were used by the Church on several occasions as temporary refuges, and although it is true, above all, that in a more permanent sense they afforded a roof beneath which the Christian cult could always find shelter, it would be absurd to regard them as the sole framework of Christian life during the faith's first few centuries. The progress of the Gospel within the bosom of pagan society must be considered against an infinitely more solid and complex background than this.

One passage from Tertullian's *Apology* has just been quoted above. In the same text he states quite clearly: 'We others, we Christians, do not live apart from the rest of the world. We visit the Forum, the baths, the workshops, the stores, the markets and all the public places. We earn our livings as sailors, soldiers, farmers or business men.' Another equally precious text, the *Letter to Diognetus*, which dates from the second century, declares that Christians do not differ from other men in their dress, their living accommodation or their food. And the account of the Lyons church itself informs us that when the persecution of 177 began there the mob hounded

---

are very far from possessing documentary evidence about all the cases of martyrdom that took place, and indeed it is certain that that which we do possess represents but a very small minority of the total. Moreover, in several cases the Christians themselves knew nothing of many of their own humble martyrs, of those unknown folk of whom their ancient inscriptions state, with extremely moving simplicity: 'God and God alone knows this man's name.'

the Christians from the squares and the public baths, fore-
seeing that they would be going there.

This mingling of the faithful among the rest of society
raised a host of practical problems; and it is this involuntary
association of two opposites that we must try to visualize. A
fair number of extant documents enable us to obtain some
idea of it. For example, when one considers the celebrated
Palatine *graffito* which represents a crucified donkey, and reads
the inscriptions accompanying it, one really imagines one can
hear one of those scraps of conversation which must have taken
place between the pagans and the advocates of the new
faith. At the school of imperial pages the pupils knew that
Alexamenos, one of their number, was a Christian: one of his
class-mates chaffed him about it by drawing the caricature on
a wall: 'Alexamenos worships his god!' And in his turn the
brave young Christian scratched the reply: 'Alexamenos remains true!' Conversations of this sort must have occurred in
all classes of society. Among the common people they were
based on evil-minded gossip, on calumnies, on tales of ritual
crime and nocturnal debaucheries. The better off gave a gri-
mace and uttered the kind of remarks recorded by Tertullian:
'He's a good fellow: what a pity he's a Christian!' or even:
'How in the world could anyone as intelligent as he is be converted to Christianity?'

In many cases the banter became more strained and verged
on the tragic. This happened, for instance, in families where
one member confessed himself a Christian and behaved as
such. Domestic quarrels, of the kind found in France during
the period of the Dreyfus scandal, give some idea of the type
of family upheavals which took place. Was not the pagan father whose son became a Christian bound to disinherit this
offspring who would no longer carry on the cult of the gods
of his *gens*? And would the pagan husband whose wife was a
Christian convert allow her to leave the house at night to take
part in the weird ceremonies around which so many rumours
raged? Here and there there were even a few comic cases, such
as the one related by Tertullian, where a husband who was
extremely suspicious of his wife (and with reason!) noticed
her suddenly change her conduct completely. When he
learned the reason for this transformation he begged her to

take back her lovers again rather than inflict on him the shame of being the husband of a Christian!

Difficulties did not only occur within the family circle. They appeared on the public plane as well. On countless occasions the collective way of life, as established by centuries of paganism, proved incompatible with Christian loyalty. Suppose a Christian merchant wanted to borrow some money; the lender would demand the customary oath in the name of the pagan gods: what was the Christian to do? What about all the Christian workmen, sculptors, painters and gilders, who worked in studios producing statuettes of the Roman idols: should they continue to work there? Here was a Christian teacher who was asked to instruct his pupils in the great stories from classical mythology: how was he to get out of this? Or it might be simply a question of an official festival—and, Zeus knows, there were plenty of those! Should the Christian go and watch the degrading spectacles in the circus? If he failed to attend this could, in times of persecution, prove an inevitable means of self-denunciation to the prosecuting tribunal. Owing to their immorality and implied support of idolatry, a fair number of occupations were prohibited to Christians: St Hippolytus lists those of brothel-keeper, sculptor or painter of idols, playwright and actor, teacher, charioteer, gladiator, priest or sacristan of temples, judge and governor (in so far as these offices gave the holder the right to condemn men to death), magician, soothsayer, astrologer, incantator and interpreter of dreams. It is clear from this that cases in which the rupture between the Christian and pagan society was inevitable were very numerous indeed.

In actual fact, did this rupture always take place? It would undoubtedly be an exaggeration to say that it did. Human nature has its weaknesses, even when it is steeped in an atmosphere of heroism. Although primitive Christianity had few apostates, although principles were safeguarded in the vast majority of cases, it must also be admitted that there were some Christians who tried to lean in two directions at once, to compromise with paganism, to play a double game. Economic necessities might justify the adoption of certain ambiguous attitudes, and also the need to preserve the faithful for the Church, and not to send them all to their deaths. However, alongside these isolated waverers there were also large numbers of heroes, of Christians whom no danger could daunt: such as the clerk who smashed his writing tablets to smithereens rather than inscribe the condemnation of one of his brothers in Christ upon them; or those soldiers who refused to carry out an order which they considered contrary to their religious principles.[2] In the measure in which Christianity conquered the upper classes, and believers found themselves invested with public offices, so problems of this kind were to become increasingly acute.

Consequently the life of the early Christians should be envisaged within the context of a number of contradictory attributes. On the one hand, the Christians mingled with the pagan society around them and their whole attitude was a valuable witness of their faith so far as that society was concerned; on the other, an elementary modesty and caution led them to adopt certain secret signs. It is highly probable that the sign of the Cross, rapidly traced across the forehead, lips and breast,[3] must have been both a liturgical gesture and also a way in which the faithful identified themselves to one another. Esoteric markings on houses, such as the drawings of a fish,[4] would have had a meaning analogous to those signs

[2] However, it should be noted that, until the end of the second century, Christians were not, in principle, 'conscientious objectors.' There actually seem to have been a fair number of them in the army, and these Christian soldiers were often missionaries.

[3] This was undoubtedly the way in which Christians inscribed the sign of the Cross at first. Several texts refer to this triple touching of the forehead, the lips and the breast, the three superior attributes of man—intelligence, love and strength—being thus placed under the protection of the Cross. Our modern way of making the sign of the Cross was to prevail in the fourth century. However, the ancient form has been retained in certain usages, e.g. it is still made at the reading of the Gospel.

[4] The idea of using mystical, secret signs must have arisen in the Christian communities in Greece and Asia. Perhaps it was an imitation of certain customs followed by the sects and religions of the mysteries. The very concept of secret pictures is akin to the systems of thought found in Gnosticism. The principal signs used were the anchor, the sailing-ship, the Good Shepherd, the lamb bearing a T or a cross, and the cross crowned by the dove from the ark; a curious engraved stone which is now in the Kircher Museum in Rome depicts them all. The most famous sign was the fish, whose use was extremely

which vagabonds and gipsies draw today to mark out the way they have gone. And it is natural to think that the religious assemblies of the first churches must have been surrounded by a certain secrecy, that secrecy whose image has been preserved until our own day by the catacombs.

## THE CATACOMBS

Even though the catacombs are not the only framework within which the young, ever-growing Christianity should be depicted, they remain, nevertheless, the predestined place where it is easiest for us to evoke the memory of our ancestors in Jesus, who sowed the Gospel seed deep in the heart of our civilization. They form the indestructible symbol of that perilous and semi-secret existence which the Church led in the very period when she was conquering the world, just as their walls still express in a thousand and one ways the two great virtues which, when all else is said and done, enabled that triumph to take place: love and faithfulness. It is impossible for a Christian to penetrate the length of these underground passages, where the air is stagnant with the stench of dampness and of burnt wax, without feeling vividly aware of a presence all about him. Here they are, those tens of thousands of believers, whose prayers filled those dark depths with their murmuring; and despite the empty tombs here they will always remain, those who sleep here in the peace of Christ.

The word which we use to designate these vast hypogeums, and which nowadays conjures up a whole picture in itself, derives, in fact, from an error of interpretation. This term already appeared on the old 'guide-books' which the pilgrims

---

common throughout primitive Christianity. It often occurs as a decoration, and in the *graffiti* it is meant as an allusion to Him who told His disciples that they would be 'fishers of men'; it reminds men of the fishes that, along with the bread, were multiplied in the miracle. But above all, in an age when Greek was the universal language, it enabled a play of words on the esoteric character. The word ICHTHUS —Greek for 'fish'—was made up of the initial letters of the five words which read 'Jesus Christ—of God the Son—Saviour,' i.e. Iesous CHristos THeou Uios Sôter. Thus, in the catacombs the representation of a fish bearing upon its back the basket of eucharistic loaves is found very frequently.

who visited Rome in the Middle Ages clutched in their hands. But it then indicated only a very small fragment of our modern 'catacombs,' namely, the area around the ancient basilica of St Sebastian, rather more than a mile to the southeast of Rome, on the Appian Way. It was the only 'region' which was well known and venerated at that time. Since it was situated in a hollow of land, it was known as 'near the dell,' in other words, in Greek, the official language of the primitive Church, *kata kumben*. When in the sixteenth century men became interested in the other sites connected with primitive Christianity, the same name was applied to all of them.

The catacombs were cemeteries: gigantic, fantastically large cemeteries in which generations of Christians interred their dead. While those at Rome are the biggest, they are also found in Sicily, notably at Syracuse, in Tuscany, in Africa, where the catacombs at Hadrumetes are famous, in Egypt, and even in Asia Minor. At Rome the oldest catacombs undoubtedly date back to the first century: the 'Vatican grottoes,' the catacomb of Commodilla on the Ostian Way, and the 'regions' of St Priscilla, St Domitilla and Ostrianus. In the last-named of these, which is situated not far from St Agnes-without-the-Walls, on the Nomentane Way, St Peter himself may have preached to many Christian congregations. The body of St Paul rested in the cemetery of Commodilla. It was not until 412, when the outskirts of the city, which were ravaged by Alaric, lost all their security, that the catacombs ceased to be used as burial-places. By the early Middle Ages the entire Roman countryside had been turned into marshland as a result of the breaking of the aqueducts, and had become a wilderness, infested with bandits. The custom of visiting these holy places—the catacombs—died out. It was almost by chance that Bosio rediscovered *underground Rome* in 1578 and indicated its whereabouts.

The custom of having subterranean cemeteries was not a new one: it had already been followed in Egypt and Phoenicia for several thousand years past, and only a stone's throw from Rome, in the heart of Etruscan country, men could see the vast burial-grounds hollowed out in the earth by that mysterious people: burial-grounds that stretched from the Tyrrhenian Sea to the slopes of the hillsides, from Viterbo to Volterra. In Roman Italy itself the Jews had practised the inhumation of their dead in various hypogeums. Several of these have been discovered alongside a number of Christian catacombs, and the adherents of Mithras also hollowed out underground cemeteries. Why did the Christians adopt this custom rather than that which was far more common—and more economical— at Rome, namely, that of cremating corpses, of placing the ashes in urns, and of setting the urns out in *columbaria*, 'pigeonries'? Possibly because inhumation seemed more respectful treatment for a body destined to be resurrected. Perhaps to conform to the custom which had been followed in the burial of Jesus. Or the explanation may be simpler still: because, according to the biblical tradition which the Christians observed, there was never any question of cremating the dead.

The oldest cemeteries were situated on land which members of the community provided for the use of the dead. This was done by Flavia Domitilla, Vespasian's niece: the converted aristocrat had a burial-ground built on the site of one of her villas for those of her family who had adopted the Christian faith; this was the 'Flavian sepulchre' whose enchanting ornamental decorations are still admired today. Then, imitating—albeit with an entirely new purpose in mind —those wealthy folk who provided a resting-place for the ashes of their freedmen and their clients, she had funeral galleries tunnelled out alongside the Flavian mausoleum, destined for the bodies of her more humble brethren in Christ. In this way vast burial-grounds multiplied along the whole length of the highways leading out of Rome, situated outside the city walls, as the law demanded. The Appian Way, where a great number of pagan funeral monuments already stood, was literally lined with them. As the Church grew, so her necropolises increased too; from the third century onwards they were to belong to the whole community, and no longer to be the private property of certain individuals. Protected by Roman law, which held sacred all land in which the dead were laid to rest, and which encouraged the poor to form themselves into funeral associations in order to acquire collective tombs, the catacombs were able, for the space of three hundred years —even in times of persecution—to erect their entrance gateways quite openly in the Roman countryside, and to drive

their galleries deep under the soil; the Government did for-
bid their use at the end of the third century, but this was
a quite exceptional act.

This was how this underground world developed, this
strange capital of the twilight and the dead, this city of hope
which offers the modern visitor to Rome such a moving display.
Into the sandy subsoil whose friability must have rendered the
work less arduous, but whose adhesive property also enabled
the builders to make excavations firm enough to allow them
to wait for the action of the air to harden them, the *fossores*,
the folk belonging to the pious corporation of the pick and
the mattock, tunnelled out their vast galleries with a patience
that is only equalled by their audacity and their skill. They
twisted them into complex patterns, they superimposed one
upon another, they organized them into prodigious labyrinths.
They plastered over mile upon mile of the inner walls, which
were destined to be decorated in brilliant colours. These grave-
diggers of God, who were almost members of the ecclesiastical
hierarchy, or at all events, their immediate assistants, played
a leading role in the primitive Church. In 217 an administra-
tor-general of cemeteries actually became pope. He was St
Callixtus I, the same man after whom one of the most interesting 'regions' of the Roman catacombs is named.

Anyone who enters this 'subterranean Rome' is overwhelmed by its size. In some places the galleries are five
storeys high, and the deepest is twenty-five yards below the
ground. What is the actual extent of this city of the shadows?
Some authorities claim that there are some four hundred and
fifty miles of galleries, or even five hundred and more. The
cemetery of St Sabina alone, which has been measured with
great care, has yielded the following figures upon excavation:
an area of 16,500 square yards, a length of 1,620 yards, and
5,736 tombs. However, this is not the largest of the catacombs.
And it is quite possible that we do not yet know about every
single one of those necropolises which Christian piety tunnelled beneath the soil of Rome, and that archaeology may
reveal the existence of others in the future.

The enormous size of these cemeteries, the placing amongst
them of a number of still vaster underground chambers, and
the symbols on the walls, suggest that they may have been

not simply the places where the living laid their dead, but also real places of worship. However, this interpretation should not be carried too far. It can be regarded as certain that the Christians—who, moreover, followed pagan custom in this respect—went there to commemorate their dead: the funeral love-feast, once christianized, could become a eucharistic banquet. The veneration of the sanctified bodies of the martyrs would have attracted numerous visitors and resulted in religious assemblies being held around them. But this does not mean that the catacombs were the normal place of Christian worship. It was only when persecution waxed fiercest that, rather than hold services in the houses of the faithful or in buildings specially consecrated for the purpose, people judged it wisest to meet deep in the entrails of the Christian earth. During the systematic persecution of the third century, the catacombs were actually equipped as veritable hiding-places, with blocked galleries, false exits and secret openings into the nearby quarries. It is the whole life of the primitive Christians —all their piety, their communal feeling, their care for the fugitives and their long-suffering courage—which survives in these necropolises as a living memory, and which makes these empty places so wonderfully crowded in our hearts.

The pilgrim should visit the catacombs in the evening, when the Alban Hills are becoming blurred against the purple sky, and the broad pines and cypresses along the Appian Way are no more than gaunt silhouettes on the horizon. The scent of sun-warmed earth, of dead grass and of wild flowers is carried along by the wind blowing down from the Sabine country. Faithful to the trysting-place given them by Chateaubriand, the mighty ruins of Claudius' aqueduct rise up, majestic, in the plain, and there, too, stands the mausoleum of Caecilia Metella, untouched by time, and easily recognizable from far away. Tens of thousands of Christians must, like ourselves, have felt the gentleness of this approaching nightfall, and the same soft-murmuring breeze, as they made their way, in small, furtive groups, to take part in the midnight communion banquet. Then one enters the gallery and, somewhat hesitantly, follows the guide's torch. The stuffy atmosphere grips one's throat; instinctively one talks in a whisper. One can spend several hours wandering along the *ambulacres,* brushing past the edges of the tombs in galleries which are often little more than three feet wide. One can spend hour upon hour looking at the long niches hollowed out of the sides of the tunnels: the *loculi*. Each one once housed a body in readiness for the Resurrection. As the light flickers on a wall or a curve of the roof one sees strange figures depicted there, easily recognizable from one's own biblical memories: Moses striking the rock, Daniel in the lion's den, Jonah escaping from the belly of the whale, or the Good Shepherd standing between two lambs. As one's eyes become more accustomed to the half-light, it is often possible to see there a delicate fantasy of beauty, a tracery of flowers, birds and leaves which the muted tones of the fresco blend into a blur of exquisite colours. But the Christian's greatest discovery in the semi-darkness is this host of names, some famous, some unknown, often badly carved on a piece of earthenware or stucco-work: the names of his long-dead brethren in Jesus. These names touch all our finest loyalties, and they are accompanied, like a refrain, by the two great words of Christian hope: *in pace*.

So, long before it conquered the capital of the Empire, Christianity had established itself all about that capital by means of the tunnels and galleries of the catacombs: a prodigious method of investment indeed!

## ENTRY INTO THE CHURCH OF CHRIST

These early Christians are the living link which binds us—the Christians of today—to the Apostolic Age and to the memory of the Saviour Himself. Is it possible for us to visualize what their inner life must have been like, to discover the concrete fundamentals of that religious experience from which our own derives? There is no doubt of the answer: though certain points remain debatable in that various interpretations can be proposed for this or that spiritual attitude of theirs, the picture as a whole seems perfectly clear to us today. Thanks to the enormous quantity of archaeological evidence provided by the catacombs, the numerous religious texts, the letters of saints and bishops, treatises and mystical compositions, all of which we shall turn to again later,[5] it is possible

[5] See the next chapter.

to clarify all the principal matters relating to primitive Christianity's faith and practice. The spiritual life of the early Christians is infinitely better known to us than that of their pagan contemporaries.

However—and this qualification is quite obligatory—despite all the documents that we possess, it is not certain that we fully understand the soul of these first Christians. Perhaps the background has changed too much for identical loyalties alone to be enough to create identical states of mind. We are now far removed indeed from those times of Revelation, and for the vast majority of Christians today the second coming of the Son of Man, which the Gospel proclaims as always possible at any time, has been lost in a nebulous future. Things were very different so far as the early Christians were concerned. On the one hand the great historical fact of the life of Jesus was still very near to them; they were within a hair's breadth of it; the Apostles' immediate disciples had told them all its details; the Holy Spirit, still bubbling up in men's souls as on the day of Pentecost, poured forth an unceasing spate of miracles. And, on the other hand, a large number of Christians, possibly the majority of them, believed that the end of the world was close at hand, that Christ was about to reappear on the clouds of heaven, and that, in short, their wretched earthly existence was but the brief prelude to an almost immediate eternity. 'May God's Grace quickly come, and this world pass away!' cries the author of the *Didache*. It is this background that we must bear in mind when considering the life of the early Christians; that life was seen as placed between the first and second comings of Christ.

How did one become a Christian? In the West today baptism marks the usual way of entry into the Church; it places the child within an affiliation, within an obedience, almost from birth onwards; though a number of adult conversions do occur, they remain exceptions to the general rule. The position was quite different during the first centuries of the Church's existence. Conversion was the general rule. Only gradually, when several generations of believers had succeeded those of the converts, were there many 'born Christians.' Even at the end of the second century Tertullian could still write: 'A man becomes a Christian: he is not born one.'[6]

Unhappily it is difficult for us to reconstruct the psychological evolution which created a Christian from a pagan or a Jew. We can recall that vast sense of expectancy which has already been noticed in the restlessness of the classical soul. We can assess the attraction of a doctrine which called all the wretched, all the disinherited of the earth, all the sufferers and all the slaves, to liberty, to complete fulfilment as children of God. We can think of all those arguments which are found so frequently in Christian dialectic, which set out to prove to those loyal to the Torah that Jesus really was the Messiah and that His message fulfilled the hope of Israel. Finally, we can award their full weight to the miracles, which were exceedingly numerous at this time, and which must have contributed to showing the pagans the truth of the Christian lesson. But this whole list leaves out the real driving force which belongs to the realms of the soul, to those dark recesses of the human mind in which God works silently and secretly.

However, one fact should be stated, for it is a fact that has symbolic value. The enormous number of conversions is striking proof of the fervour, dignity and sanctity of the early Church. It was because the Christians dared to declare their faith, whatever the circumstances, because their way of life was, generally speaking, wonderful for its feeling of love and its sense of justice, and because they died so heroically, that their community attracted so many souls to it. This man was converted after hearing a Gospel missionary preaching in some quarter of the town; that one after witnessing a martyrdom. In short, the power of example explains these conversions.

Once he had received God's call and wished to belong to Christ, the convert was not admitted into the bosom of the Church straight away. No longer was an Apostle's single speech

---

[6] '*Fiunt, non nascuntur Christiani.*' This is, moreover, a rather obscure sentence, open to three different interpretations. It is usually taken as a declaration that adult conversions were virtually the general rule; or else as an expression of the theological idea that man, being born a sinner, can only become a Christian through the sacrament of baptism. Or, thirdly, it is regarded as an implication that even children born as Christians need a preparation, a catechesis, before being received into the Church.

considered sufficient preparation for the mass baptism of the crowds it had fired with enthusiasm. As it grew Christianity had been obliged to become more prudent and cautious; it imposed a period of initiation on all those who approached it—a catechumenate—and this discipline of apprenticeship, which developed gradually over a period of one hundred and fifty years, was to assume, from the end of the second century onwards, the fixed characteristics which it retained until far into the Middle Ages.

The *catechumen*, therefore, was the Gospel apprentice, the candidate for baptism. During his compulsory period of noviciate, by following the course enjoined by the ecclesiastical authority, he was expected to assimilate all the truths of the Christian faith. At the same time he would prove, by his own conduct, that he was fit to be admitted into the bosom of the faithful. This moral, intellectual and spiritual preparation became increasingly intense as the hour when the *dignus entrare* would be pronounced over the postulant grew nearer: namely, as Easter approached, for, since a date so ancient that it is unknown, this festival had been fixed as the time when the baptismal rites took place.[7]

One very ancient text, the *Didache*, or *Doctrine of the Apostles*, which is usually attributed to the period 70–150, gives us an idea of what was taught to the catechumens in the early Christian communities in the East, where this booklet was compiled. It is a kind of summary of the obligations which the candidate for Christian baptism had to accept:

'There are two roads, the road of life, the road of death. There is a vast difference between the two.

'This is the road of life. The first commandment: you shall love God, who made you, then you shall love your neighbour as yourself, and you shall not do anything to him that you would not want him to do to you.

'The second commandment of Christian doctrine is this:

[7] But it need hardly be said that where there was any danger of death, and, in particular, the possibility of martyrdom, these delays were removed. In such cases the catechumen could be baptized even if his preparation was incomplete. It is also known that martyrdom took the place of baptism for those who died in Christ's service before receiving the sacrament.

you shall not commit adultery; you shall not corrupt young
boys; you shall commit neither fornication, nor theft, nor
magic, nor wrongful imprisonment; you shall not kill children,
either by abortion or after birth; you shall not covet your
neighbour's goods. You shall not perjure yourself, nor bear
false witness; you shall not slander nor harbour grudges. You
shall not think one way, yet speak in another, for duplicity is
a fatal snare; your words should be neither mendacious nor
empty, but efficacious. You shall be neither greedy, nor rapa-
cious, nor hypocritical, nor cruel, nor arrogant, and you shall
not hatch evil plots against your neighbour. You must hate no
one. You must bless those who hate you, and pray for them,
and, as for the rest, you must love them more than your own
life' (*Didache*, i, ii).

Anyone reading this extremely simple and noble text is immediately struck by the fact that it takes its stand almost
wholly on the moral plane, that, aside from a few strictures
more specially adapted to customs prevailing at the time of
writing (paederasty and abortion, for example), it is a direct
descendant of the Decalogue and Jewish moral tradition.
Should it be assumed, therefore, that the catechumens received only moral instruction? No, obviously not. From the
very beginning an act of faith had been expected of the individual who wished to become a Christian. When Candace's
eunuch had asked to be baptized, Philip the deacon had replied: 'If thou dost believe with all thy heart, thou mayest'
(Acts viii. 37). So Christian postulants were taught the things
they must believe. A few weeks before the baptismal ceremony, generally in the third week of Lent, they were called together, and, in the presence of their godfathers, godmothers
and relations, listened to an explanation of the *Our Father* and
of a kind of formulary which contained a summary of the essentials of the faith: *the Creed*. Next they had to pass a test:
this was known as 'the rendering of the Creed.' On the day of
baptism each new Christian had to declare that he accepted
all the precepts contained in this text, and that he agreed to
keep the rules it laid down.

In this way, after proper preparation, the neophyte was accepted for *baptism*. This was the decisive rite, the one which
made a real Christian of him. It was a very ancient rite, and

had been of fundamental importance right from the Church's beginnings, as we have seen.[8] It was a rite administered by John the Baptist on the banks of the Jordan, a rite which Christ had hallowed and transformed by Himself receiving it, a rite which the first generations of believers had interpreted, very precisely, as the one which bestowed on the recipient the bliss of belonging to Jesus. Writing to the Colossians, St Paul declared: 'You, by baptism, have been united with his [i.e. Jesus'] burial, united too with his resurrection, through your faith in that exercise of power by which God raised him from the dead' (Col. ii. 12). And this was why baptism was administered on Easter Eve: the baptized Christian died and was resurrected with Christ.

Baptism continued to be administered with water, just as it had been in the days when Christ's forerunner had conferred it at the ford at Bethabara, and this has remained its medium until our own day. Even to the unbeliever it therefore evoked all kinds of impressive traditions: the Jewish ritual ablutions, the *mikweh* which the priests had to perform before approaching the Holy of Holies on the altar; or the ceremonies which, in several countries, accompanied the manumission of a slave: the washing away of a symbolic mark on the forehead in Asia Minor, the 'bath of purification' in Mesopotamia. But in Christian eyes this rite assumed its full meaning by being linked with the declaration of faith referred to above.

We must turn once again to the *Didache* for our knowledge of the ceremonial surrounding baptism, and its spiritual meaning. 'Baptize in the name of the Father, the Son and the Holy Spirit. Baptize in running water. If there is no running water available, other water may be used, and if you cannot administer it in cold water, then do so in warm. If you have neither one nor the other, sprinkle some water on the catechumen's head three times, in the name of the Father, the Son and the Holy Spirit' (*Didache*, vii). This extract makes it quite certain that by preference the rite should be celebrated in running water, in a river, and failing this in a pool; if the

---

[8] See Chapter I, section: 'A Truly Communal Community Life,' and also Chapter I of the author's *Jesus in His Time*.

latter, too, were impossible it should be administered simply by sprinkling water on the forehead, as is the most customary form of baptism nowadays. It is striking to note with what exactitude all these different circumstances are foreseen and allowed for, proof of the liturgical development already achieved by the Church only half a century after Christ's death. Though the person administering baptism is not specified, it seems clear that he must have been a priest or even a bishop, at least at the beginning; St Ignatius states categorically that baptisms are not allowed save in the presence of the bishop.

Various related ceremonies rapidly grew up around this fundamental rite. Our own rituals have preserved their memory: the blessing of the baptismal pool (which was sometimes to be shaped like a cross), unctions of holy oil smeared on the bodies of the catechumens, those 'athletes of Christ,' the solemn renunciation of pagan errors and human temptations. In Tertullian's time the ancient rite of the *laying on* of hands, which we have already seen in use in the first Christian community in Palestine, was performed by an unction of sweet-scented oil being poured on the forehead of the new believer. Henceforth the catechumen was a member of the Church; he was a Christian in the fullest sense of the term.

## THE APOSTLES' CREED, THE 'RULE OF FAITH'

What were the contents of this formula by which the newly baptized Christian proclaimed his adherence to Christ and his membership of the Church? For the modern Christian the essential truths to which he adheres, and the dogmas which he accepts, are summed up in both the well-known Creeds: the *Apostles' Creed*, which is usually recited in private prayer, and the *Nicene Creed*, which belongs to the ordinary of the mass. The first Christians possessed texts exactly analogous to these, and our Creeds are directly descended from them: one of the most moving aspects of the history of the primitive Church is the way in which it reveals that fundamental bond that links it to the faithful of today. Our Creeds have been elaborated and completed, but they remain substantially those

of the first Christians. They are, in fact, those same texts recited by baptized folk who lived in the age of the martyrs, the
texts that Tertullian was to call the 'Rules of Faith.'

When the Church was a new-born creation, the act of faith
had been contained in four simple words: 'I believe in Jesus!'
Thus the Ethiopian eunuch had answered Philip the deacon:
'I believe that Jesus Christ is the Son of God.' And, of course,
the belief in Jesus Christ, the Son of God, is the very essential
of Christianity. During the first few decades, particularly in
communities which were in close contact with the Jews, emphasis rested almost solely on the Christological side of the
faith. Faced with Israel's unbelief, it was abundantly necessary to declare the fact of Jesus the Messiah: the Jesus who
was crucified, and who rose from the dead, as St Paul explained
it. The First Epistle to the Corinthians contains a short Credo
of the kind which men must have used at that time: that
'Christ, as the Scriptures had foretold, died for our sins; that
he was buried, and then, as the Scriptures had foretold, rose
again on the third day. That he was seen by Cephas, then by
the eleven Apostles, and afterwards by more than five hundred
of the brethren at once . . .' (1 Cor. xv. 3–7). Still later, at
the end of the first century, St Ignatius of Antioch summed
up what the faithful must believe as follows, in a letter to the
Christians of Smyrna: 'You must believe absolutely that our
Lord was the Son of God, a true lineal descendant of David
by divine will and power; that he was indeed born of a virgin;
that he received baptism at the hands of John that all should
be justly fulfilled; that his flesh was really pierced with the
nails for us, under Pontius Pilate and Herod the Tetrarch;
that we owe our life to his suffering on the cross, to his
blessed and divine Passion; that, through his Resurrection, he
has conquered all time, grouping under his standard his saints
and his faithful, those from the bosom of Judaism as well as
those from heathendom in one single body, which is his
Church' (Smyrn. i. 12). In short, the schema of Christ's entire
mission to mankind, as recorded in the Gospels, is included
in this 'Rule of Faith.'

However, a collection of dogmatic formulae was soon to be
developed. Why? The answer is quite simple. Since Christianity was a living reality, it obeyed the very law of life, which

insists that every human organism, while remaining faithful to itself, develops all its cellules, adapts itself to circumstances, reacts upon the outside world. The Christian faith had scarcely made its appearance when it ran up against contradiction; it had been worked by the leavens of the human mind. Life is a perpetual choice, a necessary option. The Church, in order to progress on her course, has a daily choice to make.

In this way she was lead to clarify more and more this or that aspect of the Master's teaching which ran the risk of being perverted by an outside enemy or a heretic. Naturally she invented nothing: she merely stated the facts clearly. For example, she set out the theology of the Trinity at a very early date. This is contained in the Gospels, but it was essential for her to explain it further in the face of certain errors and attacks. St Clement of Rome, for instance, ended one of his letters with that cry of praise which is also a dogmatic declaration: 'Glory be to God! Glory be to our Lord Jesus Christ! Glory be to the Holy Spirit, faith and hope of the elect!' Likewise St Irenaeus, Bishop of Lyons at the end of the second century, declared that 'although scattered throughout the whole world, the Church has received from the Apostles and their disciples its faith in God, the Father Almighty, Creator of heaven, earth and sea, and of all things therein—and in one Christ Jesus, the Son of God, made incarnate for our salvation—and in the Holy Spirit, who has spoken through the mouths of the prophets.' Likewise, at the other side of the Roman world, Origen in Egypt and Tertullian in Africa proclaimed similar fundamental facts. The striking thing about the variety of efforts which animated this extremely vigorous Church is the unanimity of their principles, and the steady development achieved by the Church thereby.

Very soon, it seems, all the fundamentals of the faith were assembled in one single text, which was used as the basis for the catechumens' instruction; this was the *Apostles' Creed.* The Greek word for 'Creed' suggests the idea of a sign of identification. One tradition, recorded by Rufinus in the fourth century, declares that the Apostles themselves were told by Christ that, before going their separate ways, they must compose a rule of faith designed to ensure unity of teaching in the Church, and that they had in fact drafted this Creed under divine inspiration, pooling their knowledge to do so. Later on people were to go so far as to assert that each of the twelve articles contained in the text had been drafted by a different Apostle, chosen by name. . . . The Catholic Church does not guarantee the inspired character of this text, but it is quite clear, from its contents, from its pithy brevity and its dignified simplicity, that it is closely connected with the finest writings of the apostolic period, and that its recitation is bound up with the Church's most ancient liturgy: in it is inscribed for ever an expanded Trinitarian formula, a rule of faith, and the most permanent and infallible of the Church's teachings.

The *Apostles' Creed* was certainly set out in writing simultaneously in the majority of the large Christian communities; thus there were versions of it in Jerusalem, Caesarea, Antioch, Alexandria and Rome, each differing from the rest in minor details. The modern text of the *Apostles' Creed*[9] derives from the Roman version, not as it appears in Rufinus, but as it was completed in Gaul in the sixth century (whence derives its title of 'the Gallican version'). However, by comparing the various primitive drafts with one another—drafts which have either been preserved for us by the Fathers or discovered in Egyptian papyruses—it is possible to obtain an accurate idea of the Creed which a new Christian had to recite sixteen or seventeen hundred years ago on receiving the sacrament of baptism. Here it is:[10]

I believe in God, the Father almighty,
*Creator of heaven and earth.*
And in Jesus Christ, His only Son, our Lord;
who was *conceived* by the Holy Ghost,
born of the Virgin Mary,
*suffered* under Pontius Pilate, was crucified, *dead* and buried;
He descended into hell;
the third day He rose again from the dead;
that He ascended into heaven,

[9] The *Nicene Creed* is not dealt with here. It will be studied in Chapter X.

[10] The italics denote passages in the Creed as it is recited today which would not have appeared in the oldest texts.

sitteth at the right hand of God the Father almighty;
from thence He shall come to judge the living and the dead.

*I believe* in the Holy Ghost;
the Holy *Catholic* Church;
*the communion of saints;*
the forgiveness of sins;
the resurrection of the body;
*and life everlasting.* Amen.

## THE EUCHARIST, THE 'BODY OF OUR LORD'

Once he had entered the Church, the baptized Christian shared in the whole life of the community: he belonged to Christ, he was a member of His Body. Christ! It is indeed the sublime figure of Christ Himself which shines from the centre of primitive Christianity with incomparable intensity and splendour. It was He whom the Christian of these early times considered in the reality of very recent history. No form of piety existed then which was not rigidly subordinated to the adoration of the living God.[11] It was Christ whom men

---

[11] Aside from the adoration of Christ, there were various forms of piety ranking second to it and strictly bound up with it. Just as Jesus was man's mediator before the Father, so people venerated those secondary mediators who enabled the soul to achieve unity with Christ Himself more easily. This was the way in which piety towards the saints and martyrs developed; St Jerome was to say of this: 'Their faith and works bind them to Christ: they stand before Him, like humanity's privileged spokesmen!'

Gradually one of these mediators between man and Christ became singled out from the rest: this was Mary, the mother of Jesus, to whom the angel had said: 'Blessed art thou among women.' With touching confidence, men besought her to pray to her own child for them. At first, however, she occupied a very modest place in men's minds. We find her mentioned hardly at all; properly speaking, there is no Marian liturgy. In Father Régamy's words: 'The Christian faith was to take some time to understand fully that mystery whose total acceptance rested upon total understanding.' However, the dogmatic importance of the Virgin Mother had been asserted from earliest times. The oldest creeds follow the example of the Gospels in confessing that Jesus was born of the Holy Spirit and the Virgin Mary. Against the Docetists who denied the reality of the Incarnation, the

painted on the walls of the catacombs. It was He whom men invoked by a hundred different names, all charged with meaning, wherein many biblical memories were enshrined: Emmanuel, the Star of the East, the second Abel, Melchisedek, the priest in eternity, Jonah, Jacob or Joshua; it was He who was praised, according to the Gospel phraseology, as the Fisherman, the Cornerstone, the Living Water, the Blood, the Milk, the Yeast which made the dough rise, or the Salt which never lost its freshness. It was He who was regarded as the changeless centre of time—'What Jesus was yesterday, and is today, he remains for ever' (Heb. xiii. 8)—and, for this reason, all the prayers of the day, all the festivals of the year, were organized in commemoration of His life. He was the One Model whom the least of the faithful desired to imitate in virtue and love, and He was also the One Intercessor, through whom mortal man could hope to communicate with the Ineffable Divine, the mediator who could validly implore the Almighty. 'Glory to the Father, *through* the Son, and in the

---

motherhood of Mary proved the truth of Christ's humanity. Against the heresies which sought to refuse Jesus His divinity, the dogma of the Virgin birth called attention to the transcendency of He who was made man in a fashion different from that in which other men were conceived. About 100 St Ignatius of Antioch was already saying 'Turn a deaf ear to anyone who does not confess that Jesus, the descendant of David, was born of the Virgin Mary,' and his *Epistle to the Ephesians* contains the following profound sentence: 'The ruler of this world is ignorant of the virginity of Mary, and of her travail in childbirth, and of the Lord's death: these are three resounding mysteries performed in the silence of God.' This dogmatic role, which the earliest Fathers of the Church had appreciated so clearly, gradually became blended with tenderness and veneration. The finest poems in the *Song of Songs* were to be interpreted in terms of the graces of Mary: the mysterious Chapter XIII of the Apocalypse was to be understood as a definition of her role as mediatrix. Gradually her figure appeared among the paintings on the walls of the catacombs: as the virgin to whom Isaiah foretold the miraculous birth, as the young girl whom the angel visited, and as the mother holding in her arms the Infant God. One ill-carved third-century inscription calls her *Digenitrix*. So, closely linked with Christ, and subordinate to Him, the Catholic Church's cult of the *Blessed Virgin* (the *Panagia* of the Greeks), as it was developed at the end of the fourth century and in the course of the fifth, has its roots far back in early Christian history. (See Chapter XI, section: 'The Life of the Christian Soul.')

Holy Spirit!' says one ancient formula which was used as a prayer-ending. And when Christians, faced with execution, were about to offer their final, supreme witness, they turned their thoughts towards Christ, always towards Christ: 'Lord Jesus, I bow my head as a sacrifice for your love. You live in eternity, and to you be all glory and splendour for ever and ever! Amen!'[12]

Consequently the fundamental ceremony of Christian life was the one which expressed in its single self all the essentials of Jesus' message, His teaching and His Passion. This was the *eucharist* whose Greek translation means 'giving of thanks' and which, precisely because it was regarded as the prayer of prayers, as the echo of that prayer which Christ Himself had uttered at the Last Supper, very soon came to mean what we today understand by the term: the sacrifice which reproduces the gift of the Living God.

Here the reader is in the presence of the most venerable and most ancient of all Christian rites. It existed in the earliest days of the nascent Church, and it exists today. After two thousand years it remains the supreme fact of the Christian religion. The forms in which it has been celebrated may have varied in their details; its basis remains unaltered, and though the liturgy and rites of the eucharist have become more fixed in modern times a true believer of today can derive from it that selfsame bliss and liberation of the spirit which was felt by the Christian of primitive times.

There is no doubt that the eucharist originated in a commemorative ceremony, one reproducing that Last Supper which Jesus had shared with His Apostles, and during which He had commanded them: 'Do this for a commemoration of me' (Luke xxii. 19). In the Acts of the Apostles (ii and xx) this ceremony is referred to as 'the breaking of bread,' a phrase which shows quite clearly that it was an evocation of Christ's Last Supper. Yet, at the same time, it is equally clear that the ceremony showed that it was charged with a spiritual reality. The words of Christ which immediately precede the commemorative command have a meaning which totally pre-

---

[12] The prayer of St Felix, pope and martyr.

vents this 'eucharistic meal'[13] from being regarded as a
simple commemoration alone. 'This is my body . . . this is my
blood. . . .' These mysterious words, which, at the time,
were little clarified by the words of the speech on the bread
of life, became, once explained by the drama of Calvary and
the Resurrection, a veritable pledge for every Christian, one
of those spiritual pledges which enabled them to undertake
their action in the world.[14]

This truly mystical meaning of the eucharist was already
being proclaimed in very early times indeed. St Paul declared:
'We have a cup that we bless; is not this cup we bless a participation in Christ's blood? Is not the bread we break a participation in Christ's body?' (1 Cor. x. 16–17). Christians
were never to deviate from this conviction. 'The eucharist,'
wrote St Ignatius of Antioch, 'is the body of Jesus Christ our
Saviour; his body, which suffered for our sins; his body, which,
in his goodness, the Father has resurrected' (Smyrn. vii. 1).

---

[13] As we have seen, the 'eucharistic meal' was, in origin, a proper
meal. It had been a proper meal in the case of Christ's Last Supper,
part of the Passover dinner. In the community at Jerusalem, and in
those founded by the earliest missions, the eucharist was not dis-
tinguishable from the brethren's 'love-feasts.' However, the differ-
entiation between the two occurred gradually. Why? In his First
Epistle to the Corinthians (xi. 20–1) St Paul gives the reason with
brutal frankness. Even on such holy occasions as these human nature
could gain the upper hand; these love-feasts were sometimes the
occasion for drinking bouts. Consequently the Apostle told his readers,
quite distinctly, that they should not make the eucharist celebration
into a proper meal. 'Those who are hungry had best eat at home.'
It is not possible to say at exactly what date the separation took
place, but it is certain that by the second century it was an accomplished fact.

[14] See Chapter I, section: 'Faith in Jesus and His Spiritual Pledges.'
One question still remains: in the material sense, how can we con-
nect the *love-feast* of the first Christians with the *communion* that we
know today? Lietzmann, the German historian, visualized two types
of eucharist: the Pauline type and the older, Jerusalem type (H.
Lietzmann, *Messe und Herrenmahl*, Bonn, 1926). Werner Goosens
discusses this hypothesis in his *Les Origines de l'Eucharistie*, Paris,
1931. See also: O. Cullmann, 'La Signification de la Sainte Cène
dans le Christianisme primitif' in the *Revue d'histoire et de philoso-
phie religieuse*, 1936, and, in particular, de Montcheuil's 'Signification
eschatologique du repas eucharistique' in *Recherches de science religieuse*, 1946.

And St Justin, the mighty Christian apologist of the second century, demonstrated perfectly the eucharist's central position in the Christian faith, and its full implication: 'We call this food the eucharist. No one may share it unless he believes that our doctrine is true, unless he has received the bath of baptism whereby his sins are forgiven him and he is made regenerate, and unless he lives according to the commandments of Christ. For we do not partake of this food as if it were mere communal bread or communal wine; but just as our Saviour, Jesus Christ, made incarnate by virtue of the Word of God, took flesh and blood for our salvation, so this food, which by assimilation nourishes our blood and our bodies, is the body and blood of Jesus incarnate. This is our doctrine!' (Apol. lxvi).

A text like this demonstrates admirably the dual character of the eucharistic act. On the one hand, in performing this sacred act, the believer obtains a participation in the Divine Life; he consumes the pledges of eternity. But, on the other, this operation has no meaning unless his life is completely renewed with it in mind, and, through it, consecrated to God. Communion with the Body of Christ is simultaneously the acme of mystical union and the result of man's moral effort to identify himself with the Model of models. Here is a dogmatic declaration of a loftiness which no other religion had yet attained, and which sufficed to make Christianity radically different from all the other mysteries and Eastern cults.

For a fair number of religious doctrines were already known which recorded tales of gods who had died and risen again; and the rite of 'the manducation of the god' derived from the obscure totemic traditions of the primitive races. But these completely superficial likenesses, on which the exponents of comparative religion lay such stress, are entirely unconnected with the real essential of the spiritual intention. Apart from the fact that the themes concerning 'resurrected gods' are often quite recent ones, interpreted by modern criticism in language and through a perspective imitated from Christianity, which falsifies their real meaning, it is quite obvious that their myths usually have a solely naturalistic explanation. Attis dies and is resurrected like the vegetation of the earth; he is the tree-god whom spring reanimates. Osiris germinates and pushes forth roots, and his body, which has been cut into fourteen pieces, comes to life again when the fourteen provinces of Egypt are made green once more by the Nile waters. The totemic manducation of the god is no more than a magic rite, assuring the believer of the presence of a mysterious force within him, but having no connection with any moral effort on his part, and demanding no purification of heart from him. The Eastern gods had not descended to the earth because of their love for humanity. The redemption of the human soul was certainly not one of their principal anxieties. The Christian communion stands alone as the sacred act leading to man's union with ineffable and absolute perfection, by making him share in the Passion of God.

The importance of the eucharist in Christian life was such that it assumed the central position among the Christian ceremonies right from the beginning. When the first Christians were asked what was the essential of their religion, they invariably replied by talking of the sacred meal. The liturgical assembly, which the Acts of the Apostles describes on several occasions, and of which there are many examples, recorded by numerous texts, during the first centuries of the Church's life —at Jerusalem, Antioch, Alexandria, Ephesus, Rome, and in Gaul and Africa—is essentially the celebration of the eucharist, the communion with the Living God. Gradually the liturgy was to enclose it within more complex rites; at first the eucharistic ceremony was a simple and almost intimate affair, and probably varied a good deal from one community to another. But during the course of the first two centuries it became more regularized, established itself within a framework of general rules, and added to it prayers and Creeds. As the 'giving of thanks,' it expanded in prayers which were often borrowed from the Old Testament, above all from the most sublime parts of the Psalms. As the commemoration of Christ, the God made man, it included accounts of his life, readings from those texts which were, at the same time, being made into the Gospels. And since it was essentially the ceremony of the whole community, since it gathered together all the faithful in one single intention, it would burst forth, here and there, into collective prayers, into what can be termed unanimous acclamations. In this way, in a dual mystery of union with Christ and human communion, this ceremonial whole in which the entire essential of Christian faith and tradition is fulfilled and summarized was set in working order. We call it the Mass.

## A MASS IN THE EARLY DAYS OF THE CHURCH

The text of the earliest Christian authors, archaeological discoveries and the paintings found in the catacombs enable us to obtain a fairly complete idea of what the celebration of the Mass[15] may have been like in the days of primitive Christianity, e.g. at the end of the second century or the beginning of the third.

First of all, where did it take place? It should again be emphasized that the catacombs provided its setting only in exceptional circumstances, when some martyr was being specially commemorated, or in times of violent persecution, when it was essential for complete secrecy to be observed. Thus the vestibule of the Flavians and various chapels in the Ostian cemetery, or in that of St Hermes, still show signs that they

[15] The origin of the word mass has been much debated. Some authorities think that it derives from the Latin *missa*, the equivalent of *missio* in Low Latin from the fifth to ninth centuries, meaning 'dismissal.' At the end of the ceremony the deacon spoke the words still used today: *ite missa est*, i.e. go, it is finished, you are dismissed. Others relate it to *mensa*, a meal, with the inference of a holy meal, which, in Low Latin, became *messa*. From the end of the fourth century onwards (see Chapter XI, section: 'Liturgy and Festivals') the name was applied to the entire rite. The word occurs again in the Flemish *kermis*: this originally referred to the mass of the Church, the day commemorating the dedication of a local church building, or its patron saint's festival. It also appears in the English *Christmas*. In primitive Christian times, when Greek was still the language most frequently used by the faithful, it seems that the word *eucharist* was used on some occasions, and on others the word *eulogy*, which meant a blessing. The latter eventually came to mean 'the blessed bread,' or blessed object, and it still has this meaning in the Greek Orthodox Church today. Lastly, the primitive Church frequently referred to the Mass by the general term 'sacrament.' St Augustine talks about 'performing the sacraments,' in other words celebrating Mass, the sacrament *par excellence*. The use of the word sacramentaries for the oldest missals derives from this terminology.

were used as places of worship. But generally speaking the Christians assembled fairly openly. A friendly convert, one of those rich folk whom the faith had won for Christ, would put his own house at the community's disposal. Several of Rome's churches still preserve the memory of these wealthy people who gave their homes to the Lord: Prisca, Cecilia, Pudens and Clement; and the remains of several of these mansions have been discovered beneath the foundations of the existing basilicas. Amid the sands of the Syrian Desert, the excavations at Doura Europos have brought to light yet another of these mansion-churches. Moreover, the layout of these wealthy Roman dwellings with their divisions into public and private rooms was admirably suited to the establishment of religious worship within their walls: the entrance hall could hold the catechumens in the same way as it provided a room for receiving the owner's guests; the faithful met in the 'inner court' or *compluvium*; the *tablinum*, the wide corridor leading to the family's personal apartments, provided a place for the priests, and, immediately next to it, the *triclinium*, the dining-room with its three couches, was well suited for the celebration of the sacred meal.

But very soon, the establishment of places of worship within private houses, however permanent their character, was not enough. From about the end of the first century the Christians dreamed of building 'a house for the Church.' Attendances were increasing year by year, and there they would be able to have much larger rooms. There is no doubt at all that by the second century buildings such as those which we nowadays call churches already existed in Rome, as well as at Edessa, Apamea, Alexandria and Antioch. Long before Constantine came to the throne there were several in Syria and Palestine. In some areas they must have been numerous, since on several occasions during the third century the persecuting emperors were to sign edicts ordering their destruction.

The Mass was celebrated with greatest solemnity on Sunday, the day which commemorated the Resurrection, and the day on which the Lord's Coming Again was expected (it had replaced the sabbath). The evening before was spent in solemn preparation; prayers were said, psalms recited, pious instruction given: this was known as *the Vigil*. If the Master was to come, no one must sleep. As soon as the new day began, at midnight, the service began, so that it might end *ad lucem* towards dawn: our midnight Masses preserve the memory of this extremely ancient custom.[16] The brethren and the sisters from all around were gathered together; for some of them it was not always at all easy to come to a nocturnal service; e.g. in the case of a Christian woman who had a pagan husband, or a slave who was closely watched by his pagan master. Whatever their social status, all those present mingled together on terms of perfect equality. As they arrived they greeted one another in the name of Jesus and often exchanged the kiss of peace.

The Mass began: it consisted of two main parts. The first of these was more general in character, and the catechumens were allowed to be present at it; but the second part was reserved for baptized believers alone, and in it the sacrifice and the mystery were completed. The modern Mass has retained this basic division. The man of God who presided, as a rule the bishop himself, stood facing the people. 'Peace be with you, brethren! The Lord be with you!' Many of the things that go to make up the beginning of our present-day Mass did not exist at all; there were no prayers at the foot of the altar, no public confession; the *Introit* did not appear until the fourth century, when the ceremonial character of the Mass was becoming accentuated, and the idea arose of singing a psalm of praise or a short hymn of acclamation while the bishop was advancing to the altar. Thus the Mass now celebrated on Holy Saturday, whose liturgical forms are extremely ancient, has no *introit* and starts with the *Kyrie*.

This first half of the Mass, which was a kind of introduction to the sacrifice, was intended to be devoted to prayer and instruction; for men's minds must be made ready, and their hearts opened, to receive the mystery. A deacon prayed in the name of the people; this was the *supplication*, or *litany*. According to the version in the *Apostolic Constitutions*, a fourth-century compilation which contains a collection of

---

[16] 'Rise at cock-crow,' writes St Hippolytus, 'and say your prayers! for it is the hour when the sons of Israel denied Christ and when we, having faith in Him, watch the approach of the eternal light, our souls filled with hope.'

many of the most ancient traditions of the Church, this ran as follows: 'Let us ask God's blessing upon the catechumens, that He who is all goodness and who loves men may hear their prayers and receive them favourably! May He make known to them the Good News of Christ His Only Son, may He enlighten them with divine knowledge and instruct them in His commandments!' Then followed a whole series of petitionary prayers addressed to the Lord: prayers for the catechumens and for those newly baptized, for the sick and the imprisoned, for those condemned to penal servitude in the mines, for the martyrs awaiting execution, and also, as Christian charity demanded, a prayer for those very people who were torturing them and sending them to their deaths. The faithful responded to each of these pleas with the Greek words that we still use today. *Kyrie eleison!* Lord have mercy upon us! Next, collecting together all men's anxieties and hopes in one brief and moving prayer, the celebrant pronounced the *collect*, the prayer in which all the faithful made appeal to the One: 'O Almighty and Eternal God, the consolation of all who are sad, the strength of all who labour, we beg Thee, hear the supplication of those who are suffering, so that, through their agony, all may rejoice in Thy great mercy!' Whereupon the congregation replied, in token of its agreement: 'Amen! So be it!'

At this point the readings from sacred texts took place. These varied in number, but all were aimed at making the Christian familiar with their traditions and dogmas. The *reader* mounted some steps to a raised seat or platform which St Cyprian was to compare with the tribune from which the Roman magistrates dispensed justice. There he read aloud the various texts which were ordered to complement the meaning of the festival which was being celebrated by virtue of their symbolic sense. What exactly did he read? A few pages from the Old Testament, from the Law and the prophets, some passage from a letter which one of the great leaders of Christianity had written in the course of his apostolate—and which some were still writing at the time—the Epistles of St Paul, St John or St Peter, or even those of St Ignatius or St Clement, or else accounts taken from the Acts of the Apostles. The descriptions of the various martyrdoms, of which we still possess a few extremely moving examples, for instance the description of the martyrs of Lyons, could also have been read aloud in this way. One can imagine what the faithful must have thought as they listened to these accounts—so tragically dramatic in their simplicity—of the sufferings which their brethren had just endured, of sufferings to which, as they knew quite well, several among themselves might be doomed! Between these readings psalms were said or sung, and the cry of hope and faith, the age-old cry of Israel, sprang from every breast: 'Alleluia!'

The final and most essential of these readings was taken from the *Gospel*, from the Word of God. This extract was not entrusted to an ordinary reader, but to the deacons. The passage had been chosen by the bishop himself; later on tradition was to prescribe this or that extract for different days. 'The Lord be with you!' The faithful listened to this standing, in a kind of position of attention which the Jewish congregations in the temple at Jerusalem had been accustomed to take. When the Gospel reading was over the bishop commented on it, or else had a commentary given by a preacher of his choice. This was the *homily*, the forerunner of the modern sermon. Several examples of it can be found among the works of the various Fathers of the Church.[17]

The Mass of the catechumens was almost ended. Then the priest turned to the congregation again, and with arms outstretched repeated the words which are still used today: 'The Lord be with you! Let us pray!' Nowadays no response is made to this call. But in primitive times this was when the prayers of the faithful took place. The people stood with arms stretched wide, in that very beautiful position adopted by the praying folk that can be seen painted on the walls of the catacombs or sculptured on the sarcophagi. During a silence which lasted for several minutes they would pray to Him who was about to become flesh and blood in the bread

[17] It is interesting to see that the Mass of the catechumens reproduces the liturgy of the synagogue: readings from the Law and the prophets, singing of psalms, and the homily. The Creed did not appear in the Mass until much later. At first it was a declaration of faith reserved for use in the rite of baptism and possibly in a few other very special circumstances.

and the wine. A final *collect* ended this period of profound meditation: 'O Lord, we offer Thee our sacrifices and our prayers: we beseech Thee, receive them for those who implore Thee here and for all those whose memory we are commemorating. May they pass from death into life! Amen!'

The second part of the Mass then acquired a more majestic character. The catechumens, the penitents, and also the pagan sympathizers, who were allowed to be present at the service up to this point, now had to leave. The deacons had little more to say during the rest of the ceremony. The congregation remained silent. It was the bishop, the pontiff himself, who was now to act alone. Our modern mass has retained almost the whole of the ancient ceremonial whereby the eucharistic sacrifice was prepared and consumed more than sixteen hundred years ago.

The first action to take place was the offering. In the age of the primitive Church, this included two acts which seem to us so different from each other that no one desires to reconcile them: we call them the *collection* and the *offertory*. In fact they are one and the same thing. In order to join in the sacrifice, each believer had to make an offering: someone would give the bread and wine which were to be consecrated;[18] donations would also be made for the poor, the widows and all those dependent for relief upon the whole community. The deacons separated the alms from the other offerings, and placed the bread and wine upon the altar. We do not know whether the practice of singing a hymn or a psalm during this part of the service existed before the fifth century; but when all was ready the celebrant made a collective prayer in the name of everyone present. 'Brethren, pray that my sacrifice and yours may be acceptable to God the Father Almighty.' The faithful replied 'Amen,' and then the priest, in the prayer known as the *secret* (reserved to the *plebs secreta*, the chosen race of the faithful), asked the Lord, in exchange for these

[18] Some traces of this ancient usage can be found not merely in the oft-disparaged *collection*, but also in the custom which is occasionally practised in modern France of inviting the faithful themselves to place in the pyx the host which is to be consecrated for their communion.

worldly gifts, to grant his people the gifts of heaven and eternity.

Now came the most solemn moment in the whole ceremony; through the will of his representative, Christ Himself was about to be present in the eucharistic species. The *preface* was followed by the *canon of the Mass* in which the *consecration* took place. The bishop invited the faithful to show their joy to the full. 'Lift up your hearts!' 'We have lifted them up unto the Lord!' 'Let us give thanks to the Lord our God!' 'It is meet and just!' And the celebrant continued: 'It is truly meet and just that we should give thanks to Thee, O Holy Lord, Father Almighty, Eternal God!' He enumerated God's blessings, he recalled the great mysteries of the Incarnation and the Redemption. The words of the Gospel came from his lips, in a mystical improvisation. And this supplication, this call of God on earth, ended with the thrice-repeated cry: '*Sanctus, Sanctus, Sanctus. . . .*' Stretching his hands over the bread and the wine, just as we can see one celebrant doing on a painting in the catacombs, the priest was to repeat the very words spoken by Jesus at His Last Supper. The Holy Spirit descended among the believers, the sacrifice was accepted by the Almighty.

Finally came the last part of the mass: the *communion*. The priest broke the bread in the same way that Christ had broken it: this was known as the *breaking of bread*. Owing to its importance, the name often indicated the whole Mass. At this point a most charming prayer was said, the prayer for unity, which is recorded for us in the *Didache*: 'Just as the bread was, in its elements, scattered upon the hillsides, and was made one here, so, O Lord, may Thy Church be gathered up from all the ends of the earth. . . .' This was the place in the service at which all those present came up to share the sacred meal. For all partook of it, all who were pure and holy: the rest were forced to leave, expelled by a categorical formula which aptly quoted the Gospel words: 'It is not right to take the children's bread and throw it to the dogs!'(Matt. xv. 26). The communicants—the word has its full meaning here—gave one another the kiss of peace. Each approached the bishop, who had himself just communicated, being followed by the priests and deacons. The bishop placed a morsel of bread in the right hand of each believer, with the words: 'Corpus Christi.' 'Amen!' the communicant would reply, filling the single word with a wave of faith and hope. 'I believe in Him! I believe in this Christ who is about to become present in me!' Then the deacon held out the chalice containing the wine, saying 'Sanguis Christi calix vitae,' and the communicant drank a sip from it. When all was done, whilst some consecrated hosts were being set aside for subsequent administration to the captives and the sick, those who had communicated returned to their places, in a silence fraught with religious fervour.

Now the Mass was over. A collective prayer of thanksgiving was said by the celebrants, thanking God for His blessings. 'We give thanks to Thee, Heavenly Father, for Thy holy name, which Thou hast made to dwell in our hearts, for the knowledge which Thou hast given us, for the faith and everlasting life which Thou hast revealed to us through Jesus. . . .' The congregation responded with a cry of gladness, a loud hosanna. Then, on their knees, they received the bishop's blessing, and listened to that 'prayer said over the people' which held them together before God for the last time in the ceremony. 'Go, it is finished!' Already the dawn was breaking in the east. The faithful returned to their homes, their hearts overflowing with happiness, their souls filled with the wonderful symbols. Life might offer them little save sufferings and dangers: but they had Christ within them.

## A Way of Life Hallowed by Prayer

Unlike all too many modern Christians, the believer of primitive times did not think of God merely once a week, during the Mass: 'While we live, we live as the Lord's servants, when we die, we die as the Lord's servants; in life and in death, we belong to the Lord' (Rom. xiv. 8–9), said St Paul, and on another occasion: 'For me, life means Christ' (Phil. i. 21). The baptized believers were to translate these declarations into deeds.

While He was living on earth, a man among men, Jesus had, on several occasions, stressed the necessity of prayer, and, in this field as in every other, had provided a personal example for His followers to emulate. Through prayer He had prepared Himself for the great event of His life; in prayer He had found peace and strength; and by means of prayer He had frequently rejoined His Father. Consequently prayer was a permanent accompaniment of the true Christian's life, or, to put it more accurately, his whole existence, once consecrated to God, became a prayer: life should therefore be one perpetual orison.

St Clement of Alexandria, the great thinker who lived at the end of the second century, expressed this idea in such admirable terms that the entire extract deserves to be quoted. 'We should make our whole life one blessed festival, knowing as we do that God is everywhere and in everything, and that in working we praise Him, and while we are relaxing we are singing hymns of thanksgiving. If I may dare to phrase it thus, our prayer is like a conversation with God. Although we may supplicate Him in silence, or with scarcely moving lips, we are praying inwardly. Our heads uplifted, our arms raised heavenwards, we remain, even when the spoken prayer is ended, drawn towards the spiritual universe in the unseen quivering of our souls. The Christian is praying while he walks, while he talks, while he rests, while he works or reads: and, when he meditates alone in the secret retreat of his own soul, and calls upon the Father with groans that are no less real because they are unspoken, the Father never fails to answer and draw near to him' (Strom. vii. 7).

Turning towards the East—for the East signified Christ, *Oriens ex alto*, and in the East lay the Promised Land, the earthly paradise, and also the terrestrial Jerusalem—the Christian would pause to say his prayers several times a day. He would raise his hands in that gesture of appeal which is as old as man himself; he clasped them in supplication; he prostrated himself or fell on his knees in order to confess his humility, his human wretchedness; and, making the sign of the Cross three times upon his forehead, his lips and his breast, he signed himself with the Master's seal, while—the words varying according to the circumstances of the moment—he uttered a particular formula acknowledging that he belonged to Christ alone. 'Every morning and every hour,' wrote Aristides *c.* 140, 'the Christians say their prayers, praising God for His great goodness towards them. And, in like manner, they give thanks for their food and drink.'

Is it possible to make a list of the principal times of prayer? They were extremely numerous! There was the morning prayer, said at cock-crow, at daybreak, when, as we have already seen, the eucharist was celebrated. This corresponded with the vesperal prayer, which followed the setting of the sun, and was said before the lamps were lit. There were the prayers associated with all the essential actions of the day: rising, sleeping, eating. These followed a pattern which many modern Christians have retained. But there were also prayers to complement even the most insignificant deeds, prayers connected with visits to and from friends, with the day's work, with travel. The Christians also practised a custom inherited from Judaism. This was the custom of holding rather more ceremonial prayers at three particular times of the day, at the third, sixth and ninth hours. Monastic services still recall this custom, in the same way that they honour the memory of that extremely ancient Christian habit of rising in the middle of the night in order to pray yet again.

What sort of prayers did these magnificent Christians recite? We are very far from knowing them all, and in all probability they did not have that rigid and stereotyped character which satisfies all too many of our modern believers. Of course the 'Our Father,' the Christian prayer *par excellence*, was used a very great deal indeed. It is certain, too, that the early faithful borrowed many of their prayers from the most beautiful pages of the Old Testament, which had been handed on to them by the Judaic tradition; men used the biblical psalms in their appeals to the Almighty, as the Church still does today. Even when they did not quote the actual words of the biblical texts, the Christians derived much of their literary expression from the styles of the Chosen Race—allusions and rhythms, for example—just as the Blessed Virgin had done in the Magnificat. But they rejuvenated and transformed these Jewish memories by permeating them with the philosophy of Christ, prophetically present throughout Israelite symbolism, and the

supreme goal of Israel's long-awaited hope.[19] It is within
frameworks such as these, far larger than our own, that ancient
Christian prayer should be considered. It was spontaneous in
character, owing much to improvisation, but nourished by biblical references and sustained by an ardent faith.

We have preserved very few of these ancient prayers, at
least in their oldest forms. But those that we do know have
an intensely moving ring; more especially since many of them
have been handed down to us in the *Acts of Martyrs*, that is
to say, they express the faith and hope of men who have
reached the final moment of human experience, and who are
face to face with death. Here, for example, is the prayer of
St Polycarp, which the saint recited at his martyrdom in 155:

'Lord God Almighty, Father of Jesus Christ, Thy well-be-
loved and holy Child, who hast taught us to know Thee, God
of angels, principalities and all creation, and of the race of
the righteous who live in Thy presence! I thank Thee for having judged me worthy of this day and this hour, worthy of
taking my place in Thy company of martyrs, in the Chalice of
Christ, in order that I may obtain eternal resurrection of the
body and the soul, in the incorruptibility of the Holy Spirit.
May I be admitted today into Thy presence, with all Thy
martyrs, a rich and pleasing sacrificial victim! That fate which
Thou hast foretold to me is now to be accorded me, O God
who never liest, O God of truth! For this, as for all Thy
mercies, I praise Thee, I bless Thee, I glorify Thee, through
the Eternal and Heavenly High Priest, Jesus Christ our Lord.
Through Him, glory be to Thee, with Him and the Holy

[19] This is the symbolic interpretation of the Old Testament which
was followed so thoroughly by almost all the Fathers of the Church
(particularly those who lived during the second century) and by
medieval Christians. It explains a host of allusions which can still
be plainly seen in the breviary. Each Sunday the faithful are reminded of it in the choice of Epistles and Gospels, and the sculptures
of our cathedrals, too, have turned it into a host of material masterpieces. For instance, the Resurrection is placed in line with the
flight from Egypt or even the story of Jonah; the Circumcision with
the spring of Horeb; while the crossing of the Red Sea or the Flood
are symbolic of baptism. . . . Claudel has been a vigorous and often
admirable defender of this tradition in modern times, for it is one
which Christians have probably abandoned far too much. (See
Chapter VI, section: 'The Fathers of the Church.')

Spirit, now and for evermore! Amen!' This cry of love which the saintly bishop of Smyrna uttered before the martyr's stake was no different from that which sprang to the lips of all the faithful every hour of the day.

In order to understand the true significance of these prayers, it is essential to listen to them in the sense indicated earlier in this section, namely, to remember that they were said with intentions that are not exactly the same as ours, and by people whose spiritual attitude differed somewhat from our own. For the modern Christian the emphasis is more often placed upon the efficacy of prayer: men make their requests to God and expect them to be answered (which does not imply that these requests are always pragmatic or selfish in intention!). But while the early Christians understood and asserted the *efficacy* of prayer and of the sacraments, they had more understanding than we of their true *meaning*, of the symbolic and mystical purpose behind them. In their eyes prayer was analogous to a conversation with the living Jesus, a conversation like that which the disciples had had with Him at Emmaus, and which each individual believer would have with Him on the eternal tomorrow, in glory. For them communion meant sitting at the very table on which the Last Supper had been laid, whose details are familiar to us all, and, at the same time, taking their place at that eternal eucharist which they were so soon to see celebrated. This spiritual attitude shines through the works of St Cyril of Jerusalem, of the Pseudo-Denys and of Maximus the Confessor; it has a truly wonderful ring, and it is a matter of regret that such an attitude is all but forgotten today.

The same mystical intention also explains the way in which the first Christians wanted to hallow time. By marking the year, the month, the week, with festivals and prayers they were making what is most perishable in our human lives pass into immortality; it was a kind of means of establishing an immediate connection between our nature, which is bound to the ephemeral, and the supernatural order of divine eternity. Time, like the individual life, must be consecrated to God, for everything had to be given to the Lord! Consequently the week revolved around Sunday, the day of the Resurrection, which became its starting-point; thus Wednesday and Friday readopted the Jewish tradition of fasting,[20] though with a change of days to avoid confusion with Old Testament practice, in order to remind the faithful of the need for penitence; and Saturday, preserving something of the ancient sabbath, became a day of preparation for the glory of Sunday. Likewise the whole year was gradually organized into a liturgical cycle in which all the months, seasons and days were dedicated to God. At first only one great Church festival seems to have existed: this was *Easter*. The whole of time, of which the Resurrection was the ultimate end, converged upon it; but very soon, even before the fourth century, other episodes in the life of our Lord were also being specially commemorated. First and foremost among these was the *Nativity*, which was certainly celebrated at a very early date indeed, though estimates of its exact beginnings vary. *Pentecost*, or *Whitsuntide*, the ancient Jewish feast which had become a Christian festival through the descent of the Holy Spirit upon the Apostles, was also celebrated very early in Christian history.

In this way the Christian's entire existence was illuminated by God. Christian life began with baptism, and the great ceremonies connected with it, in which the believer affirmed his faith. It was to continue on the same path, from beginning to end, marked out by prayer, orientated towards God, touched by a perpetual symbolism which made it the first step towards eternity. And when the end came it was prayer again which accompanied the deceased Christian to the threshold of eternal bliss: like everything else, burial became a Christian act; it was a moment of rejoicing, for the soul had reached its goal. When the body had been washed and made ready for burial, the last prayers, taken from the verses of the psalms, were sung over it: 'My broken bones shall rejoice!' (Ps. li). 'Thou

[20] Fasting consisted of abstaining from all food, and even all drink, until the ninth hour, that is to say, until the middle of the afternoon. The Friday fast commemorated the death of Christ; the Wednesday fast was probably observed in expiation of Judas's betrayal. In addition to these weekly fasts there were the annual fasts which preceded Easter: these were fixed to forty days, in memory of the time spent by Christ in the wilderness, and this custom, dating from the first century, is the origin of *Lent*. The first chapter of this book contains an account of how the Christian fast took the place of the Jewish fast. (See section: 'It is Impossible for us to Refrain from Speaking.')

art my refuge in tribulation!' (Ps. xxxii). 'Even when I walk in the shadow of death, I fear nothing, for thou art with me, Lord!' (Ps. xxiii).

## MORALITY AND PENITENCE

A sanctified life: this then was the Christian's ideal. But obviously this also implied a life that was morally transformed. Had not this been the great call of Christ Himself, the call that echoes throughout the whole of His message to mankind: 'Change yourselves completely!' Living in Him, and living according to His example, meant effecting as complete a transformation as possible within oneself. And such is the basis of Christian morality; it is not just the doctrine of a philosophy to whose precepts one can, and indeed should, pay attention; it is an effort at resemblance, at self-identification with a perfect Model. In several passages in his Epistles, St Paul makes it perfectly clear on what bases the morality of the baptized should be founded: upon resemblance to Christ, upon identification with Christ. Be pure, for 'your bodies belong to the body of Christ!' (1 Cor. vi. 15). Be generous, like Christ, who gave His all, even His life! 'You do not need to be reminded how gracious our Lord Jesus Christ was; how he impoverished himself for your sakes, when he was so rich, so that you might become rich through his poverty' (2 Cor. viii. 9). Be regardless of self, like Jesus: 'His nature is, from the first, divine, and yet he did not see, in the rank of Godhead, a prize to be coveted; he dispossessed himself, and took the nature of a slave, fashioned in the likeness of men, and presenting himself to us in human form; and then he lowered his own dignity, accepted an obedience which brought him to death, death on a cross!' (Phil. ii. 7–8). Husbands, 'show love to your wives, as Christ showed love to the Church!' (Eph. v. 25). There is not a single principle of morality which is not transfigured in this way by the idea of a supernatural resemblance.

The different Christian thinkers, the first Fathers, expanded this fundamental notion, which is found in all the texts of the primitive Church, according to their personal temperament. Some were to derive from it a very simple and humane moral concept. A thinker along these lines was the author of the *Didache*, who contented himself with borrowing his precepts from the Scriptures. Another was Hermas who wrote *Pastor*, and who defined the ideal of the true Christian as follows: 'They should be constantly unaffected and happy, having no bitterness towards one another, filled with compassion for everyone, and showing a childlike candour.' Other thinkers, like St Ignatius, were to lay stress on the mystical side of the moral effort, and still others, such as Clement, for whom life was a 'spiritual battle,' emphasized the ascetic aspect of it. In short it was simply a question of shades of interpretation. What mattered was the will for personal transformation which Church leaders constantly demanded of their flocks. They set before them this perfect image of man, made incarnate in Jesus, on which to meditate.

Take, for example, the problems of marriage and sexual life. We know how acute these were in Roman society. Divorce and the lack of desire to marry were ruining the foundations of the family, and slavery, because of the opportunities it afforded the master towards his female slaves, was, here as everywhere else, a demoralizing agent. It was usual for Christians to marry. St Paul had already set out very soundly the principles governing the marriage of the faithful. Not only did the Church abide firmly by these, but she strongly opposed the heretics who condemned marriage. Tertullian declared: 'Let us show the blessedness of marriage! The Church welcomes it, the offering confirms it, the blessing seals it, the angels recognize it, the Father in Heaven ratifies it!' Had not Christ Himself ordered the bride and groom to become 'one flesh' and never to leave one another? Consequently, for the Christian, divorce was inadmissible and celibacy could be envisaged only in the light of a loftier achievement, in terms of a mystical union with Sovereign Purity.[21]

[21] The Christian conception of virginity is linked to the same ideal. Long before the appearance of monasticism, the Church included many men and women who had renounced marriage to devote themselves to God. This was a custom which had existed in Israel, among the Nazirs and the Essenes. In the primitive Church, dedicated virgins were more numerous than celibate men, for those men who wanted to devote their lives to the Lord became priests. From very early times, e.g. at Antioch, under St Ignatius, the virgins formed a separate group in the Church, and were highly venerated. St Cyprian

However, according to Christianity, marriage itself acquired a new meaning. It was quite different from pagan marriage, although, in external appearances, it adopted the latter's principal customs: processions, bridal crowns and festive rejoicing. The harmony of two hearts which the pagans still acknowledged as indispensable in several cases—*ibi Gaius, ubi Gaia*—was not sufficient in itself. The social necessity of bringing children into the world, the family duty whose principles are perfectly set out by Clement of Alexandria, and in whose name the emperors had legislated all in vain, were not the real bases of Christian marriage. The man and the woman must be united in God, in a spirit of love and purity resembling that which Christ bears towards his Church. And Tertullian calls to mind those married couples who 'sustain one another in the way of the Lord, who pray together, who go together to God's table, and who face all their ordeals together.' Marriage was no longer just an institution, under the protection of the best of the laws, but a sacrament. When society as a whole became Christian, therefore, it would rediscover one of those bases of its existence which had been most shaken in the pagan world.[22]

---

was to call them 'the Church's crown.' And Origen declared: 'An immaculate body—here is the living host which is agreeable to God!' It is indeed in the dual sense of a perfection in the ideal of purity and of a mystical marriage with Christ that we must conceive this specifically Christian institution. Virginity was spoken of as a veritable substitution for martyrdom, abounding in graces, and the Spanish Council of Elvira, *c.* 300, which declared all those Christian virgins who had broken their vows to be excommunicate, was probably simply confirming an accepted custom. It is in this concept of virginity, as the superior virtue, and the means of union with Christ, that we should seek the origins of the celibacy of the priesthood, which had not been practised at all by the Apostles or the first disciples and which did not become general for a very long time to come.

[22] The primitive Church was to show itself very hostile to remarriage. Nevertheless St Paul had said that young widows ought to remarry (1 Tim. v. 14). But second marriages were strongly criticized, and certain communities actually prohibited them altogether. Athenagoras called them 'adultery made respectable.' It cannot be denied that there is a certain grandeur in this view of marriage as the single gift of both spouses, hallowed in and by God, which not even death can break, since eternal life is certain. 'For whom are you making the offering,' one man, who had remarried, was asked, 'for

A similar change was effected in men's attitude towards the material goods of this world. Not that the faithful Christian was expected to reject them systematically! It would be quite wrong to imagine the members of this primitive Church as made up of monks and violent ascetics. 'We remember the gratitude we owe to God,' says Tertullian. 'We should not refuse a single fruit of His works!' What Christianity condemned was the abuse of wealth, the excessive love which man had for these worldly goods, and which made him blind to their true meaning and limited value. Clement of Alexandria and several of the other Fathers of the Church vigorously denounced the luxury of the age, the richly coloured gowns, 'the slippers embroidered with gold, decorated all over with spirals of studs,' and the immoderate gluttony of the wealthy, the over-fancy meals, and 'the empty skill of the pastry-cooks.' Men should use all the things which God had given them in a spirit of gratitude, in moderation, without ever forgetting those celestial riches which would never pass away, and the celestial food which was 'the only enduring and pure pleasure.' Herein lay the whole of the Church's teaching on this subject.

So far as money, the real ruler of imperial society, was concerned, Christian teaching resulted in a complete change of attitude. 'Those of us who loved money in the olden days, now give away all that we possess,' writes St Justin. This did not imply that money, in itself, was condemned, nor private property. Already Hermas was noting, in his *Pastor*, that the Church contained both rich folk and poor. The Fathers, and in particular Clement of Alexandria, returned to this topic on many occasions. From these early Christian writings there emerges a veritable theory on the Christian attitude to money and property, which remained vividly alive in the best of the Church's traditions, and to which the modern Church is increasingly tending to return. Wealth was not evil in itself, but it could only be justified by the use to which its owner proposed to put it. The rich man was to be regarded as a kind of administrator, using his own property for the superior in-

___

your dead wife or for your living one?' In other words, which wife would he regain at the Resurrection? But this rigorism did not last, and the Church was soon to tolerate these second marriages, probably in order to avoid worse abuses.

terest of the community. Moreover, it should never be forgotten that the riches of the earth were perishable, and that the only true wealth was that of paradise, which was eternal.

So it can be said that there is a political economy implicit in Christian morality; and, supporting and conditioning it, there is a sociology also: that of charity. It is touching this point that the Gospel principles brought about the most complete transformation in a society which was hard-hearted and rigid, and full of crushing injustices. It was charity, in other words the absolute law of love which Christ had taught, and which all the great Apostles, St Peter, St Paul and St John, had repeated ceaselessly, which transformed men's relations with one another. It was charity which made Christianity—which was far from being a social theory—into the most active of social ferments in the classical world. 'Because they all have one single Father, God,' in Tertullian's words, the Christians were truly one another's brethren. They were united by an entirely new feeling, which St Ignatius of Antioch called *agape* —united love—a feeling that was so powerful that the word soon became synonymous with the whole Christian community, with the Church. The Church was love! 'See how they love one another!' the pagans declared with significant astonishment when they saw the Christians. And St Cyprian was to go so far as to write: 'Perpetual charity has a value equal to baptism in the dispensation of God's mercy.'[23] The Christian looked beyond the bounds of social class, and the differences of race or language, and knew himself united with his fellow Christians in a reality far beyond his own comprehension. His whole moral life had perforce to be permeated with the sentiment of love which made each individual beloved of Christ.

[23] Charity must have been socially organized in the Church at a very early date. Though the practice of placing the whole community's individual possessions in a common pool, which has been noticed at Jerusalem, did not prevail (it had, moreover, been entirely voluntary), the *Didascalia* refers to a tithe which the faithful paid of their own free will. Funds for the relief of the widows and orphans of the martyrs were soon set up everywhere. In the East, the custom of offering the first-fruits of the harvest to God was established in very primitive times: the *Didache* alludes to it. The medieval tithes and our modern 'church rate' thus have very ancient foundations.

Were all the Christians true to this extremely lofty ideal? The question springs immediately to mind when we consider the kind of creature that man is, and the difficulties every noble principle encounters when attempts are made to apply it practically. Though exalted by a young and vigorous faith, the baptized remained ordinary men and women, and they cannot be looked upon as a breed of wholly saintly people. On the contrary, one of the most touching characteristics of all primitive Christian literature is the fact that it does not try to conceal the flaws that crept into Christianity. The first Christians were exposed, like ourselves, to the kind of temptations we know all too well; in addition, still more serious dangers threatened them, stemming from the circumstances of the age in which they lived: the appeal of the all-encompassing paganism, and the seduction of apostasy when the danger became pressing.

Consequently the Church was soon faced with the problem of deciding what attitude she should adopt towards those children of hers who had betrayed, perhaps seriously, perhaps not so seriously, the promise of their baptism. At first it seems that she made no haste to organize the power given her by Christ, through the mediation of Peter, to pardon sins. Baptism, being conferred on adults, was sufficient to do this in most cases, and for the less heinous sins penance could be done by fasting, alms-giving and prayer. It is not possible to say exactly when the codification of penitence was made. In the second century there seem to have been two conflicting trends in the Church on the subject. The one alleged that serious sins committed by the baptized, and especially the three offences of idolatry, adultery and murder, could not be absolved; even if the guilty regretted and repudiated them, they had no hope whatsoever of being reconciled with God and the Church. This rigorist viewpoint, to which various great minds such as Tertullian, Origen and Hippolytus subscribed to some extent, did not prevail; the popes acted in the contrary direction. St Callixtus seems to have been particularly concerned with this problem; the Church, more faithful than some of her own sons to the true teaching of Christ, who had forgiven the woman taken in adultery and promised Paradise to a repentant thief, admitted the principle of penitence. The idea is already very clearly expressed in Hermas' *Pastor*, written *c.* 150. At the end of the second century every Christian found guilty of a serious sin was obliged to give restitution to the community as a whole. He was temporarily cut off from the Church, and forced to perform various harsh exercises and humiliating acts until the day when the bishop, by the laying on of hands, readmitted him among the faithful. Thus we have a public expiation of sins and a solemn pardon, in a spirit of brotherly love and mercy: penitence, in the full sense of the word. In allowing man to free himself from himself, in thus giving him the chance to reacquire the weapons to fight the battle of life, Christianity instituted a means of moral transformation which was of capital importance. Until now it was something which no philosophy and no religion had possessed.

## The Churches and the Church

Whatever aspect of primitive Christianity one studies, one is always struck by its collective and social character; the individual was never alone in it. He was a part of a group, an element in one unity. In this way the sublime paradox of Christ's message is made manifest in its actions: though our Lord addressed Himself to all that was most personal and most private in each individual, though He spoke in a voice which was unique to each of his listeners, yet at the same time He bound to one another all those who hearkened to that voice; He welded them together with love. The promise of salvation that He gave was of no value to the egotists, to those who had no interest in their fellow men. No one can save himself alone! Each is responsible for all![24]

Such is the fundamental meaning of the word which, ever since the earliest Christian times, has been used to indicate the gathering of men and women that is born of Christ: the

[24] It is interesting to note that the great letters of the first Church leaders were scarcely ever addressed to individuals, but to whole communities. St Paul wrote to this or that church, just as St Ignatius, St Polycarp and St Clement were to do. Also, when a community took part in some great event, for instance if it had just been ravaged by persecution, it would send the news of this to the other Christian communities.

*Church*. This word rapidly increased and accentuated the fraternal meaning of the Greek *ekklesia*, which, at the time, meant simply 'assembly.' Already, in the Old Testament, where it had been used to translate the Hebrew *qualiâl*, it implied very much more than an ordinary meeting of men. 'The Assembly of the Lord, the Church of the Lord,' which is referred to in Deuteronomy (xxiii. 1, 9) is a consecrated entity whose members are mysteriously linked to one another by the Promise and by faith. St Paul, a genius here as in everything else, had made the quadruple meaning of this word abundantly clear by the ways in which he had used it: the Church, which is the assembly of the faithful and the community of believers, is, even more, the mystical proof of Christ's presence upon earth and, in heaven, the holy company of all those whom He has saved.

In this way, therefore, the Christian assembly was very conscious of being different from all the other kinds of groupings that had been known up to that time. It was not a 'synagogue' after the Jewish pattern, for in the synagogue men were grouped according to their geographical origins or affinities, or their social rank. It was not a 'college,' one of those guild-colleges in which the pagans met in order to organize mutual relief among themselves and ensure that all the members had decent funerals. It was not a 'sect' like the many Eastern religions and mysteries, which only the initiated could enter. It was something entirely different, a reality whose unique characteristics were to be defined more and more in the future by Christian theologians.

Wherever there were any Christians there was a community, a church. In theory one existed in each 'city,' that is to say, in the administrative centre on which each imperial region depended. Within the city there was one single church, in contrast to the synagogues, which could be numerous and diverse in character in one district alone—there had been thirteen of them in Rome in the first century—and in contrast, also, to the groupings of the adherents of Isis and Mithras, which limited the number of their members, and divided themselves up once a certain figure had been reached. The Christians who were scattered throughout the region were attached to the church in the city. This explains why St Ignatius sometimes called himself Bishop of Antioch, and on other occasions Bishop of Syria. In theory each church was established in such a way that it could live an independent existence. This was essential in an age when persecution could strike a community and isolate it from the rest. Each church, therefore, had its own head, its clergy, its members, its economic organization, its social works and even, to a large extent, as we have seen, its own customs and liturgy. But this autonomy went hand in hand with one element which balanced it and gave it its real meaning: above the churches there was the *Church*.

It is easy to show that the three characteristics which are traditionally acknowledged as fundamental to the Church—universality, apostolicity and sanctity—are in no sense the recent inventions of theologians, but that ever since the faith's earliest days all Christians have regarded them as absolutely essential.

For them the Church is *one*. Thereby she obeys the wish expressed by Christ in His last prayer: 'I pray for those who are to find faith in me through their word; that they may all be one; that they too may be one in us, as thou, Father, art in me, and I in thee . . .' (John xvii. 20–1). Countless primitive texts confirm this principle: it is found in the letters of St Paul and in the writings of St John; the *Didache* calls to mind 'this Church, gathered in from the four corners of the earth'; St Clement prayed in exactly the same terms, and, using for the first time a word which was henceforth to denote this characteristic of unity as applied to the Church, St Ignatius wrote: 'There, where collectivity should be, where there is Jesus Christ—there is the *Catholic* Church.' In doctrine as in organization, sometimes radiating through differences of appearance, but always maintained in substance, and defended against certain heresies with a savage energy, there is this splendid idea of *catholicity*, in other words of universality, which was always to remain the motivating idea of the Church, right into our own time.

This Christian collectivity was not merely defined as being *one*. It knew itself to be *apostolic*. Above all, this word should be understood in terms of a very recent historical reality, in the sense in which we have already evoked it several times. For example, let us consider Irenaeus, Bishop of Lyons *c*. 180. He had known Polycarp of Smyrna personally: the latter had been on affectionate terms with Ignatius, the aged Bishop of Antioch, who in his turn had certainly known the Apostle John, and had possibly been called to Christ by him. Here is a perfectly direct link binding these Christian communities to their divine founder. Consequently apostolicity was a pledge of the authenticity of their religion, a justification of their faith. 'Christ came from God,' writes St Clement of Rome, 'and the Apostles came from Christ, and it was the Apostles who, finding their inspiration in the Spirit, instituted certain men as bishops.' Likewise St Irenaeus, when setting out the principles of the Church, indicates as fundamental 'her preservation of the tradition of the Apostles.'

Finally, for the first Christians, as for the Christians of all ages, the Church was *holy*; here is her most decisive characteristic, the one which sustains all the rest. She is holy because she has been founded by Christ, because she is His prolongation upon earth, because she is His bride and His body, because she is the new Eve born of the new Adam, springing from the gashed side whence the blood flowed. Countless passages in the Epistles, the Apocalypse, and in the works of the Apologists, the first Fathers, affirm this intimate relationship between the Church and the God Incarnate. In his First Epistle to the Corinthians St Paul goes so far as to call the Church herself 'Christ' (xii. 12), and St Augustine was to speak in similar terms: 'Christ preaches about Christ, the Anointed Bride preaches about the Anointed Bridegroom.'[25] From this it follows that Christians, being a part of Christ, ought to be a society of saints; Hermas' *Pastor* already says so categorically; naturally this sanctity was only relative, it was to be perpetually broken into by the defects of human nature. But it was a sanctity which echoed like a battle-cry in the conscience, and which ensured that the Christian never considered himself a man like other men, but the very repository of God.

Thus the Church was looked upon by her members in the light of characteristics which are often described as *theandrical*, in other words, simultaneously human and divine. It is

[25] And Bossuet was to say: 'The Church is Jesus Christ in His entirety diffused among us and communicated to us.'

this duality within unity which defines 'the mystery of the Church,' that mystery which her adversaries have never been able to comprehend and which was to be at the bottom of all the misunderstandings and all the hatreds. Because she is human she must be a society possessing her own organization, methods and public attitudes; but the goal of this society will never be limited to the boundaries of the earth, and, though enclosed within human history, the action of the Church remains, in intention, transcendent to all history, and orientated towards the kingdom of God. Such, in short, is the secret of her strength. Her methods of action, and her fortunes, have probably never been better expressed than in this sentence of one eminent theologian: 'The Church is the permanent Incarnation of the Son of Man.'[26]

## THE CHURCH ORGANIZES HER RANKS

Since she was a human society, the Church needed an organization from the moment of her birth. For this reason, as we remember, Jesus Himself had laid down the foundations of an administration by establishing, first, the Twelve, and then the Seventy-Two. We possess evidence regarding the existence of ecclesiastical ranks which dates back to the very earliest times: Chapter XI of Acts refers to the elders or 'presbyters,' and Chapter XX to the supervisors or 'bishops.' Throughout the first hundred years or so of the Church's life, these institutions were to become increasingly defined and consolidated, so that, from about the year 100 (the date at which St Ignatius speaks of them), their general features are fairly clear.

The principle behind these institutions was one of authority. Although a Church leader was chosen by his flock, his prestige and his authority were absolute. Was he not the representative of Christ, the witness of the Spirit? Consequently it was the idea of hierarchy which dominated the whole organization. St Clement of Rome told the Christians that the army was an example of this idea, with its methods and its discipline, or even the human body, where the function of

[26] Moehler, the German theologian.

each different member was subject to collective usefulness. 'It follows that each one of us should be subject to another, according to the particular qualities he has received.'

All the same, this principle does not easily explain the way in which the ecclesiastical hierarchy was established in the primitive Church. It is actually one of the most debated points in its whole history. The writings of St Clement, and the *Didache*, only refer to two hierarchical categories: the bishops and the deacons; each community would appear to have been led by a college of bishops or presbyters (the two names seem to be synonymous in this period). Beneath them were the deacons, subject to their orders. But in the works of St Ignatius of Antioch we are faced with a three-tier system: 'Let everyone show reverence to the deacons, just as they revere Jesus Christ. And let them also revere the bishop, who is the image of the Father, and the presbyters, who are the Senate of God, the Assembly of the Apostles.' And it seems that from this epoch, that is to say from the beginning of the second century, this system was accepted in the Asian churches as a general rule.

Perhaps the answer to this apparent conflict can be found in the functioning of the two streams of thought which could be equally fundamental in the primitive Church. In her capacity as a human society what did the Church desire? Above all she wanted virtuous, energetic, learned and generous-hearted leaders. Many of the ancient texts lay stress upon the moral qualities necessary to bishops, priests and deacons: St Paul, for instance, in his First Epistle to Timothy, or St Ignatius or St Polycarp. But in so far as she was a divine society, the Bride of Christ, the Church desired above all to see as her leaders men who were directly linked with the apostolic tradition, descendants of those first bishops whom St Paul, St Peter or St John had established. Consequently a clergy must comprise the wisest and most saintly of the faithful, but above it was the bishop, the representative of God, His 'visible sign'; the hierarchies of the earth were, in a way, the image of the celestial hierarchies. Here is another illustration of the Church's *theandrical* character, and the organization which was to be permanently established during the second century may well be the synthesis of these two aspirations.

At the bottom of the hierarchy, in immediate contact with the faithful, and very close to them, were the *deacons*. They played some part in religious ceremonies, but, in the beginning at least, they worked primarily in the practical sphere, keeping order during the religious meals, collecting the offerings for the Mass, and administering charity to the needy. There were a number of women among them, who were known as *deaconesses*, and who were highly respected on account of their age and virtue. A goodly number of the Church's heroes and martyrs, and many of her most efficacious missionaries, came from this class of humble auxiliaries. At the time of certain persecutions, or great plagues, it was the deacons and deaconesses who showed themselves the most admirable of Christ's witnesses.

Above the deacons were the *priests*, the *presbyters*, who performed the kind of functions that we are accustomed to see exercised by present-day priests, albeit in a rather different fashion. Their importance in the Church rested not so much on their individual title as on their character as a collective group. The *presbyterium* was a veritable 'Senate of God.' It helped the bishop, advised him, and supported him in the fullest sense of the word, being his substitute in the case of his absence or death. The priests represented the wisdom and collective experience of the whole community; beside the episcopal principle of authority, there is evidence here of a principle which can aptly be called democratic. It would be wrong to regard them as a counterweight to their leaders, but their role was undoubtedly a very important one.

Far above the rest, dominating the whole community, the object of enormous respect, was the *bishop*. He exercised very great authority indeed. As the Church expanded and organized herself, the bishoprics, based roughly on the imperial system of the 'cities,' were mapped out one after another. Each see produced an episcopal dynasty whose members' names were to be piously preserved by the community. Chosen, it seems, by agreement among all the Church members—here is another glimpse of the democratic principle at work—the bishop was consecrated with unique and solemn ceremony. He was invested with a character that placed him quite apart from all the rest of the faithful; he was the true leader, the incarnation of the principle of authority, the shepherd of his flock.[27]

The bishops' duties fell into four categories. The first, and the most important, it seems, in the eyes of the Christians, since they were intimately linked with their own sacramental life, were the *liturgical duties*. Just as, at Jerusalem, the Israelite religion could only be performed by the high priest and the Levites (it was St Clement who made this comparison), so, in the Church, the great sacramental rites depended upon the bishop. St Ignatius of Antioch says that no one could be baptized, or receive communion, without the bishop; he even thinks it advisable to ask the bishop to preside at the marriages of the faithful 'so that all that he approves may be approved by God, and thereby made completely sure and valid.'

The bishops' second duty was to give *religious instruction*. The *Didache* asserts that, as the direct successors of the Apostles, they filled 'the ministry of prophets and doctors.' And, in his *Apology*, St Justin portrays the bishop, during the course of the morning Masses, and after the reading from the Gospel, as himself giving the commentary upon the sacred text, and drawing lessons from it. This teaching role was to be particularly decisive in the epoch when the first internal dissensions appeared in Christian philosophy, and it became necessary to defend the doctrinal integrity of the faith against the various heresies.

[27] How were ordinations and consecrations carried out? For the deacons and presbyters, the ceremony which conferred on them their strictly religious powers would have been quite a simple one; the ancient rite of the laying on of hands would have been the essential basis of it. If we can believe the information given in a ritual of ordination left us by St Hippolytus at the beginning of the third century, the principle must have been the same in the case of the bishops, but the ceremony was a much more solemn one: the *Apostolic Tradition* describes it as follows: 'When the bishop has been nominated and agreed upon, all the faithful shall assemble, together with the presbyters and the deacons, on the Lord's Day. All the bishops present shall lay their hands upon the proposed bishop, whilst the priests and the assembled company stand motionless, praying in silence that the Holy Spirit may descend upon him. After that one of the bishops shall have the honour of laying his hands upon the new bishop, thus ordaining him. He shall pray over him, assisted by all the rest.'

A more pragmatic side of their function was the *administration* of the community's goods and property. Several texts emphasize the qualities which the bishop ought to possess for this task. It was he who distributed the offerings made by the faithful at Mass. He was responsible for the welfare of Christian widows and orphans, and it was he who welcomed and gave hospitality to the Christian stranger passing through his territory, the believer who had been forced to flee into hiding. The heavy administrative duties which are the lot of our modern bishops thus have their origins in the very remote past.

Finally, and summing up all the rest, their most essential duty was the moral and spiritual supervision of their community (the word bishop means 'supervisor'). Every believer had his modest place in the Church, each priest and deacon had his task to do, according to his hierarchical rank; the bishop took them all upon himself, he was responsible for everyone. He attended to the community's discipline and morals; he ensured that accord existed among his flock. Should one of them waver or behave badly, or apostatize, the bishop would feel these faults as wounds inflicted upon the mystical Body. One Asian bishop considered himself responsible for the soul of a young Christian who had turned brigand. Like the father of a family who feels himself personally stricken by the sin of a son or a daughter, the bishop was the guarantor before God and before men of the community entrusted to his care.

It is clear that the episcopal system was one of the fundamental elements of Christianity during that decisive period when it conquered the world. To this system the faith owed its steady flexibility, its doctrinal soundness and its material efficacy. We do not know very much about many of these early bishops who were, in truth, the foundations upon which the Church was built. But how many of those about whom we do know appear haloed in an aura of genius and sanctity! We have only to think of Ignatius of Antioch, Polycarp of Smyrna, Denis of Corinth and Irenaeus of Lyons, then, later on, of Cyprian of Carthage and Hilary of Poitiers, and of all those mighty bishops who, at the dramatic turning-point at the end of the fourth century, were to emerge as the real leaders of society as a whole! Without this system, and without these men, Christianity would not have been able to play the role we know.

## Apostles, Prophets and Doctors

By the end of the second century, therefore, the ecclesiastical organization was fixed. The main features that we know today already existed; they were to be further defined in the direction described in the last section. But aside from these official administrative grades, this primitive Church contained a number of elements of which we have scarcely any idea today. Their role appears to have been considerable during this period, but it was to grow progressively weaker as Christian society became more firmly established.

Once again we are concerned with the spiritual facts relating to the double idea that the coming of the Spirit was still an event of the very recent past, and that His second coming was believed to be imminent. Thus various manifestations which we find somewhat disconcerting occurred within the bosom of the different communities. Sometimes a liturgical assembly would be interrupted by a sudden shout, an improvised song, a speech or a flow of words. Some man or woman in the congregation had suddenly felt the Holy Spirit speaking within in an irrepressible voice; a 'charism' occurred; the gift of words, or 'glossolaly,' had been divinely granted to a humble believer, who was very often a poor man, uncouth and uneducated, and, in a silence mingled with fear, the whole assembly would listen to their inspired brother in Christ. Like the people who had been present at the first Whitsuntide, these people sometimes talked, during their trance, in tongues which they did not normally know. These were strange phenomena indeed. Claudel has compared them with those which were to reveal Sts Vincent Ferrer and Francis Xavier preaching straight away in the language of the peoples they were to convert, or the great ecstatics, such as Catherine Emmerich, speaking in Greek or Arabic. At all events, in these days of mighty faith happenings of this kind were very far from being regarded as a sign of insanity pure and simple, and, although the Church became increasingly circumspect in the matter, the 'gift of tongues' was unanimously venerated as a manifestation of the Holy Spirit.

It is against this rather special background that we must consider three categories of persons whose saintly character is unquestionable, but who do not belong to the regular ranks of the hierarchy and who acted in accordance with a particular kind of inspiration. They already existed in the age of St Paul; the First Epistle to the Corinthians lists them: 'God has given us different positions in the church; apostles first, then prophets, and thirdly teachers' (1 Cor. xii. 28). A large number of Christian texts refer to them: Hermas' *Pastor*, the *Didache* and several others.

We do not know much about the *apostles*. They were the men who had received the divine call to spread the Gospel, and who, contemptuous of all dangers and all fatigues, set out across the world shouting aloud the Good News, exactly as in the time when St Paul had been preaching it. Was not the task of evangelization still an enormous one? Did not gigantic areas still exist where the Cross had never been planted at all? They were, if one wishes to call them so, missionaries, in the sense in which we use the word. But they were missionaries without a mother house, without a hierarchy, and without organization. The Church bade a joyful welcome to these travellers of Christ, but, being prudent, she was wary of those who might assume the outward appearances of Christ's spokesmen in order to sponge on the faithful; she advised believers not to give them more than three days' lodging, to provide them on their departure with only sufficient food to reach their next resting-place, and, in particular, to give them no money!

The *prophets* were those people in whom the Holy Spirit spoke: not in an exceptional manner, during a sudden outburst that was never to be repeated, but all the time. In a way they were the direct successors of those astonishing figures found in the Old Testament, the heirs of John the Baptist. There were sometimes women among them, like the four daughters of Philip the deacon, who, according to the Acts (xxi), 'possessed the gift of prophecy.' As the witnesses of God, the inspired spokesmen of the Lord, the prophets were undoubtedly highly thought of and deeply respected, being regarded as direct messengers of the Word. Had not the prophet Joel declared of old that the gift of prophecy was to be one of the signs of the Messianic era? And were not several very great saints—men holding high ecclesiastical office—also invested with this extraordinary power, for example St Igna-tius, the famous Bishop of Antioch, who in his letter to the Trallians says quite categorically that he has direct knowledge of celestial matters? Thus the prophet is encountered right through the first centuries of Christian history. Men welcomed him and listened to him. In words as enigmatic as they are admirable, the *Didache* declares that it is men's duty to hearken to the message of the prophets since the latter work 'for the good of the cosmic mystery of the Church.' However, here too the Church counselled prudence: she was anxious that these inspired wanderers should be carefully examined before being given credence, that they should be judged by their way of life, which ought to be exemplary. When one of their number, Montanus, inclined in a direction that was more than suspect, she condemned him, but until this se-rious crisis of the Montanist heresy arose there was no oppo-sition between the hierarchy and the prophets.

As for the *doctors* (or *teachers*), they were the intellectuals, the scholars, who were divinely endowed with the gift of study-ing Christian doctrine, and of spreading their knowledge among their fellow men. To some extent they were like suc-cessors of the Hebrew scribes and Doctors of the Law, who, in ancient Israel, had devoted their whole lives and all the resources of their learning to penetrating the secrets of the Scriptures; in another respect they were the heirs and rivals of the Greek philosophers. Many of them were extremely familiar with classical dialectic, and they would argue with its protagonists from a sound basis of knowledge for the glory of Christ. At Alexandria the Jew Philo had founded a school of wisdom by creating a system of wisdom, a *didascalia*, in which Greek methods of logic were applied to Israelite themes. The Christians, in their turn, made the same synthesis start-ing from the Christian standpoint. St Justin was a typical ex-ample of these Christian scholars. He was a philosopher of the Greek school, the equal of the Athenian thinkers. Living in Rome, a convert to Christianity, he brought to the service of his new faith an immense wealth of learning, the fruits of a mind well versed in all the technique of classical philosophy. Tatian and Origen, the Christian scholars of Alexandria, were similar in type, as were one or more alarming personages, such as Marcion, the heretic. For, though the doctors' labours were eminently useful, though the gnosis[28] could, before losing its way along strange byways, greatly help the Gospel cause, the dangers in this sphere were many and serious. The Church, which reserved a place of honour for the doctors, and which gave them willing encouragement, knew how to be prudent, on this point as on all the rest; though she used the doctors, she never ceased to control them.

The existence of these different types of men, all equally devoted, body and soul, to Christ, and consumed by their zeal for the faith, gives us an extremely vivid idea of the youthful vigour of the primitive Church. Each of these categories of God's servants corresponded to a profound intention of Christianity; each brought an element of life itself to the common task. The members of the hierarchy were the guardians of the faith, the keepers of the sacred trust and the agents of the sacraments, the means whereby this spiritual authority, this living force which Christ had bequeathed to his followers, could be transmitted to others. The apostles were the sowers, the tireless messengers of the Word, who were less concerned with the work done than the work still to do, whose mission lay, not in the sound, tilled ground, but in the hazardous fields that still remained, where men waited, in the night of ignorance, to hear the Good News. To the prophets fell another task, of an apocalyptic and eschatological nature. Father Danielou has expressed their function very aptly: it was 'to prevent the Church from taking up her abode in the world, to remind her constantly that she was foreign to it, and that her real home was elsewhere.' Finally, the doctors, the didascali, were essentially the servants of the Word, the witnesses of that light which had come into the world, and which every Christian had to try to make shine more brilliantly. Thus in

---

[28] The word gnosis usually brings to mind the heretical trend which is better known as Gnosticism. There was a legitimate Christian gnosis, just as there had been a Jewish gnosis: legitimate, that is, until its course deviated. See the following chapter, section: 'Oportet Haereses Esse.'

these various aspects of one common effort each kind of Christian found something to exalt, sustain and satisfy him. The young Church sprouted and grew in all its many aspects, in every direction.

Little by little these scattered forces were to be incorporated in the hierarchical system. As she expanded the Church increased her discipline, and the apostles, prophets and doctors either took their place among the clergy or else saw their functions assumed by the priests as a whole. By the third century these manifestations of primitive enthusiasm scarcely existed any more as separate entities. The Catholic concept absorbed and put to the service of certain well-defined ends the energies which, if acting in their original unco-ordinated way, would probably not have been sufficiently efficacious when the time came for the final struggle.

## THE UNITY OF THE CHURCH AND THE PRIMACY OF ROME

Would the immense organizational effort which we have seen the primitive Church carrying out in all her fields lead her to settle the institutional problem of her unity? As we have seen, the feeling of unity was deeply ingrained in the Christian conscience. Was it not to be made manifest in deeds? While Christ's Apostles lived they had been able to control the communities they had founded themselves, and by preserving the bonds of friendship between them all had simultaneously embodied and guaranteed the brotherhood of the faithful. When the Twelve died the same affectionate relationships survived them. Consequently one of the most attractive features of primitive Christianity is this constant exchange of men, news and letters between the different churches. Friends wrote to friends, brethren visited brethren. When one community had a splendid example of faith to offer, for instance a heroic martyrdom, it told the rest all about it. If one possessed texts worthy of common meditation, it passed them on to the others; it was in this way that the different letters of St Paul or St Ignatius became widely known.

But relationships and friendly connections of this kind

might be only those of a federation of churches,[29] which were striving to preserve intact the sacred trust of the faith, to put Christ's charity into practice and to maintain the spiritual meaning of Christian unity. Is it admissible to go further than this? Is it possible to say that from the earliest times one of these communities had played a pre-eminent role among the rest, and had been acknowledged by all the others as being invested with a special authority? This is a problem which has been debated an infinite number of times, naturally enough, since it concerns the very foundations of the present-day Catholic Church. However, the texts we possess appear to solve it.

About 95, at the end of Domitian's reign, various dissensions occurred in the church at Corinth, the most important of all the Christian communities in Greece. The faithful in Rome were then undergoing a cruel ordeal. Scarcely had the persecution ended when the church in the Eternal City sent her Greek sister an embassy consisting of three men, who bore a letter which Clement, the Roman bishop, had written expressly for the Corinthians. This letter was a model of wisdom and moderation, a magnificent testimony of the writer's intelligence and charity. Clement addressed several pieces of good advice to this troubled community, which was threatened with secession and exhausted by internal intrigues. He spoke with striking authority, giving his instructions quite categorically, in the tones of a man who intends to be obeyed. Had he been consulted on this matter? This would imply that his pre-eminence was already recognized at that time. Or had he acted on his own initiative, which would mean that the prestige of the Roman Church and its leader was such that an action of this kind could be taken as a matter of course? At all events we have no evidence that the step caused any irritation or jealousy at Corinth. Consequently this incident is indisputable evidence of the Roman community's primacy, in fact at least.

There are other proofs of it too. Here are the words in which

[29] From the earliest times councils were certainly convened to study the problems of the Church, like that held by the Apostles in Jerusalem. But in the second century they probably remained regional in character. We know of councils held in Asia, in Pontus; in Gaul; in Osrhoenia; at Corinth; and at Rome.

St Ignatius of Antioch addressed the Roman Church: 'To the church which presides in the city of the region of the Romans, worthy of God, worthy of honour, worthy of blessing, worthy of praise, worthy of being heard by the Lord, worthy in chastity, and president of the brotherhood of the faithful, according to the law of Christ.' Are these sentences simply examples of Eastern hyperbole? No, the answer is not so simple as that. The saint does not use this kind of tone in his other dedications, and two expressions from it deserve to be particularly emphasized: *which presides in the city of the region of the Romans*, an expression which seems to imply something special, something differentiating Rome from the other churches, which are simply called by the name of their city: 'the church of Antioch,' 'the church of Tralles' or 'the church of Smyrna'; and *president of the brotherhood of the faithful*, in Greek, the agape—*united love*—a word which, we should remember, meant, so far as primitive Christianity was concerned, Christian unity itself, in other words the Church.

Ignatius wrote these words in 106. Some thirty-five years later Hermas, the author of *Pastor*, a mystical treatise full of strange visions, ended his work by entrusting the Bishop of Rome with the task of passing it on to all the other churches. Shortly after this a Phrygian bishop named Abercius was drafting his own epitaph, in readiness for his death. In it he related, in symbolic language reminiscent of the Apocalypse, that he had gone to Rome at the call of the Good Shepherd 'to contemplate there a sovereign majesty and a princess clothed in gold, with golden slippers on her feet,' and that he met there 'a people bearing a shining seal (baptism).' And a few years later still St Irenaeus, the Bishop of Lyons, while defining the purity of Christian dogmas against the Gnostic heretics, quoted as his conclusive reference the doctrine of the Church of Rome: 'All churches, in other words, all the faithful scattered throughout the world, must in fact be in harmony with this church, on account of its lofty pre-eminence. In her Christians of every land have preserved the apostolic tradition.'

It seems established, therefore, that from primitive times, at all events by the second century, the whole Church recognized that Rome possessed a primacy relating simultaneously to doctrine and control. When in 1924 the German Protestant historian Harnack completed the great work he had begun at the end of the nineteenth century, he made the following assertion, which, coming from so great a scholar, has considerable weight: 'Twenty-two years ago, in my capacity as a Protestant historian, I exposed the fact that *Roman* equals *Catholic* in my *Manual of the History of Dogmas*, albeit with certain reservations. But since then this thesis has been strengthened, and Protestant historians should no longer be shocked by this proposition: that the basic elements of Catholicism go back to the apostolic age. . . . Thus the link appears to be complete, and the concept which Catholics have of their history is triumphant.'

It only remains to ask: what was the reason for this primacy? Why was this authority acknowledged? Why did so many early Christians want to visit Rome: men like Abercius, and Polycarp of Smyrna, and Irenaeus of Lyons, and the Palestinian Hegesippus, and the Samaritan Justin—and, later on, Tertullian of Carthage, Origen of Egypt and so many others? Was it merely the political prestige of the capital of the Empire which was reflected in the waters of Christianity and illuminated in its image? No. As St Irenaeus declared, what the faithful venerated in Rome was her *apostolic tradition*. The tradition which, as we have seen,[30] links the foundation of the Church of Rome with St Peter's apostolate, its growth with the work of St Paul, and its double consecration with the blood of both saints shed there for it at about the same time, certainly goes back far into Christian antiquity. The pilgrims who came to Rome were little interested in the imperial palaces and the dazzling riches of the different 'forums.' They

---

[30] At the end of Chapter II. Regarding the subject of the primacy of the Roman pontiff, one very remarkable fact still remains to be quoted. In 95 St John the Apostle was still alive, probably the only survivor of those who had personally known Christ. He was, it is true, a prisoner, but after emerging unscathed from the ordeal of immersion in boiling oil he must have had considerable renown among the Christian communities. If, on his journey from Rome to the forced labour camp at Patmos, he had happened to pass through Corinth, the usual port of transit for the East, how much attention would have been showered upon him! However, it was not John who was asked to settle Corinth's religious difficulties! (This point is made by Father Delhostal, S.J.)

wanted to see the 'confession of Peter' at the Vatican, the 'chair of St Peter' on the Nomentane Way and the places where the memory of St Paul, prisoner and martyr in the city, was preserved. In his letter St Clement alludes to the two Apostles quite categorically as the pillars of his Church. These were the pillars which supported the increasingly glorious throne of that Bishop of Rome for whom, three hundred years later, the name of *Pope* was to be reserved.

And yet how insignificant these first popes seem, in the half-light of the age of the catacombs! The majority of them mean no more than a name to us. The Church has inscribed them all upon her roll of martyrs, for all must have given their blood or at least their labour in the arduous work of that heroic pioneering period. We can compose a probable list of them from a catalogue of names written down by St Irenaeus: St Linus, St Anacletus and St Clement, who were probably the first three successors of St Peter, during the first century, of whom only the last-named stands out at all clearly; in the second century, St Evaristus, St Alexander, St Xystus or Sixtus and St Telesphorus, who were undoubtedly four Greeks and of whom only the fourth is slightly known, owing to his martyrdom under Hadrian; then St Hyginus (?136–?40), St Pius (?140–?54), St Anicetus (?154–?65), who received St Polycarp, St Soter (165–74) and St Eleutherius (175 –89), who was the friend of St Irenaeus. How many modern Christians still regard these names as having much meaning?

But this obscurity which enshrouds the successors of St Peter has something symbolic and significant about it. We can picture them either as powerful personalities or as very ordinary shepherds of their flocks; it matters little either way. It is not their personalities that count; what is important is the idea which they made incarnate, this wonderful idea of an affiliation, and a permanence which, even today, gives the Roman pontiff his influence and his authority. Their power was to increase from the third century onwards. A more and more unanimous veneration was to surround them. Their remains were gathered together in a special crypt on the Appian Way, and this was to become so famous that it acquired the name of *The Cemetery*, just as though it were the only cemetery in all Rome. Henceforth, whatever the ordeals suffered by the Church, and whatever the character of each individual pope, nothing would be able to shatter the link which, through Peter, the Prince of Apostles, joined the Bishop of Rome to Jesus Christ, the founder of the Church.

## THE THIRD RACE

Thus we have here an increasingly sound and well-defined human organization; a society whose foundations are completely new ones; and a type of man different from all those whom the world has known in the past. These are the three fundamental facts which emerge from a picture of primitive Christian life. When, in his Epistle to the Galatians, St Paul had told the Christians that they were no longer 'Greeks and Jews,' that they comprised a new race of men, a historical reality different from all the others, it was these three elements which his intuitive genius had discerned within the very substance of the Gospel message; these defined the Revolution of the Cross, and were to make its triumph a certainty.

Henceforth, from the end of the second century onwards, the Roman world was to go into decline, and—'like a river rushing towards the abyss which is to swallow it up,' in Nietzsche's words—classical civilization was to sink faster and faster into decadence. All those corroding forces which it is possible to discern in the Empire even in the period of its splendours, but which were still having little effect on it during the first two centuries A.D., were to become increasingly active and formidable. But at the very moment when classical Rome was about to give way, the relieving force was already in process of preparation; Christian Rome had been born.

The imperial organism suffered increasingly violent crises. The progress of centralization and bureaucracy weighed more and more heavily upon it, and it felt itself gradually stricken with paralysis; its administrative machinery disintegrated, its hierarchies ceased to have a realistic basis. But at the same time the Church was becoming stronger and stronger, and her organization was constantly improving.

In the same way Roman society, increasingly wormeaten with vices against which all rules and regulations were powerless, was rotting away where it stood. The real period of decadence commenced at the beginning of the second century, and the Late Empire was to offer a more and more degrading manifestation of it. Socially unbalanced, morally stricken, classical society possessed nothing which could save it from itself. But another society had established itself within its very bosom, a society founded on very different principles. This society was to grow within the old, and would, in the end, replace it.

Finally, man himself was to change: his principles, the concept he had of himself, his role on earth and his destiny. A new humanism was in course of preparation, namely a new synthesis between the historical facts of the age and the permanent values of the spirit. And, as always happens in the case of spiritual revolutions called upon to make the world change fundamentally, this new synthesis absorbed many elements from the past and transfigured them. Greek intelligence and Roman order were integrated with the Christian reality and transubstantiated in it. From this was born that admirable entity which for fifteen hundred years was to give our history its characteristic appearance, and which our own epoch is in process of losing: the civilized man of the West.

It is very necessary to grasp this modification of all the fundamental attributes of civilization if we really want to understand the future triumph of Christianity. Let us repeat: Christian life is a totally changed life. Consequently everything pertaining to this life is transformed too. Just as Christianity embodied a private morality which forbade divorce and excessive luxuries, and a commercial morality which stipulated honesty, so it also contained a social morality which completely modified the very perspectives in which one regarded institutions such as slavery. There was to be a Christian way of dressing and teaching. There would even be a Christian way of spending one's leisure, of amusing oneself, of conceiving the circus spectacles. Naturally a Christian literature would emerge which, as we shall see, was of exceptional importance. Here let us dare to make a statement which may appear paradoxical: 'The world's very bases were to change.'

In this sense it is particularly interesting to consider art, as the first Christians conceived and practised it. At first, when they began to decorate the corridors and crypts of the catacombs, or when they desired to give one of their famous dead a sarcophagus worthy of his qualities, they could only imitate the pagans; their frescoes arc in Pompeian style, and their sculpture faithfully reproduces, feature for feature, the Roman sculpture of the period. Then, very gradually, a Christian intention creeps in, shining through images that are still pagan in outward form, according to the laws of a moving symbolism. Look at this young, handsome, beardless shepherd, carrying a sheep upon his shoulder! Is this a representation of Hermes or of the Good Shepherd? And this Orpheus charming the animals: does he not make us think of another figure, and call to mind the picture of another, far greater, spokesman of consoling truths? The Church leaders, who were doubtless preoccupied with all their other duties, did not yet take much interest in what probably seemed to them to be merely a simple matter of decoration. Then, during the second century, they realized how art could be used for educating the faithful; and it became their ally in the tasks of instructing and moralizing. From then onwards the Christian revolution permeated art; new forms were imperative. Good Shepherds, praying figures and Virgin Mothers all appeared, and these unforgettable pictures were permeated with a delicate fervour which radiated through the clumsiness of their artistic execution. Since it was entrusted to ordinary artisans—for there would not have been sufficient professional artists to carry out such vast schemes—the technique necessarily became more simple and less skilful; these Christian painters and sculptors were only aiming, in their work, to glorify God and to edify their brethren. But herein, precisely, lies the miracle! It was this sober treatment, this submission to reality, this humility, which was to rejuvenate man's creative mind. Classical art of the age of decadence might founder in excessive facility, fluency and artificiality; close beside it a new art was growing up which had borrowed the old art's tools, an art which radiated a splendour never before known, and whose youthful vigour was not to wait much longer before springing into the full light of day.

Thus in aiming solely, not at the principalities of this world, but at the kingdom which is not a part of it, primitive Christian life actually effected the revolution which was, at that time, quite essential. Long beforehand Christianity was pre-

paring the means of relief that history demanded. Were the
folk who lived this splendid adventure aware of the role that
devolved upon them? It seems so. At the beginning of the
second century, the *Letter to Diognetus*, which is undoubtedly the earliest Christian masterpiece we possess aside from
the scriptural texts, contained these wonderfully clear-sighted
sentences: 'The Christians are to the world what the soul is
to the body. Just as the flesh hates the soul and is continually
waging war upon it, so the Christians are in permanent conflict with the world. And just as the captive soul preserves the
body which keeps it prisoner, so the Christians preserve the
world.' A ferment and a protection to the society in which it
developed; such was indeed the dual role assumed by the
Christian race, this new race, this living link between the past
and the future, this *tertium genus* of which St Augustine was
to speak.

# THE SOURCES OF CHRISTIAN
# LITERATURE

## FROM THE LIVING WORD TO THE FIRST
## WRITTEN TEXTS

JESUS HAD written nothing down, save on one single occasion, and then He had only written on the sand. He had certainly not founded a school of thought, a philosophic sect. He had not troubled to set down on papyrus the words He had spoken. However, before the end of the first century the essentials of His life and His message already existed in the form of books: books which we still read today. And before the end of the second a veritable Christian literature had been established, capable of comparison with that of the pagans, founded solely on His doctrine, and intended to renew the spiritual seeds which He had sown. It is this final characteristic which reveals the vitality of the nascent Church. Its intellectual fecundity was wonderful: just as wonderful as its strength to influence and to conquer, its heroism in the ordeal of persecution, and its organizing genius; the effects of this fecundity have endured into modern times.

This Christian literature was not to stem from the will of a handful of talented individuals, who were desirous of expressing themselves in the written word. It was to be born of life itself, of necessities and circumstances, simultaneously the medium and the evidence of action. Here once again the simile of a plant rises to mind, a plant whose beginnings are small, but which adapts itself wonderfully to its soil and pushes out roots in all directions. It ends by becoming a mighty tree, by virtue of a power of organic development which is both irresistible and imperiously logical. The mustard seed was a very small thing indeed, but it housed within it the Spirit of God.

How did this history of Christian literature, which was to rise to such heights of glory, begin? In a very humble way.

Jesus had not written anything down but He had talked a great deal. And how skilfully and powerfully! The temple guards had not dared to lay their hands upon Him, and had confessed: 'Nobody has ever spoken as this man speaks!' (John vii. 46). Countless people declared themselves astounded by his authority. He had spoken simply and clearly, in a way that the most illiterate of his listeners could follow. His words had a fine fragrance of natural things: the tilled earth, the tree heavy with fruit, the wind-swept water, the ripe corn glistening beneath the skies of June. But one sensed the great mysteries that lay behind these words; strange phrases, not capable of analysis, burst from His lips, and struck His hearers to the heart.

How had He talked? In the traditional manner of Jewish speech, the kind of oratorical style which still exists in Middle Eastern countries. All the methods used by the prophets, which can be grouped together under the heading 'oral style,'[1] were familiar to Jesus. He manipulated them superbly: the play of parallelism, which made the memory almost automatic; the use of parables, which struck the imagination so forcibly, and gave reality to the moral lesson; the skilful technique of repetition, which turned certain key words into kinds of pegs upon which the main thought of the argument could be hung: all these tools belonged to an art that was popular and refined at one and the same time, and that derived from the experience of generations. Jesus had possessed them all. We need only read aloud a Gospel passage, such as the following, in order to feel for ourselves His power of style and rhythmic perfection:

'Whosoever, then, hears these commandments of mine and carries them out, is like a wise man who built his house upon rock; and the rain fell and the floods came and the winds blew and beat upon that house, but it did not fall; it was founded upon rock. But whoever hears these commandments

[1] The basic works on this question in French are those of Father Marcel Jousse, particularly his Le Style oral et mnémotechnique chez les Verbo-moteurs, Paris, 1925. See also the note on this subject at the end of Father de Grandmaison's Jésus-Christ. As we have already seen, St Paul used the same technique (Chapter II, section: 'An Art Form Inspired by the Holy Spirit').

of mine and does not carry them out is like a fool, who built his house upon sand; and the rain fell and the floods came and the winds blew and beat upon that house, and it fell; and great was the fall of it' (Matt. vii. 24–7).

After Jesus' death it was this marvellous art of words which helped His teaching to survive. It is fairly certain that during His lifetime none of His disciples—not even those like Matthew, who were far from uneducated—had committed what they heard to writing. They had no need to do so. In Israel, just as in nascent Islam later on, or in old Madagascar, or among the North American Indians, the real medium for passing on ideas was the human memory. The golden rule of the rabbi's pupils was that they must listen to the master, and then repeat his maxims with scrupulous accuracy. 'A good disciple,' it was said, 'is like a well-constructed tank, which does not allow the smallest drop of water to escape from it.' The Mishna of the Talmud, and the Koran were both to be handed down orally for a considerable period, before being put into written form. The rhythmic, pictorial style, crammed with alliterations, comparisons and keywords, was actually intended to help this process of memorization. The Apostles scrupulously repeated the words of Christ, just as the rabbis' pupils repeated the maxims of their masters, and thus had no difficulty in handing down an accurate version of His doctrine.

Now let us imagine a gathering of the adherents of the new faith assembling under Solomon's Porch after the prayers said at the ninth hour were over. Some of those present would have known Jesus, would have seen Him and heard Him speak; others might just have been converted: but all possessed the same passionate desire to learn more about His teaching, and to hear His friends describe what He had been like. Then one of the Apostles would rise to his feet, possibly Matthew, the former tax-collector. Christ's sentences were so deeply engraved on his memory that he had forgotten not a single one of them. 'In those days . . .' In a single phrase he evoked the hillside of the Beatitudes, as it had looked that June day when Jesus preached there. 'Blessed are the poor in spirit; the kingdom of heaven is theirs. . . . Blessed are those who mourn; they shall be comforted. . . .' And no one present in the group would ever forget these words again.

326 THE CHURCH OF APOSTLES AND MARTYRS

This is the way in which the first catechesis should be visualized. St Paul calls it simply 'the tradition,' and the Acts refer to it as 'the way of the Lord.' This oral transmission would have been extremely simple, and might have actually tended to further simplification of the original: no one indulges in philosophical conferences with the masses. It would have turned on a few important doctrinal ideas and the essential biographical facts. It would also have tended to gather together in one sequence the various elements of Christ's message which the different events of His life had separated. In this way, little by little, a kind of teaching method was developed. So far as the biography of Christ was concerned, it became customary to divide it into four main sections, the same four which are still found in our Gospels today: the preparation for His ministry and His action in Galilee; the stay in Judaea; the Passion; and the Resurrection. His teaching was grouped together in large blocs: the Sermon on the Mount, the parables, His advice to His disciples, and His eschatological speeches on the future of the world and the Last Judgment.

This situation was to continue for twenty or thirty years. All this time the Christians simply spoke their tradition, without thinking of writing it down. The Church, the community which Jesus had founded, handed the divine message down to them. It was she who guaranteed its authenticity. Was not Peter here among them, the living witness, the authority instituted by Christ Himself? Men talked, men taught, men repeated everything that they knew regarding Jesus' life and message. Their teaching was called 'the Good News,' meaning both the news of the marvellous gift which our Lord had made of Himself and the news of the divine gifts which He had brought with Him; and, deriving from a Greek word which had originally meant 'gratuity for the bearer of good news,' but which had been applied to the good news itself ever since the Greek Golden Age, was expressed in the word *euangelion*, which in modern times is the root of our English word *Evangelists*, as applied to the writers of the Four Gospels, and of the French *l'Evangile*, meaning the Gospel itself.

How did this oral transmission become converted into writing and why? Several reasons must have contributed to the process simultaneously. As time went by, and the Church became larger, the danger of inaccurate oral reporting would grow greater. When it emerged from its Jewish framework to penetrate Greek-speaking and Greek-thinking circles, the Good News found itself working on very different ground, where the mnemotechnic customs of oral style scarcely existed at all. Since it was essential for the missionaries to be equipped to teach their audiences the basic facts about Jesus' life and message, the practice arose of giving them little booklets, which were like a kind of manual, and which were probably written in Greek for the benefit of the hellenized Jewish circles in Jerusalem, and were later produced in Antioch, where two languages, Aramaic and Greek, were equally used. In the first paragraph of his Gospel, St Luke makes a clear allusion to these preliminary drafts which had preceded his own work. These booklets were certainly incomplete compilations, varying in their scope, being merely simple schemas, notes or outlines. They aimed at supporting the oral expression of the Gospel tradition, which still remained the essential teaching medium.[2]

This co-existence of written and spoken teaching was to last for a very long time. Seneca had declared that he valued 'the living word' more than books. For many years to come this was to be the Christians' attitude too. What they long liked best was to hear those who had personally known the Master speaking about Him. Then, when these first witnesses died, they flocked to listen to their disciples, or the disciples of their disciples. This attachment to direct relationships, this handing down of the Word from man to man, has something exceedingly moving and attractive about it. About 130 Bishop Papias of Phrygia confessed that he preferred 'things spoken by the living, perishable voice' to the contents of books. Likewise, later still, St Irenaeus was to tell how he had kept all that St Polycarp had taught him 'not on paper, but in the heart,'

[2] We can get some idea of what these booklets, these 'rudimentary Gospels,' must have been like by reading the little speech which Peter made in the presence of Cornelius, the centurion, which is quoted in the Acts of the Apostles (x. 37–41). He there sums up all the essentials of Jesus' life and teaching in about a dozen very simple lines, arranged under the four headings indicated in this section.

and this concerned things that Polycarp had learned from St John himself. But long before this, fearful of possible deviations from the truth and also motivated by the superior demands of her missionary endeavour, the Church had set down the Good News in final textual form.

## MATTHEW, MARK AND LUKE, THE FIRST 'EVANGELISTS'

The modern Christian who wishes to learn about Jesus' life and teaching betakes himself to one volume divided into four parts; or rather to four separate little works assembled together in a single volume: this is the *Gospel*, comprising the *Four Gospels*. However limited his critical curiosity, numerous questions immediately spring to mind. These accounts are our most precious and almost our only source of knowledge about Jesus: when were they written? Why do three of these texts contain so much material in common that they appear to have been written after the same model, whereas the fourth, without differing from them in its fundamentals, has quite a different tone and style, and was clearly written with a different intention behind it? Why are there certain divergencies even among the first three Gospels? The Gospels present many problems, which exegesis has been tirelessly examining for the past two thousand years; but today it is possible to offer a reasonable explanation for them, and one which is fairly generally accepted.[3]

Let us try to envisage the conditions in which these books were written. Each of those writers whom we call 'the Evangelists' was interested simply and solely in reporting Jesus' message faithfully; each effaced his own character before the radiant figure of his subject, and humbly submitted himself to the Divine Inspiration which was impelling him to write. These Evangelists did not wish to produce literary masterpieces, but testimonies of faith; for that matter men were not to speak of 'the Gospel *of* Matthew, or *of* Mark, or *of* Luke, or *of* John,' but of 'the Gospel *according to* . . . ,' and this slight difference in emphasis is fundamental. Nevertheless these men who

[3] For a more detailed study of all these questions the reader is referred to the introduction of the author's *Jesus in His Time*.

wrote as the Spirit dictated still remained ordinary men; they had their own temperament, processes of thought, style and ability. And then some account must be taken of the kinds of information which they had at their disposal: personal memories, the living tradition, the teaching manuals referred to in the previous section, and such eye-witness knowledge as they would collect. Nor was this all: in these fervent communities where the Word of God was men's life-blood, an evangelical text which was in process of compilation must surely have been analysed, discussed and compared with other documents; new quotations and other additions were endlessly possible. Finally, as Christianity progressed its horizons changed: one book might be primarily addressed to the Jewish circles in Jerusalem, while another was aimed at the Hellenists of the *diaspora*; one was thinking of an ordinary, humble audience of simple folk, while another would be seeking to attract the attention of educated people. When considering the origin of the Gospels, it is quite essential to bear in mind this whole collection of infinitely complex intentions and resources, of reciprocal influences and varying techniques; these first Christian texts carry the strong impress of men, environments and epochs, that is to say the impress of the very life which engendered them.

Our first three present-day Gospels were certainly written first also: no one disputes the fact that John's book is later than those of Matthew, Mark and Luke. These three contain so many analogies with one another that they can be arranged in three columns wherein the number of their paragraphs almost coincides. This is why they have acquired the title of the *Synoptic Gospels*: they are texts which can be read simultaneously.

Eusebius, the Church historian who lived in the fourth century, drew up a rather curious statistical table in which he showed that if the Gospels were divided into sections corresponding with an idea or development, a very large number of these fragments repeated themselves from one synoptic to another: for instance, St Matthew contains only 62 individual extracts out of 355, and St Mark only 19 out of 233. In this case, it may be asked, why preserve all three books? Or rather, why are there a number of unquestionable differences between these three brother texts? It is here that the factors relating to personalities, intentions and documentation, which have been referred to above, come into play.

The first writer to set to work was undoubtedly Matthew, the former publican from Capernaum whom Jesus had snatched from his tax-collector's table: Matthew was a Jew with a smattering of Greek ideas, but he remained profoundly Hebrew at heart. About 130 Papias asserted that 'Matthew arranged the Lord's sayings, in Aramaic,' and a little later on St Irenaeus states precisely that 'Matthew committed the Gospel to writing, among the Palestinians, in their own language, while Peter and Paul were preaching in Rome and founding the Roman Church.' Our information, therefore, is quite clear. Somewhere around the years 50–5, Matthew, who was living in a completely Jewish environment at the time, wrote his book. He thought as a Jew; he wrote as a Jew. Does he not describe himself as 'a scribe perfectly instructed in the things concerning the Kingdom of Heaven'? Does he not make specific allusions to a letter of the Hebrew alphabet, and to the tricks and quibbles of the Pharisees? Because he had a thorough understanding of his compatriots and of their Messianic expectancy, he laid special stress upon the imminent approach of the Kingdom of Heaven. But in addition, since he was still very close to the age in which Jesus had spoken, since he saw as his essential task the teaching of the Master's doctrine and the bearing of His Divine Message, he constructed his book around Christ's five great fundamental speeches, contenting himself with placing them soberly in their setting, without laying too much emphasis upon the biographical details. Matthew was an eye-witness who reported what he had seen.

We no longer possess this first Gospel in its original version. Eusebius, and later Clement and Origen, actually record a tradition according to which Pantaenus, the founder of the Christian school at Alexandria in the second century, went to the Indies and found there, in one of the communities established by St Bartholomew, a copy of this Aramaic Gospel according to St Matthew: but this remains no more than a tradition. The Hebrew features of the first Gospel show through the later, Greek, version of it, but others too have been superimposed upon the original material, for by the time the translation was made the two other Gospels had already been written.

Some years went by. Peter had already been established in Rome for a long time. Probably *c.* 55 he was joined by a disciple, a Hellenist Jew, who may have originally come from Cyprus, but who had been living recently in Jerusalem. This man's name was John, surnamed Mark. Mark had not really been Jesus' disciple, being probably too young at that time,[4] but he had adhered to the new faith at a very early date. He had humbly taken a minor position in the community, but he had performed various useful tasks as a secretary and catechist in an admirable fashion for several of its important leaders. He had worked with the wise Barnabas, and even, for a short time, with St Paul; he had known Peter since his boyhood. Mark was a man of the people, but he could speak Greek; he did not manipulate the language of Homer particularly well, but he was direct and realistic, like ordinary folk. When he reached Rome—possibly after the death of Barnabas, his master—he devoted himself to Peter. He listened to Peter preaching; he noted the striking features of his catechesis, and, since the Prince of Apostles was himself a man of the people, holy rather than learned, what Mark recorded was not particularly literary, nor well arranged, but it contained the full pungency of the faith. And this was how, possibly some time between 55 and 62, Mark wrote down what he had heard from Peter, at the request of the enthusiastic Christian community in Rome. In addition, he had for reference a few rudimentary manuals, in particular an account of Christ's Passion. The whole comprises a slim volume of some fifty pages, rather untidily set out, but full of an astonishing vigour and a rare freshness of vision.

Once again it is Papias who tells us how the second Gospel originated. 'Mark, who had been Peter's interpreter, wrote down accurately all that he remembered about the Lord's say-

---

[4] Mark was the son of the Mary who, in 44, sheltered the Christians in a house situated in a deserted spot of the outlying quarter of Jerusalem; some authorities have wondered whether the land belonging to this house may not have been the scene of Jesus' arrest, and whether Mark himself may have been the young man whom he describes (xiv. 51) as trying to follow Jesus, whom the guards attempt to catch, and who fled naked into the night.

ings and actions, but not in an orderly sequence. Peter had chosen his teaching according to the needs of the moment, without attempting to set it out in order. Consequently Mark was not to blame for writing it all down exactly as he remembered it being said: he was anxious only to omit nothing and to record nothing but the truth.' And if we read the text we can see clearly the circumstances in which the drafting was done: when Mark explains that the Jordan is a river, when he gives a Romanized version of various Jewish expressions, when he explains laboriously the ritual customs of Israel, this is because his readers are not Jews alone, but ignorant Roman pagans too, honest but uneducated people for whom it is quite essential to dot all the i's.

Luke is quite different. In the literary sense his book is a masterpiece, the first masterpiece that Christianity was able to inscribe upon the honours roll of the world's outstanding literature. He writes in a fine, measured Greek, full of flowing harmony, and showing great delicacy of touch. The writer shines through his text: sensitive, intelligent, artistic and well educated. Theological arguments do not interest him very much. His overriding desire is to make his readers feel the living presence of Christ, and make them love Him. And how wonderfully he succeeds, this biographer of the Good Samaritan, the pardoned harlot, and the prodigal son to whom the father opened his arms in welcome! Dante calls him 'the scribe of gentleness.'

Who was Luke? Very probably he was the 'beloved physician' whom St Paul mentions several times in his Epistles, the travelling companion of the Apostle of the Gentiles on the latter's marathon journeys. St Irenaeus declares explicitly that Luke committed to paper 'the Gospel which Paul preached.' He was a citizen of Antioch, familiar with the problems facing Christianity and the world; and he was a physician, in other words a scientist, accustomed to reflection, to intellectual study, to referring back to sources. That he was, in addition, extremely talented is clear from the published result we see before us. He came to Rome with Paul. Did he write his Gospel for the better-educated elements in the Roman community? Or was it written, as some traditions aver, for the church at Corinth, which was so dear to Paul's heart? Luke probably started work on his book *c.* 63. From Paul he gathered a great deal of material which came direct from the Apostles; during the course of some prolonged visits to Palestine he had questioned many eye-witnesses of Christ, possibly including Mary herself, the mother of our Lord, from whom he may have obtained his precious chapter on Jesus' infancy, and possibly, also, a certain Joanna, the wife of Chuza, Herod's steward. He was certainly helped by Mark's text, which had already appeared. This he uses quite obviously, as well as certain translated passages and partial summaries from the Aramaic manuscript of Matthew. And, writing with far more narrative sense than the others, following a considered plan, he produced the Gospel which probably moves us most deeply.

And it was now at last that the first Gospel assumed the form in which we read it today. A number of fragmentary attempts had been made to translate Matthew's Aramaic text, which was extremely popular among the primitive communities.[5] Papias alludes to these. The Church was anxious to organize them in a permanent form: a collective version was undertaken, possibly *c.* 64 and during the following few years. But by this time Mark's and Luke's Gospels were in existence, and, in the course of their difficult task, the translators judged it useful to reread closely anything that was already written in Greek, e.g. Mark's text, and this resulted in certain additions and modifications to the original Aramaic version. Was it Matthew himself who translated his work? At all events, by keeping his name on the book the Church confirmed that nothing of substance from the original version had been altered. Though the last of the synoptics in its modern form, Matthew's Gospel remains, at heart, the first.

## THE APOSTLES' OWN ACTIONS
### AND WRITINGS

Jesus had returned to His Father in heaven. The Gospel contained the essentials of His message. But was this all? Was it

---

[5] St Matthew's Gospel remained the one most commonly used in the ancient Church. Writing in the middle of the second century, St Justin quotes it no less than 170 times.

enough? Men's curiosity about the Lord was so great! Their souls hungered and thirsted for yet more of the divine truth! A number of men had survived Jesus, men who had been His privileged eye-witnesses. They were His disciples. He had chosen them and taught them. Was it not vital, therefore, to collect their words and note their actions, not, of course, in the same way as Jesus' message and life had been preserved—for, holy though they were, they remained mere mortals for all that—but as the reflections and torchbearers of Him who had been the Light Eternal?

It was this apostolic loyalty, which was such a fundamental feature throughout the whole of the early Church, which was to give birth to an entirely new chapter of Christian literature. 'Have the example of the excellent Apostles before your eyes, all the time!' wrote St Clement of Rome to the Corinthians; and had not St Paul, who, though not one of the Twelve, had received his call direct from the Master, already declared that: 'This secret of Christ's . . . was never made known to any human being in past ages, as it has now been revealed by the Spirit to his holy apostles and prophets' (Eph. iii. 5–6)? The Acts of the Apostles and the collection of Epistles were born of this conviction, which was shared by all the early generations of Christians.

The book of the Acts of the Apostles (this is its Greek title) is the quasi-unique document which we possess regarding Christianity's very earliest beginnings: if we did not have it, we would know scarcely anything of those vital thirty years during which the mustard seed of the faith was being planted far and wide. The life of the Jerusalem community, the evangelization of Judaea and Samaria, the origins of the mission into Gentile territory and the conversion of Cornelius the centurion; then the bulk of the biographical details concerning St Paul, his conversion, his great journeys, his travels in Greece, his arrival in Italy: we know all these facts from this one little book. Moreover, it is a vivid, stirring and often picturesque piece of writing: modern Christians do not often read it, and this is a very great pity; it has no equal of its kind in the whole of Christian literature.

According to a tradition which dates back to the first Christian writers, and which, moreover, is confirmed by a close examination of the text itself, the author of the Acts is the same man who wrote the third Gospel: in other words, it is more than probable that the Acts were written by Luke. The opening sentences of the two works, with their message to the 'noble Theophilus,' the unity of style, intention and doctrine, all support this traditional attribution. The 'beloved physician' probably wrote the book of Acts at the same time as his Gospel, or immediately afterwards. It is clear from the book's ending that it was finished in between Paul's first and second periods of captivity in Rome: if we assume that it was published between 63 and 64 we must be very near the truth. We find in it the mark of that same well-educated, well-informed and intelligent man that we see in the third Gospel. Luke had an acute mind, capable of studying his facts critically, and he certainly took good care to provide himself with every possible documentation before he started writing: he had questioned the actual eye-witnesses of the events of the earliest days of Christianity, when he met them in Jerusalem; he had observed and noted the deeds and gestures of Paul, his master, and his text contains (in the fragments where he uses the pronoun 'we,' which the critics have analysed so thoroughly) the actual notes that he took on the course of his journeys. All this goes to make a singularly rich book; obviously one that is not complete in every sense, because Luke was no historian, but a propagandist, and because his real aim was to throw into relief the realization of Jesus' own prophecy: 'You are to be my witnesses in Jerusalem and throughout Judaea, in Samaria, yes, and to the ends of the earth!' (Acts i. 8), and because, moreover, he was not much of a theologian. But in point of fact, as if to complete this narrative, the Church ordained that it should be followed by a collection of other texts, moral, spiritual and theological in their content: these are the *Epistles*, outstanding among which are the Epistles of St Paul.

It is the Epistles, more than any other documents, which make the reader fully aware of the extent to which the creation of a Christian literature was really the actual work of life itself, of the extent to which the written word was linked with men's actions. For example, we have but to look at any one of those thirteen letters which we know for certain were written by St Paul; we hear the man himself talking through them, they are pulsating with the breath of life. Paul dictated these letters himself, to some secretary or other, during a halt in the very midst of his missionary labours. With his own hands he wrote in the final good wishes and his signature, so that his scrawling handwriting, clumsily formed on account of his poor eyesight, should sweep away any suspicion of faking. He sent these letters to correspondents who were personally known to him: disciples, whole communities and occasionally to simple and ordinary believers. In them he alludes to precise incidents, and to immediate contingencies, mingling with these the most lofty considerations upon the spiritual life, for in these times of great faith material problems and spiritual questions comprised but one single reality, one single subject for reflection. How very close to life all this is, above all when it is expressed in this sparkling style—ironical, yet tender, enthusiastic, yet sympathetic—the style of the polemicist and the mystic who was the Apostle Paul!

And it was this very breath of life which the Christians wanted to find when they read or listened to these texts. No sooner had a community received a letter from one of the Apostles than a copy was made and sent on to the other churches. St Paul had expressly meant several of his to be published. St Peter alludes, as though to something well known, to the collection of letters written by his 'beloved brother, Paul' which were available for study in the churches. We possess a great deal of evidence to prove that the various Epistles which we still read during Mass were already being read eighteen hundred years ago. In the account of the trial of the African martyrs of Scillitum, we have seen how Speratus, one of the accused, when questioned about the books found in his possession, replied that they were 'our holy books and the letters of Paul, a good and upright man.' These texts were the living links which bound the communities to one another. They were also a wonderful medium for the development and definition of the moral and theological topics whose principles had been laid down by Christ.

This is why the Church, when she came to fix the canon of the Scriptures, wanted to place a certain number of these letters, whose value she considered outstanding, immediately

after the Gospels and the Acts. And first of all she awarded
a place to those of St Paul, for in every respect they are the
most important. Written throughout the length of his missionary life, spaced out in time between 52 and 66, differing
considerably from one another as to length (a number are
simply short letters, while others are veritable treatises), tone
and even style, they constitute an essential step in the development of Christianity. Of course they do not add to Jesus'
message, but they interpret it with truly marvellous lucidity,
and bring it much closer to human preoccupations. So many
souls of that epoch bore within them the longing for redemption and salvation: it was Paul who proved conclusively that
Christian doctrine provided complete satisfaction for that
longing. The conflict between reason and faith had already
begun, and was to continue constantly down the centuries: it
was Paul, once more, who indicated how it could be resolved.
The vigorous seeds of everything that was, in the future, to
grow into Christian theology and Christian philosophy can be
found in his thirteen Epistles. There is no problem either of
his age or of any other age which he did not see and for which
did not offer the answers born of his brilliant genius.[6]

Set beside the writings of the great missionary of the Gentiles, the other Epistles appear rather more insipid, even the
Epistle to the Hebrews, which is in Paul's tradition, and goes
by his name, but which cannot be definitely said to be his
work. However, there is not one of them that leaves the reader
unmoved, that does not add a stone to the edifice of the faith.
The Epistle of St James, 'the brother of the Lord,' the first
bishop of Jerusalem, whom St Clement of Rome admired very
deeply, is valuable on account of its moral teaching. The two
Epistles of St Peter, which were to be much venerated by the
Fathers of the Church, are, simultaneously, a precious record
of the quality of Christian faith in the period when the aged
Prince of Apostles was writing them, and, in the sobriety of
their rustic style, sublime calls to hope and charitable love.

[6] The list of St Paul's Epistles and their classification have been
given earlier in this book, in Chapter II, which is devoted to the
Apostle's life, work and writing (see the note in Chapter II, section:
'Christ is Proclaimed to the Gentiles'). On the question of the
Epistle to the Hebrews, see also the same chapter.

The short Epistle of St Jude, or Thaddeus, brother of James, one of the Twelve, which was written *c.* 66, at the time when Jerusalem could see the terrible holocaust prophesied by Jesus drawing near, is a perfect description of the purity of heart which the righteous must possess when the Last Day comes. The list of Epistles is completed by the three letters which the same name and the evidence of the same inspiration link with the fourth Evangelist, St John, the man who, together with St Paul, stands out as one of the great pillars of Christian wisdom in the earliest days of the Church's history.

## THE WORK OF ST JOHN

'At the beginning of the second century a group of five texts, connected with one another by various complex links, existed among the Christian communities in Asia Minor. They were attributed to one author, by the name of John, whom ecclesiastical tradition subsequently considered to have been the same John who was the son of Zebedee, and the disciple of Jesus.' This is how the liberal Protestant historian Lietzmann sets out (and apparently settles, in the space of two sentences) the much-debated problem of the Johannine texts. These texts consist of an 'Apocalypse,' a Gospel—our fourth—and three short Epistles, the two first Epistles being addressed to a community whose name is not indicated, and the third to a certain Gaius, clearly a great friend of the sender. They give rise to two questions: were all five documents written by the same author? And was this author the man whom the Church claims he was: John, Christ's Apostle?

Today the attribution of the whole collection to one individual is more easily accepted than it was some fifty years ago. No one can deny that there are some very obvious differences between the Apocalypse and the Gospel, and if, as tradition maintains, the latter was written after the former, it cannot even be said that the passage from one to the other is marked by any progress in style, or by the usual literary evolution that might have been expected. But these differences seem less serious if we consider that a book of 'apocalyptic' visions is not likely to be written in the same way as an ordinary historical or theological work, and if we accept, as a number of exegetists do, the hypothesis of a secretary for one or other of the works. It is clear that all five texts contain the same distinctly 'Johannine' expressions, and possess a profound identity of spiritual attitude. The most recent studies on the language of these documents have demonstrated that the Apocalypse and the Gospel prologue both employ the same poetic technique of regular strophes and stanzas, marked by the seal of a similar talent. If, therefore, it is concluded that one author wrote all five texts, can it also be immediately assumed that this author was, indeed, the Apostle John?

Free-thinking criticism, relying on a somewhat obscure document by Papias, who was writing c. 125, has maintained that this author could not have been the Apostle, but, instead, a certain 'John the Elder,' namely a presbyter of some Asian community. The word disciple—and not Apostle—which the Evangelist freely applies to himself, supports this argument too: although there seems no reason why one of Christ's own immediate disciples should not stick to this name. The Church has some very strong reasons to put forward in justification of the original attribution. First of all, the Gospel itself states categorically that it is the work of an Apostle: 'the disciple whom Jesus loved' (John xxi. 20); and confirmation of this fact can be seen in the modesty which results in the author never mentioning by name either John, or James, his brother, or Zebedee, his father, or the Salome who was probably his mother and whom all the Synoptic Gospels call attention to at Calvary, on the evening of the Crucifixion and on Easter morning: a true signature of humility. Moreover, all the recent works on the subject have shown that this writer possessed outstanding geographical accuracy; of all four Evangelists, his topographical sense is the most exact, and it is from his information that the reader is best able to refer back to specific fields of action: his descriptions and allusions are those of an actual eye-witness. Finally, the tradition which attributes these five texts to the Apostle John is an extremely ancient one: Polycarp of Smyrna c. 150, Melito of Sardis c. 160, Irenaeus of Lyons a little later, then Polycrates of Ephesus, Clement of Alexandria, and the 'Muratorian Canon'—a catalogue of sacred books compiled c. 200—all confirm that their author is, in St Irenaeus's words, 'John, the disciple of the Lord, the same who rested upon Christ's breast.' Textual analysis shows him possessed of Jewish habits of thought and style transposed into the Hellenic framework. And in reply to those critics who marvel that a humble Galilean fisherman could have written works of such sublimity as these, it should be pointed out that the greatest rabbis of Israel—men like Rabbi Akiba, Rabbi Meir and Rabbi Johanan—were themselves only ordinary manual workers, cobblers, cooks or joiners, and that, in addition, a total of sixty years had elapsed between the epoch when John was fishing on Lake Tiberias and that in which he wrote his books, a whole lifetime of apostleship and religious meditation: what a moulding of character could have taken place within that time!

In this way the tradition which claims the author of these five Johannine texts to be none other than the youngest of the Apostles, the young man who watched at the foot of the Cross, Jesus' favourite disciple, is an extremely compelling one: a grand old man, weighed down by years, by sanctity and by fame, combining, with his character of one of the Messiah's actual eye-witnesses, the hieratical dignity of a great priest and the flamboyant violence of a prophet. After a miraculous escape from execution, and release from exile, he ended his days at Ephesus, amid universal respect.[7] If John the Apostle did not write these five texts, if their author was but an ordinary 'presbyter,' how was it that the Church, which as we shall see, was to show itself exceedingly severe in its choice of sacred texts, rooting out several other 'apocalypses' in a most ruthless fashion, was prepared to accept these writings, whose tone was so novel and so different from that of the synoptics?

This difference is self-explanatory. Very many years elapsed between the writing of the first three Gospels and the Pauline Epistles and of the Johannine texts: at least thirty or forty. The Apocalypse dates from 92 to 96, the fourth Gospel from 96 to 104. By this time the historical background had completely changed. The life of Christ was well known to all the faithful in its main features: anyone wishing to deal with it further needed to look at it in an entirely new light and to use bare facts only when they were necessary to complete the earlier

[7] See Chapter III, the first section.

accounts. Persecution had become a historical reality which weighed heavily upon the Christian soul and forced it to envisage the coming of the Kingdom of Heaven through perspectives of ordeal and frightful torment. St Paul had been working on another plane and his philosophical genius had profoundly influenced Christian understanding of the Master's teaching; he had defined problems and formulated solutions which no one could ignore. By conclusively emerging from its original Jewish framework in order to develop itself upon Hellenic soil, Christianity had encountered currents of thought and modes of expression of which it was bound to take cognizance: e.g. the Platonic concept of Logos, the Word, which had been developed by Philo of Alexandria, and which is easily and legitimately found, in its complete form, in Christian truth. Finally, within the bosom of Christianity itself, a number of tendencies were manifesting themselves which needed careful watching: heresy was beginning to circulate; there was already warning of the *Docetists*, who denied the divinity of Christ, the first *Gnostics*, who were to compromise that divinity amid nebulous systems of abstractions, and the *Nicolaics*, who wrongfully claimed descent from one of the first deacons, and who, under pretext that the flesh is despicable, encouraged the grossest immorality. At the end of his life St Paul had been more or less aware of all these facts; c. 90–100 a mighty mind like St John's was bound to conceive his work in terms of them.

About 92–6 John was living on Patmos, one of the islands belonging to the Sporades group, between Naxos and the coast of Anatolia, having been deported there by Domitian. In Rome he had witnessed, and probably taken part in, the tragic drama of the persecutions. His soul was profoundly shaken by the black hurricane which was buffeting the Church. As one of God's prophets, and as a witness of Christ, he felt bound to react to the anguish which tore at his heart, bound to shout his lamentations aloud! And he reacted as men of his race so often reacted. The Apocalypse is his cry of anguish. How strange and mysterious it seems to us, with its torrent of images, its flood of wild visions, its fantastic catalogue of beasts, its blinding symbolism! It is a book which generation after generation of Christians have read continously in the hope of

being able to find therein the secret of their own destiny!
But it would have seemed far less bizarre to a man of the
first century than it does to us, if only because it was in the
direct line pursued by traditional Israelite writing over the
previous six hundred years. As we have seen,[8] the apocalyptic
current had been ceaselessly working through Jewish literature
from the prophetic books of Daniel and Ezekiel right up to
contemporary writings. There was the Book of Enoch, the Book
of Jubilees, The Testament of the Twelve Patriarchs, the
Ascension of Moses and several others besides, all in this *genre*.
They comprised quite a library which John could use as a
model when he wanted to express the fundamental and ago-
nized cry of the Christian soul in distress, in the same way as
the Jewish apocalypses had expressed the anguish of the imprisoned and humiliated soul of Jewry. Thus John followed the
same literary methods of his predecessors: the mysterious com-
binations of numbers, and the esoteric descriptions, enabled
him to allude to the existing situation in a way which meant
that only the very folk to whom he was speaking would understand him. Like his predecessors, by taking as his starting-
point the tragedy of the moment, and by making constant
references to it, his mind eventually travelled far beyond it;
he attained far wider horizons, those of the essential drama of
man, and of the fundamental opposition between the world
and the Divine Word; he embarked upon his terrifying descriptions of the end of the world in order to find therein the
promise of Christ, the hope of salvation, the Hope Divine!
. . . Here indeed is the supreme lesson that emerges from all
these grandiose developments, a lesson that the Christians of
John's epoch most badly needed. No outburst of temporal
violence could prevail against the ultimate sovereignty of the
Saviour, and, however terrible the jolts of history might be,
one reality remained immune from them, a reality upon which
history itself would turn until the end of time: the Word of
life, the revelation of the Lamb.

Some years later, after his liberation, John wrote his Gospel
at Ephesus. Circumstances now gave him other preoccupations,
and though his goal remained always the same—to make the

[8] See Chapter I, section: 'The Glad Voice of the Heralds.'

message of Christ ring out far and wide—the situation that gave him the opportunity to do so was very different. The Asian communities amongst whom he lived besought him to commit his memories to paper. This he did, right at the end of his life, and, to the information given in the three synoptics, which he knew very thoroughly, he added his own personal sources. In this way he produced an infinitely precious work of which about half (106 sections out of 232) owes nothing to his predecessors. But his book is even more original in its emphasis and its echoes. The upsurge of philosophy was very lively in Asia at the end of the first century. The hellenized circles who were interested in Christ wanted, more than anything else, to know what His revelation consisted of, what connection He had had with God the Father, and how He had communicated the understanding of the things ineffable to men. Besides, in the Church herself, there were already a number of nonconformists, heretics who denied that Jesus had been the Christ or that the Son of God could have been made incarnate. Consequently it was necessary to reply to all these expectant queries, and to all these errors. This was why, as Clement of Alexandria was to say, 'seeing that the other evangelists had only dealt with material facts, John, the last of them all, wrote the spiritual Gospel in response to the prayers of his friends and with the divine support of the Holy Spirit.'

This is the explanation of the extremely striking originality of the fourth Gospel: its perspectives are not those of the synoptics. Conjointly with the work of St Paul, it stands on the brink of what was to become Christian philosophy and Christian theology. Its author exposes, with extreme artistry and skill, a number of elements which already existed in the work of his predecessors, but which when isolated acquire their true prominence, and he shows us a Christ who is simultaneously very real and loftily metaphysical. Each account of a miracle is notable for the spiritual meaning which emerges from it: the multiplying of the loaves proclaims the bread of life; the resurrection of Lazarus promises life eternal to us all. This Gospel, wherein the whole man is found, grasps the whole reality and lifts it towards God.

The summit of this lies in the prologue. This conclusively

344  THE CHURCH OF APOSTLES AND MARTYRS

expresses the doctrine which is John's own contribution to
Christian thought, the revelation of the Word incarnate. 'At
the beginning of time the Word already was; and God had the
Word abiding with him, and the Word was God. . . . And
the Word was made flesh, and came to dwell among us . . .'
(John i. 1, 14). We are so accustomed to these musical cadences that the mystery expressed in them has become
blunted, and few Christians recognize their complete originality any more. It would have been very different for John's
own hearers! This grandiose concept of the Word, Logos, the
Word which created, ordered and revealed, had already been
sketched out by the philosophers in a myriad of approxima-
tions. The expression was widespread throughout all those
eastern Mediterranean lands that had bathed in the tide of
Greek learning. Plato had recognized in it the origin of ideas;
the last book of the Old Testament had seen the Divine Wisdom therein; Philo, a loyal Jew, had just interpreted it in
his way, by recognizing in it the intelligible world, the imperfect representation of God. St John gave the certain solution to all these groping attempts at the truth; he joined all
these interpretations of the expression under one head. The
divine power which St Matthew and St Luke had seen made
incarnate as a child in the Virgin's womb, the Creator of man
and of the world, the Discoverer of God, who is God Himself: the fourth Evangelist describes all this under the name
of the Word, and links it with Christ; the Word is no longer
an abstract principle, but a personal being; Logos means Jesus.
This conception was already implicit in St Paul's Epistle to
the Colossians and in the Epistle to the Hebrews; but St
John gave it formal expression. In this way, by 'christianizing'
words and philosophical formulae, he did what so many Christian thinkers were to do after him: he took over ideas that
were strange and unknown and gave them their final meaning.
Here is his essential originality: through him the theoretical
God of the philosophers became henceforth the God of love.[9]

[9] St John's three Epistles are contemporary with his Gospel: the
first, which is by far the most important in every respect, lays principal stress on Jesus' Messianity and divinity; the two others denounce the errors of the enemies of Christian dogmas, and explain
the answers that should be given them.

## The Church Lays Down Her Choice:
### the Canon

The Johannine texts close the list of works which today figure in our Bible, constituting there the Book of the New Testament, in other words, the book of the New Covenant.[10] Just as the Israelite texts which are assembled together in the Bible were the age-old commentary on the Covenant established between Yahweh and his people, so, for the Christians, the New Testament books are the written pledge of the New Covenant which Christ came down to earth to establish between God and men and which He sealed with His own blood. These texts, numbering twenty-seven altogether, form the canon of the New Testament, that is to say, the rule, the correct measure, the model. How was the choice of them made? And by whom? It was made by the Church, who, having existed long before any of these documents were written, possessed, in her capacity as Jesus' witness, the right of detecting which works were literally scriptural and which were not; and the Church made her choice during the final decades when the breath of the Spirit was still blowing cool and fresh upon the faces of her children.

Nascent Christianity was quickly compelled to make this choice. It must have felt the necessity to do so less than a century after the Master's death. In the extreme fervour of these primitive times, in the naïve and touching desire to know as much as possible about the details concerning Jesus, many other writings had sprung up, composed at about the same time as the Apostles' works, in which the workings of popular imagination tended to infiltrate in a highly indiscreet fashion. Moreover, as theological arguments became more general, as actual doctrinal deviations occurred, a number of texts might well be put into circulation by over-facile interpreters, or

[10] The Hebrew *berith*, meaning alliance, was translated into Greek (by the Septuagint) by the word *diatheke*, which usually means document, and can thus be applied equally well to a treaty as to a testament. In Latin *diatheke* was translated (possibly by Tertullian) into the word *testamentum*, which limited the Greek meaning, and, compared with the Hebrew, modified it noticeably.

even by downright heretics, in order to favour certain specific ideas. In short, ever since the earliest days of the Church, that type of literature known as *apocryphal* has been in existence: a literature that depicted a bizarre world, divorced from reality, a mixture of truths and disordered imaginings, from which the Middle Ages was to derive several artistic themes, whose content is by no means all unacceptable, but which the Church was wise enough to treat with the utmost reserve.

In this way the Gospel of the Hebrews, which St Ignatius would have known, and which is also mentioned by Clement of Alexandria, Origen and Eusebius, had enjoyed a wide circulation among the Judeo-Christian communities. The Christian communities of Egypt had possessed their own version, which was very ascetic in tone, and already strongly tainted with Gnosticism. The Gospel of Peter, a document full of a wealth of details about the Passion, the Crucifixion and the Resurrection, but tinged with Docetism, in other words unfaithful to the dogma of the Incarnation, was tremendously popular with several churches. From the Gospel of Nicodemus men sought details about Jesus' trial, and about 'the Acts of Pilate,' and could find a weird and very grandiose vision of the descent into hell. This literature was to appear throughout the whole of the second century; Gospels of the Holy Infancy multiplied in number. These dealt with Jesus' birth and boyhood, were spiced with fabulous details, and displayed a taste that was often more than dubious. People wanted to learn more about our Lord's family too: there was to be an account of the Dormition of Mary, her death and her Assumption.[11] A History of Joseph the Carpenter also appeared. The Apostles were to be equally victims of this indiscreet and tendentious curiosity; there were Acts of Peter, Acts of Paul and Acts concerning Andrew and John, and Thomas, and Philip, and Thaddaeus, not to mention several apocryphal Epistles and some five or six apocalypses attributed to famous Christian figures. This unrestrained riot of imagination was to continue

---

[11] These texts, although not canonical, are regarded as orthodox, and as expressing an ancient tradition which is certainly a completely authentic one.

until the end of the fourth century, but by that time the Church's canon had been fixed for a long time.[12]

Faced, therefore, with all this mass of more or less suspect documents, the Church made her choice of twenty-seven of them, and guaranteed their authenticity. She declared that these twenty-seven texts were *inspired*. What should be understood by this expression? 'Inspiration,' said Leo XIII in his encyclical *Providentissimus Deus*, 'is a supernatural impulse whereby the Holy Spirit inspired and encouraged the sacred writers, and assisted them while they wrote, so that they preserved with absolute accuracy, desired to report faithfully, and expressed with infallible truth everything that God commanded them, and wrote only what He commanded them to write.' But then what were the signs whereby the texts inspired by the Spirit could be recognized?

The choice was not made rigidly, *a priori*, *ex cathedra*; the decision was born of living experience alone, and came naturally and quite serenely. There were undoubtedly a number of tentative choices, of afterthoughts, and probably a number of discussions too. Eusebius describes how Seraphinus, the Bishop of Antioch, was presented with the Gospel of Peter, with which he was unacquainted. First of all he gave permission for it to be read, but then, having examined it more closely and discovered traces of Docetism in it, he prohibited it. Hermas' *Pastor*, the book which is so closely linked with the early years of the second century, was considered inspired for some time. It was then banished from the Western churches, but was to remain highly regarded by the Church of Egypt for a long time to come; Origen was still to consider it as divine writing.

One thing is certain. The Church was to show extreme severity in the methods which she employed to enforce her choice. About 200 Tertullian relates that some thirty years earlier a book called the Acts of St Paul had appeared in the province of Asia. In this document the Apostle was portrayed as converting a certain Thekla, a young pagan woman, where-

---

[12] There are various editions of these apocryphal works in French and English. In French, see also the numerous critical works by Lépin, Variot, Le Hir, etc. . . . Art historians, notably Émile Mâle, have also studied them a great deal. See also the author's own *Les Évangiles de la Vierge*, Paris, 1948.

upon she immediately began to preach the Gospel herself, in a most admirable fashion. Tertullian describes how, since this account appeared to be suspect, its author was immediately sought and apprehended. He was a priest, more well intentioned than prudent, and he was immediately degraded. In addition we have but to read the apocryphal texts alongside the canonical ones to see on which side all the prudence, wisdom and moderation lie and to realize how delicately and how tactfully canonical Scripture fixes and limits the claims of the supernatural and the miraculous.

The two criteria determining the Church's choice were, essentially, catholicity and apostolicity. A text was accepted as canonical when all the communities recognized it as being faithful to true Christian tradition, to the true message of our Lord. As the liturgy became more codified, the custom of reading various pages from the Epistles and the Gospels during the Mass meant that the contents of these passages were put to the test of public opinion: as soon as the Christian conscience had decided that certain of these bore the mark of the Spirit, the choice was made. And since the apostolic connection was of fundamental importance to all these primitive communities, those that were retained were the ones where living testimonies made it clear that they were directly related to Jesus' disciples.

A number of questions arise in connection with this choice. Do these twenty-seven texts contain all that we can legitimately know about Christ's life and message? Do we possess all twenty-seven in the actual form in which their original writers composed them? Is their order due to mere chance or to a positive intention?

It is probable that the New Testament may have allowed a few crumbs of the bread of life to escape it, but no more than a few; in the writings of certain Fathers of the Church, and even in the apocryphas, we come across certain phrases of Christ's—*logia* or *agrapha*, expressions not contained in the Scriptures—and various historical details which have the ring of truth; thus Clement of Alexandria reports the following admirable sentence, surely worthy of the Divine Master: 'If thou hast seen thy brother, thou hast seen thy God'; thus we search in vain in the Gospels for a statement of Christ's descent into hell, which is, however, included in the Credo, and, in the Scriptures as a whole, for any account of the Assumption of the Blessed Virgin, which is, however, accepted by Catholic tradition going back to time immemorial.

Moreover, the veneration with which Christians regarded Jesus' teaching was related more to the content than to the actual text, which was perfectly natural in an age when oral instruction still existed, as we have seen. Consequently this or that little fragment whose inspired origin seemed certain would be added to the texts after the first drafts had been written. For example, the famous episode about the woman taken in adultery, one of the jewels of St John's Gospel, seems to have been inserted after the final draft of the original text had been made, possibly by the Apostle himself, possibly by posterior tradition, and, it would appear, after some discussion, so outspoken in its moral outlook did it seem! And a number of very ancient New Testament manuscripts, e.g. the Codex Bezae at Cambridge, contain small additions to the customary text. But in general these are unimportant matters, mere gleanings from the field where the good harvest had grown and been gathered in.

It merely remains to ask why the Church desired to preserve these twenty-seven texts in the order in which we know them, with their occasional divergences on points of detail, and their particular emphases. It seems that it would have been a simple matter to amalgamate all these elements into one whole, so making them into a system of doctrine. For the Four Gospels, in particular, it would have been easy to arrange a combination whereby the life and message of Jesus would have been related in one single text. And, in fact, a number of attempts were made along these lines. About 150–60, Tatian, who was one of St Justin's disciples, wrote an extremely skilful single Gospel, the *Diatessaron*, which the Syriac Church was to hold in high esteem; a fragment of it has been found among the excavations at Doura Europos in Upper Mesopotamia. The heretic Marcion, whose story we shall be telling later on in this book, was working in a similar direction at about the same date. The Church did not take this course, and her attitude in this respect is one of the strongest proofs of the absolute truth of these twenty-seven texts. Out of respect for those who had written them, and certain also of their apostolic origin and divine inspiration, she was to place them alongside one another, with all their individual characteristics and differences left untouched. The testimony which they give is all the more striking for this.

By the close of the second century the choice had been made. We possess an extremely precious document to prove this: the *Muratorian Canon*, called after a librarian at the Ambrosian Library in Milan, who discovered and published it in 1740, from a manuscript dating from the sixth or seventh century. This document is only a catalogue, a table giving the contents of the Holy Scriptures, but it certainly dates from about the year 200, and was written in Rome. It shows that in this epoch the Roman Church possessed the same canon as Christians do today (with the exception of the Epistles of St James and St Peter), that she rejected *The Pastor* by name, whilst authorizing the reading of it, and, more categorically, rejected various writings containing Gnostic tendencies. Some one hundred and fifty or two hundred years later, catalogues of the canon are found in much greater abundance; they have been discovered in Africa, Phrygia, Egypt and at Rome; in 397 the Council of Carthage was to lay down the final list of sacred books which was to be readopted in the sixteenth century by the Council of Trent, in the face of the threat of Protestantism.

Thus the New Testament was fixed in its permanent form. As a book, its success increased continually. Henceforth anyone wanting to study Christianity would be obliged to refer to it. The Fathers of the Church, the doctors of Christian learning, quote 'the twenty-seven texts' in exactly the same way as the rabbis of Israel had been wont to quote the Old Testament books. Papyrus rolls or bound booklets containing the New Testament texts[13] were to be found among the

[13] Here we are leaving out the question of the material transmission of the scriptural texts from generation to generation. The first copies must have been written on papyrus, then, in several places, on sheets of papyrus which were bound into small books. Of course we do not possess any of these fragile documents; however, a minute fragment of one was found in a tomb in Egypt in 1935. It dates from about 130 and has on it a short passage from the eighteenth chapter of St John: it can now be seen in the Rylands Library, Manchester. Later

Christian missionaries' personal baggage, and as common objects in Christian churches and private homes. For the faithful of these heroic times, here indeed was the living treasure, the inexhaustible source of faith, the sum of all necessary understanding. Tertullian was to say: 'The first article of our faith is this: that there is nothing beyond this that we need believe.'

## THE FATHERS OF THE CHURCH

There might indeed be nothing to believe beyond what was inscribed in the books of the New Testament, but did it follow, therefore, that one was forbidden to meditate upon these texts, forbidden, too, to scrutinize them closely, and comment upon their content? By no means. St Irenaeus was to say: 'It was like some precious material that was enclosed in an excellent vessel: the Spirit rejuvenated it constantly, and communicated its youth to the vessel which contained it.' The age

---

it became usual to write copies on parchment, 'the leaf of Pergamum,' that is to say, on stretched sheepskin: the great Codes (Codex-Codices) were compiled in this way. We are still able to admire them, and the oldest surviving examples date from the fourth century: *codex Vaticanus, codex Sinaiticus;* there were about four thousand fairly complete copies made up to the time that the art of printing was developed. It goes without saying that, being transcribed by hand, with all the attendant risk of unintentional or intentional mistakes, the text could suffer many grievous outrages. In the third century Origen wrote: 'Today it is quite clear that our manuscripts contain many diversities, which are due either to the negligence of certain scribes, or to the perverse audacity of others, who make so bold as to try to correct the original text.' *Textual criticism's* task was to pick out the truth from amongst a host of flaws of detail: from the fourth century onwards, and, in particular, from the time of St Jerome, a real critical effort was to be undertaken, but it was not really until the sixteenth century that this effort was to be systematically carried through.

It should be noted that, in the case of the documents to which we can refer—the first Codes, dating from the fourth century—there is a gap of no more than three hundred years between the writing of the New Testament texts and the earliest known copies. The significance of this fact can best be appreciated by remembering that in the case of the works of Aeschylus, Sophocles, Aristophanes and Thucydides the gap is one of fourteen hundred years; sixteen hundred years in the case of Euripides. For a further discussion of these problems see the introduction to the author's *Jesus in His Time.*

of inspired Scripture was ended; a literature in the real sense
of the word was beginning, a literature created by men, but, as
Bossuet declared, by men who were 'nourished on the wheat of
the elect, full of that primitive spirit which they imbibed
from very close at hand, and, more than abundantly, from the
source itself,' by men who learned from the example of the
Apostles and who directly participated in the conquest of the
world by the Cross. It is this vast collection of literary figures
which started in the second century and which was to grow
even vaster in the centuries to follow which is designated
under a heading that is more famous than explicit: the
*Fathers of the Church*.

*Fathers of the Church*: the phrase conjures up a vision of
the majestic series of quarto volumes published by the Abbé
Migne a century ago under the general title of *Patrologiae
cursus completus*, which holds an honoured place on the
shelves of our religious houses and seminaries, comprising 217
volumes of Latin 'patrology,' and 161 of Greek. But the learned
collector of all these texts, in establishing his gigantic plan of
collective scholarship, on the one hand confined himself to the
Latins and the Greeks by leaving out all the Syriac, Coptic
and Armenian Fathers, who also contain many gems of learning, and, on the other, extended the phrase in the chronologi-
cal sense, going, so far as the West was concerned, right up to
the death of Innocent III (1216), and, in the case of the East,
up to the fifteenth century. It is, for example, only by such
an extension that St Bernard can be called a 'Father of the
Church'; the early Fathers, those who really founded Christian
philosophy, were those scholars who lived in the five first centuries A.D. which preceded the collapse of the Roman Empire.
Indeed they constitute a whole world to themselves. Their influence was to be fundamental right down the centuries, fer-
tilizing both the mind and the soul; Orthodox Greeks and
Protestants are as attached to them as Catholics. There is no
great Christian writer who is not linked with them in some
way or other, and though the ordinary mass of Christians
reveres them more than it knows them, it is important to draw
attention to a modern revival of interest in this source, whence
springs a river of faith that is truly mighty.

The word *Father* was originally used of the leaders of the

churches, the bishops; it is the meaning it has retained in relation to the first of all the bishops, the Bishop of Rome, the
Pope. As we have seen, all authority resided in them, doctrinal
as well as disciplinary. Later on the word was principally applied to the defenders of doctrinal orthodoxy, notably to those
men who battled for the faith against the heretics, even if they
did not actually hold episcopal office. From the fifth century
onwards the word is used in theological treatises and conciliar
documents in the sense in which we understand it. What conditions must a writer fulfil to be awarded this splendid title?
The answer is not easy to express. All the Christian authors
who have written about religious subjects have not qualified
as Fathers; as a general rule it is necessary for their orthodoxy
to be outstanding, for them to be closely linked with the great
tradition of primitive times, and for the sanctity of their personal lives to be a guarantee of the holiness of their philosophy;
yet Tertullian, Origen and Eusebius, who all fulfilled these
three conditions in a somewhat unequal manner, are, nevertheless, firmly inscribed on their list; consequently we must
look for the explanation of this designation more in a general
approbation given to an individual's work by the Church, and
in a profound and unanimous feeling of approval bestowed
by the Christian community at large.[14]

The material which the Fathers covered was enormous:
truth to tell, it is as vast as the world itself, and quite inexhaustible; it is indeed the whole of Christianity. Certain pages
stress moral teaching first and foremost, giving advice on
men's way of life, calling the faithful to penitence, and de-

---

[14] The expression 'Doctor of the Church,' which is often linked
with that of Father, is not synonymous with it. 'Doctor' indicates a
more exalted position: all the Fathers are not doctors. At first the
word was used to designate all those who studied the message of
Christ (see preceding chapter). Gradually it was reserved to a few
great minds whose outstanding scholarship, rigorous orthodoxy and
exemplary sanctity gave them an authority which everyone acknowledged. The Church recognized and named as doctors a small group
of very select men, and she has continued to award the honour, extremely sparingly, until modern times. The Byzantine Church holds
three doctors in veneration: St Basil, St Gregory of Nazianzus and
St John Chrysostom; Rome adds a fourth Easterner, St Athanasius,
and four Westerners, St Ambrose, St Jerome, St Augustine and St
Gregory the Great; these are the eight 'great doctors' of the Church.

nouncing sins and errors with an outspoken vigour of a kind
with which our modern world is no longer familiar. Others are
primarily concerned with putting forward the mystical realities: they are principally an encouragement to union with God.
Yet others develop the science which was soon to be called
*theology*, the process of systematic reflection upon the great
fundamentals of doctrine and upon their implications in real
life; one of patristic literature's most essential contributions
lies in this effort to define intangible dogmas by giving them
tangible expression and in making the great revealed truths
more intelligible to mankind. Thus in one flight of learning the
Fathers were to accomplish a triple effort; their works are simultaneously moral, mystical and theological, sustained as
they are by the breath of supernatural life.

Two of their characteristics should be emphasized particularly: they are *scriptural* and *pedagogic*. Moreover, these two
features are directly linked with their most fundamental
characteristic, that of being a living literature, intimately
bound up with the very existence of the Church and her development. The action of a man or of a society is not really
fruitful unless it finds its exact equilibrium between the past
and the future, between the values of tradition and the
audacities of venturing into the unknown. This the Fathers
of the Church realized instinctively.

Their literature is *scriptural* because they knew that their
roots could find their vital sustenance only at the very sources
where Jesus had made the living water flow. The foundation
of their whole structure, their corner-stone, consisted of the
Gospels and all the other New Testament texts. 'To ignore the
Holy Scriptures is to ignore Christ,' so St Jerome was to say.
It was the duty of the human mind to make the sacred repository which God had entrusted to mankind bear fruit; the
Fathers devoted themselves magnificently to this task. They
analysed the minutest details of the Scriptures, they sought
to discover their most trifling secrets: in this way they originated the science of the Scriptures which we call *exegesis*.
They did even more than this: by going back to the books of
the Old Testament, which, as the New declared time after
time, had foretold the coming of Christ, by adapting to Chris-

tian realism the concepts of certain Jewish thinkers such as
Philo, they carried out a conclusive annexation of the Old
Bible by the New, and, between the two historical realities of
the destiny of Israel and the coming of Jesus, established close
links of imagery and fundamental meaning. Justin, Irenaeus
and Clement of Alexandria were the creators of this symbolic
interpretation, of this *typological exegesis* which is one of the
mysterious treasures of Christianity, and without an understanding of which the whole of our medieval art is virtually
incomprehensible.

However, the danger of a profound knowledge of the written
word lies in the possibility that it may tend to imprison the
mind within narrow, limited perspectives, and sterilize the
forces of action. This had happened in the case of the doctors
and scribes of latter-day Israel. But nothing comparable occurred so far as the Fathers of the Church were concerned.
They were not writing for writing's sake; their textual analysis
was not undertaken with the passionate but limited zeal of the
scholiast or the archivist. They were writing that their writing
might be a means of action and creation. Their writing is
*linked with life*, or, if another term is preferred, *pedagogic*;
its aim is to teach the message of Christ, to enlighten men's
minds and to mould their souls. It goes without saying that
literary artistry, which was very considerable in the case of
some of the Fathers, was regarded by them simply as a tool
for the task in hand, exactly as it had been by St Paul and
St John, both of whom were also wonderful writers. All that
they thought and said had been conceived within the living
reality of the communities whose members they were, and
where the creative force of the faith was impelling men's souls
towards the future.

It is this dual character which explains the influence which
this simultaneously austere and fascinating literature has exercised right up to modern times. Therein Christianity is seen
to embrace man's entire past and also his entire future. Bossuet
was to say: 'In those who study them, their works produce an
infinitely precious fruit.'

## THE APOSTOLIC FATHERS

The first group of these writers are usually known as the *Apostolic Fathers*. They are those linked with the first two generations of Christians; we can say of them what St Irenaeus wrote to St Clement: 'They still had the Apostles' voices in their ears and their example before their eyes.' The first of them—St Clement, St Ignatius, St Polycarp and the unknown author of the *Letter of Barnabas*—were certainly contemporary with the last years of St John. If the usual span of a man's life is added to this, the last of them would be living *c.* 1701–80, or at all events before the end of the second century. Who were these early Christian scholars? Though they all wrote in Greek—fairly pure Greek at that—they belonged to every race and nation; among them were Romans like Clement and Hermas, Syrians like Ignatius, Asians like Polycarp and Papias, and probably Egyptians such as the authors of the letter attributed to Barnabas and the Odes of Solomon. They came from all classes; Clement, Ignatius, Polycarp and Papias were bishops, but Hermas was an ordinary, humble believer, and certain anonymous texts seem to express the collective philosophy of a whole community, the actual voice of the Christian masses. Caught as they are between the supernatural brilliance of the inspired writings of the canon and the forceful work of their successors, these texts of the 'Apostolic Fathers' are certainly far from all being masterpieces. But they provide us with invaluable and unique information about the age in which the Gospel was germinating. This is their real quality; they form irreplaceable documents relating to those far-off beginnings which we should be unable to reconstruct without them. It is through them that we can envisage that very first Church of Apostles and Martyrs. It is through them that we understand the fundamentals of Christian doctrine, supernaturally illuminated by an utterly admirable faith; the mystery of the One God in Three Persons, the mystery of the Incarnation, the mystery of the Church which is simultaneously human and divine. When we read them we can grasp the main issues with which the faithful of this age were preoccupied, their reactions to the problems raised by the growth of Christianity, by the separation from Israel, by relations with Rome, and—even more important—we can feel the quality of a faith which was inspired, by the expectant belief in Christ's imminent return, to an ideal of perfection which has never since been surpassed.

First of all there are the bishops' letters, the Epistles, written by some of the Church's great leaders, composed, moreover, for quite specific occasions. However, their apologetic value caused them to be preserved by the communities as a whole, just as St Paul's letters had been before them.

To *St Clement of Rome*, St Peter's third successor (*c.* 90–100), tradition attributes not only four 'apostolic' texts but some rather fanciful writings as well, of which the *Clementines* and the *Recognitions* are veritable romances. His literary fame rests on his authentic Epistle to the Corinthians, whose importance in relation to the ecclesiastical organization of the period and the pre-eminence of the Roman Church has already been noted.[15] This wise and moderate document, the expression of a profoundly humane and gracious Christianity, remains, in the main, rather a dull grey in tone. However, it glitters with one or two passages of fervent colour, such as the one in which the saint-bishop—unique in the whole of classical Christian literature in this respect—exalts the beauty of the world which was created so that it, in turn, might praise the Creator, or that wonderful concluding prayer to the Lord God Almighty, 'who chooses from among the nations those who love him through Jesus.'

*St Ignatius* was the mighty, fiery-hearted Bishop of Antioch, the heroic figure whose progress to execution was to serve as an example for all the martyrs who followed in his footsteps.[16] The conditions in which he wrote were strange indeed. In 107 Ignatius, under sentence of death, was being taken to Rome, fettered to ten soldiers, to be thrown to the lions there. However, during the journey he dictated seven letters, which were subsequently collected and circulated throughout the whole Church. Their success was so considerable that various Asian forgers were to alter their content and add some passages of dubious material to them. Packed with facts to bursting-

[15] See the preceding chapter.
[16] See Chapter IV, section: 'In Asia: Two Princes of the Church.'

point, and somewhat rough and ready in style, these seven
letters are nevertheless the masterpieces of this period, and
are certainly one of the pinnacles of Christian literature. Ignatius teaches us several things about the meaning of the Church,
and her organization, and about the sacrament of holy eucharist; he counters the budding heresies of the day with some
extremely powerful arguments. But nothing equals the splendour of his letter to the Romans, where, leaving aside all
matters of doctrine, the martyr simply lets his faith blaze
forth in pure brilliance. He is sublimely contemptuous of death:
he radiates his desire for heaven, and feels so strongly that his
life is consecrated to Christ that to him the only necessity
consists of giving Christ that life.

Although a less important literary figure, *St Polycarp* is a
man of the same stamp and stature as St Ignatius. Polycarp
had welcomed Ignatius to Smyrna during the latter's journey
to Rome; from him he received a letter of gratitude and good
counsel; after the great bishop's death the younger man busied
himself in passing the account of his martyrdom on to the
different churches. A letter of Polycarp's announcing the imminent arrival of this document to the folk of Philippi is still
extant. The text is somewhat commonplace, but it contains
the following lines, which surely sum up the whole of the
Christian faith: 'Let us keep our eyes constantly fixed on our
hope and the pledge of our justice, namely on Jesus.' Polycarp's glorious martyrdom, in 155, under Antoninus, was to
make him famous: the Christians of Smyrna sent an account
of it to all the other churches, and later on his old pupil, St
Irenaeus, was to relate his life story and exalt his lessons.[17]

These eminent bishops did not ignore the more concrete
problems of the Church, but these hold a much larger place
in one extremely precious little book: the *Didache*, or *Doctrine
of the Apostles*. This was rediscovered in 1873 in a library in
Constantinople, at a time when it was considered lost for ever.

---

[17] St Irenaeus also had an extremely high opinion of St Papias,
Bishop of Hierapolis in Phrygia, 'the pupil of John and the friend
of Polycarp.' He wrote an *Explanation of the Sayings of Our Lord*,
in which it is thought he used much material collected from oral
tradition. Unfortunately this work is now lost, and we know of it
only through a few small fragments quoted by Eusebius and Apollinaris.

It enjoyed such tremendous popularity among the early Christians that it was regarded as an inspired work. Its author is unknown: it is generally thought that he was born in one of the Eastern communities, in Syria, Palestine or Egypt; according to the whim of various critics, his dates have been set somewhere between the limits of 70 and 200. The *Didache* is a kind of catalogue of the moral, individual and social obligations imposed on the first Christians. It has much of the character of a catechism or liturgical manual, and, besides, contains meditations of lofty moral philosophy and spirituality. As we have seen, anyone studying the history of the primitive Church is bound to quote it frequently. It gives us specific information on the conditions surrounding baptism, on fasts and prayers and on the eucharistic meal. The *Didache* tells us most of what we know concerning things which have disappeared from present-day Christianity, such as the function of the wandering 'prophets' in the Church. In its pages we can really see how a Christian community lived. At the beginning and end of the book, however, there are two chapters that soar to flights of mysticism. The first chapter is a moral fable of an elevated character which sets side by side 'the two paths' which man is free to take—the path of light and the path of darkness, the path of life and the path of death—and which calls on the Christian to make his choice.[18] The final one

---

[18] This fable of the 'two paths' seems to have been extremely widespread among the first Christian communities. It is found again in the *Letter of Barnabas*, an Alexandrian text which probably dates from the middle of the second century and which is fictitiously attributed to St Paul's companion. The necessity of choosing between acceptance or rejection of Christ is at the root of this symbolism; this option obviously brings to mind that of Israel. This is why an Egyptian Jew, who had been converted to Christianity, but who remained permeated by the methods and philosophies of the rabbis, applied it to the tragedy of the Chosen Race, who had refused Jesus and preferred to take the path of darkness. The *Letter of Barnabas* is an important document dealing with the resistance to Jewish influences in primitive Christian circles. It is also the first attempt at a spiritualistic interpretation of the Old Testament in terms of Christian symbolism, a symbolism that is often exaggerated. Finally, it is, in part, a mystical work, which speaks about the soul—'that spiritual temple built to house the Lord'—in language which St Teresa of Avila would not have repudiated.

is a kind of acclamation to the God who is soon to come, to the Christ whose return is very near. It is so fervent, so vehement, and, without a doubt, was so profoundly traditional at the time of writing, that the old Aramaic words spring to the suppliants' lips as of old, words like those which the Apostles must have uttered at the last Passover, words which St Paul, too, had used: '*Marana Tha!* Come, O Lord!'

Thus all these apostolic writings, whatever their aim, bask in a faith that is very alive indeed. Some of them are solely interested in proclaiming that faith, in exalting the spiritual life, in commenting upon the love of God and the problems of the soul in lyrical terms. This is the starting-point of Christian mystical literature. The most curious of the texts of this type is *The Pastor*, by Hermas. It is certainly a strange and at first sight disconcerting work, evoking emotions similar to those which the modern reader must feel on opening Dante's *Divine Comedy* or Blake's *Prophetic Books*. Symbolism reigns there and visions abound. It is not possible to pick out those details deriving from genuine prophetic inspiration from those inserted as mere literary artifices. The *Muratorian Canon*, which is slightly posterior to *The Pastor*, asserts that its author, Hermas, was the brother of Pope Pius I (?140–?54), during whose pontificate the book was written. Hermas himself declares that he is of Greek and Christian origin, and that he was sold as a slave, when very young, to a Christian noblewoman who gave him his freedom. He wrote his book after various ordeals, family tribulations and reverses in his personal fortunes, with a profound awareness of the meaning of expiation. The general theme is a call to penitence. Contrary to the theses of the rigorists, Hermas assures his readers that penitence always obtains the pardon of God. This theme, which would not appear to need to borrow very much from the fantastic, is developed in most abundant fashion in the *Visions*, the *Precepts* and the *Similitudes*, or *Parables*. The first half of the book is the strangest. At the call of the Angel of Penitence, 'the shepherd to whom the soul of Hermas was entrusted,' the visionary is placed face to face with a number of extraordinary spectacles all charged with profound meanings. A mighty tower is rising above the waters, made of square brilliant stones, whilst other stones are left, rejected, on one side, and others, again, are being recut. The tower is the Church, standing on the waters of baptism; the stones are men—abandoned if they are sinners, reshaped if they are repentant, and square and shining if they are saints. Only when the tower is completed will the end of time occur. The Christians of primitive times were passionately fond of these mysterious pages, and although the Church removed *The Pastor* from the canon, she did not prevent it from being regarded, by many devout souls, rather as we today regard the *Imitation*.

The *Odes of Solomon* possess a very different character, but it is a character which touches us more deeply. Their mystery stems from the silence which entombed them from the fourth century until 1900, when they were discovered in a Syriac version, and from the problems of their authorship. The view most widely accepted is that the Odes are a work dating from the middle of the second century, deriving from an Alexandrian community of Christians which was permeated by Jewish influences; their author wrote them, fictitiously, under the name of the great poet-king of Israel; and they abound with constant memories of the Old Testament, particularly of the Song of Songs and the Proverbs. The least one can say is that this collection of poetry is a masterpiece of Christian spirituality, and if it were better known it would probably seem very close indeed to the finest psalms in the biblical canon. Rarely in the whole of the mystical literature have the love of God, His presence and His efficacy been so exquisitely expressed as here. 'As the honey from the comb, as the milk from the breast of woman, so my hope flows toward thee, O my God! As the strings sing when my hands play upon the zither, so, in my love, my very body rejoices in the Spirit of the Lord. . . . Open your hearts, I say, open them to the joy of the Lord, and let your love flow from your hearts to form the words that spring to your lips!' This book, which never refers to Jesus by name—on account of the fiction of its title—but which alludes to 'the beloved son through whom the sun was created,' is undoubtedly the most profoundly evangelical of all the writings of this epoch.

Thus, though so far removed from us in time, the *Apostolic Fathers* are not far away at all in spirit. Circumstances have changed profoundly. All too many modern Christians have forgotten that they live in peril and only for a permanent conquest of the world. Today the words found in the *Didache* are scarcely ever repeated any more: 'Come, Divine Grace, and let this world pass away!' Liturgical formulae and religious customs are no longer the same. . . . And yet what believer can remain unmoved by words like these, words which express a faith and hope he recognizes as his own? Jesus is present even in the least of these ancient texts; it is His love which animates them, and against that love all the dust of centuries cannot prevail.

## THE NEED FOR PHILOSOPHY

This early Christian literature, then, is modest in character; its aims and its means of expression are strictly limited. But very soon, from the second half of the second century onwards, it was to extend its scope and climb to new heights of brilliance. As the Christian plant grew larger, internal factors conditioned its progressive expansion and the strengthening of its roots; at the same time, with admirable flexibility and power of absorption, it took from the exterior forces which it encountered anything which could assist its own development.

At first the Church had included few intellectuals in her ranks. St Paul wrote to the Corinthians: 'Consider, brethren, the circumstances of your own calling; not many of you are wise, in the world's fashion, not many powerful, not many well born' (1 Cor. i. 26). This predominance of humble folk of little learning was to last for almost two hundred years. The Christians acknowledged it: their enemies noted it with irony. But from Hadrian's reign onwards the better educated classes of society had been touched by the faith. By the end of the second century there were clearly a large number of Christian intellectuals who had thought out their faith according to the philosophical methods with which they were familiar and who intended to defend it against those who criticized it on their accustomed ground. A Christian philosophy was about to emerge.

In order to assess the strength of this philosophical need to which Christianity was to be subjected, it is necessary to take into account the intellectual activity which enlivened the Graeco-Roman society of the first few centuries A.D., and its taste—nay, even its passion—for ideas. In some rather curious pages the philosopher Seneca describes to Lucilius how, in his youth, he fanatically followed the instruction of his teachers, and observed with genuine delight the ascetic rules which they enjoined upon him. Philosophy was all the rage. At several schools large numbers of the public thronged to the classes, just as the Parisian public of yesterday thronged to hear Bergson's lectures. Snobbery, of course, played its part in the craze, but there were also a number of sincere folk who were trying to find, in these philosophical doctrines, an answer to the great problems of the universe, something that would bring peace to their troubled hearts. There was a Peripatetic renaissance as a result of Andronicus of Rhodes's edition of Aristotle's works, and a Platonic revival which was embodied in the persons of Plutarch of Caesarea and Apuleius, but which, in addition, influenced the Neo-Pythagorism of Moderatus of Gades and Nichomachus of Gerasa; in particular, there was a spectacular expansion of Stoicism, which, in the first two centuries A.D., could boast the three brilliant names of Seneca, Epictetus and Marcus Aurelius. Thus the Christian intellectuals found themselves faced by a force which was truly considerable.

Consequently the natural reaction of educated Christians was to desire to demonstrate that they had been fully justified in adopting the faith in Christ, that their religion was not a barbarous superstition which they ought, according to Celsus, to 'get over,' that, intellectually, Christianity could 'hold its own.' Such were the feelings that prompted Christian intellectuals to take the first steps along the road of Christian dialectic, where they were subsequently to be followed by philosophical giants like Origen, St Augustine and St Thomas Aquinas. It was a road which was not to be without its difficulties. The professional philosophers, who, in this epoch, discoursed primarily upon moral problems and who liked to be regarded as spiritual directors, were irritated to see their function passing into the hands of preachers who quoted as their authority principles which were unknown, and doctrines which

had no renown whatsoever. Minucius Felix, the apologist, declared that the majority of the philosophers did not conde-
scend to listen to the Christians and blushed to answer them.
This was not true everywhere, for, during the trial of St Justin,
we shall see evidence, in the shape of the large crowd which
came to watch and listen, of an intense curiosity about the
individual involved, and about his ideas. But something else
that Minucius Felix said was even truer, namely that, though
disdained and criticized, and playing a part that was a singularly difficult one, the Christian intellectuals felt themselves
carried forward by an invincible force: 'Perhaps we do not
talk about very important matters—but it is we who possess
life!'

The affirmation of the dignity of Christian philosophy: this
then was the first aim. Now, is not the best way of fighting a
doctrine to borrow its own weapons? The pagan philosophers
quoted reason as their authority. But was not Christ Himself
reason incarnate, the Supreme Wisdom? Did not the Greek
systems of thought contain certain elements which could be
annexed to Christianity? Down the centuries the Church was
to be wonderfully aware of how to utilize every system in the
universe to her own advantage; the Christian scholars who
lived c. 150 already realized the need to do this, and inaugurated the method whereby it could be achieved. They were to
borrow, not so much from the great Stoics, who were, however, sometimes so near them in their vocabulary of evangelical expressions; no, they borrowed their ideas principally
from Plato, going so far in this direction that it is possible to
speak of the *Platonism of the Fathers*. While noting the gaps
in his doctrine, his erroneous concept of the pre-existence of
matter, and the numerous aberrations in his moral philosophy,
the Christian intellectuals were to regard the wise Hellene as
a superior and prophetic being, in whose mind the echo of
certain Christian declarations had pre-existed. They were to
follow Plato's methods when they appealed to reason to justify
the existence of God, the immortality of the soul, the distinction between good and evil, and judgment after death. It was
St Justin who inaugurated this technique of using pagan philosophy as a Christian ally; Origen was to make it his decisive
life's work, and so, later on, was St Augustine.

Besides, the Christians found themselves forced into this engagement on the intellectual plane. The pagans began to be interested in Christianity on their own initiative, and writings hostile to the new faith sprang up in large numbers. At first these took the form of spiteful witticisms and contemptuous allusions, such as Epictetus' remark that the Christian martyrs were nothing but obstinate fanatics. Then Fronto, Marcus Aurelius' tutor, under pretext of refuting Christianity, produced his collection of all the anti-Christian commonplaces and popular calumnies. Finally, crowning them all, came Celsus' *True Discourse*, which appeared *c.* 178. This was the first really important anti-Christian text, and so serious was the threat it raised that seventy years later Origen was to work to refute it. Sufficiently conversant with Christianity to give the impression of being fully documented on the subject, Celsus made extremely skilful use of arguments which were to become famous. He jeered, not without spirit, at the idea of a revelation being made to men: 'Once upon a time there were some blind bats who declared: "It is to us that God has revealed himself!"' He discovered the comparativist method in order to assert that the Resurrection was no more than the ancient idea of the transmigration of souls, that the wonderful stories of the Old Testament had their counterparts in Greek mythology, and that the Christian Credo was a clever mixture of Stoic, Eleatic, Jewish, Persian and Egyptian elements. He fiercely criticized the idea that a God could be made incarnate, regarding it as an absurdity. Philosophical pamphlets of this type needed answering. Whether they wanted it or not, the Christians found themselves dragged into the war of ideas.

In this way the task forced upon them was of a triple nature: to place Christian doctrine on the plane where the pagan philosophers held the field; to annex to it everything in pagan thought which might be of some service; to answer the criticisms of their intellectual adversaries. One man had preceded the Christians in this triple effort: *Philo*, the Alexandrian Jew. Philo was a rabbi, a Doctor of the Law, with the qualifications of so many of his forbears in Israel. He was permeated by the Jewish sacred texts, and was the distinguished possessor of the minutest details of the Torah; but he was also a Jew of the Alexandrian *diaspora*,[19] in other words, he had grown up in the society where the legalist spirit had become most receptive. We do not know much about his life: we only know that the family into which he was born was of considerable standing (his brother Alexander had been steward in the house of Antonia, Claudius' mother), that he had received an extremely careful and thorough education, and that his temperament inclined him, simultaneously, to philosophy and action. The same man who made a retreat in the desert, after the Essene fashion, showed himself capable of making the arduous journey to Rome, in his old age, to protest to Caligula about the extortions of the imperial officials. Philo was born twenty years before the start of the Christian era, and died c. A.D. 40. He would, therefore, have been Jesus' exact contemporary. He was a man of mighty faith, 'drunk with sober rapture,' as he was fond of saying, a man who was very sensible of God's presence and who strove only to reach that presence, and he left behind him an immense quantity of exegetical writing and religious philosophy. 'When the righteous man searches for the nature of all things created, he makes this one admirable discovery: that all is grace. Everything in the world and the very world itself manifests the blessing and generosity of God.'

Such was the man, who, by readopting and carrying through designs which had previously enjoyed a limited currency among the Jewish scholiasts of Alexandria, had consciously made use of Greek culture in order to put it to the service of his own faith. Philo was a devout Jew, and he had remained faithful to Yahweh; he rejected none of the great traditional ideas of Israel: the holiness of God, His mercy, and man's obligation to repent and to beg forgiveness from the Lord. However, like the developed Jew he was, he interpreted the application of these ideas on the inward, individual plane, and no longer understood them in national or social terms. For Philo, the Kingdom of God existed in the soul. Consequently his education, his environment and his own attitudes of mind led him to include in his system the philosophical ideas which he knew so thoroughly. The 'great' and 'very holy' Plato

19 On the tendencies of the Alexandrian *diaspora* in Philo's time see Chapter I, section: 'Hellenists and Judaizers.'

had been the teacher to whom he referred most constantly, but he had also leaned upon the authority of Aristotle, Heraclitus, the Pythagoreans and, in particular, the Stoics. A meeting of two streams as vigorous as these could not have failed to give birth to a mighty river.

Two themes from Philo's philosophy had had considerable importance and were to have substantial future influence: his method of scriptural explanation, and his doctrine of the Logos. In order to reconcile Greek philosophy with the sacred texts of Israel he had accepted the fact that God had wanted to set out the spiritual history of humanity under the letter of Holy Scripture, and that, in short, the Bible gave material appearances to the principles expressed by the Greeks in abstract terms. For instance, for Philo, Abraham was the soul who passed from the world of lying illusions (Chaldea) to that of reality and truth (the Holy Land); he first married Agar, representing human values, and then Sarah, representing the abundance that is the Spirit's. . . . This allegorical exegesis is not quite in line with the Christological exegesis of the Fathers, and, indeed, in viewing the Old Testament as totally historical in content, in wiping out the ascent to the Messiah which is apparent therein, it was not without its dangers. However, transferred to the Christian framework it was to be extremely fruitful, and, on this point, Philo's true successors were to be the Christian philosophers of Alexandria, notably Clement.[20]

As for his theory of the Logos, this was an entirely analogous attempt directed, with a skill that borders on genius, at bringing together the tradition of Israel and the great philosophical themes on the notion of God. Certainly, Philo's Logos, the thought of God, the immanent link with the world, the archetype of creation, was not yet the Word made flesh which St John was to make men acknowledge forty years later, but there is no doubt that this philosopher-rabbi had made human thought clear a most important stage, and on this point also Christians were to remember him.

Finally, he had pointed the road for them to follow in yet

[20] The reader should remember that the *Letter of Barnabas*, referred to earlier in this chapter, is of Alexandrian origin: it is directly in the tradition of Philo.

another way, by composing two treatises addressed to the pagans in which he defended his fellow Jews against Gentile calumnies and lack of understanding. Philo, the ancestor of the theologians, and the outstanding exegetist, was to be one of the teachers of the Christian thinkers who lived at the end of the second century; Philo, the defender of his Jewish brethren, is in fact the precursor of the men known as the *Christian Apologists*.

## THE APOLOGISTS OF THE SECOND CENTURY: ST JUSTIN

Around the year 120 a new type of Christian literature made its appearance, that of the *Apologists*. Catechesis handed down by authority or founded on sentiment was no longer enough: the apologetic testimony given by the martyrs during their interrogations, or even in the course of their actual executions, needed to be explained. It was to these tasks, which we have acknowledged to be essential, that the Apologists were to devote themselves henceforth.

About fifteen of their names have been preserved, but there were certainly a great many others, and we possess only fragments relating to several of them. The remains of this vast collection of material are sufficient to show its considerable interest. The Apologists were better writers than the Apostolic Fathers, and were often distinguished philosophers. Their very intention obliged them to set out Christianity in terms comprehensible to non-Christians, to underline the points of contact and the differences, and all this makes them much more accessible to the modern reader. In addition, in order to answer the calumnies of their enemies, they were led to evoke the dignity and sanctity of the Christian life. In so doing they painted a picture which is as splendid as it is useful. Certain of their expressions are somewhat arguable; their theological language is still imperfect; but it is impossible not to experience a feeling of profound admiration before the vigour of their faith and the intrepidity of their attitude.

The very idea of writing these 'Apologies' of Christianity may seem rather strange. Is it not incredibly naïve to address oneself to the people who hate and despise you, and to the Caesar who is persecuting you, in an attempt to teach them the truth? At first sight it is astonishing to see Justin asking the emperors to give his text their official stamp, and Athenagoras using all kinds of delicate flatteries towards Marcus Aurelius and Commodus. These actions prove that, at this period, the conflict between Rome and the Cross was still not regarded as inexpiable, and that the Christians dreamed of reconciling the Church and the Empire. It was a kind of policy of the outstretched hand, made whole-heartedly, and in complete sincerity.

Christian apologetics were born in Greece, the motherland of ideas. While Hadrian was on the throne (117–38) an Athenian named *Kodratos* or *Quadratus* wrote him a letter in which he set out the Christian religion: unhappily this document is lost and all that we know of it is a sentence quoted by Eusebius. Very soon afterwards *Aristides*, who actually proclaimed himself 'a philosopher of Athens,' published an Apology, which, after being missing for a very long time, was rediscovered some fifty years ago. He develops his thought along two axes: on the one hand, supporting himself on the notion of God, he shows that the Christian concept of this notion is very much more lofty, noble and pure than that possessed by the Barbarians, the Greeks and the Jews; on the other, he evokes the evidence of the Christian way of life in order to prove the beauty of the Christian religion, stressing especially, with extreme delicacy, Christian charity, the expression of the love of Christ. As for the *Letter to Diognetus*, a small, anonymous text, which it is thought may date from the time of the Antonines (*c.* 110 and the years following), it is a veritable jewel: its author was possessed of an outstanding brain and a simple and pure soul, and its style, with its Athenian echoes, is brilliant. Renan admired it. It is a kind of extension of St Paul, but of a Paul with the style of a true classicist, a Paul whose anxieties have been strained away, and who is at perfect peace. Was it addressed to the Diognetus who taught the young Marcus Aurelius? No one knows. At all events, certain of its elaborations on the situation of the Christian 'who is in this world, yet is not of it,' or on the reasons which explain why God delayed so long in sending men their Redeemer, have scarcely any equal in the whole of Christian literature; these pages deserve to be read far more than they are.[21]

It was under Antoninus (138–61) that the greatest and most famous of the Apologists made his appearance. His name was *Justin*. How deeply he touches us, this man who groped in the dark so long for the Way, the Truth and the Life! How similar are his problems to our own! His heart beats in a rhythm that we know so well! This philosophy, which is eighteen hundred years old, sounds a kind of Pascalian echo in our ears; in this distinguished dialectician there is a receptiveness, and an openness of soul, which modern believers might do well to emulate. The Christianity which emerges from this densely packed, badly organized work, with its often dubious style, is singularly near to that which we cherish.

Justin was born in the very heart of Palestine, in the settlement of Flavia Neapolis which had just been rebuilt upon the site of the ancient Sichem and which is nowadays known as Nablus. He was the son of well-to-do farming stock, most probably of Latin origin. When still very young he acquired a taste for philosophy, in the sense in which the word was understood at that time; not in the sense of speculative research, but as the active pursuit of wisdom and truth. 'Philosophy is a very precious blessing in God's eyes,' he was to say, 'for it is philosophy which leads men to Him.' At all events, philosophy did indeed play this beneficent role in Justin's own spiritual progress, which followed the stages which he himself has related to us. First of all, Justin entrusted himself to a Stoic, but this doctrine seemed to him to be limited, and disappointing in its metaphysics. A Peripatetic philosopher disappointed him equally quickly, when he revealed to Justin, by his own personal, sordid attitude, that the methods of Aristotle were not sufficient to effect a change in men. However, a Platonist enabled him to clear a decisive hurdle when he showed him that philosophy's only true goal was to acquire

---

[21] Some idea of the tone of this wonderful text is conveyed by these simple sentences: 'Christianity is not a worldly invention, it is not even a collection of human mysteries. Christianity is the Truth, the Holy Word, the Inconceivable, sent to men by God Himself, the Almighty, the invisible Creator of the Universe.'

knowledge of God. Justin spent some time in a retreat on a sandy waste near the seashore, meditating long and carefully on this new truth. Would it still the dreadful torment of his mind? Not completely. The contemplation of these ideas raised his spirits, but did not touch his soul.[22] It was then that he made the acquaintance of a wise old Christian at Palestinian Caesarea. Taking the young man's Platonism as his starting-point, this pedagogue drew all sorts of conclusions from it. He demonstrated to this well-intentioned soul that Christianity was the true philosophy, the completion of those partial truths which the ancients, especially Plato, had grasped. In that moment the link between the Platonist soul and the Christian soul, so dear to Péguy's heart, was forged, and the famous phrase of Pascal was justified long before it was written: 'Go to Plato in order to incline to Christianity.'

Once converted—probably c. 130—Justin did not forsake philosophy in any way. Quite the contrary: he wanted to make 'the fire which had been kindled in his soul' shine forth to the world. 'God will call to account the man who, once enlightened, does not testify in favour of the truth!' He founded schools of Christian philosophy at Ephesus, first of all, and then, from c. 150, at Rome. Taking up residence 'at Martin's house, near the thermal baths of Timotheus,' he began to teach, using exactly the same methods as the pagan philosophers, but lecturing according to the principles of Christ. He had his disciples, and a real audience. He spoke at public meetings, contradicting the theories of the pagans, and his work was so efficacious that the other philosophers became extremely worried and jealous about it. This was an important step in the history of Christian philosophy: Justin had forced men to take it seriously.

---

[22] The same process of restless questing is seen in another text, almost contemporary with these events. This is the *Clementine Homilies*, one of the works connected with Pope Clement. Here too the hero is searching for the truth. He goes to Egypt to seek it from the priests. On the subject of the survival of the dead, and the opportunities of communication with them, he learns a great deal. But these scraps of knowledge seem insufficient; they needed the addition of Christianity. The need to know God, anxiety about eternal life: are these not two of the profound causes of the religious restlessness which is still being felt in our own time?

We possess only three of Justin's texts today: but his literary output must have been far more considerable than this. The three still extant are all important: they are the *Dialogue with Tryphon* and the two *Apologies*. The first is a reply to the Jews, to the rabbis imprisoned within the rigidity of the Law and the sentiment of exclusivism; the Apologies are both speeches in which the author defends the Christians against pagan calumnies, describes their exemplary way of life and exalts their virtues, and doctrinal expositions in which, re-adopting the methods used by Philo, and going decidedly further than St John, he annexes to Christianity the processes, vocabularies, and even some of the substance of the classical philosophies.

For St Justin Christianity is truly the only complete philosophy, and even more than a philosophy, a total revelation, being both a perfect concept of the world and a rule of life, a method of understanding and a method of salvation. But does it follow from this that all the efforts made by human philosophy for so many centuries past have all been vain and empty? Not at all. Every man shares in the reason which is 'the seed of the Divine Word.' Thus 'all those righteous principles which the philosophers have discovered and expressed have been discovered thanks to their having achieved a participation in the Word.' And this Word, this Logos which has progressively enlightened human intelligence in this way, is none other than the Christ, as He has been revealed in Jesus, through whom all philosophy and life itself have found their true meaning. This wonderful idea, which was to make all the Platonism and Philonism and expectant heart-searchings of past generations merge into the truth of Christianity, certainly bears the seal of true genius! From St Augustine to Miguel de Unamuno countless Christian thinkers were to take it up once more. For all of them Christianity was to be a permanent value of the human spirit which had been given its real meaning and full significance by the Incarnation! St John had laid down the definitions of the principle of the Word made flesh, transcendent, spiritual and personal at one and the same time; St Justin recognized it in the evidence of intelligence, and created a universal method of philosophy from the philosophy of the Logos. Firmly established in the faith, the Christian thinkers were, from now on, fully aware of the philosophic reasoning implicit in it; later on, in the conflicts between the gnosis and the antignosis, we shall witness an effort at the development of this reasoning along Christian lines and the definition of its methods.

Consequently St Justin's work was a truly immense one. And it was a labour which touched on a hundred and one problems. It was Justin too, who, borrowing Philo's method of scriptural interpretation, conclusively orientated the science of exegesis towards the symbolic explanation of biblical texts. Aside from the concrete historical meaning of their work, the inspired authors of Holy Scripture had wanted to superimpose another symbolic interpretation. Philo had already said so; but whilst the Alexandrian Jew had seen only the signs of moral and spiritual realities in the biblical scenes and characters, St Justin—even more than the anonymous author of the *Letter of Barnabas*—recognized these realities in Him who had made them incarnate, in other words, in Christ. 'All the commandments of Moses are models, symbols and indications of what would be achieved in Christ.' It is therefore due to Justin's example that we are accustomed to see the forewarning of Calvary in Abraham's sacrifice, and that, as the Gospel had already pointed out, the Resurrection is foreseen in Jonah's escape from the whale's belly.

Justin then was a profound commentator on scriptural revelation, a brilliant teacher of the spiritual life and an apologist who described Christian virtue in terms that can never be forgotten by anyone who has once read them. But we must not omit the factor which gives Justin's work its full meaning: the fact that he sealed it with his own blood.

This man, who had never wanted to be a priest, who considered himself merely 'a humble member of the Christian flock,' had acquired such renown that he was regarded in Rome as one of the leaders of the Church. He was denounced by a pagan philosopher named Crescens, whom he had criticized somewhat harshly, and was arrested in 163, along with six of his pupils. When Justin was interrogated by the prefect Rusticus, he set out his beliefs, yet again, with courageous fervour. He was threatened with flogging and execution, but he retorted, quite simply, with an act of faith. His persecutors beheaded him.

The impulse which St Justin had given to Christian philosophy was not to be halted. Throughout the final years of the second century many other apologists followed his example. Of course they did not all possess his generous mind, his inexhaustible capacity to welcome new ideas. Thus the Assyrian *Tatian*,[23] Justin's pupil, a brilliant but paradoxical mind, a kind of philosophical polemist, indulged in apologetics which smacked of the clenched fist rather than the outstretched hand, and, moreover, swept along by his own fanaticism, was to become engulfed in the 'Encratistic' heresy, a kind of precursor of Jansenism, which claimed to prohibit marriage, regarding it as fornication pure and simple. But *Athenagoras*, 'the Christian philosopher of Athens,' followed directly in St Justin's footsteps; Bossuet admired his *Supplication for the Christians*, the title of the Apology which he addressed to the 'philosopher-emperor' Marcus Aurelius and to Commodus. He replied in detail to the three crimes imputed to his co-religionists: atheism, immorality and cannibalism. *St Theophilus of Antioch*, a pagan scholar who was converted to Christianity in middle age, becoming a bishop of the Church, wrote a considerable quantity of philosophical work, including a short Apology in which the word Trinity is used for the first time, in order to express the distinction between Father, Son and Holy Spirit, and in which we can read this wonderful sentence: 'Show me the man that you are, and I will show you my God.' Other Apologists—Miltiades, Apollinaris, Melito of Sardis, and Hermias—are no more than names to us, for almost all their writings are lost. This abundance of apologetic material shows the extraordinary vitality which Christian philosophy had acquired at this period.

One little masterpiece, 'the pearl of apologetic literature' according to Renan, must be set apart from the rest: this is the *Octavius*, by Minucius Felix. Whilst all the other Apolo-

---

[23] The reader should remember that Tatian was the author of the *Diatessaron*, the one Gospel compiled from a fusion of the four, which has already been mentioned in the section: 'The Church Lays Down Her Choice: the Canon.'

gists had written in Greek, this .........
time (probably some time betw..........
in Latin. The author was a Roma.........
He was a devout Christian, but also.........
tication. His book is the man of the.........
Apology which, as is fitting, is easy to rea.........
matic, a simple Introduction to the Tru.........  The
language is elegant, the literary skill consu........, the style
classical. The reader might almost think he w..e reading Cicero or Seneca. At the baths at Ostia, Minucius Felix talked
to two of his friends, Octavius, a Christian like himself, and
Coecilius Natalis, a pagan from Cirta (Constantine), both
men of noble birth. Coecilius had bowed before the statue
of an idol: his friends expressed astonishment at this. Sitting
by the edge of the baths all three engaged in a lengthy argument. Why was Coecilius a pagan? Did he believe in the gods
of mythology and in stone statues? No, but in view of man's
absolute ignorance regarding the meaning of his destiny, he
judged it simplest to adhere to the traditional religion, the
benevolent national institution, which preserved law and order in society. Moreover, were the Christians not reprehensible? There were lots of tales abroad concerning the secret
society that they had formed, which was impious and wicked
in intentions and practices. Consequently why should he,
Coecilius, be interested in them? Why change his religion?
After all, truth consisted of uncertainty, as the wise men belonging to the Academy proclaimed. . . . Octavius replied to
this statement. He proved the existence of God, and demonstrated the action of Providence; he criticized the absurdity
of polytheism, which had, in addition, been abandoned by
the philosophers; he absolved the Christians of all the dis-
gusting accusations brought against them by the mob and concluded with such a fine and noble description of Christian
morals that Coecilius was almost overcome and demanded
only a little more information before becoming a Christian.
Anyone who reads these vivid, elegantly fervent pages can almost hear the sound that rang from a lofty soul, guided by an
alert intelligence, when it was struck by the Word of God.

## 'OPORTET HAERESES ESSE'

The ferment of ideas which characterizes the primitive age of Christianity was not without its attendant dangers. Could not the interest shown in religious matters lead, in the heat of many impassioned arguments, to a number of distinct doctrinal deviations? For at least four or five centuries the eastern Mediterranean had been a crucible in which various doctrines had moulded themselves into weird syntheses. When the Christian faith was enticed into this whirlpool would it always be able to resist these insidious influences and remain inviolate? So many points in its message might be conducive to temptations, so many of its mysteries could incite men to erroneous speculations! The very person of Christ, the mystery of the Incarnation; the signs of His coming again, which were liable to be interpreted in too precise a fashion, in a climate of frenzy and terror; Christian morality, which, taken in its most limited sense, seemed to be easy to follow, but, when taken to extremes, could lead to excessive austerities. There were also the subtle influences of the pagan mysteries—ancient Persian dualism, the hermetic speculations of the Neo-Pythagoreans, ideas from the Egyptian cult of Isis—and these threatened to taint the Living Water with their own impure waves. And then too there was the still unsettled question of Christianity's connections with its Judaic loyalties, which could always give rise to argument. And, in conclusion, heresy was as old as Christianity itself. St Paul and St John had both had to oppose it. During the second century the problem became extremely serious. Three crises, though unequal in their respective importance, disturbed the Christian conscience in this period.

The characteristic of heresies is the inflation of orthodox teaching in dogma, tradition or morality to the point where it is totally falsified. For example, in the primitive Church there was an extremely widespread idea that Christ would not long delay His return to the earth, and that men were soon to see Him reappear, majestic and terrible, for the Last Judgment. This idea, when linked with a certain Jewish legend fixing the temporal reign of the Messiah at a thousand years, and linked also with a tendentious interpretation of the Apocalypse, resulted in a semi-heresy, called *millenarianism*, which asserted that Jesus would reign upon earth in person for a thousand years with the righteous, who would enjoy a thousand pleasures during that time, after which the Last Judgment would take place. Papias professed this doctrine to a large extent. In the third century Nepos, the Bishop of Egypt, was to give it his vehement support, but it was rejected by Pope Damasus.

A similar concept of the imminent coming of the Kingdom, of the return in glory, was also mingled, in certain hot-headed individuals, with the belief in a constant manifestation of the Holy Spirit in the person of certain favoured Christians. The gift of prophecy, which, as we may remember, had been recognized by the early Church, was gradually becoming rarer; at the end of the second century the Phrygian *Montanus* claimed to be its repository. Flanked by two women visionaries, *Maximilla* and *Priscilla*, who were as irrational as he was, and who had left their husbands in order to follow him, he hurled himself into a frenzied campaign of evangelization through the Near Eastern provinces. The world was nearing its end! The Paraclete, heralded by Jesus, was soon to appear, clothed in glory! The wonder that had been but vaguely hinted at at Pentecost was soon to acquire its conclusive meaning! Glory be to the Spirit! Glory be to Montanus, its interpreter, its living presence, 'the vibrant lyre singing beneath God's bow'! This propaganda met with rapid success in the East where mysticism was readily excited. Theologically, the doctrine was not very exhausting; morally, the austerities which it encouraged were no surprise to an area which had witnessed the Galli practising self-castration in order to enter the Phrygian mysteries. The fanatical teaching which made martyrdom into an obligation, towards which men were required to run, found echoes in many souls who had been robbed of all their senses by the prevalent atmosphere of conflict and terror. From about 170 onwards a wave of semi-insanity was let loose upon the world. It travelled through many Christian communities in the East, and later in the West as well: Montanist churches sprang into being.

*Gnosticism*, the other great heresy of the second century,

was more subtle, more insidious, and on the whole much more dangerous. If Montanism was an aberration of character, gnosticism was an aberration of the mind, the abuse of the research and speculation which had been applied to the mysteries of God. It is not easy to find our bearings in the nebulous and chaotic universe into which this heretical current sweeps us. The numerous studies on the subject have neither fully enlightened, nor even completely explored, the horizons of this strange world. In order to recognize its fundamental elements, it is necessary to make a distinction between two factors in it; on the one hand, a method of philosophy which is also a spiritual attitude; on the other, an infinitely complex system, offering an explanation of the world, of life and of God. We shall reserve the name *gnosis* for the first of these: the second is properly *gnosticism*.

What is gnosis? The word, in Greek, means 'understanding,' 'knowledge.' Now, is not God the primordial object of all knowledge? Therefore gnosis is man's effort to grasp the divine, an effort which he must carry through completely, with all that is in him, in order to acquire the power to understand, to feel, to achieve spiritual union with God, to imagine Him in all His fullness. It is, simultaneously, an attempt to force an entry into the ineffable secrets of the divine and, in adhering to them, a means of obtaining salvation. It is the point at which intelligence unites with ecstasy, where speculation and faith mingle intimately. The final truth, the truth that will ensure our eternal salvation, is beyond an invisible barrier, beyond the screen of the world; it is essential to pass through these.

Thus defined, in the sense of an attitude of mind, gnosis was considerably older than Christianity. It had existed in India, Greece, Egypt and Persia. It formed a part of that vast current of thought which, particularly since Hellenic times, had been carrying the human soul towards the desire for a more profound religious understanding, the fruit of an inner illumination. In many quarters gnosis appeared an ideal way of seizing hold of the divine, an esoteric way, which had been transmitted down the centuries since time immemorial by a series of initiates. It could be applied to all religions, with the claim of giving each a deeper meaning. For that matter there had been an Egyptian gnosis, which interpreted the traditional theology of Osiris and Isis according to this method; in Samaria there had been a Jewish gnosis, which has been associated with the figure of Simon the magician.[24] A perfectly orthodox Christian gnosis was quite conceivable, and in fact had existed since the very earliest days of the faith. St Paul had stated quite categorically that there was a Christian gnosis, the mystery of God (1 Cor. ii. 8); and St Clement of Rome and the *Letter of Barnabas* had spoken of that 'gift of the gnosis which God implants in man's soul,' enabling him to understand the meaning of the Scriptures better and to attain perfection. But it was absolutely essential that those who aimed at ends of this kind should be firmly rooted in orthodoxy by a singularly strong faith. In these perspectives it was extremely tempting to regard the Revelation as a kind of mysterious Grace which was given to men through the medium of intelligence, a concept which cancelled out the indispensable role of Christ and the Church.

The danger became obvious when the gnosis, spreading like a spiritual cancer, absorbing elements from almost every possible source—from the Docetist heresy, Platonism and Pythagorism, and also from Persian dualism and possibly even from Buddhism—claimed to knead and reshape the dogmas of the Christian faith. This vast religious current encountered Christianity at the very beginning of the second century, and set loose upon it a wave of truly formidable heresy, the heresy of knowledge. Gnosticism is this complex mixture of Christian ideas and heterogeneous speculations, which resulted in a world of aberrant reflections.

The starting-point of this heresy was far from being an ignoble one. Gnosticism was founded on two ideas: that of the sublime elevation of God, borrowed from the latter-day Jews, for whom Yahweh had become infinitely distant and mysterious, the Almighty, the Great Silence, the Unfathomable; and that of the infinite misery of man and his abject state. Gnosticism was obsessed by two problems, the very problems which continue to attract human minds: that of the origins of matter and life, the very obviously imperfect works of a

[24] See the note in Chapter I, section: 'The Work Done by St Peter and Philip the Deacon.'

God who was said to be perfect, and that of the evil which existed in man and in the universe. When the Christians replied: 'The world was created perfect by God, but man's sin introduced evil into it, an essential rupture of the divine order,' the Gnostics rushed into the most complex explanations. God, being unique and perfect, was absolutely separate from beings of flesh and blood. Between God and men intermediary beings existed, called *aeons*, who emanated from Him by a continuous process of degradation; the first aeons resembled God, but they had engendered those who were less pure, who in their turn . . . and so on. Esoteric calculations enabled the number of types of aeons to be counted: the whole formed the complete world, the 365 stages, the *Pleroma*.

In the middle of the succession, one aeon had committed a sin: he attempted to go beyond the ontological boundaries and equal God; he was thrown out of the spiritual world and forced, with his descendants, to live in the intermediate universe, and in his revolt he created the material world, an evil work, marked by sin. Some of the Gnostics called this traitor-aeon the *Demiurgos*, and others identified him with the Creator-God of the Bible. What did man become, seen in these perspectives? In himself he was not wholly bad, since, as the supreme emanation of the aeon, he housed a divine spark, a spiritual element which was the prisoner of matter and which longed to be freed. The fault lay in the very fact of his existence. The evil was life itself. Those who were satisfied with merely living were irrevocably lost; those who, through the gnosis, understood the way of salvation—the 'psychics'—could progress towards divine peace; while those who had renounced life completely—the 'spirituals'—the superior initiates and most noble souls, would be saved.

Even such a brief *résumé* as the above makes very clear the extent to which speculations of this kind conflicted with Christianity. The historic Jesus disappeared and Christ became no more than one member of the divine hierarchy of aeons, His human flesh merely a kind of illusory case for the divine spark within it. The Christian ideals of the redemption of the whole man, both body and soul, through the suffering and death of Christ incarnate, and of the realization of the

Kingdom of God, were replaced by a kind of call to Nirvana, by the deliverance of the soul that had been snatched from the abjections of the material world. Christian morality, which was so sound and so humane, yielded to quite another sort of morality which, being violently hostile to the body, sometimes led to excessive asceticism, while on other occasions, by despising the flesh, it became complaisant and allowed free rein to man's basest instincts.

The history of Gnosticism consists of the development of this complicated schema in all directions. On encountering the Church, the Gnostic stream infiltrated into her, taking up a position within her very bosom.[25] There was a Syriac-Christian Gnosticism in the persons of Satornilus, and later Cerdo. Basilides founded an Egyptian Gnosticism, which was violently hostile to the God of the Jews. Above all, and most remarkable, there was the Gnosticism of Valentine, which started in Alexandria and later spread to Rome. This was a rather touching attempt to reconcile the Gospel with the most audacious Gnostic speculations, but it foundered in extravagant absurdity. Such a list does not take into account the various more or less quackish Gnostic sects: the Cainites, who exalted Cain as the hero of antimorality; the Ophites, who worshipped the serpent of the temptation in the Garden of Eden; the fanatical devotees of Judas, who wrote a gospel named after him. Gnosticism was like a mighty river, a veritable flood which beat against the Church on all sides during the second century. Phrygia, Asia and the West were all attacked by it. Rome, where Valentine lived from 135 until 165, contained a fair number of Gnostic supporters; a group of them is depicted on a fresco in the Aurelian Catacomb. St Irenaeus denounced the ravages of the heresy in Gaul, particularly among the women there, for in the Gnostic com-

[25] In order to help their own propaganda, the Gnostics drafted a number of works which they tried to insert into the Scriptures. A number of apocryphas are impregnated with Gnosticism: the Book of Baruch, the Pseudo-Acts of St John, the Pseudo-Gospel of St Thomas and several others, including the Gospel of Judas! The Gnostic trend was to survive in philosophy and literature until modern times. Thus we find clear traces of it in William Blake's work in the eighteenth century, and in that of Martinez de Pasqually, in the nineteenth.

munities women could be priests, officiating at the religious rites, and prophesying. Its vague mysticism, its fundamental pessimism and its air of mystery, which made Christian dogma seem too commonplace and too simple, made Gnosticism well suited to attract men's minds in a world in perdition, in a profoundly disturbed society, obsessed with the desire for deliverance, but having lost all understanding of its ultimate objective, rather like India had been six hundred years earlier, in Buddha's time. The Christian faith was in danger of being engulfed by it.

We must find a place in this stormy world for yet another heretic, *Marcion*. Marcion was really a Gnostic, but only a partial one, having acquired a smattering of Gnostic doctrines from Cerdo the Syrian. But by nature he was certainly no speculative thinker; quite the contrary. Marcion had a fiery temperament and a fervently religious nature. No one ever questioned his own moral probity. He was an energetic figure, a real man of action and a good organizer into the bargain. Marcion was born at Sinope, on the shores of the Black Sea, where his father, a bishop, was forced to excommunicate him, because his adolescent zeal revealed him to be so undisciplined and unorthodox. He settled at Smyrna, where he followed his trade as a shipwright, and where the saintly old bishop, Polycarp, dubbed him 'Satan's first-born.' Then he came to Rome, where a gift of two hundred thousand sesterces ensured his being held in high regard initially. But he rapidly came into conflict with the leaders of the Church there, and in 144, when his deviation from the true faith became apparent, he was immediately excommunicated; his money was handed back to him and he set up a counter-Church.

The fact which decided the rupture was the collection of ideas which Marcion set out in his one book of *Antitheses*. Like all the Gnostics, Marcion was obsessed by the problem of evil, and when his rather simplifying mind traced it back to its origins he asked himself why the Creator-God had established evil in the world; why He had created scorpions, serpents and crocodiles; and why mankind's noblest action, that of giving birth to new life, was linked with rape and impurity. In addition, he had read the Old Testament; he had been totally insensitive to the spiritual impulse which marked it throughout, to the moral grandeur of the prophets, to the faith of the Psalmists; he had set himself against St Justin's confession that this mass of strange facts contained much symbolic material; he confined himself rigidly to the literal meaning of the text, to the brutality of a temperamental God of retribution, to the harshness of the allegedly divine faith, to the violence and injustice proclaimed in so many of its pages. And these two observations led him to a conclusion expressed in the following dogmatic declaration: there were two Gods. One, inferior and contemptible, was the Creator, the Demiurgos, and, at the same time, the frightful retributive judge of the Bible; the second God, who was all love and goodness, had come to undo the work of the first, to annul creation, to render the declarations of the Old Testament null and void. All this is, if one wishes to call it so, a kind of Gnosticism, but it is a simplified sort of Gnosticism, systematized to the extreme, and a Gnosticism in which the emphasis was laid, not on an effort of the mind, but on a sentimental impulse. In order to be saved man must love the God of love, hurl himself into His arms, and drown himself in His adorable depths. Everything else—the principles of the Law, the rigours of the ferocious Old Testament God—did not count at all. Marcion simultaneously annulled the whole of creation and the entire morality of the Old Testament without taking into account that, at the same time, he was wiping out the flesh, in other words the Incarnation, and the Messianic revelation, namely, the Redemption. He did not understand that he had reduced to nothing that Jesus whom he adored, and whom he spoke of with such profound tenderness.

These doctrines, somewhat simple theologically, but touching in tone, seduced many minds in an epoch when Christianity could not escape the currents of restlessness and confusion which were circulating everywhere. Marcion was a good administrator, and he established his Church on a sound basis. Arrogating to himself the right of selecting sacred texts, he compiled his own canon, rejecting anything that embarrassed him, and relying on St Luke and St Paul, both of whom, moreover, he expurgated a good deal. The sect progressed rapidly. St Justin was speaking of it with anxiety as early as 150; at the beginning of the following century Tertullian declared that Marcionite teaching had invaded the entire Christian world. Marcion's churches were to endure after their founder's death in 160; they became primarily country communities, and survived until the sixth century. He had few really important successors, with the exception of Apelles, who was to make Marcion's theses more flexible: later on part of the Marcionite stream was to unite with the third-century river of Manichaeism.

The Montanist crisis, the Gnostic crisis, the Marcionite crisis: in order to assess their danger to the Church, it is essential to remember that at this period Christianity resembled a citadel besieged by the enemy, in which the heretics, even when they behaved as fervently as true believers, up to the point of suffering martyrdom, as many of them did, were literally rebels and traitors. Celsus, the Christians' great adversary, used the existence of the sects as an argument against the Church. He jeered at these discords which were threatening a unity that claimed to be divine. However, if we think of the role which these rebels themselves finally assumed in the development of Christianity, we feel inclined to echo St Paul's words: '*Oportet haereses esse.*' 'Parties there must needs be among you, so that those who are true metal may be distinguished from the rest' (1 Cor. xi. 19). Not everything along the paths which swept souls towards heresy is to be rejected: the vehement faith which Montanus gave to a life consecrated by the Spirit; the fearless speculative demand of the best of the Gnostics, their desire to solve the problem of evil and probe the mystery of God; Marcion's over-exclusive preference for what is, notwithstanding, the core of Christianity, the religion of love. Heresy forced the faith, not simply to recognize 'the true metal,' but to trace a path through all this tangled undergrowth of ideas. Practically speaking, and in accordance with a dialectical law which is often to reveal itself in the future, notably at the time of the Counter-Reformation and the Council of Trent, the action of the heretics incited the Church to firm decisions and to new efforts. In compiling his own canon Marcion must have contributed to making that of the Catholic Church more sound and more necessary; and it was at the time of the great antiheretical controversies that a new team of Fathers of the Church made such progress in the fundamental religious sciences, exegesis and theology.

## THE CHURCH'S REPLY: ST IRENAEUS

The first reaction of loyal Christians to the outbreak of heresies was one of dismay. 'My God,' cried St Polycarp sadly, 'what a dreadful age you have made me live in!' But the second immediate emotion was the realization of the need for counter-attack. Strengthening their bonds with one another, the various churches combined to struggle against the new dangers. Each community gathered around its leader, the rightful repository of orthodox tradition. Christian institutions became more clearly defined and rigid, so that the acid of heresy would not corrode them. And a competition sprang up among orthodox intellectuals: who would battle best for the truth? Who would fight the scourge most energetically?

There is scarcely one writer of the second century who does not make some allusion to heresy and oppose it with his particular arguments. Several of the Apologists had been anti-heretical controversialists at the same time. St Justin, for example, had written a work, which is now lost, entitled A *Treatise Against All the Heresies*, in which, according to Irenaeus, he made a particularly strong attack on Marcion. Similarly St Theophilus of Antioch and Miltiades had battled against the Gnostics, Apollinaris of Hierapolis and Theophilus against the Montanists. In this way veritable battalions were drawn up for the theological struggle. Every error and every deviation had their sworn enemies in the orthodox camp. Against Montanus there were Apollonius, Caius, and even the authors of various anonymous lampoons; against the Gnostics, Rhodo, a pupil of Tatian, and Hegesippus, a converted Jew who, between 155 and 175, made a thorough investigation of the whole Church to find out exactly where its true faith lay. At the end of the second century and the beginning of the third, St Hippolytus, an important specialist in these problems, wrote a work of such monumental proportions that it was to be called *The Labyrinth*; in it he set out and refuted all the false doctrines, all their variations and all their derivatives:

the whole comprised ten volumes, dealing with thirty-two heresies!

Nor was this battle without its difficulties. The first stemmed from the fact that in its early stages a heresy was hard to distinguish from the true faith; at first men merely considered that differences of temperament or shades of meaning were concerned; only later did the positions become more clearly defined; meanwhile the ambiguity helped the evil to make progress. But there was an even more serious difficulty. The men who hurled themselves energetically into the conflict were, substantially, strong, ardent spirits, the type of people who enjoyed a battle of pamphlets, in a word polemists; and God knows well enough how hard it is to keep such people from going to extremes! Consequently a number of them, in the very act of defending orthodox doctrine with all their vigour, might actually deal it some rather cruel blows. For example, the priest Caius, who battled vehemently against Montanism, conceived the idea of expurgating, and even suppressing, the writings of St John and anything that seemed to him to be too closely linked with the doctrine of the Spirit, of the Logos, in order to improve his own case. This heretical tendency of his was known as *Alogos*, but it enjoyed only a limited success. Later on we shall see St Hippolytus quite simply seceding from the Church, under pretext that the popes were not displaying sufficient energy against the heretics! But the most famous instance of this danger is the tragedy of Tertullian. Tertullian began as an outstanding and distinguished defender of the true faith, a tireless opponent of the Gnostics and Marcion. However, he allowed himself to be carried away by an intemperate zeal complicated by illusionism after the style of Montanus, and in this he foundered and sank.[26] It was not easy to detect the true wisdom, to maintain a sense of proportion and prudence, in the midst of these battles of

---

[26] Even St Irenaeus, that model of faith and wisdom, has one aspect which the Church was to consider alarming. In some of his work he supports the thesis of millenarianism, which was generally considered suspect, though without being expressly condemned. As for Tertullian, whose life straddles the end of the second century and the beginning of the third, he is studied later, in Chapter VII.

ideas. One can only admire all the more the straightness of the road which the Church knew how to trace.

The great interest of these anti-heretical controversies lies in the fact that, in the best cases, they went beyond the bounds of simple polemics and led certain brilliant minds to make an effort of doctrinal construction which was to give Christian philosophy its decisive foundations. One name sums up this effort, one personality dominates all others in this field: that of St Irenaeus, Bishop of Lyons.

This noble figure first appears on the scene in 177, in the middle of those terrible years when persecution was ravaging the Christian population of the Gauls. Although decimated and crushed, the Church of Lyons nevertheless possessed the strength to be preoccupied with the superior interests of Christianity as a whole. The faithful of Lyons heard tell of the disturbances provoked in Asia by Montanus, and of the measures taken against him. This news troubled them a great deal, and they wrote a letter to the Pope, in order that peace might be re-established among the Church's sons. They entrusted this letter to a bearer whom they declared to be 'extremely zealous for the testament of Christ,' Irenaeus.

Irenaeus was an Asian, for the metropolis of the Gauls, now an important centre of trade with the East, contained many Asian-born people. He was born probably at Smyrna, c. 135, and had had the great good fortune—still extremely rare at that period—of learning the faith from Christian parents. His religious fervour manifested itself early in his youth. He himself relates how, as a boy of fifteen, he sat with his schoolfellows at the feet of the saintly Bishop Polycarp, never tired of listening to the old man describing what John the Apostle had taught him of Jesus. Irenaeus was therefore a direct witness of the apostolic tradition, one of those outstanding guarantors to whom those studying the origins of the Scriptures and the way in which they were handed down delight to refer.[27] In addition, Irenaeus had had a good classical education. He was familiar with classical philosophies, and had studied doctrine, possibly at Rome itself, and, at all events, knew St Justin well. He had an upright, profoundly sincere

[27] See the first section of this chapter.

and evangelical soul, a generous and receptive heart and a temperament that inclined him to moderation and wisdom; he was quite the opposite of a sectarian, of an embittered, angry polemist. Does not the very etymology of his name make us think of peace and its attendent virtues? Even at the height of the struggle against the Gnostics, Irenaeus never forgot that Jesus' first commandment was one of love.[28]

Irenaeus was chosen Bishop of Lyons on his return from Rome. The Asian, the Roman and the Westerner all had a part in his character, making him, so to speak, a living synthesis of the whole of Christianity. As a bishop he was first and foremost a man of the Church, following in the footsteps of those great martyr-bishops upon whom he modelled himself, Clement, Ignatius and Polycarp. He led his flock with tireless devotion. Besançon and Valence almost certainly owed to him their conversion to the faith. Irenaeus learnt to speak the native tongue of his Gallic neighbours; he always refers to them with deep affection and exquisite tenderness; and he probably wrote his *Demonstration of Apostolic Preaching* for his Gallo-Romans. This is a short exposition of Christian doctrine, aimed at a popular readership, the first of the catechisms. But he soon saw that the flock entrusted to his care was threatened by a ferocious beast. He had heard talk of the Gnostic danger when he was in Rome; in his own territory

[28] One incident in his life gives excellent proof of his profoundly good and peace-loving nature: the dispute regarding the *date of Easter*, which broke out during the pontificate of Pope Victor (189–98). The Church in Asia Minor was accustomed to celebrate Easter on the exact anniversary of the traditional Jewish date, 14th Nisan. Rome celebrated it on the Sunday following this. St Polycarp had tried in vain to achieve unity in this matter in 155, in the name of Pope Anicetus and the Asians. Pope Victor wanted to settle the matter in an authoritarian fashion, and convened councils throughout the whole Church in order to get the date of Sunday accepted. The Asians refused, out of loyalty to their ancient customs, and Victor excommunicated the disobedient bishops. On hearing this news St Irenaeus was grief-stricken; the measure seemed to him excessive. He wrote a letter of protest to the Pope and begged him to show more moderation. This followed. And the peace-making intervention of the saintly Bishop of Lyons was to be crowned with success, since by the beginning of the third century all the Asian communities celebrated Easter on the Sunday following 14th Nisan, as we still do today.

the heresy was making progress in the Rhône valley. The truth had to be upheld against these false theses, and Irenaeus applied himself to the task.

It was a formidable undertaking. The result was *The Exposition and Refutation of the False Gnosis*, generally known, right up to the present day, under the name of *Adversus Haereses*. It consists of five large volumes, and although the reader sometimes receives the impression that they were written rather hurriedly, the requirements of the general plan being violated on numerous occasions, the beauty of many of their sentences, the striking precision of several of their expressions, shine out from a delectable Greek that is pleasantly mixed with Gallo-Roman elements. The enterprise has a dual interest. In the first two volumes St Irenaeus analyses in detail all the heresies of his day (and, as a result, gives us a great deal of information about them), because, as he says, 'it is by exposing their systems that we conquer them, just as a dangerous animal is rendered harmless by being snatched from the undergrowth and placed in the full light of day.' In the second section, comprising the three final volumes, the author sets out orthodox doctrine so clearly that he makes the possibility of heretical errors permanently impossible. From this a system of philosophical and theological thought was created, sound rather than new, but which was henceforth to serve as a basis for the whole of Christian thinking.

The reader will remember that the Apologists, and St Justin in particular, had wanted to annex to Christianity that sovereign ideal of humanity which Greek philosophy called reason; they had caught a glimpse of the intimate harmony which exists between reason and faith. But the experience of the gnosis had shown that reason could go astray in a very strange fashion. It was consequently necessary to keep it within bounds by means of an exact consideration of Christian principles. In brief, St Justin had made it clear that faith included reason; St Irenaeus explained that without faith reason erred.

Now what was the force which was to prevent such deviations? *Tradition*. Herein undoubtedly lies Irenaeus' essential contribution: for the first time he expressed what had been implied or hinted at—or, at all events, shown in the general feeling of their work—by St Clement, St Ignatius and St Justin, and which was henceforth to be the fundamental principle of the Catholic Church. The Gnostics had claimed the right to know God and the mysteries of faith through the medium of human intelligence, and we have seen to what madness they descended. Intelligence needs a guide, and tradition supplies one. What is tradition? Materially it is not that of a sequence of alleged initiates, whose thinking is difficult to verify; it is that of the Church, which every believer can recognize, of the bishops, whose list can be established, and of Rome, which holds an eminent place in that tradition.[29] Spiritually it is not a fossilized idea which scoffs at intelligence; it is a principle of life 'which the Spirit constantly rejuvenates,' a principle which controls reason and assigns it its proper end.

It is this traditionalist basis which supports the whole of Irenaeus' work, and makes it so rich and so fruitful in every direction. It guarantees the rule of faith; it enables the great problems of mankind to be resolved: e.g. those of the knowledge of God and the nature of man. The Gnostics had hurled God into such a deep abyss that He had become inaccessible. St Irenaeus replied that though God was indeed unknowable through the natural forces of reason,[30] Christianity had assured us that He had been revealed through that supreme manifestation of love which was the Incarnation, and that accordingly He reveals Himself to those who love Him. He readopted the valid ideas contained in Marcion's thesis of the God of love. As for man, creation and the flesh, which the heretics despised completely, had they not all been consecrated and redeemed by Christ, the new Adam, who *recapitulated* (according to a phrase of which St Irenaeus was very fond) in Himself entire humanity? 'If the flesh be not saved, then the Saviour has not redeemed us!' The power of love which is the sovereign knowledge: this is the idea which was to be evoked down the centuries by all the mystics and by

[29] It was when writing his theses on tradition that St Irenaeus was led to affirm the primacy of the Church of Rome, as already noted in Chapter V, section: 'The Unity of the Church and the Primacy of Rome.'

[30] That is, with the exception of His existence and of certain attributes, which according to St Paul can be known by unaided reason.

Pascal. A total concept of man, a being who is simultaneously flesh and spirit—'and the spirit itself is carnal,' as Péguy was to say—this is the starting-point of all Christian philosophy, sociology and politics.

There is another direction in which the idea of tradition was to carry St Irenaeus towards an essential development, a direction in which he encountered exegesis and the philosophy of history simultaneously. It need hardly be said that, so far as exegesis was concerned, he was resolutely in favour of the symbolist method of typology so dear to St Justin and to all subsequent Fathers of the Church. But whereas his predecessor, even while he proclaimed, in opposition to Marcion, the unity of the two Testaments, believed that God had given the Law to the Jews as a lesser evil, in order to maintain them in a certain loyalty, St Irenaeus was far more deeply aware of the harmony which existed between the two halves of the Bible. The immensity of tradition includes the whole history of the Chosen Race; God has progressively educated man through the intermediary of Israel, and the two Testaments are two moments in that education, two complementary stages in man's march towards truth. This is indeed a grandiose idea, containing at the same time a whole Christian conception of history. As the mystical body of Jesus, and His witness down the centuries, is it not the Church's mission to make humanity progress continually towards its supreme goal, towards the fulfilment of the Kingdom of God?

The vast scholarship of St Irenaeus contains innumerable doctrinal ideas which have had a decisive influence upon the evolution of Christian thought. Of all the Fathers of the Church, few indeed seem so close to us as he does, and so concerned with our own immediate problems.[31]

---

[31] Nothing certain is known about Irenaeus' death. St Jerome is the first to declare, in 410, that he must have been martyred. Lyons was partly destroyed and pillaged in 197; in 200–2 persecutions struck the Lyons community. St Irenaeus probably suffered death on one of these occasions.

## THE MISSION OF CHRISTIAN PHILOSOPHY

So, as the second century draws to a close, Christian philosophy finds itself established on firm foundations, so firm that nothing would ever destroy them.

In this extremely short period four stages had been cleared. The first Christian generation, that of our Lord's immediate disciples, had, under the very aegis of the inspiration-giving Spirit, set out the basic elements of Christ's message in a fixed form; and, without intending to erect either a philosophy or a theology, St John and St Paul had, each in his own way, pondered deeply on the fundamentals of these. The second generation, that of the Apostolic Fathers, had understood and proclaimed that it was essential to make the capital they had received bear fruit; though not intensely speculative, they were profoundly spiritual, and they had initiated those developments from which emerged a metaphysical ideal which was, later on, to become Christian philosophy. With the third generation, that of the Apologists and of St Justin in particular, philosophical development had been considerable: for the first time the Christians, by drawing on the valid elements of pagan philosophy, had laid down, in theory, that a certain use of reason, a certain concept of nature, could serve the faith, thereby opening up to the Christian mind limitless horizons of research and speculation. Finally, this team of anti-heretical writers, and notably the great Bishop of Lyons, in their reaction against the internal dangers threatening the Church—especially Gnosticism—forced the Christian mind to examine the supernatural truths more and more, thus making Christianity into the soundest system of religious philosophy in the world, beside which the pagan theologies appeared feeble and inconsistent.

Such was the achievement of the literature whose early stages we have just been studying. Naturally its importance should not be exaggerated: it alone would not have been sufficient for Christian philosophy to conquer the world. For that task the living force was the prime essential, the mysterious power which made the grain of mustard seed sown by Jesus

Himself germinate and grow. However, in their very number, their variety and their wealth of talent, do not these Christian scholars themselves give the impression of a brilliant manifestation of this force? Had they never lived, would Christianity have been what it is today?

Historically the work of the Fathers of the Church filled a twofold need. Undoubtedly the value of an intellectual doctrine is not sufficient to endow it with the force of a total engagement, able to permeate souls to the very core. St Justin remarked: 'No one believed Socrates until he died for what he taught.' And it was for reasons far removed from literary ones that so many Fathers of the Church sealed their work in their own blood; they died for the faith because they were brimful with the love of Christ. On the other hand, could Christianity have penetrated the ruling classes and the intelligentsia, had these men not been there to demonstrate to them, in their own language and according to their own methods, that the message of Jesus was so valuable that men were prepared to live and die for it. Their missionary role was therefore considerable.

It was not the only one. In order to vanquish classical society and ensure the triumph of the Revolution of the Cross, the whole concept of the world had to be transformed and reshaped by the valid elements of the past and the fundamentals of Christian Revelation, an intellectual synthesis on which civilization could live. The intuitive genius of St Paul had already seen the need for the Christian conscience to seize the world and remodel it; his action had a powerful influence upon the future. The Fathers of the Church pursued the same intention by applying the same sacred principles to circumstances and events. 'No revolutionary action without revolutionary doctrine!' declared one man who was particularly well versed in revolutionary matters;[32] without a doctrine to sustain it, control it and explain it, Christian activity would not have had the results we so greatly admire. All the vitality of Christian missionary endeavour, all the heroism of the martyrs, would have served little purpose had this effort to make the world think in terms of Christ not been accomplished

[32] Lenin.

simultaneously. This was to become increasingly apparent as the Cross on earth grew larger, and the way was made ready, throughout the tragic third century, for the decisive relief of the Empire by the Church.

# SELECT BIBLIOGRAPHY

It is hoped that the following selective list, which has been taken from M. Daniel-Rops's much more extensive bibliography in the French edition of this work, will be of value to French-speaking readers who wish to study aspects of the period described in greater detail from some of the author's own sources. Those which have been translated are given in their English versions, and Father Philip Hughes's *History of the Church* has been added to the list of general works.

## GENERAL WORKS

*L'Histoire de l'église*, ed. A. Fliche and V. Martin: vol. i, *L'Église primitive*, by J. Lebreton and J. Zeiller, 1934; vol. ii, *De la fin du IIᵉ siècle à la paix constantinienne*, by J. Lebreton and J. Zeiller, 1935; vol. iii, *De la paix constantinienne à la mort de Théodose*, by J. R. Palanque, G. Bardy and P. de Labriolle, 1936.

P. Hughes: *A History of the Church*, vol. i, 2nd ed., 1948.

P. Batiffol: *Le Catholicisme, des origines à saint Léon: I. L'Église naissante et le catholicisme*, 1927.

Dom Henri Leclercq: *La Vie chrétienne primitive*, 1928.

Dom C. Poulet: *L'Histoire du Christianisme* (4 vols.), 1933–48.

## Chapter I. 'SALVATION IS TO COME FROM THE JEWS'

On Jesus Christ and the origins of the Church, the reader is recommended to M. Daniel-Rops's (Eng. trans.) *Jesus in His Time*, 1955, and to the books referred to therein.

On Palestinian Judaism see:

J. Bonsirven: *Le Judaïsme palestinien au temps de Jésus-Christ*, 1934, and *Les Idées juives au temps de Notre-Seigneur*, 1934.

On the *Diaspora* see:

E. Beurlier: *Le Monde juif au temps de Jésus-Christ et des Apôtres*, 1900.

On the Church's very earliest days see:

L. Cerfaux: *La Communauté apostolique*, 1943.

On Judeo-Christian relations see:
M. SIMON: *Verus Israel*, 1948.

## CHAPTER II. A HERALD OF THE HOLY SPIRIT: ST PAUL

A. The following are some recent works dealing with Paul's life and with his work in general:
F. PRAT: *Saint Paul*, 1922.
A. TRICOT: *Saint Paul, apôtre des Gentils*, 1927.
E. BAUMANN: *Saint Paul*, 1925.
E.-B. ALLO: *Paul, apôtre de Jésus-Christ*, 1942.
J. HUBY: *Saint Paul, apôtre des Nations*, 1943.
G. RICCIOTTI: *Paolo Apostolo*, 1947.

B. Works dealing primarily with Paul's doctrine include:
F. PRAT: *The Theology of Saint Paul*, 1957.
F. AMIOT: *L'Enseignement de saint Paul*, 1938.
L. CERFAUX: *La Théologie de l'église selon saint Paul*, 1942.

## CHAPTER III: ROME AND THE REVOLUTION OF THE CROSS

See the author's *Jesus in His Time*, and *L'Histoire de l'église*, ed. Fliche and Martin, previously cited. See also:
E.-B. ALLO: *L'Apocalypse*, 1933, and *L'Évangile en face du Syncrétisme païen*, 1930.
G. FOUARD: *Saint Jean et la fin de l'âge apostolique*, 1922.
A. OLIVIER: *Les Cahiers de littérature sacrée*, 1947.
A. HARNACK: *Die Mission und Ausbereitung des Christentums in den ersten Jahrhunderten*, 1916.
MGR L. DUCHESNE: *Les Anciens recueils de légendes apostoliques*, 1895.
G. DE REYNOLD: *La Formation de l'Europe*: vol. iv, *L'Empire romain*, 1945.
L. HOMO: *Nouvelle histoire romaine*, 1941, and *Le Siècle d'or de l'Empire romain*, 1947.
J. TOUTAIN: *Les Cultes païens dans les provinces latines de l'Empire romain*, 1907–20.

## CHAPTER IV: SACRIFICE OF BLOOD: THE CHURCH'S FIRST MARTYRS

P. ALLARD: *Histoire des persecutions* (5 vols.), 1903–8; *Le Christianisme et l'Empire romain*, 1908; *Dix leçons sur le martyre*, 1910.

E. Causse: *Essai sur le conflit du Christianisme primitif et de la civilisation*, 1920.

L. Homo: *Les Empereurs romains et le Christianisme*, 1931.

M. Viller: *La Spiritualité des premiers siècles chrétiens*, 1930.

## Chapter V: CHRISTIAN LIFE IN THE AGE OF THE CATACOMBS

Dom Henri Leclercq: *La Vie chrétienne primitive*, 1928.

G. Fouard: *Saint Jean et la fin de l'âge apostolique*, 1922.

E. Amann: *L'Église des premiers siècles*, 1928.

Works more specially relating to spiritual life, religious practices and liturgy include:

M. Viller: *La Spiritualité des premiers siècles chrétiens*, 1930.

H. Daniel-Rops and A. Hamann: *La Prière des premiers chrétiens*, 1952.

Mgr L. Duchesne: *Christian Worship*, translated by M. L. McClure, 1950.

On the primacy of Rome see:

P. Batiffol: *Cathedra Petri*, 1939.

F. Mourret: *La Papauté*, 1929.

On the Catacombs see:

H. Chéramy: *Les Catacombes romaines*, 1932.

N. Maurice-Denis and R. Boulet: *Romée ou le pèlerin moderne à Rome*, 1948.

On the Church and the exact meaning of the word see:

L. Cerfaux: *La Théologie de l'église selon saint Paul*, 1942.

## Chapter VI. THE SOURCES OF CHRISTIAN LITERATURE

J. Huby: *L'Évangile et les évangiles*, 1940.

L. Cerfaux: *La Voix vivante de l'évangile au début de l'église*, 1946.

F. Cayré: *A Manual of Patrology and the History of Theology* (2 vols.), 1929.

J. Tixeron: *Précis de patrologie*, 1918.

G. Bardy: *La Vie spirituelle d'après les pères des trois premiers siècles*, 1935.

P. de Labriolle: *La Réaction païenne*, 1939.

L. Bréhier: *Les Idées philosophiques et religieuses de Philon d'Alexandrie*, 1925.

L. de Faye: *Gnostiques et gnosticisme*, 1925.

# Image Books

# Image Books

### ... MAKING THE WORLD'S FINEST CATHOLIC LITERATURE AVAILABLE TO ALL

**ON THE TRUTH OF THE CATHOLIC FAITH**
*Summa Contra Gentiles Book II: Creation. Newly translated, with an Introduction and notes by James F. Anderson*   D27—95¢

**ON THE TRUTH OF THE CATHOLIC FAITH**
*Summa Contra Gentiles Book III: Providence. Newly translated, with an Introduction and notes by Vernon J. Bourke*
  D28a Book III, Part 1—95¢
  D28b Book III, Part 2—95¢

**ON THE TRUTH OF THE CATHOLIC FAITH**
*Summa Contra Gentiles Book IV: Salvation. Newly translated, with an Introduction and notes, By Charles J. O'Neil*   D29—95¢

**THE WORLD'S FIRST LOVE**
*By Fulton J. Sheen*   D30—85¢

**THE SIGN OF JONAS**
*By Thomas Merton*   D31—95¢

**PARENTS, CHILDREN AND THE FACTS OF LIFE**   *By Henry V. Sattler, C.SS.R.*   D32—75¢

**LIGHT ON THE MOUNTAIN:**
*The Story of La Salette*
*By John S. Kennedy*   D33—75¢

**EDMUND CAMPION**
*By Evelyn Waugh*   D34—75¢

**HUMBLE POWERS**
*By Paul Horgan*   D35—75¢

**SAINT THOMAS AQUINAS**
*By G. K. Chesterton*   D36—75¢

**APOLOGIA PRO VITA SUA**
*By John Henry Cardinal Newman   Introduction by Philip Hughes*   D37—95¢

**A HANDBOOK OF THE CATHOLIC FAITH**
*By Dr. N. G. M. Van Doornik, Rev. S. Jelsma, Rev. A. Van De Lisdonk. Ed. Rev. John Greenwood*   D38—$1.45

**THE NEW TESTAMENT**
*Official Catholic edition*
  D39—95¢

**MARIA CHAPDELAINE**
*By Louis Hémon*   D40—65¢

**SAINT AMONG THE HURONS**
*By Francis X. Talbot, S.J.*
  D41—95¢

**THE PATH TO ROME**
*By Hilaire Belloc*   D42—85¢

**SORROW BUILT A BRIDGE**
*By Katherine Burton*   D43—85¢

**THE WISE MAN FROM THE WEST**
*By Vincent Cronin*   D44—85¢

**EXISTENCE AND THE EXISTENT**
*By Jacques Maritain*   D45—75¢

**THE STORY OF THE TRAPP FAMILY SINGERS**
*By Maria Augusta Trapp*
  D46—95¢

**THE WORLD, THE FLESH AND FATHER SMITH**
*By Bruce Marshall*   D47—75¢

**THE CHRIST OF CATHOLICISM**
*By Dom Aelred Graham*
  D48—95¢

**SAINT FRANCIS XAVIER**
*By James Brodrick, S.J.*
  D49—95¢

**SAINT FRANCIS OF ASSISI**
*By G. K. Chesterton*   D50—65¢

11

# Image Books

*...making the world's finest
Catholic literature available to all*

**VIPERS' TANGLE**
*by François Mauriac*    D51—75¢

**THE MANNER IS ORDINARY**
*by John LaFarge, S.J.* D52—95¢

**MY LIFE FOR MY SHEEP**
*by Alfred Duggan*    D53—90¢

**THE CHURCH AND THE RECON-
STRUCTION OF THE MODERN
WORLD:** *The Social Encyclicals
of Pius XI.* Edited by T. P. Mc-
Laughlin, C.S.B.    D54—$1.25

**A GILSON READER:** *Selections from
the Writings of Etienne Gilson.*
Edited by Anton C. Pegis.
D55—$1.25

**THE AUTOBIOGRAPHY OF
ST. THERESE OF LISIEUX:** *The Story
of a Soul.* A new translation by
John Beevers.    D56—75¢

**HELENA**
*by Evelyn Waugh*    D57—75¢

**THE GREATEST BIBLE STORIES**
A Catholic Anthology from
World Literature. Edited by Anne
Fremantle.    D58—75¢

**THE CITY OF GOD**—St. Augustine.
Edited with Intro. by Vernon J.
Bourke. Foreword by Etienne
Gilson.    D59—$1.45

**SUPERSTITION CORNER**
*by Sheila Kaye-Smith* D60—65¢

**SAINTS AND OURSELVES**
Ed. by Philip Caraman, S.J.
D61—95¢

**CANA IS FOREVER**
*by Charles Hugo Doyle*
D62—75¢

**ASCENT OF MOUNT CARMEL**—
St. John of the Cross. Translated
and Edited by E. Allison Peers.
D63—$1.25

**RELIGION AND THE RISE OF
WESTERN CULTURE**
*by Christopher Dawson*
D64—85¢

**PRINCE OF DARKNESS AND OTHER
STORIES**
*by J. F. Powers*    D65—85¢

**ST. THOMAS MORE**
*by E. E. Reynolds*    D66—95¢

**JESUS AND HIS TIMES**
2 Volumes    D67A—95¢
*by Daniel-Rops*    D67B—95¢

**ST. BENEDICT**
*by Justin McCann, O.S.B.*
D68—85¢

**THE LITTLE FLOWERS OF ST. FRANCIS**
Edited and Translated by
Raphael Brown.    D69—95¢

**THE QUIET LIGHT**
*by Louis de Wohl*    D70—95¢

**CHARACTERS OF THE REFORMATION**
*by Hilaire Belloc*    D71—85¢

**THE BELIEF OF CATHOLICS**
*by Ronald Knox*    D72—75¢

**FAITH AND FREEDOM**
*by Barbara Ward*    D73—95¢

**GOD AND INTELLIGENCE IN
MODERN PHILOSOPHY**
*by Fulton J. Sheen*  D74—$1.25

If your bookseller is unable to supply certain titles, write to Image
Books, Department MIB, Garden City, New York, stating the
titles you desire and enclosing the price of each book (plus 5¢
per book to cover cost of postage and handling). Prices are subject to change without notice.    **21**